Management

A Concise Intro   on

Richard Pettinger

Principal Teaching Fellow (Reader) in Management Education
University College London

palgrave
macmillan

First published 2012 by
PALGRAVE MACMILLAN

Palgrave Macmillan in the UK is an imprint of Macmillan Publishers Limited, registered in England, company number 785998, of Houndmills, Basingstoke, Hampshire RG21 6XS.

Palgrave Macmillan in the US is a division of St Martin's Press LLC, 175 Fifth Avenue, New York, NY 10010.

Palgrave Macmillan is the global academic imprint of the above companies and has companies and representatives throughout the world.

Palgrave® and Macmillan® are registered trademarks in the United States, the United Kingdom, Europe and other countries

ISBN: 978–0–230–28535–4

This book is printed on paper suitable for recycling and made from fully managed and sustained forest sources. Logging, pulping and manufacturing processes are expected to conform to the environmental regulations of the country of origin.

A catalogue record for this book is available from the British Library.

A catalog record for this book is available from the Library of Congress.

10 9 8 7 6 5 4 3 2 1
21 20 19 18 17 16 15 14 13 12

Printed in China

For Rebecca

Contents

List of figures and tables

Figures

Tables

Preface

The economic, social and political turbulence that exists in the world has created great uncertainty both in countries and regions, and also in business and public service organizations in all sectors and localities. The collapse and bankruptcy (moral, as well as financial) of organizations in the political, financial and energy sectors in the recent past has called into question and examined in minute detail the conduct and expertise of those who held top, senior and key positions. The consequent pressure on financial and other resources now means that those responsible for leading, directing and managing organizations for the future have to be able to get higher levels of effective performance out of a greatly diminished resource base.

The ability to lead and direct people, and to create and sustain organizations that are capable of survival and effectiveness, has therefore never been so great. The key priority is to know and understand the expertise that is required of those who are to lead and direct – to manage – the organizations of the future.

This in turn requires that 'management' is recognized, understood and valued as:

- having a defined, agreed and accepted body of knowledge, understanding and expertise;
- having a professional and expert standpoint that commits those who find themselves in positions of responsibility, authority, influence and accountability to particular levels of conduct, behaviour and performance;
- making the critical difference between organization success and failure, and knowing and understanding all those factors that contribute.

If this position is adopted, some things start to become clear. It is clear that the effective and successful practice of management is founded in knowledge and understanding of the environment; of how companies and organizations behave and operate; of products, services and markets; of finances and investment. It is clear that those in positions of authority and responsibility have to be able to serve (and in many cases, reconcile) the legitimate, divergent and often conflicting demands placed on them by their constituents and stakeholders. It is also clear that all organizational activity is founded on a fundamentally competitive basis – that at any given moment there is competition for products and services, competition for staff and their expertise, competition for customer and client bases. There is competition also between staff for opportunities and promotions, competition between organizations and departments for resources, competition between regions for jobs and work and the prosperity that goes with it.

There is therefore a drive towards the professionalization and professionalism of management. In many cases, those who would quite rightly hold to account those in positions of authority responsible for medical errors, would themselves be horrified if they were to be made accountable for their actions just because they were managers. This in itself is enough to define the need for a clear body of knowledge, understanding and expertise that all managers ought to have before being allowed to practise.

So there has to be a different approach. The drive has to be towards defining management in professional terms, with its own clear body of expertise, ideally with some kind of core pre-qualification that is demanded before anyone can be placed in any position where they have authority, responsibility and accountability for their actions; and for their impact on the very future of organizations and therefore other people's lives.

However much one may know about the law or medicine, those aspiring to practise have to have qualifications in order to do so. This therefore needs to be the same with management. It is not enough to have people placed in managerial positions – positions of leadership, power, authority and influence – without qualifications, simply because they seek progression and advancement, or because organizational history and trends require that people are promoted to management rather than having the necessary expertise to practise.

It is clear finally, that all of this takes place in an ever-changing economic, political and social environment, and one that is increasingly technologically driven. All of this brings clear commitments, as well as expertise, that ought to be the foundation of professional management practice.

The core of management is defined as:

- using and consuming resources effectively and in the pursuit of stated aims and objectives;
- achieving things through and for people;
- delivering performance and making a profit;
- coping with change and uncertainty.

This has to be delivered in the context of what is possible and feasible within the existing and developing environment. It has to be delivered both for the immediate, and also for the long term. There is a great variety of courses and education available in management; and this means that there is a collective recognition that management needs to be taught and learned, as well as applied. This in turn means that the principles and foundations of management can be taught and learned – they do not just appear or materialize.

This book is therefore presented as a foundation stone for management education, covering the range of skills, knowledge, attitudes, behaviour and expertise required of all those who aspire to positions of responsibility, authority and accountability. The book is targeted at:

- those on undergraduate and postgraduate business and management courses;
- those on post-experience, certificate and diploma courses in supervisory and management studies;
- those on programmes of professional study in areas where there is an ever-increasing demand for managerial, as well as professional, expertise (for example computer science, engineering, architecture);
- those on specific practice development programmes (for example Chartered Institute of Personnel and Development, Chartered Management Institute, Chartered Institute of Marketing, Institute of Administrative Management) which again require a foundation, knowledge and understanding of the principles and practice of management as part of their programmes.

The book is divided into four parts:

1 The foundations of management, setting out the main principles of effective management and the context in which these principles have to be taught, learned and applied effectively.
2 Management and organizational behaviour, covering the foundations of collective and individual behaviour and the skills, qualities and expertise necessary to know and understand how and why people behave in particular ways in organized settings.
3 Management and business, covering the strategic and operational aspects of management, including the context in which business practice is established and the nature of marketing, financial and other performance.
4 The practice of management, bringing everything together so as to be able to learn and understand how knowledge and expertise are implemented effectively.

Icons

Icons are used throughout the book in order to be able to indicate the source of some of the complexities, and also to provide points for reflection along the way. These icons are:

best practice indicating standards, levels and applications of what is understood to be the highest form of practice (at least at present).

just a minute designed to ensure that there are regular pauses for reflection throughout the text.

expert view quoting from those who are either authoritative or demonstrably successful in their field.

point of view in which either an alternative or complementary point of view is presented, which again should be used as a point of reflection.

true story illustrating good and bad organizational and managerial practice in the context in which it is delivered.

in brief at the end of each chapter, there is a series of 'In brief …' points, again as points of reflection and reference.

Acknowledgements

As always, a great number of people have contributed to this work, and it would have been impossible to complete it without their help and support. The comments of those who reviewed the manuscript have helped very greatly with the content. I am very grateful to Ursula Gavin and Ceri Griffiths at Palgrave Macmillan for their enormous patience and support over the entire period of the work and to Bryony Allen and everyone at Aardvark Editorial for their efforts in making this work into something we can all be very proud of. I have, as always, had great support from all the staff and students of the Department of Management Science and Innovation at UCL. Finally, I am very grateful to Paul Griseri, Hasna Chakir, Roger Cartwright, Mike Hutton, Ken Batchelor, Keith Sanders, Jamie Pollock, Jia Jia Ye, Pamela Sekhon, Ram Ahronov and Stephen Gruneberg for everything – over what is now very many years!

Richard Pettinger
UNIVERSITY COLLEGE LONDON
May 2012

The foundations of management

The principles, practices, profession and discipline of management have evolved into an evermore apparent body of knowledge, understanding, expertise and skills which have to be taught and learned, and which must be capable of application in whatever situation aspiring and practising managers find themselves.

The purpose of this part is therefore to identify and illustrate the foundations on which leadership, executive and managerial expertise is built, and which is capable of being delivered effectively. In order to be fully effective, the key priorities of profit, working with and for people, and delivering results have to be known and understood, and these are addressed by way of introduction in the first chapter.

The rest of Part One deals with the other key issues that form the foundations of effective management. It is essential to know and understand the nature of the environment, and of all the factors present. How to understand, analyse and evaluate the environment is dealt with in detail in Chapter 2. The nature of change and its effects on all aspects of organizational and managerial practice are addressed in Chapter 3. The nature of ethics and standards, and the need to be able to address questions of conduct, behaviour and performance are addressed in Chapter 4. At the end of Part One, Chapter 5 deals with management in practice – an introduction to how the relationships between what it is necessary to know and understand, and what it is necessary to be able to do, begin to interrelate.

Additionally, the content of Part One forms the foundations for the material covered in Parts Two and Three; and these then interrelate to form the foundations for the material covered in Part Four.

1

Introduction

'If you don't like, trust, respect and value people and their contribution you should not be a manager.'

In this chapter:

- what management is
- the complex disciplines and expertise of management
- developments in management expertise
- the professionalization of management

Introduction

'Management' is a body of knowledge, skills and expertise that must be applied in ways demanded by the particular organization in which the individual manager is working; and in ways demanded also by the particular environment in which activities are conducted. The knowledge, skills and expertise required are as follows:

- achieving things through people;
- achieving things for people;
- making a profit and delivering performance;
- using scarce resources; and planning, organizing, controlling and accounting for resources;
- improving and developing products, services, service and processes;
- coping with change and uncertainty.

Management is conducted in organizations; and organizations operate in their environment. Organizations may be described as: 'systems of inter-dependent human beings' (Pugh and Hickson, 1996); a 'joint function of human characteristics, the task to be accomplished and its environment' (Simon, 1967). Organizations are therefore combinations of resources brought together for stated purposes. Organizations have their own life, direction, permanence and identity; and are energized by people, and their expertise, skills, talents and commitment.

Achieving things through people

Achieving things through people is a key priority because no managerial activity takes place in isolation from staff and their expertise. People's capabilities have to be harnessed in ways that are of value to the organization; and their willingness to work has also to be engaged. This part of management expertise is therefore to engage, energize and harmonize the organization's staff in pursuit of the stated goals, targets, aims and objectives. To do this effectively requires a knowledge and understanding of organizational, collective and individual human behaviour, with especial reference to how people act and react in particular situations and circumstances; and how people act and react in response to crises, emergencies and change.

just a minute

Think about any organization from which you have had bad service; and then decide: was this because the staff were incapable of giving good service or unwilling to give good service? The answer is almost invariably the latter!

expert view

'If you don't like, trust, respect and value people and their contribution you should not be a manager.' – **T. Peters** (1992)

'In the Virgin organisation, the staff come first. Only by having top quality, committed and motivated staff can you deliver the company performance that we ask for.' – **R. Branson** (1998)

'Truly professional staff require the minimum of supervision and the maximum autonomy in order to carry out their jobs for lasting effective performance.' – **C.B. Handy** (1993)

'If you want to get the best out of your staff, you have to promote and provide full and genuine equality of opportunity and treatment.' – **R.M. Kanter** (1985)

Achieving things for people

Achieving things for people, in particular meeting and responding to the legitimate demands and expectations of customers, suppliers and shareholders, is the next key priority. Each of these groups has particular requirements of every organization. These requirements must be satisfied or the customers will go elsewhere, suppliers will seek other outlets for their materials, and backers will seek alternative organizations and ventures in which to put their funds.

Customers require confidence in the products and services on offer, and that their demands for quality, durability and volumes of products and services are met. Customers expect to be able to return to the company or organization for product and service upgrades, maintenance and repairs. The implication is therefore that successful organizations are managed for the long term as well as to give immediate satisfaction.

Suppliers require steady and assured volumes of business; and so they will gravitate towards those organizations that deliver this. Again, the clear implication is the need to be confident that organizations being supplied will remain in existence over the long term.

Shareholders require assured levels of returns, both in share values and also in dividend repayments, as a prerequisite to investment; otherwise they will move their investments elsewhere. Overall therefore, achieving things for people is based on perceptions and understanding of expectations, assurance and permanence which, together with the delivery of good quality products and services, all add up to immediate and enduring confidence. Confidence in managerial terms is hard to define more precisely. The presence, knowledge and understanding of confidence is an absolute priority in achieving things for people; and it is also the case that, where confidence is lost or not fully assured, organization decline quickly sets in.

Stakeholders and management

A stakeholder is anyone who has a particular interest in any aspect of the organization. Stakeholders include:

- shareholders, backers, financiers, and financial institutions and their representatives;
- stock markets, stock brokers and financial advisers;
- organization directors and shareholders' representatives;
- public service organization governors and those charged with responsibility for gaining finance and backing for public ventures and enterprises;
- the organization's functional directors, managers, staff and their representatives;
- suppliers and distributors;
- customers, clients and end-users;
- industrial and commercial markets;
- the communities in which activities take place;
- the media, business, financial and management journalists and media analysts;
- pressure groups, lobbies and vested interests.

Organizations inevitably have dominant stakeholders – those whose interests must be served above all else; or more insidiously, those whose interests are served as a priority, whether or not this is the correct course of action for the particular organization.

The financial interest is invariably found as a dominant stakeholder. The best organizations also place their staff, suppliers and customers at this level. It is also true that any group that has cause to raise legitimate concerns about organizations and their activities should be treated as a dominant stakeholder until the issues have been addressed.

Serious problems can arise when the interests of the dominant stakeholders are served in spite of conflicting or divergent concerns from less influential sources.

The key lesson is, therefore, knowing and understanding which interest is being served at a particular time. It is additionally essential to know and understand whether specific interests are being served at the expense of others, or whether every interest is being served as far as possible. Whichever line is taken, there are opportunities and consequences that are certain to affect overall organization performance, and also the ways and means by which performance is delivered.

Achieving things for people, and balancing these interests, is therefore a major management issue at all times.

Making a profit

All managers must 'make a profit'. 'Profit' needs to be defined by all organizations and their managers in their own terms. This definition requires attention to the following.

- Surplus of income over expenditure. A version of this is calculated, by law, for all organizations on an annual (and increasingly half-year and quarterly) basis. The managerial discipline additionally requires knowledge and understanding of product and service surpluses and losses on an individual basis; and 'individual' means surpluses and losses per location and per customer, as well as per product and service unit, product and service cluster and in terms of overall output.
- Increasing organizational reputation and confidence, as the result of the ways in which products and services are delivered, as well as attention to absolute expectations in meeting product and service volume and quality demands. Increasing reputation and confidence feeds people's expectations and perceptions of products and services; and increasing quality and demand for products and services feeds reputation and confidence.
- Costs, cost-effectiveness and cost efficiency. There is a key organizational and managerial issue here, in that efficient and effective cost management can lead to a much greater income margin per product and service. The problem lies where cost management is the only, or overwhelming, driving force towards profit; and this can then go seriously wrong.

Frozen fish

Helmont Ltd is a fish processing and cannery company located at Walsall, West Midlands, UK. Until recently, it took its supplies of fresh and frozen fish from Ocean Going Trawlers

Ltd, a fishing fleet based in Liverpool. Helmont Ltd was a very successful and profitable company that supplied to all the main brands, including John West, Bird's Eye and Ross. Helmont also supplied fresh, frozen, canned and processed fish products to the supermarket chains for sale under their own brand names.

Following new quota arrangements introduced by the EU, the prices of the landed fish catches in the UK rose by 10%. Accordingly, Helmont decided to look around for alternative supplies. After extensive research, the company found that the port and fishing fleet of Cadiz, Spain, were prepared to supply it with the volumes of fish and the regularity of deliveries required. Helmont unilaterally cancelled the contract with Ocean Going Trawlers of Liverpool and took up with Cadiz. The catch prices in Cadiz were 53% lower than those from Liverpool; and the full cost, including transport, worked out at 38% cheaper than the Liverpool supplies.

The key lesson is that there is a simple cost advantage, and this is apparent to all. However, Helmont's previous suppliers were barely 100 miles away, and it was therefore much easier to manage any difficulties if things did go wrong. The new suppliers would be over 1,000 miles away; and consequently, there was a much greater propensity for things to go wrong. All of this, in practice, has to be paid for out of the cost advantages.

This venture failed because everything that could go wrong did go wrong. Refrigeration units on the lorries broke down. There were strikes and disputes involving the border authorities between France and Spain with the result that the lorries were held up on their journeys (in spite of the fact that the EU is notionally an open market, the Spanish in particular retain an active border presence). There were hold-ups at the Channel ports in Northern France. The lorries were then faced with the problems of negotiating the overcrowded UK motorway network, in particular the M25 around London and the M6 through the West Midlands, before they could get back to the company's headquarters and factory.

Helmont tried to reschedule deliveries to meet its own new limitations, and to ensure that the customers would remain satisfied. However, the customers – the branded goods and the supermarket own brands – had contracted with Helmont in good faith, and now did their best to hold them to the agreement. In order to remain viable, Helmont now had to return to Ocean Going Trawlers in Liverpool and to do their best to renegotiate the contract. This they did, but the conditions in the contract were now to be very much more onerous.

Clearly, not every cost-saving exercise goes wrong; and all managers at all times need to be actively managing their costs and maximizing and optimizing their resources. However, it is essential that the full context and range of issues are addressed. Simply to concentrate on one priority at the expense of all others is invariably a recipe for disaster.

- The 'profit' delivered by public service organizations is a function of the speed, effectiveness and completeness of service delivery, as well as the ability to stick within financial and other resource constraints. The profit delivered by public services is also, in practice, a function of the ability to respond to political directives, raise funds from external sources (for example hospitals selling flowers and books for the patients and other relatives), and develop their services according to particular local and environmental needs (for example schools providing evening classes, sports clubs and playgroups outside normal hours).

- The 'profit' delivered by not-for-profit organizations and charities is a function of the extent to which they can, and do, raise the levels of funding and resources required to serve the particular client bases. As above, not-for-profit work ultimately takes place in a competitive environment; and consequently those responsible for the management of foundations and charities have to arrive at a clear view as to whether they are competing with other charities (for example 'If people give to me, they will not give to others'); or whether people will give anyway (for example competing for customers' disposable income overall).

As required by law, Sony always produces quarterly and annual financial results. In the company annual reports however, as well as attending to immediate issues, Sony always makes clear its long-term prospects, performance and intentions; and this is to underline the fact that its priority is long-term viability and existence.

'Making a profit' requires delivering the performance that is demanded; and performance can only be delivered in relation to purpose, aims and objectives. If the purpose, aims and objectives are not clearly stated then it is not possible to evaluate anything for success, failure, achievement or otherwise.

'Performance' is covered in detail in Chapter 15. At this stage, however, it is essential to recognize that establishing the basis, boundaries and context of performance is a key management task and a core plank of managerial expertise. It is also a collective and organizational discipline, and needs to be addressed in full detail, to include:

- financial performance and targets;
- production, productivity and service output targets and aims;
- staff performance;
- market performance and standing;
- reputation management and development;
- new product and service development;
- new market development;
- long and short-term planning;
- risk assessment and evaluation.

Too many organizations and managers concentrate solely on the financial figures and targets without recognizing the impact of each of the above.

Using scarce resources

Managers are required to organize, prioritize, use and consume – and produce a return on – those resources that are placed at their disposal. All resources are ultimately finite; and, even where resources are plentiful and assured for the present and foreseeable future, they should be used and consumed as efficiently and as effectively as possible. This gives a lead to every organizational and managerial activity that everything is valued; it establishes a discipline for the use and consumption of the scarcer and more valuable resources; and it is also the case that even plentiful resources can, and do, become expensive (for example oil in the 1960s, 1970s and early 21st century).

Organization production, service and information technology, property, premises and equipment are resources with capital and operational values. Each represents a part of the total organizational investment, and the returns required and demanded must be known, understood and accepted. Organizations and their managers need to know, understand and be clear about the need for all technology and equipment, the returns required, and whether circumstances might change and affect the nature, levels and spread of returns.

Staff expertise, willingness and commitment are the primary organizational resources. Expertise and commitment are both required; neither is effective in isolation from the other. Organizations that have expertise and commitment, targeted at known, understood and agreed priorities, outperform those that do not. Organizations that have expertise but no commitment lose staff to other organizations where there is a greater sense of overall purpose; and these organizations tend to retain staff because of their commitment to themselves and their own individual interests, rather than to the organization and its products and services.

best practice

Manchester United Football Club has always sought to attract good players who want to play for it. The club has only sought to attract the very top players if this commitment could always be demonstrated. And as soon as the commitment begins to waver, the club moves the players on. For example in January 2012, the club sold Ravel Morrison, described as one of the best players of his generation: the club nevertheless found itself unable to deal with Morrison's erratic and sometimes difficult behaviour.

Improvement

Everything that is done in organizations and by people is capable of improvement. Customers, clients and product and service users expect improved and enhanced quality and volumes of what they require and demand. Staff expect improved wages, salaries, and terms and conditions of employment; improvements in the quality of their working environment and working relationships; and improved opportunities and interest in their jobs and careers. Shareholders expect improved returns on their investments, and will seek to invest in organizations that promise or give a clear understanding of improvements in these areas.

Meeting the requirements and demand for improvement is a fundamental human desire, as well as a priority placed on organizations and managers. The consequence is therefore that managers must know and understand the full range of activities carried out in their domain, how these activities interact with each other; and from this, seek to improve processes, attitudes and behaviour, as well as products, services and outputs.

Coping with change and uncertainty

Coping with change and uncertainty requires a full and detached knowledge and understanding of the organization; its products and services; its staff and their priorities, hopes, fears and expectations. It also requires a full and detailed knowledge and understanding of the external, economic, social, political and operating environment, and of the forces that are present within it. It is essential to know and understand, and be able to respond to, the effects of the following.

- Natural disasters including earthquakes, floods and drought. While it is never possible to predict the precise dates or locations in which these will happen, it is absolutely certain that each will occur at some time; and so the key is to be prepared and able to respond when they do occur.
- Terrorist attacks. And again, while it is not possible to predict when and where these will happen, it is certain that they will occur and so, again, it is essential to be able to respond at these times.
- Economic crises brought on by, for example, stock market crashes; runs on particular currencies (and upward valuations of others); oil crises (as above); energy shortages.
- Political crises and uncertainties, which are at their most visible in war-torn regions of the world, but which can occur anywhere (for example the sudden uprisings across the Middle East in early 2011; the formation in the UK of the first ever peacetime coalition government in 2010).
- Market crises brought about by losses in consumer, wholesaler and investor confidence; and which are increasingly set to be brought about as the result of macro-market choices to invest either in India or China, or in Western Europe, North America and Japan, but not both.
- Market and activity shifts brought about by the availability of expertise and technology in different parts of the world. Some of the recent effects have been to seek the movement of manufacturing activities from Western to Central and Eastern Europe, as well as the Far East; and the outsourcing of specific activities to parts of Asia and Central America because of the (perceived) lower labour and technology costs in those regions.

The above are all macro issues affecting the activities, operations, effectiveness – and performance – of organizations when they do occur. This is not to say that each will occur, or occur on a regular basis. It is for managers to know, understand and be able to respond when they do.

At a micro level, the ability to respond depends on the overall efficiency and effectiveness of product and service delivery, and of organizational processes, attitudes, values and behaviour. For example:

- A competitor's new technology may render that of other organizations obsolete; or it may appear to do so; or it may not do so (however attractive it may look at first sight). The need therefore is to be able to take a fully informed view as to whether or not the competitor's technology requires that all other organizations in the sector replace their technology, rather than jumping to the conclusion that it does.
- A new entrant to a particular market may gain immediate share, and cause concern among existing players. Whether the new player sustains and develops the market for itself is very much up to the ability of the existing players to respond.

Change and uncertainty remain constant features in the employment of staff. The stability, commitment and engagement of the staff and workforce can only be assured so far, however good the wages, terms and conditions, and managerial and supervisory style and relations. The key issues for all organizations to be aware of as employers of staff are: the effects of new employers (especially large employers) moving into the area; the effects of large employers leaving the area; increases in demand for relatively mobile staff (for example professionally qualified people) elsewhere; and gaining and losing road, rail and air infrastructure and transport connections.

Alongside this, it is essential for managers to know and understand every aspect of the bond between organization and staff, and to be fully aware of the strengths, and especially the shortcomings, present. Organizations and their managers must know and understand that, in some cases, individuals will move on for their own reasons. Organizations and their managers must also know and understand that if there are demonstrable known and understood weaknesses in the bond between employer and employee, they ultimately have a clear choice to make between remedying these issues, or managing the constant problems each time they arise.

just a minute

It is necessary to remember always that when people say 'they hate their job', this is invariably not the case – in practice, they either dislike or distrust their manager, or their work colleagues; or else they see no future for themselves at the organization.

A summary of the foundations of management in this way clearly illustrates the range of skills, knowledge, understanding and expertise involved. For those who aspire to be truly expert managers, delivering effective products and services in whatever organization and circumstances they may find themselves, there is no substitute for acquiring and developing this range of skills, knowledge, understanding and expertise. The sheer complexity has driven others to seek quick, easy and assured solutions to problems, development, enhancement and improvement through the adoption of faddish approaches.

Fashions and fads

The opposite to the rigour of developing expertise and a body of knowledge is to take a prescriptive and simplistic approach. 'Fashions and fads' is a useful way of describing directive, prescriptive and simplistic approaches to management issues and problems. Some current issues are as follows.

- **Job evaluation:** the analysis of job and work activities according to present criteria in order to rank them in importance, status, values and place on the pay scale. In practice, job evaluation tends to be rigid, inconsistent and divisive.
- **Business process re-engineering (BPR):** attention to administration, supervision and procedures for the purposes of simplicity, clarification and speed of operation. The premise is that these improvements are always possible. In practice, BPR tends to be applied prescriptively to all functions without reference to organizational effectiveness or wider aspects of operations.
- **Business analytics:** at its best, business analytics requires that every issue is 'blitzed' with data and information from as many sources as possible and then evaluated from all points of view so that decisions and initiatives are all substantiated at all stages. At its worst, it becomes another consultant-led 'numbers speak for themselves' driver of expedient and short-term fixes for problems that managers would rather not have to take responsibility for themselves.
- **Total quality management (TQM):** attention to every aspect of organizational practice in pursuit of continuous improvement, the highest possible standards of practice, products, services and customer service. In practice, TQM tends to be prescriptive in approach and dominated by paperwork and administration systems rather than attention to products and customers.
- **Right first time, every time:** this rolls easily off the tongue/pen; it is a direct contradiction of the view that everything can be improved. It is also a denial of humanity – after all, everyone makes mistakes!
- **Benchmarking:** benchmarks set standards of activity against which other activities can be compared and rated; benchmarking also applies to placing people on salary scales, activity scales, job importance scales and other matters to do with status. In practice, it is usually rigid, inconsistent and divisive. Some organizations also seek to benchmark their salaries, terms and conditions against other employers; while this is useful knowledge to have, ultimately all organizations have to be able to stand alone and independently.

- **Virtual organization:** organization structures based on technology rather than physical presence. A useful concept that tends to get drowned, either by cost-cutting or technological processes; or conventional, adversarial supervision.
- **Outsourcing:** especially the practice of outsourcing manufacturing, production and service delivery activities to locations in Central America, the Pacific Islands, South-East Asia, and the Indian subcontinent. The driving force behind this form of outsourcing is to take advantage of the reduced labour costs, and less stringent labour laws present in these locations. The downside of this form of overt cost saving is that it is a lot harder to manage and resolve problems and issues when they do arise in a rural location thousands of miles away, than if the same problems and issues do arise on the spot.

The major contribution of each (and all fashions and fads) is to broaden the debate on management issues, and to get people thinking about progress and improvement. Their weakness is apparent when they are grasped as perfection, the absolute truth, and instant solutions to all-round management problems.

Management research and literature

There is a great range of management research and literature, including textbooks, how-to books, personal and organizational histories, professional and commercial journals and periodicals, computer-based packages, databases, leaflets, checklists; and also university and commercial research programmes, monographs and learned papers. This can be broken down as follows.

- Some of it is intellectually extremely challenging. The ability, both to understand and to be an effective practitioner also in certain aspects of the managerial sphere, requires a high degree of intellectual capacity, higher education and a basic grasp of some mathematical and economic theories as well as behavioural and operational matters.
- Some of it addresses precise or defined issues that have a direct bearing on the business sphere. This is especially true of the areas of leadership, motivation, perception, and the formation of attitudes, standards and values which have both their own body of knowledge in their own right, and which then require translation into particular managerial situations in different ways.
- Some of it dwells heavily on empirical research, case histories and anecdotal examples. This enables studies of the relationships between variables in given situations to be undertaken and assimilated, and 'what if?' and other hypothetical discussions to take place in relation to real events of the past, but in overtly 'safe' situations at present. The body of the general knowledge and experience of the manager is thus developed and extended, as are his critical faculty, awareness and overall view of the sphere.

- Some of it illustrates particular successes and failures; this is especially true of the swelling array of books produced by successful business people. The lessons to be drawn here are often in the mind of the reader. Such books tend to reinforce certain aspects only of the whole managerial sphere. They provide a very useful library of what has worked in practice for comparison against a theoretical or academic base, although one by-product of this has been to create and develop a faddish approach.
- Some of it illustrates the amount of attention to detail and sheer hard work that is required of anyone who wishes to become a manager (and/or business leader or entrepreneur). Television series such as *Dragons' Den* and *Undercover Boss* are primarily entertainment, though behind the pictures presented they do show how hard it is to become and remain successful.

Over the years, management research and literature has concentrated heavily on all aspects of organizational and managerial performance, and the skills, knowledge and expertise required of those placed in management positions and responsibilities. To date however, there remains no firm, understood and agreed body of knowledge, skills or expertise; nor, as above, are there any qualifications required of those who come into managerial and executive positions as a condition of appointment.

The continuing professionalization of management

The continuing professionalization of management has led to attempts to classify the disciplines involved, as well as to crystallize the body of skills, knowledge and expertise required. This has led in turn to the rise of summary classifications, as follows.

The reflective practitioner

The 'reflective practitioner' approach emphasizes the ability to think things through, and to know and understand why things turned out in particular ways. This requires analytical and evaluative capabilities and expertise, as well as a detailed and comprehensive body of knowledge and understanding so that for any given set of circumstances, a detailed and precise critique can be conducted.

The thinking performer

The 'thinking performer' approach is an attempt to summarize the expertise required under the following headings:

- **personal drive and effectiveness**, which requires individuals to set out their own personal as well as professional objectives;
- **people management and leadership**, requiring capabilities in the management and leadership of people and the expertise that goes with it;

- **business knowledge and understanding**, of the specific needs and wants of whatever organization is being served at the time;
- **professional and ethical competence**, and a commitment to serve the standards of all professional bodies of which the individual is a member;
- **continuing learning**, a discipline required of all those in the traditional professions of law and medicine; and a personal commitment of anyone who aspires to excellence in any field at all;
- **analytical and creative/intuitive thinking**, to develop the capability to evaluate any situation, proposal, venture or initiative, and to be able to implement what is intended in the particular given set of circumstances;
- **customer focus**, a commitment to serve to the best of one's ability all those who seek to take advantage of the particular professional and expert capability;
- **strategic capability**, the capability to see the wider interests and ranges of issues, as well as being able to respond to specific requests;
- **communication, persuasion and interpersonal skills**, and this includes active listening as well as the ability to communicate actively, early, positively and with integrity.

The excellent performer

The excellent performance perspective requires that managers adopt the personal as well as occupational (professional) commitment identified above; the key is knowing and understanding what to commit to. Peters and Waterman (1982) identified a series of timeless and universal elements as follows:

- a belief in being the best;
- a belief in the importance of the staff and individuals as well as in their contribution to the organization;
- a belief in, and obsession with, quality and service;
- a belief that organization members should innovate and have their creative capacities harnessed;
- a belief in the importance of excellent communication among all staff;
- a belief in the concept of simultaneous loose–tight properties – measures of control that allow for operational flexibility;
- a belief in the continuous cycle of development;
- and a recognition that there is always room for improvement;
- attention to detail – the necessity to ensure that whatever the excellence of the strategic vision, it must always be carefully and accurately carried out;
- a belief in the importance of economic growth and profit motive;
- a belief in action rather than procedures and processes;
- a belief and commitment to constant innovation and improvement in products, services, service, working practice and staff capabilities;
- a belief and commitment to the core business of the organization.

These factors ought to indicate points of priority and concentration for any manager in all organizations, regardless of location, size and activities. The question of managerial professionalization and expert management development is considered in full detail in Chapter 19.

Management and leadership

The relationship between management and leadership is complex. On the one hand, managers at all levels are required to inspire and generate loyalty, enthusiasm and commitment among their staff, and this is clearly a leadership priority (see also Chapter 10). On the other hand, many organizational leaders, inspirational and expert though they are, clearly need senior, middle and functional managers to implement organization strategy, policy, direction and priorities.

point of view

Management as common sense

Rosabeth Moss Kanter, the then Dean of the Harvard Business School, was interviewed by Tom Mangold for the BBC *Business Matters* television series. She was asked to consider the view that all of this was 'just common sense'. Rosabeth Moss Kanter replied:

'Sense, yes. It all sounds intuitively right, and there is plenty of evidence that where these managerial characteristics are in place, organizations perform well, and remain profitable. Common – that is a different question. If this "sense" was truly "common", then we would not have the organizational, managerial, economic and social crises that we have today.'

Source: BBC (1998) 'They Did It Their Way' – *Business Matters.*

These kinds of approaches have reinforced the crystallization of 'the professionalization of management', which may be summarized as having and developing proficiency and commitment in the basic body of knowledge, skills, expertise and understanding, as above. Many professional managerial bodies now run their own certificate and diploma level qualifications, management education schemes, foundation programmes and introductory courses so that those who seek to join them and to practise in their name are known and understood to have an agreed level of competence; and this also applies to many organization-based management training schemes.

Conclusions

The overall purpose here has been to illustrate the complexity, range and scale of the subject matter that is to be considered, the widely differing standpoints from which it has been tackled, and the progression of it as a field of study. The balance of the material quoted reflects the particular concern with it over the period since 1945 and its emergence as an area critical to both business and economic success, and also the wider prosperity of society at large.

It is not at all an exhaustive coverage. However, it does attempt to itemize major staging posts and fields of inquiry, and to illustrate the variety of studies that have been undertaken. Each study indicated addresses different parts of the business and management sphere. Each makes its own particular contribution to the whole field; none provides a comprehensive coverage of it. What is clear, however, is that it is an ever-broadening sphere. The work illustrated here demonstrates just how far this has developed and the variety of approaches that have been taken in the pursuit of this.

There is no doubt that there has been a shift in approach to regard management as an occupation in its own right. What has been less certain is what the actual composition of this occupation and profession is. This chapter has attempted to illustrate the basis of this and to introduce some of the major concepts, studies and ideas that have contributed to the state of its development.

Some more specific conclusions can also be drawn from this material. Management direction and leadership are separate from the functions, operations and activities of the organization. Ability to generate confidence, loyalty, trust and faith of all those in the organization is essential. It is necessary to establish the identity of a common purpose to which everybody in the organization can aspire and to which all the resources of the organization are concentrated. People must be rewarded in response to the efforts that they put into the achievement of the organization's purposes. Both the organization and its managers must have knowledge of, and ability to operate in, the chosen environment and to influence this as far as they possibly can. Within particular constraints, organizations establish their own ways of working, cultural norms, procedures and practices, as part of the process of making effective their daily operations. There is the recognition that business and managerial practice takes place in what is both a global and turbulent environment. The ability to operate within this is critical to continuity and success.

It is additionally critical to note that much of the pressure that exists on and in companies and organizations at present has arisen (and continues to arise) because of the lack of managerial expertise and an understanding of what makes companies and organizations effective and profitable, and how to get staff to do the right things at the right time. The banking and political crises of the period since 2008 arose because of decisions taken by leaders and managers; these crises did not cause themselves to happen. There have therefore to be other ways of doing things, that ensure enduring viability and profitability in the present and evolving environment; and this has to be a major challenge for those who are to lead, direct and manage organizations in all sectors and locations for the future.

This represents the context in which the rest of the book is written. It enables a broad understanding of where the current state of the management art/science/

profession is drawn and where the current matters of importance and concern within it lie. It also indicates the range and complexity of the qualities, expertise and capacities required of all leaders and managers, whatever the size, structure, location or activities of their organization may be.

- Understanding the full range and complexity of the skills, knowledge, expertise, attitudes, behaviour and experience that goes into 'management' is essential.
- There is a responsibility on individuals who seek to become professional managers to develop their own knowledge, skills and understanding in each of the areas indicated.
- A major part of management is about organizing and involving people, and their capabilities and commitment; and so it is essential to understand human behaviour in as much detail as possible.
- In terms of companies and organizations, the key management priority is long-term profitability and viability; and so managers need to know and understand every element that contributes to this profitability and viability in particular situations.

Further reading

Branson, R. (1998) *Losing My Virginity.* Virgin Books.

Drucker, P. (1999) *Management Challenges for the Twenty First Century.* HarperCollins.

Hammer, M. and Champy, J. (1996) *Reengineering the Corporation.* Harvard.

Handy, C. (1993) *Understanding Organizations* (4th edn). Penguin.

Kanter, R.M. (1990) *The Change Masters.* Free Press.

Peters, T. (1992) *Liberation Management.* Pan.

Peters, T. and Waterman, R. (1982) *In Search of Excellence.* Harper and Row.

Pettinger, R. (2007) *Introduction to Management* (4th edn). Palgrave Macmillan.

Pugh, D. and Hickson, D. (1996) *Writers on Organizations.* Penguin Business.

Simon, H. (1967) *Organizations.* Harper and Row.

2

Organizations, managers and the environment

'No organization exists in isolation from its environment.'

In this chapter

- the nature of the business and managerial environment and its complexities
- assessing the different aspects of the environment
- using analytical tools and techniques
- using the results of the analyses

Introduction

Everything in business and management takes place within its environment; nothing ever happens in isolation. Everything that happens affects the organization and the ways it is managed, and the ways in which managers have to act, react and respond. The environment, and everything that goes on within it, provides opportunities for exploitation; and also provides constraints within which companies and organizations have to be able to operate effectively. Consequently every manager needs to be an expert in the environment overall, and especially the parts of it that directly affect their areas of responsibility and accountability.

The environment in which organizations operate, and in which managers have to manage, is ever-changing and complex. New organizations enter particular markets and activities; existing players take their activities elsewhere. Regulations and statutes change. Energy and commodity prices change. Each of these factors brings pressures under which companies and organizations and their managers have to be effective and successful. It is therefore essential that all managers learn as much as they possibly can about the environment. The purpose of this chapter is therefore to indicate the main areas that have to be learned, and the ways in which this knowledge and understanding are acquired.

The nature of the environment

As above, in order to stand any chance of being successful, managers have to be able to operate within the constraints and complexities present. It is therefore essential to know and understand the forces within the environment as a whole, and to be able to assess and evaluate these forces in detail, in the context of the given organization, its products and services, and markets served and in response to stakeholder demands and interests.

The environment in which organizations and managers have to operate may be summarized under the headings of:

- external factors;
- the immediate environment;
- internal factors.

External factors

The external factors and forces that have to be understood are the economic, social, political and legal constraints that form the basis of the wider overall operating environment. These forces include: the present and evolving nature of the trading environment; the nature of competition and rivalry; and whether the given markets are expanding, stagnant or contracting. This has to be seen in the further context of: inflation and interest rates, and currency exchange rates; wider volumes of economic activity; political stability and/or volatility; degrees of confidence in the trading environment; and the ways in which political, financial and economic interests manage change and develop each of these elements.

Economic forces are directly affected by the actions of government and the central banking system through the use of interest rate and currency valuation policies, changes in rates of taxation, and specific initiatives such as regional development.

Wider social issues refer to: the mobility of population; availability or scarcity of skills and expertise; pay and reward levels in given sectors; and the volumes of jobs and occupations available. This is related to and influences: absolute levels of prosperity; and relative levels of prosperity by occupation and location. And this additionally influences the capability and willingness to spend money on goods and services.

The population structure and demographics have to be considered, and it is usual to evaluate this through reference to: age structures; cultural and social issues; and the wider general expectations and perceptions of what the society ought to provide. Social issues are additionally affected by taxation levels as above, and related also to the capability and willingness of the population to pay taxes, and compulsory and near-compulsory charges for public services and utilities.

Legal issues refer to the present state of the law and to envisaged changes in the law. Of particular present concern to organizations and managers are: the ever-greater protections for staff at work; and strengthening health and safety legislation, including the possibility of introducing corporate manslaughter for negligence at disasters. Other areas of present and enduring concern relate to advertising and marketing; the materials used in production and packaging; and strengthening demands for accurate descriptions of products and services.

The other parts of the external environment that require continued assessment and consideration are: technology, information and telecommunications infrastructures; the strengths, opportunities and constraints of the transport and distribution networks and infrastructure; and the energy charges that arise as the direct consequence of having to use these infrastructures.

Knowing and understanding the environment means keeping up to date with everything that is happening in the business world. As well as informing your own managerial knowledge and practice, this is part of a continuing professional commitment.

The immediate environment

Knowing and understanding the immediate economic, social, political and legal environment requires taking the wider concerns, as above, and relating them directly to the location or locations where activities are taking place. Particular priorities are:

- availability of staff skills and expertise;
- property and transport prices in the particular localities;
- competitive demands for staff skills and expertise from others in the area;
- competition for supplies and the distribution network in the immediate area;
- the quality of the energy, transport and telecommunications infrastructure in the immediate area;
- specific issues concerning replacement, maintenance and upgrades of all organizational technology, equipment, expertise and resources.

There is additionally the question of the overall aura or climate of the organization and its industrial or commercial sector, which can, and does, affect the capability of organizations to attract and retain staff and expertise. In many cases, this capability is not so much a function of competition for staff and expertise from other organizations, but rather a wider malaise within the sector that cannot easily be remedied.

Attracting and retaining staff in the NHS

In its primary functions of medical care, sickness and emergency treatment, and overall healthcare provision, the UK National Health Service (NHS) continues to experience difficulties in attracting, recruiting and retaining staff to work in its core professions of medicine, surgery and nursing. These problems have been caused in part by depressed levels of salary, which has resulted in nursing and junior medical staff not being able to afford to buy property, and partly by the extremely stressful working conditions that are generated by staff shortages and lack of medical technology resources.

The problems have been compounded by continued restructurings in the NHS overall, and by the consequent pressures on local managers as the result of having to constantly change their aims and objectives to meet the latest rounds of political targets.

The net result is that for individual hospitals and other health service facilities in many areas, it is impossible to attract any staff at all to train or work in these professions. Local managers have therefore to find alternative solutions to the particular problems.

The wider lesson for all managers and students of management is to know and understand the fact that these extreme constraints can apply within any sector, and to use whatever influence they have to structure work as effectively as possible within these extreme constraints. It is additionally the case that anyone working within these constraints will always have operational problems, whatever the location or nature of the organizational and operating environment.

Internal factors

The internal environment of the organization is a reflection of its capability and willingness to operate within the wider external and immediate forces present; to create effective working relationships and conditions; and to deliver products and services whatever the constraints. Priorities for managers include the capability and willingness to:

- improve cost bases so as to be able to remain effective at times of rising energy and fuel costs, interest and transaction rates, and budget constraints;
- respond to changes in employment, production and service law while keeping disruption to a minimum;
- respond to the arrival of new employers into the area;
- respond to new competitors and entrants into the sector;
- fill any gaps left by competitors leaving the sector.

The professional management discipline required is therefore to know and understand where the pressures and forces are likely to come from, where the information that supports this is available from, and how to use it. This then defines the conditions that are needed within organizations, departments, divisions and functions that enable the required responses to be made. It is therefore in turn necessary to be able to conduct each of the following activities:

- analyse the environment;
- set effective priorities and targets;
- take effective decisions, and create effective series of decisions;
- form the basis for an effective management style;
- understand the wider constraints of the limitations present.

Analysing the environment

In order to analyse the environment effectively, it is essential to be able to identify, separate out and classify the forces and factors that are present. The information required needs to be gathered from wherever it might be available or found. All managers therefore need to know and understand where information can be found; and this will include access to public, industry, national, regional and local databases that cover every aspect of organization activities. Market, product, service, technological and customer knowledge is required. Matters such as access to staff and expertise, and pay and reward levels, have to be understood. The activities of competitors and alternatives have to be assessed and evaluated. Possibilities of changes to the law and regulations and their effects have to be known and understood. Financial data has to be available and current. So managers and organizations need to be able to gain access to any sources where comprehensive and reliable data in these areas is held; and they also have to be able to open up and use effectively their own primary data and information sources.

Environmental analyses

The environmental analyses required are:

- SWOT analysis;
- PESTLE analysis;
- Five Forces (industry analysis);
- competitor analysis;
- customer and client analysis.

Each of these analyses is conducted to ensure that as much knowledge and understanding as possible is gained about every aspect of the organization, and that its competitive and general environment and operating pressures are clearly understood. The detail of each of the analyses used now follows.

Strengths, weaknesses, opportunities, threats: SWOT analysis

The purpose of SWOT analysis is to help organizations learn, clarify issues, and identify preferred and likely directions (see Figure 2.1).

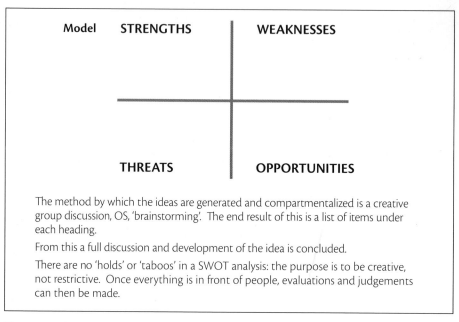

The method by which the ideas are generated and compartmentalized is a creative group discussion, OS, 'brainstorming'. The end result of this is a list of items under each heading.

From this a full discussion and development of the idea is concluded.

There are no 'holds' or 'taboos' in a SWOT analysis: the purpose is to be creative, not restrictive. Once everything is in front of people, evaluations and judgements can then be made.

Figure 2.1 *SWOT analysis*

In this activity, issues are raised, highlighted and categorized under four headings:

- **Strengths:** the things that the organization and its staff are good at and do well; that they are effective at; that they are well known for; that make money; that generate business, and reputation.
- **Weaknesses:** the things they are bad at, or do badly; that they are ineffective at; that they are notorious for; that make losses; that cause hardships, disputes, grievances and complaints; that should generate business, but do not. This aspect requires a degree of candour.
- **Opportunities:** the directions that they could profitably go in for the future that may arise because of strengths or the elimination of weaknesses.
- **Threats:** from competitors; from strikes and disputes; from resource and revenue losses; from failing to maximize opportunities or build on successes; this also includes matters over which the organization has no control.

Opportunities and threats are representations of the external environment and its forces. The information thus raised and presented is then developed, researched or investigated further. It can be done for all business and managerial activities, and to address wider global and strategic issues. It is an effective means of gathering and categorizing information, of illustrating or illuminating particular matters, and for gathering or articulating a lot of information and ideas very quickly.

Whenever you do carry out a SWOT analysis, it is essential to make sure that nothing is prejudged. Once everything is out (however wild and wacky some of the things may be), judgement and prioritization come later.

Political-Economic-Social-Technological-Legal-Environmental: PESTLE analysis

The purpose of PESTLE analysis is also to help organizations learn, but the material arising is much more concerned with the analysis of the wider strategic situation and the organization in its environment.

- **Political:** the internal political systems, sources of power and influence, key groups of workers, key departments, key managers and executives; externally, it considers particular considerations in the establishment of markets, by-products, location, ethics, and values.
- **Economic:** the financial structure, objectives and constraints (for example budgets and budgeting systems) at the place of work; externally this considers the market position, levels of economic activity, and commercial prospects and potential of the products and services offered.
- **Social:** the social systems at the workplace, departmental and functional structures, work organization and working methods; externally this considers the relationship between the organization and its environment in terms of the nature and social acceptability of its products and services, its marketing, and the regard with which it is held in the community.
- **Technological:** the organization's technology, and the uses to which it is put, and the potential uses of it; and the technology that is potentially available to the organization and others operating in the given sector.
- **Legal:** the need to work within statutory and regulatory constraints; the ability to respond to changes in the law or statutory obligations; the ability also to influence changes in the law and regulations, and the ways in which these are introduced.
- **Environmental:** the ability to work effectively within the constraints of the environment; the ability to respond to macro and micro environmental pressures; the ability to understand the effects of operations and activities on the environment; the ability to manage particular 'environmental' elements, especially waste and effluent management, noise and light pollution, energy and other resource usage.

Again, the information thus raised can be further analysed and evaluated. It establishes in more detail the wider background against which particular product or service initiatives are to take place; and raises wider issues or concerns that may in turn require more detailed resource and analysis.

The SPECTACLES approach

For the specific purposes of developing the discipline of analysing the environment in full, and to ensure the maximum completeness of coverage, Cartwright (2001) proposes the SPECTACLES approach.

Cartwright stated that it was not enough to limit consideration to political, economic, social and technological issues (the PEST elements); and so the wider view required was developed under the acronym SPECTACLES:

- **Social:** changes in society and societal trends; demographic trends and influences.
- **Political:** political processes and structures; lobbying; the political institutions of the UK and EU; the political pressures brought about as the result of, for example, the Social Charter, market regulation.
- **Economic:** referring especially to sources of finance; stock markets; inflation; interest rates; government and EU economic policy; local, regional, national and global economies.
- **Cultural:** international and national cultures; regional cultures; local cultures; organizational cultures; cultural clashes; culture changes; cultural pressures on business and organizational activities.
- **Technological:** understanding the technological needs of business; technological pressures; the relationship between technology and work patterns; the need to invest in technology; communications; e-commerce; technology and manufacturing; technology and bioengineering; technological potential.
- **Aesthetic:** communications; marketing and promotion; image; fashion; organizational body language; public relations.
- **Customer:** consumerism; the importance of analysing customer and client bases; customer needs and wants; customer care; anticipating future customer requirements; customer behaviour.
- **Legal:** sources of law; codes of practice; legal pressures; product liability; service liability; health and safety; employment law; competition legislation; European legal pressures; and whistle-blowing.
- **Environmental:** responsibilities to the planet; responsibilities to communities; pollution; waste management; farming activities; genetic engineering; cost–benefit analyses; legal pressures.
- **Sectoral:** competition; cartels, monopolies and oligopolies; competitive forces; cooperation within sectors; differentiation; and segmentation.

Cartwright states that his intention is:

'to widen the scope of analysis that needs to be carried out in order to include a more detailed consideration of the environment and culture within which an organization must operate, the customer base, competition within the sector, and the aesthetic implications, both physical and behavioural, of the organization and its external operating environment.'

This approach requires managers to take a detailed look at every aspect of their operations within their particular environment and niche. It requires managers to understand fully the broadest range of environmental constraints within which they have to conduct effective operations. It is also much more likely to raise specific, precise, detailed – and often uncomfortable – questions that many managers (especially senior managers) would rather not have to address.

Industry structure or five forces analysis

Industry structure analysis is based on evaluating and analysing 'five elemental forces of competition', drawing on the framework developed by Michael Porter (1980), who defined the five forces as follows:

1 **The industry competitors:** the nature and extent of rivalry among those organizations currently operating in the field and the implications of this for the future (for example reduced profit margins where price wars occur; reduction in capacity where there is over-provision).
2 **Suppliers:** the extent to which they dominate the sector through the supply of a key, critical or rare component; their ability to integrate forwards into the market itself; the range of choice of suppliers available; and the ability to use alternative supplies; the overall bargaining position of the suppliers.
3 **Buyers:** the extent to which they dominate the sector either because they purchase high volumes from it, or because they control the final outlet of the product in question; their ability to integrate backwards into the market itself; the number and type of operators in the buyer group; and the ability to generate and supply alternative buyers; the overall bargaining position of buyers.
4 **Potential entrants:** the extent to which organizations operating in other sectors have product, service, technology and staff capacities to gain entry to the sector in question; and the extent and nature of the entry barriers that surround the sector.
5 **Substitutes:** the extent to which the organization's product is a matter of choice on the part of the buyer; the extent to which equivalent benefits can be gained from a product that is similar, but not the same.

It has subsequently become clear that there are other forces that ought also to be considered, as follows.

- **The threat of regulation**: the threat of regulation and legal changes can have major effects on the costs of activities. Examples include regulations concerning: product contents (a major current issue for the food industry); service delivery (of continuing concern for the low cost airline industry): employment practice (the need to actively address the conduct, behaviour and performance of recalcitrant employees without having to pay the costs of employment tribunals).

- **The threat of deregulation**: allowing others into what have hitherto been restricted and enclosed areas, bounded by regulations, in which the operating companies have been able to establish dominant positions because of their capabilities in working within the bounds of the regulations.

- **The threat of re-entry**: re-entry is an issue where (often) large and dominant companies re-enter markets that they have allowed to lie dormant for a period. Examples are: supermarkets going back into clothing and hardware (challenging the clothing and hardware specialist companies); low cost generic medicines (challenging small and specialist pharmacies); and banks reopening estate agency chains (creating competition for existing specialist estate agencies and real estate businesses).

- **The threat of technology**: the main threat from technology is the potential for inventions that can and do destabilize the whole existing ways of working and cost bases of particular sectors. For example, production technology has revolutionized the clothing and textiles industries both in terms of the ability to produce new designs en masse quickly, and also in terms of where production can be located. Elsewhere, surgery that required major interventions can now be carried out using lasers or keyhole techniques.

The purpose here is to understand the nature and strength of all of the above as forces prevalent in particular sectors; and especially to understand which are the dominant forces, and the consequent effects on organizational and managerial practice. For example, if an organization is dependent upon a single key supplier, this clearly becomes the dominant force; or if the organization's core products and services are only valuable until something else can be substituted, then this too becomes a dominant force. Five forces analyses and evaluations should be carried out on a continuous basis, especially where it is known and understood that there is a large range of potential entrants and substitutes, or where the supply side is volatile.

just a minute

Always make sure that you have analysed and evaluated the strength of all the forces. Even where you have come to the conclusion that one force is dominant, make sure that you do not underestimate the strength of the others. It is also essential always to keep an open mind on potential threats and changes: the potential for regulation/deregulation; the potential for substitution and the creation of alternatives; the potential for changes on the supply side or in customer behaviour.

Competitor analysis

Competitor analysis involves an assessment and evaluation of the other players in the field. It considers the initiatives that they may themselves take to promote their own strategic advantage and also to measure their likely responses to such initiatives on the part of the organization in question (see Figure 2.2).

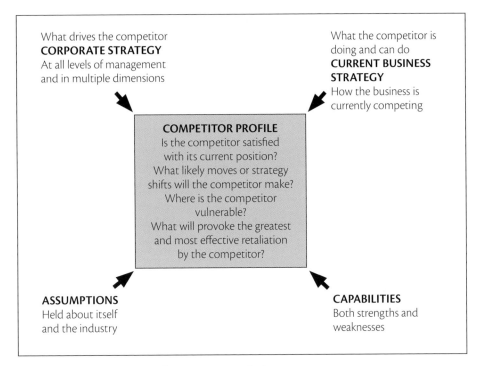

What drives the competitor
CORPORATE STRATEGY
At all levels of management
and in multiple dimensions

What the competitor is
doing and can do
**CURRENT BUSINESS
STRATEGY**
How the business is
currently competing

COMPETITOR PROFILE
Is the competitor satisfied
with its current position?
What likely moves or strategy
shifts will the competitor make?
Where is the competitor
vulnerable?
What will provoke the greatest
and most effective retaliation
by the competitor?

ASSUMPTIONS
Held about itself
and the industry

CAPABILITIES
Both strengths and
weaknesses

Figure 2.2 *The components of a competitor analysis*

The components of a competitor analysis are:

- the strategy of the competitor, its driving and restraining forces;
- its current business operations, capacities, strengths and capabilities;
- the assumptions held about both the competitor and the industry itself;
- a detailed profile of the competitor, its current satisfaction with its current position; its likely moves and responses to moves; its position in the market; its under- or overcapacity.

This constitutes a detailed discussion to be devised and conducted by sectoral, corporate, strategy specialists and experts and to be used as the basis on which both offensive and defensive strategic moves are made. Presentation to an organization's top management and directorate will normally be limited to the matters arising, the results of analysis, the conclusions and recommendations drawn from a detailed competitor analysis.

Customer and client analysis

The purpose of conducting customer and client analyses is to ensure that the business or public service relationship is considered from the point of view of customers, clients, consumers and end-users. It should form a major component of strategic analysis. This is necessary in order to:

- test assumptions and received wisdom concerning the attitudes of customers and clients to the particular organization, its products and services;
- ensure that these assumptions are not taken as absolute fact;
- assess the extent to which organizational direction is based on generally favourable responses and attitudes, rather than real customer and client demands;
- ensure that customer behaviour is not taken for granted.

In order to build up as much understanding as possible, it is necessary to make detailed enquiries along the following lines:

- Why do customers and clients use us/why do they not use us?
- Why have customers and clients increased/decreased the value or volume of business that they conduct with us?
- Why have customers started using us/stopped using us?
- Where does our product or service come in the customer's order of priority? Do we serve wants or needs?
- What causes customers to use us/what causes customers not to use us?
- Under what circumstances would customers use us more/use us less? Under what circumstances would customers increase/decrease the value and volume of their business with us?
- What are the alternatives available to customers if they do not do business with us?
- What do competitors provide that is better than us? What do competitors provide that is worse than us?
- Why do customers use us/why do customers use our competitors?

These are direct and precise questions, requiring accurate answers. In particular, if the answer to any question is either available in general terms only, or is simply not known, then lines of inquiry should be opened as a matter of urgency.

Once accurate answers are produced as above, it is then possible to understand and classify customers and clients as:

- **Apostles:** apostles demonstrate ultra-loyalty. The apostle is delighted with the service or product, and delighted to be associated in any way with the particular organization. They identify very strongly with the organization and its products and services. Apostles carry out part of the marketing function for the organization. They are highly loyal and delighted, and they tell their friends and relations.
- **Loyalists:** loyalists form the key important component of any customer base. All organizations need to be able to accurately identify where their loyalist customer

base lies, and to ensure that this is maintained, preserved and developed where possible. The ability to satisfy loyal customers on a long-term basis lies at the core of all enduring commercial success.

- **Mercenaries:** mercenaries are the hardest customers to deal with as they are basically a-loyal. They tend to go for the cheapest or most convenient option. They are difficult to deal with because they may well be satisfied but are not loyal. Or they may demonstrate product loyalty but brand a-loyalty; or brand loyalty but supplier a-loyalty. They may well move from brand to brand or supplier to supplier. If asked why they moved, the answer may be in terms of cost or convenience, but it may well be just a desire for change.
- **Hostages:** hostages are the individuals that make up 'captive markets'. Hostages are overwhelmingly the customer base of public utilities, public services, and public transport. Hostages are also found in isolated communities where, for example, there is only one convenient shop, garage, pub or restaurant.
- **Defectors and terrorists:** these are customers who once used a particular organization, but now do not do so. Defectors may move from a position of loyalty simply because there is now a much better or more convenient alternative source of supply; or they may move because they are actively dissatisfied with what has previously been on offer, but have simply said nothing about it.

Terrorists

In practice, terrorists have invariably been extreme loyalists or apostles and so therefore, when they switch their allegiance, are determined to make sure that everybody knows about it. Cartwright (2001) states that:

> 'Many of those who appear on consumer affairs television programmes have been previous apostles. On being let down, they have no problem in letting the world know about it.'

To this list others may be added:

- **Browsers and window-shoppers:** those who have a general interest in what particular organizations have to offer, and who may make unconsidered occasional purchases from time to time.
- **Passing trade:** in which particular customers and clients find themselves confronted with something that they are interested in purchasing by chance.
- **Convenience customers and clients:** who use a particular organization purely because of its overwhelming convenience to them on their own terms. This is especially important in the case of business to business activities, when organizations become the clients of suppliers purely because of the quality of relationship between themselves and the suppliers' representatives.

Customer and client types

It is also possible to distinguish the following types of customers and clients, and customer and client behaviour:

- **Passive loyalists:** those who think very highly of particular organizations, but who seldom or never use their products and services.
- **General loyalists:** those who think very highly of particular organizations, but who only use those organizations once, or very, very infrequently (this is an especial problem in the luxury goods and services industries, and also in the medium, high and top quality holiday package industry).
- **Passive apostles:** customers and clients who always used to use an organization, its products and services, but who do so no longer – either because they have ceased in their need for it, or because it is no longer convenient to get to. They nevertheless continue to praise the organization, often years after they have last used it (for example, this was an especial problem in the decline of Marks & Spencer: everyone who the company asked concerning the reasons for declines in sales continued to speak very highly of the company as an entity, and so the problems of product sales were never addressed).
- **Loyal mercenaries:** customers who come to an organization for the first time as mercenaries may be translated into loyalists as long as the product or service quality can be demonstrated. This was the basis on which the Japanese car and electrical goods manufacturers built their industrial base in the UK, USA and Western Europe in the 1970s and 1980s. Customers and clients had no particular affinity for the Japanese (indeed many still had vivid memories of brutal treatment at the hands of the Japanese military during the Second World War). Nevertheless, when the product and service quality was demonstrated, they were persuaded to change their buying habits.
- **Anticipatory terrorists:** this is an enduring present problem for those needing to avail themselves of public services. Because of media coverage that gives the overwhelming impression of the decline in quality of healthcare, education and social services in the UK, clients of these services use them on the basis that they are going to receive poor quality service, badly delivered. They therefore tend to look for the bad rather than the good in the service; and this gives rise to a culture of client complaint and compensation. So far, the strategic management of these services has not begun to address this issue.

The outcome of looking at customers and clients in these ways ought to be a full understanding of the perspective from which particular groups come to do business with the organization.

It is therefore clearly essential that organizations and their managers analyse their customer and client bases and behaviour in as much detail as possible. The outcome needs to be a clear understanding of where and why customers and clients come to particular organizations; and why they start to cease coming and change their attitudes and behaviour. It is then possible to plot particular customer and client bases on a loyalty matrix (see Figure 2.3).

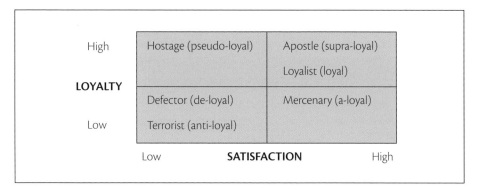

Figure 2.3 *The loyalty matrix*

Customer and client analysis is a key management priority. It is also more complex than organizational or environmental analysis because it requires time, energy and resources to be consumed in understanding the precise nature and requirements of those with whom the organization is to do business. It therefore becomes very easy to neglect this, to take customer and client attitudes on trust, or to understand them in general terms only. Specific points of inquiry are required, as follows, in order to establish precise understanding of:

- the price that customers/clients are willing to pay for particular products and services;
- the value and quality that they expect from particular products and services;
- making products and services as convenient as possible to the customer and client bases served;
- length, frequency and intensity of usage;
- depreciation/appreciation and re-sale aspects;
- maintenance, repair, replacement and upgrade elements;
- personal feelings of esteem and worth that accrue from ownership and usage;
- fashionable and faddish elements (especially important in clothing, cars, computers and furniture);
- feelings of exclusivity, luxury, desirability;
- returns on financial and emotional investment;
- particular demands and requirements of individual customers.

Much of this is therefore clearly subjective. Purchases made by different customers of the same item, for the same purpose, for the same price may result in widely differing levels of satisfaction. Customers and clients may be prepared to go to one organizational location for a given set of purposes, but not others. Customers and clients may also be persuaded to use (or stop using) an organization or location when it is known, perceived or believed to be in their interests to do so.

The Millennium Dome and the O2 Arena

In order to celebrate effectively the 2nd Millennium of Christianity in the year 2000, the Millennium Dome was conceived by the UK government in 1994. The Millennium Dome was to be built on a former naval site on the south bank of the River Thames at Greenwich, south-east London. As well as celebrating 2000 years of Christianity, the Millennium Dome would provide an exhibition and demonstration of everything that was best about the British way of life.

The project failed. The visitor numbers (projections were estimated at 30,000 per day every day for the year 2000) never materialized; the quality of the exhibitions and presentations was variable; and transport access and egress was never fully resolved.

From the point of view of analysing the environment in this way, the best that could be said for the project was: the micro-environmental issue was addressed because it meant that the pollution present on the site had to be cleared up before the Dome could be built; and from an aesthetic point of view, the Dome was a particularly distinctive design.

From every other point of view, there were shortcomings however. Society had changed, and people would only visit such an exhibition if it was both of a high quality, and also convenient for them to do so. The political issues, especially in terms of who was to take responsibility, were never fully evaluated; nor were the economic questions of cost; or the cultural, aesthetic and customer demands for the quality and variety of actual presentation and exhibition content. Wider environmental and sectoral demands in terms of the quality of the transport infrastructure, or specific questions of what constitutes 'a good day out' for those visiting London were not addressed. It was additionally the case that the Millennium Dome was located many miles from the majority of tourist attractions, the rest of which are in central London.

It was not until 2005 that a commercially viable use was found for the site. The Dome was renamed the O2 Arena, and for the first time now had a clear purpose in life – a concert, entertainment and events venue. Over the period since 2005, the venue has been extremely successful in terms of attracting top performance from all branches of entertainment to perform there and in generating the large numbers of customers necessary to make these events successful.

A full customer analysis would have concluded that the original Millennium Dome would never have been viable; and that, given an active purpose to go to the site for particular events, the venue could have been made successful in those terms.

Setting priorities, aims and objectives

A full understanding and analysis of the environment, and classification of the pressures and constraints present, establishes the context in which priorities, aims and objectives are set. Establishing effective and achievable priorities, aims and objectives is the foundation for measuring and assessing all aspects of organizational and managerial performance.

Drucker (1996) summarized this as 'management by objectives'. To be fully effective, management by objectives required the establishment of specific targets and priorities that were capable of achievement within the constraints of the operating, competitive and wider environment. This clarity of approach, and attention to the environment, was essential, whether establishing overarching goals and targets for organizations as a whole, or whether establishing specific achievements and results desired and demanded of particular departments, divisions, functions, groups and individuals.

Within these constraints, the establishment of priorities, aims and objectives, concentrates on the following:

- key tasks, key results and performance standards;
- work improvement plans, setting key tasks against action plans, target dates and intended outcomes;
- regular performance reviews based on participation;
- attention to future directions, as well as assessment of the present;
- previewing and reviewing the potential of staff, products, services and inventions.

For each of these to be effective, management information systems are required; and these have to be kept fully up to date at all times. Information has additionally to be capable of delivery in ways that are useable by those who have to take decisions for the future; and again, this refers to both those at the top of organizations and also those with specific responsibilities at more junior levels.

Establishing priorities, aims and objectives in this context enables the tangible and high profile aspects of organizational performance to be addressed. These areas are:

- market standing, reputation and position;
- sales performance;
- innovation, enterprise, pioneering, research and development;
- productivity and output levels;
- assessments of resource utilization: premises, technology, capital goods and equipment, expertise and the human resource.

Assessing these areas in this context ought to lead additionally to developing the capability of addressing and assessing the less tangible areas of organizational cohesion and performance: managerial performance and development; staff performance and attitudes; and the nature of responsibility and accountability towards the public and the wider environment.

Approaching priorities, aims and objectives in these ways gives a basis for the judgement of likely overall profitability and effectiveness; and also for assessing the value and actual profitability and effectiveness of activities presently in hand.

To be fully effective, attention is necessary in each area. While the balance clearly varies between organizations, neglect in any one area is likely to weaken the whole. Setting priorities, aims and objectives additionally has the purpose of ensuring that the organization is not blinded by extremes of performance in one area to the detriment of the others. For example, excellent sales performance may lead to feelings of complacency and lack of attention to the need for new products, or to any assessment of potential declines in sales, should environmental circumstances change.

Simon (1967) further highlighted the difficulties of establishing effective priorities, aims and objectives within the constraints of the environment; and these constraints were related to the capability of the organization to deliver sustained levels of excellent performance within the changing nature of the operating and competitive environment.

Simon identified three levels of performance:

- excellent: sustained high achievement, output and quality, leading to high levels of profit, effectiveness and satisfaction, but in reality achieved by very few organizations;
- unsatisfactory: low levels of achievement, unacceptable to stakeholders, and leading to losses, inefficiency, ineffectiveness and dissatisfaction;
- satisfactory: achieved by most organizations most of the time, satisfactory performance requires producing acceptable levels of output, volume and quality, leading to enduringly acceptable – and therefore satisfactory – levels of profit and effectiveness.

Simon found that the drive for satisfactory performance was influenced by a lack of capability in predicting future pressures within the environment; and a lack of capability additionally in being able to respond effectively to changes in these pressures. Simon found that in many organizations and industries, there existed therefore a consensus that satisfactory performance represented an acceptable level of achievement; that in practice, the top priority of senior managers was to ensure that satisfactory levels of performance were achieved. Simon also found that this approach was a major influence on decision-making processes.

best practice

Whatever the strength of performance, you should always look for areas where improvements can be made. If it appears that no improvements can be made, then make sure that you can say why; and make sure that you keep coming back to the area just to make sure that no improvements are possible at some time in the future.

Organizational considerations

The organizations that have to operate within the environment, and whose managers are responsible for taking and implementing decisions, have to be considered from a variety of different points of view. Organizations have legal status, a presumption of permanence, and a presumption that they will deliver the products and services stated.

The legal status of organizations refers to their constitution and composition. The main forms of legal status are:

- **Commercial organizations**: sole traders, partnerships, private limited companies, and public limited companies (plc). Each of these organization forms may additionally be: local, regional, national, international and global; part of a joint or multi-venture; a specialist subsidiary; or an organization constituted for the purposes of single project delivery, after which it is disbanded.
- **Friendly or mutual society or cooperative**: in which the profits and rewards are shared among members.
- **Charities and not-for-profit organizations**: charities and not-for-profit organizations raise funds for particular purposes and are normally constituted for stated purposes and with a clear financial base that depends on raising money from particular sources (including small individual public donations).
- **Public bodies and public corporations**: these organizations are the institutions of central, regional and local government functions that normally have the remit of providing essential public services, providing for civil and military defence, and maintaining the desired and anticipated quality of life on the part of the nation, region or part of society concerned.
- **Non-governmental organizations**: non-governmental organizations are autonomous entities funded by government and constituted for a particular purpose; this includes the constitution of bodies for the independent regulation of specific activities.
- **Churches and other religious foundations**: this includes charities that are funded by donations and other receipts for stated purposes; and these funds are then distributed in the areas with which the charity is concerned.
- **Transnational organizations**: transnational organizations include the United Nations (UN), World Health Organization (WHO), and International Monetary Fund (IMF). These and other bodies have a general influence on the ways in which organizations operate and interact with their environment; and may, from time to time, make specific pronouncements, recommendations and interventions in given locations, affecting directly the activities of other organizations in those areas.

It is essential to note that the legal status of organizations can, and does, change. Governments privatize public services; commercial organizations undertake merger and takeover activities, and open and close subsidiaries. Changes of legal status can, and do, also occur as the result of changes in international, corporate and company law.

Beneficiaries

The beneficiaries of an organization are those people for whom the organization is especially constituted, and whose interests it seeks to serve.

The primary beneficiaries of an organization are normally its staff, customers, clients, shareholders and suppliers.

The ultimate beneficiaries of an organization may also be the staff, customers, clients, shareholders and suppliers. However, problems do occur when top and senior managers and (in public services) powerful political interests use organizations in practice for their own ends. Powerful and influential figures and groups tend to disrupt the effectiveness of organizations in the interests of pursuing their own position and reputation. Short-term shareholder drives disrupt the long-term effectiveness of commercial organizations; political ambitions disrupt the enduring effectiveness of public services.

Changing beneficiaries occurs when organizations change their status. Newly privatized public services have suddenly to run under the financial regimes of the new owners; and a proportion of the funds raised will be redistributed in the form of share dividends, rather than going straight back into the services. Mergers and takeovers mean that staff, customers, shareholders and suppliers of the previous organizations have to get used to new ways in which they are to be dealt with, and any, or all, of these groups may cease to benefit from the new organization (though these groups are also often replaced by new beneficiaries who find the new organization attractive to them).

Non-beneficiaries are present where organizations do not deliver what they state that they will deliver; and where customers and clients do not receive the products and services expected and anticipated. Attention to non-beneficiaries is a prime concern when changing or varying the quality, range and coverage of all public services; and in ensuring that customers continue to receive adequate quality of supplies following the privatization of infrastructure and essential commodities of life, especially water, gas, electricity, heating and lighting.

Management style

The nature of the operating environment, the priorities identified and established, decision-making processes, and the legal status of the organization all impact heavily on the management style of the organization. Effective delivery of products and services is dependent upon managerial expertise, capability and willingness to operate within these constraints; and this leads to the design and emergence of preferred approaches to staff, workloads, priorities and decision-making.

In this context, the key to an effective management style is founded in the chosen approach to the staff of the organization. This approach is normally one of the following:

- **Unitary:** in which the aims, objectives, hopes, fears, aspirations and ambitions of the individual must be harmonized and integrated with those of the organization – and where necessary subordinated so that the overall purpose of the organization remains the main driving force.

- **Pluralist:** in which the organization recognizes the divergence and often conflicting aims, objectives and drives of the people who work for it. Organizations that take this view normally include opportunities for personal and professional (as well as organizational) fulfilment. The basis is that by recognizing this divergence and attending to all needs, organization needs will be satisfied.

- **Radical:** in which it is recognized that there can be no long-term productive effort and harmony unless everyone involved is given a substantial and meaningful stake in the organization. This used to be regarded as the Marxist approach, and has therefore fallen into some disrepute. However, many organizations take the view that by offering staff substantial shareholdings in the company for which they work, or substantial profit-sharing arrangements, they therefore engage the direct interest of the staff in their own future and economic prosperity. For example, John Lewis, the department store, divides 15% of its retained profits between its staff; Semco divides 23% of its retained profits among its staff.

- **Mutual:** normally founded on the abolition of status and rank in favour of occupational and organizational effectiveness; however, this normally only works where there is full openness and availability of information, knowledge of activities and understanding of the value of every contribution.

- **Cooperative:** in which the organization establishes a psychological and behavioural basis of partnership and involvement based on the value of the contribution that everyone is to make.

- **Confrontational:** an adversarial approach to staff. This is based, at best, on the recognition that harmony of objectives is impossible, leading to the creation of systems and processes for the containment and management of conflict. At worst, it is based on mistrust and coercion, often stemming from a lack of genuine value placed on staff.

best practice

You should always evaluate management style in terms of areas that can be improved. On the other hand, where it is clear that the management style is very strong, it is essential never to lose those strengths in the pursuit of other things.

Psychological contract

Organizations may be viewed from the nature of the psychological contract that they engage in with their staff. This is the result of implications and expectations that arise as the result of the given organizational, occupational, professional and personal relationships in specific situations. They vary between all organizations and situations, and may be summarized as:

- **Coercive:** whereby the relationship between organization and staff, and also organization and customer, is founded on a negative. An example of this is prison – the prisoners are there against their will. It is also present where sections of the community are forced or pressurized into using a monopoly or near-monopoly for an essential commodity or service – examples are electricity, telecommunication, petrol and fuel. It also can be present in institutions such as schools and colleges where the children or students attend because they are required to do so by the society.
- **Alienative:** whereby the relationship between staff and organization is negative. This has traditionally applied to large and sophisticated organizations and especially to those staff working on production lines and in administrative hierarchies where they have no, or very little, control over the quality and output of work.
- **Remunerative:** whereby the relationship between staff and organization is clearly drawn in terms of money in return for efforts and attendance. It is normally to be found as the dominant feature where there is also a low level of mutual identity between staff and organization.
- **Calculative:** whereby the staff have a low commitment to organization goals and a high commitment to current levels of earning and satisfaction – it is again a key feature of the wage–work bargain for production and administrative staff. For those with high levels of professional and technical expertise, the calculative relationship is based on the ability to practise, the need to find an employer and outlet for those skills and individual drives to serve and become expert.
- **Normative:** whereby the individual commitment to organizational purpose is very high. This is found in religious organizations, political parties and trade unions. It is also increasingly found in some business organizations when a normative (that is, committed quarrel) approach is taken to the wage–work bargain as well as the economic. It is effective as long as the wage–work bargain itself is sound and the organization accepts a range of obligations and responsibilities to ensure that it is maintained.
- **Internalized:** whereby individual and collective commitment to organization purpose, activities, attitudes and values is unquestioning.

Viewing organizations from a variety of positions in these ways indicates the background against which aims and objectives are to be drawn up. It also indicates the source of some of the limitations and constraints that have to be taken into account when considering the capabilities of organizations and the nature and relationship of these with the purposes that are to be pursued.

point of view

It is also essential to understand the psychological contract from the point of view of the staff, and what makes them come to work and do the jobs that they do, for the given organization at the present and evolving stage of its life. This then ought to give a clear indication of the sorts of staff, personalities and capabilities that can be attracted to work. It also gives a clear indication of where the sources of collective and individual staff motivation and commitment truly lie (see also Chapter 17).

This also gives rise to conflicting and divergent aims and objectives as those with managerial responsibility either seek to reconcile these divergences, or else prioritize some (often their own interests rather than those of the organization) at the expense of others (see Figure 2.4).

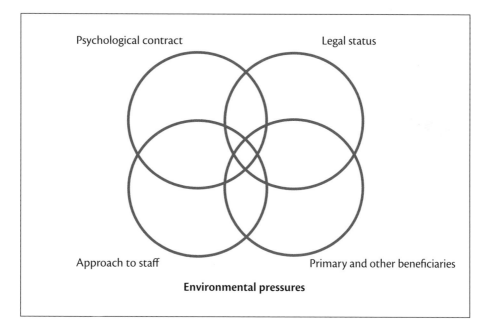

Figure 2.4 *The foundations of management style*

Conclusions

As no organization exists in isolation from its environment, the nature and extent of the relationship and interactions must be considered. Organizations are subject to a variety of economic, legal, social and ethical pressures which they must be capable of accommodating if they are to operate effectively. In some cases, there are strong religious and cultural effects, and local traditions that must be capable of effective harmonization also. More specifically, organizations need access to workforces, suppliers, distributors, customers and clients; and to technology, equipment and financial resources.

It is clearly essential that organizations, and their managers, understand the environmental pressures and constraints under which they have to operate. It is also clear that this is an extremely complex process, requiring time, energy, resources and commitment. Because of this, this aspect of managerial understanding is often not considered at all, or else not attended to in full. The position is further complicated when this part of management expertise is summarized as follows.

- There is clearly no best way to organize; as the environment changes so systems, aims and objectives must be flexible and responsive.
- The environment changes in both predictable and unpredictable ways; it changes in ways that can be controlled and influenced and in ways that cannot be controlled and influenced. The problem for managers lies in the extent of their understanding of their environment, and in their ability to anticipate the unexpected by building systems that are capable of accommodating these pressures.
- Because of the nature of the relationship with the environment, organizations need to spend time on external issues, assessing and understanding the environment, and the changes and turbulence within it.
- Decision-making processes have to be both structured and effective within the context and environment in which they are undertaken. No decision can be taken in isolation from either internal or external pressures.
- Each input process/output cycle changes the nature of the organization's social and technical resources, presenting an opportunity to strive for optimization and improvement.

Above all, the environment is dynamic and not static or rigid, allowing for limitless opportunities for change to occur: investment in environmental adaptation and transformation are as essential to success as investments in capital, equipment and staffing. The more complex and turbulent the environment, the more essential this form of investment becomes.

Environmental, technological, market and competitive pressures, as well as social changes, are the primary causes and inspiration for organizational improvement, development, enhancement and change.

Social, legal and ethical constraints constitute the main limitations placed on the activities of organizations. These require that specific approaches are adopted to all aspects of activities in order to meet standards prescribed by law or laid down by the prevailing values and morals of society.

The purpose of this chapter has been to summarize and indicate the various forms of organization, the different points of view from which they may be considered and the wider context in which they operate. No organization operates in isolation from, or without reference to, its environment. The environment provides staff, customers, resources, technology and equipment; and also confidence and expectations – the context in which successful and effective activities take place.

- The ability to analyse the environment in full is critical. This is a key part of business and management teaching, and ought to translate into professional practice.
- When assessing organizational and managerial priorities, you need to be clear what is driving them; and if it is anything other than enduring levels of performance, you need to be prepared for problems.
- When evaluating the psychological contract between employees and organization, it is essential to be aware of the strengths and weaknesses – and you need to have ideas about removing the weaknesses if at all possible.
- When evaluating the management style of an organization, you need to be aware of why it exists and whether it works; and if does work, you need to know why; and if it does not work, you need to know why also with a view to making improvements.
- In overall terms, you need to be aware of the extent to which all interests are being served, and what improvements ought to be made to ensure that the expectations of everyone are being met.

Further reading

Cartwright, R. (2000) *Mastering Customer Relations*. Palgrave Macmillan.
Cartwright, R. (2001) *Mastering the Business Environment*. Palgrave Macmillan.
Christensen, C. et al. (1987) *Business Policy*. Irwin.
Drucker, P. (1996) *The Practice of Management*. Heinemann.
Porter, M. (1980) *Competitive Strategy*. Free Press.
Simon, S. (1967) *Organizations*. Harper and Row.

3

Managing in a changing environment

'Clear aims and objectives are required when proposing change.'

In this chapter

- the nature of change and how it affects organizations and their managers
- identifying priorities and drives and restraints for change
- change as a process
- the nature of changes in organizational practices and activities

Introduction

As stated in Chapter 1, a key managerial task and expertise is to be able to operate effectively within the constraints of a changing environment. Social, economic and political changes in society over the recent past have deeply affected the management of organizations. These changes may be summarized as:

- **Technological:** affecting all social, economic and business activities; rendering many occupations obsolete and creating new ones; and opening up new spheres of activity, bringing travel, transport, distribution, telecommunication, industry, goods and services on to a global scale; the development of fledgling virtual industries; the development by companies of virtual activities.
- **Social:** the changing of people's lives, from the fundamentals of life expectancy and lifestyle choice, to the ability to buy and possess items; to travel; to be educated; to receive ever-increasing standards of healthcare, personal insurance and information; to be fed; to enjoy increased standards of social security and stability, increased leisure time and choice of leisure pursuits; and all commensurate with increases in disposable income and purchasing power, and choices of purchase.

Changing demographics

In many parts of the world, the fundamental structure of society is being radically affected by changes and movements within the population. The migration of people from areas where there is no work to those places where they can find employment is a major political issue. In other parts of the world, the issue of ageing population has also to be addressed. Elsewhere still, the great expansion of youthful population means that there is the pressure to provide work in those areas.

Whichever of these issues has to be faced in particular locations, it produces a major impact on the particular environment, and therefore a critical pressure for organizations working in those locations.

- **Economic:** pressures to change and develop are brought about by the ability of organizations to locate production and service delivery functions in the locations of their choice based on their own priorities (especially cost reduction); the opportunities to develop markets in hitherto unfamiliar locations; and the opportunity to recruit staff from an international pool. Economic change also refers to fluctuations in currency exchange rates, interest rates and inflation rates; and these in turn are reinforced again by the ability of organizations to trade with those whom they choose, anywhere in the world.
- **Macro-political:** the creation of trading blocs and superstates (the EU), and the expansion of hitherto national currencies to become the currency of choice elsewhere (for example the US dollar is now the currency of choice in Ecuador). These and similar moves have led some countries to be able to advance and enhance their political influence with a clear implication that there is a commercial advantage to be gained for their own organizations, and therefore their own domestic economies.
- **Macro-organizational:** the ability of organizations to locate their activities wherever they choose. This has led, for example, to the practice of outsourcing particular activities to areas where technology and expert labour are cheap and plentiful; and to establishing flexible patterns of employment so that those who work with technology can do so wherever they happen to be at a given time; and the creation of transnational and global organizations, able to shift priorities and volumes of activity wherever they may be demanded (and able to remove them very quickly from areas where they are suddenly not demanded).
- **Eco-political:** resulting in changes in all governmental forms; the state of flux and expansion of the EU, and the adoption of supranational laws and directives, and the single market; the emergence of Russia as an economic power; the emergence of Brazil, North and South Africa, and the Middle East as spheres of

political and economic influence; the rapid expansion of China and India as dominant spheres of economic, and therefore political, influence; the potential for the rest of Africa, Central and South America to develop along similar lines.

- **Environmental:** pressures on organizations to manage, maximize and optimize their use of resources so that waste and effluent are kept to an absolute minimum and can be disposed of effectively and without lasting effect on the environment; pressures on organizations to manage their transport and distribution activities so that these are as energy and environmentally efficient as possible; wider questions of the use, availability and sourcing of scarce resources.

- **Expectational:** the development and enhancement of people's expectations as the result of their increased ability to gain access to products and services from all over the world; what was previously acceptable is now very often superseded by the presence and availability of substitutes and alternatives from a much wider range of organizations.

In order to achieve the degrees of permanence, order and stability essential for the sustenance of long-term commercially viable products and services, and effective public services, the turbulent and changing environment has to be accommodated. The result is that pressures on managers for change, development, enhancement and improvement come from the following sources:

- the changing nature of markets, and their size, scope, scale and location;
- the changing nature of technology, combined with the ability to locate it and use it effectively anywhere in the world;
- the changing nature of work patterns, again in relation to the ability to locate and source workforces anywhere in the world;
- the drive to maximize the return on investment on indigenous and domestic workforces through the creation and implementation of flexible and non-traditional patterns of work;
- the changing nature of competition, recognizing that competitive pressures, products and services can come from any organization, anywhere in the world.

just a minute

You should always remember that change is a process as well as a series of events. Any change that is made now will affect the ways in which things are done in the future, and provide opportunities (and constraints) for future activities and initiatives.

The drive for change

The main drive for change is concerned with maximizing and optimizing returns on investment. This in turn requires that organizations get a greater return on the investment that they make in premises, technology and expertise in the pursuit of producing and delivering effective products and services. This has to be delivered in the context of changes in the economic, social and political environment as above; and within the constraints of the changing nature of market demands, and the pressures to produce and deliver public and other services.

The drive for change has also to be seen in competitive terms; meaning that even excellent and high performing organizations will lose their edge if they do not constantly adapt and develop, and so leave themselves at the mercy of those that do. Effective managerial approaches to change have to be seen, above all, in terms of recognizing and addressing the barriers to change that exist everywhere.

Barriers to effective change

When addressing either the need to change, or the barriers to change, it is essential to be able to present what is proposed in terms of:

change – from what – to what – when – where – how – why?

If any of these elements is not clearly addressed, barriers to change are certain to exist. Barriers to effective change, and the ability to respond to organizational, environmental and market pressures, may be classified as either operational or behavioural.

Operational barriers

- **Location:** this is a barrier when, for whatever reason, it becomes impossible for the organization to continue to operate in its current premises. Relocation has consequences for the resettlement of families, retraining and organization development. Even where the new premises are close by, it may affect access, work and attendance patterns. For greater distances, the consequences of widespread disruption have to be addressed. As well as personal consequences, this includes attention to organization culture and structure.
- **Tradition:** this is a problem where there has been a long history of successful work in specific, well-understood and widely accepted ways. This may be underlined where a whole community has grown up around a particular industry or organization and where this is a major provider of employment and prosperity (for example coal mining, iron and steel, shipbuilding, engineering). If this has been steady for long periods, there are strong perceptions of stability and permanence.
- **Success (and perceived success):** if the organization is known or perceived to be successful in its current ways of doing things then there is a resistance based on: 'Why change something that works?' This is especially true if there is a long

history of stability and prosperity. It is often very difficult in these circumstances to get workforces to accept that technology, ways of working and the products themselves are coming to the end of their useful life.

- **Failure:** this is a barrier to change where a given state of affairs has been allowed to persist for some time. The view is often taken – by both organizations and the staff concerned – that this is 'one of those things', a necessary part of being involved in a given set of activities. Resistance occurs when someone determines to do something about it – again, upsetting an overtly comfortable and orderly status quo.

just a minute

You should always remember that success and failure are value judgements to a greater or lesser extent. The only way to at least begin to rationalize success and failure is to assess what was achieved against what was intended.

- **Technology:** this is a barrier for many reasons. It is often the driving force behind jobs, tasks, occupations and activities. Their disruption causes trauma to those affected by the consequent need for job and occupation change, retraining, redeployment – and often redundancy. Technological changes may also cause relocation to more suitable premises. Technological change in turn causes changes to work patterns and methods. It has been one of the driving forces behind the increase in both home working, where employees can be provided with all the equipment necessary to work without the need to come together at the employer's premises, and part-time working where the demands for maximization on investment in technology and increases in customer bases have led to extended opening and operational hours. Technological change disrupts standard and understood patterns of behaviour and interaction; and this can lead to changes and loss of identity with work groups and colleagues. It has led to flexible working, away from traditional job titles, restrictive practices and demarcation. Technological change has also disrupted traditions of representation and membership of trade unions, and professional and occupational bodies. Some jobs and occupations have become obsolete, others have been created, and others still have changed out of all recognition from their traditions and expectations.
- **Vested interests:** changes are resisted by those who are, or who perceive themselves to be, at risk of obsolescence or loss of influence. Vested interests are found in all work and occupational areas. They include senior managers threatened with loss of functional authority; operational staff faced with occupational obsolescence; people in support functions no longer considered necessary; and those on promotional and career paths for whom the current order represents a clear and guaranteed passage to increased prosperity and influence.

Lobbies and vested interests

Lobby groups and vested interests are present in all organizations, and in relation to the environment in which activities are carried out. Lobbies and vested interests have to be managed whatever the present state of the particular organization. It is essential to recognize the nature and extent of the influence of lobbies and vested interests, and where, when, why and how they are able to exert this influence. The main lobbies and vested interests that have to be managed within a changing environment are:

- **Management groups:** as stated in the text above, especially where their own interests and priorities are threatened.
- **Trade unions:** especially when faced with loss of influence in workforce representation.
- **Shareholders' representatives, stockbrokers and other financial interests:** when, for example, a change of ownership or direction is muted or strongly indicated.
- **Customer, consumer and environmental groups.**
- **Overmighty and over-influential individuals, groups, departments, divisions and functions:** especially where organizational restructuring or changes of direction mean that this influence is to be diluted or lost.
- **Environmental lobbies:** concerned with the effect of activities or proposed activities on the quality of the environment; examples include – the effect of construction blight when road-building schemes are considered; the ability to dispose effectively of toxic waste and effluent; concerns for environmental blight brought about by noise, lighting and dust.
- **Managing the media:** especially the ability to respond effectively to questions raised, both legitimately and otherwise.

The lesson here is that these groups each expect to have their concerns addressed. In most cases, the concerns raised are legitimate even if delivered from a biased or partial point of view. Those responsible for managing in a changing environment need to understand this. It is additionally the case that the ability to respond to concerns raised by such groups meets their expectations; the inability to respond to the concerns raised by such groups, on the other hand, calls into question the strength, probity and integrity of what is proposed.

- **Managerial:** the managerial barrier is a consequence of 'the divorce of organization, ownership and control' (Marx, 1867, cited in Harvey, 2010), where there is a divergence between the organization's best interests and need for long-term survival, and the needs of individuals and groups of managers to preserve their own positions. Existing patterns of supervision may again provide both general order and certainty, and specific career and promotion paths.
- **Bureaucracy:** the bureaucracy barrier occurs where patterns of order and control have grown up over long periods in the recording and supervision of activities and

in the structuring of organizational functions. The problem is worst where the bureaucracy is large and complex, and a significant part of the total range of activities.

- **Redundancy and redeployment:** this is referred to above. It is a barrier in its own right because in the current context any proposed change carries redundancy and redeployment as possibilities, and because it has so often been a consequence of other changes.

You should never make people redundant except as a last resort. Reducing the size of the workforce is superficially attractive and gives the impression of change and progress. You need always to ensure that redundancies are only carried out when everything else has been considered.

Behavioural barriers

The main behavioural barriers are as follows.

- **'It cannot be done':** this is a barrier to both confidence and understanding, and is based on a lack of true, full and accurate information concerning the matters that the organization is proposing.
- **'There is no alternative':** this comes in two forms. First, it is adopted by the workforce and interest groups in and around it (for example trade unions) that have a vested interest in the maintenance of the status quo either because it is familiar, or because any change will result in loss of influence. This is especially true where business has been conducted in an effective and productive steady-state for a long period of time. The other side of this is where directorates and managers adopt this as the one and only explanation for a change that is to take place. Conducted in isolation, 'there is no alternative' simply becomes a challenge for others to think of alternatives. The matter requires explanation and communication in order to demonstrate to all those affected that alternatives have indeed been considered and that what is now proposed represents the chosen strategic direction.
- **Lack of clarity:** if organizations have not sorted out the basis of the changes that are proposed, neither staff nor customers will go along with them with any degree of confidence or understanding; aims and objectives must be clearly understood as the prerequisite to successful and effective change, and communicated to those concerned in their own language.
- **Fear and anxiety:** these are human responses to concepts and situations that are unknown or uncertain. They are the initial response (or part of it) to any change that is proposed; and if allowed to get out of hand, can become an exercise in the devising and promulgation of hypothetical scenarios that could, in certain circumstances, become problems on the changing landscape. Not only does this

constitute a waste of organizational resources and a diversion from actual purposes, but such interaction among the staff feeds on itself, generating negativity and unnecessary internal turbulence.

- **Perfection:** at the point at which change is proposed suddenly everything concerning the status quo becomes 'perfect'. Anything that is proposed as an alternative has therefore to address this barrier. It is another manifestation of familiarity and comfort, and faced with the loss of this, such elements become highly worthwhile to retain.

Each of the barriers indicated above in practice comes about if one of the **change – from what – to what – when – where – how – why?** factors is not present. In practice, people are willing to change if it is made clear to them that they have to do so and if, as far as possible, it is made in their interests to do so.

For all barriers, the main issue is to avoid leaving a vacuum. Organizations have therefore to understand where the proposed changes are to lead and what their consequences are. Early communication is essential for the benefit of all concerned. The best employers give every opportunity to their workforce to be a part of their future before casting around outside for new staff and expertise.

In most cases most of these barriers, operational or behavioural, are present. The influence of each barrier depends upon the particular situation, the nature and extent of the changes to be made, and whether they are strategic, operational, locational, attitudinal, structural or cultural. Whichever is present, the keys to effective and sustainable progress are:

- integrity, directness and clarity of what is proposed;
- clarity of purpose, strategy, direction and priority, easily understood by all affected;
- clarity of communication, and this includes sustaining the directness of communication over the period of change;
- clear monitoring, review and evaluation processes, so that problems and teething troubles are addressed as soon as they become apparent;
- consultation, counselling and support for individuals and groups that know, believe or perceive themselves to be most at risk from particular changes;
- a capacity for addressing specific problems, issues, quirks and anomalies as these become apparent.

Changing cultures and structures

Effective, lasting and operationally successful change is achieved only if attitudes, values and beliefs are addressed and the same universal importance placed on change as on operational and technological factors. They all impinge on each other: for example, the introduction of an automated production line leads to new job requirements, which leads to new job descriptions, which leads to new ways of working, which leads to revised staff handbooks and work agreements – and so on.

Consequently, attempts to introduce an operational change in isolation (for whatever reason – and a common one in the UK used to be trade union pressure) simply result in the old stance being conducted less effectively on the new machine. While there may be a short-term gain in terms of expediency in the avoidance of a labour dispute; in the longer term, both operation and production will suffer.

It has to be recognized that what is currently in place is undesirable for a variety of reasons. The desired state of affairs must be articulated; and a strategic approach adopted to ensure that the required conclusion is reached.

There are two standard approaches:

- **Unfreezing-transforming-refreezing** (see Figure 3.1). It is important to recognize that the idea of 'refreezing' incorporates aptitudes of flexibility, dynamism and responsiveness. It is essential to note also that the statement of 'refreezing' ought to directly address the 'change – to what?' element of the overall process.
- **Force field analysis** (see Figure 3.2). This is where the forces that drive change and those that restrain it are separated out. The drivers are then energized and pushed on; the restrainers are either removed, neutralized or else re-energized in ways productive to the required outcome. Effective force field analyses deal in detail with the elements of 'change – from what – when – where – how – why?'

UNFREEZING	TRANSFORMING	REFREEZING
– consultation – high quality open information – getting people used to the idea	– introduction of new technology, work patterns, products, services, attitudes	– the new becomes the steady-state and familiar – note the danger of becoming rigid or set anew

Figure 3.1 *Unfreezing–transforming–refreezing*

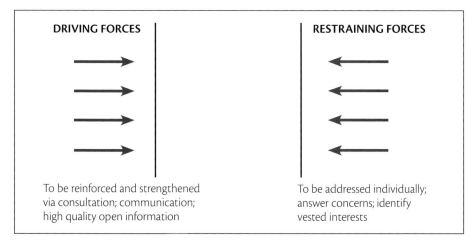

Figure 3.2 *Force field analysis*

The key problems with both the unfreezing/refreezing and the force field approaches are that:

- the history of organization development indicates that structures are easier to put in place than they are to change, dismantle or rearrange;
- the need for change, as we have seen, may neither be apparent nor recognized;
- the structure has often provided a career progression path through the organization that has been one of the attractions of working in it and staying in it.

Change catalyst and change agent

In response to the pressures, drives and constraints outlined above, organizations create their own opportunities for change, development and improvement. These approaches may be:

- structured and strategic, in which clear catalysts and agents are sought for something that is already to be implemented;
- opportunistic, in which the senior managers of an organization are sufficiently expert to take advantage of opportunities when they do present themselves, and to engage in wider programmes of change;
- ad hoc, in which changes, developments and enhancements are conducted in isolation from the overall purpose and direction of the organization.

Whichever is chosen, the change process must be capable of being summarized as:

- 'Change – from what – to what – when – where – how – why?'
- 'Is this possible or feasible in the given state of the organization and its environment?'
- 'Are there any possible or potential circumstances or conditions which may change or arise which will prevent what we want to achieve from occurring?'

The catalyst for change may be an event or series of events; or a person or group. Whichever it is, the outcome is that for whatever reason, it is agreed that the present state of affairs is no longer adequate. Progress of some sort has therefore to be made, and so the organization has to be galvanized into action.

The change agent is the person who galvanizes the organization into action, and sees through what is proposed to its conclusion. The change agent may be the person who has decided that things do have to progress; or they may be someone who is either given the job to see things through, or else brought in from outside. Outsiders may be experts taken on to the payroll for the given purpose. Additionally, many organizations use management and specialist consulting firms as catalysts and agents of change; though it is vital to be absolutely clear about what the consultants are there to achieve.

If you do bring in change agents and catalysts from outside, make sure that they clearly understand the brief that you have given them. Failure to do so can cause lasting damage and so make sure that when you do bring in outsiders, effective communications with everyone continue to be maintained.

Changing attitudes and approaches to quality, value and expectations

Whatever the purpose or catalyst for change, the priority is the ability of the organization and its managers and agents of change to concentrate on quality, value and expectations in all areas. All organization stakeholders have presumptions of the quality and value that they are to gain from the organization, and expectations that their own collective and individual aims and objectives will be met.

Customers expect improved ranges and quality of products and services. Shareholders and backers expect improved share values, returns on investment, and dividend payments. Staff expect better pay and rewards, and greater opportunities for recognition and advancement.

It is important to note that these expectations are not always delivered. Quick fix approaches that have the purpose of increasing share values in the short term (for example outsourcing of functions) very often settle back to previous levels as the particular matter becomes institutionalized (and in some cases, operational problems start to emerge). Rebranded and redesigned products and services have to deliver additional benefits of value to the customers, otherwise they will be dismissed as fashionable, faddish or transient only, not suitable to the enduring needs and wants. Staff restructuring rarely delivers increased opportunities or rewards for staff; indeed, most staff expect that restructuring will lead to job and opportunity losses, and reduced career paths. Meeting the demands of quality, value and expectations in managing within a changing environment requires that the following priorities are addressed by the change agent, leader or director if the above concerns are to be met.

- **Obsession with customer satisfaction**, in terms both of the products or services offered, and the ways in which they are delivered by the organization. This must cover the whole process from the acceptance of orders, through delivery and dispatch, to after-sales service. In many cases, this is instrumental in the generation of repeat business. There is thus a strong element of long-term investment inherent in any true genuine approach and attitude that has quality at its core.
- **Obsession with staff excellence**, in terms of their expertise, skills and knowledge. This must be underpinned, however, by a commitment to them that

ensures that they are instilled with the attitudes necessary to deliver this expertise in the ways in which the organization and its customers require. They must be paid and rewarded adequately. They must have their expectations and aspirations accommodated in the intention and pursuit of excellence. Again, this is regarded as a long-term mutual investment and commitment between staff and organization. It is not regarded as a purely instrumental or functional approach, or concept of employment.

- **Obsession with constant improvement,** the recognition that each and every aspect of the organization, its products and services, its practices, procedures and operations can be made to work better and more effectively in the pursuit of quality and excellence. Levels of investment in production methods and capacities, standards and life span of production plants and equipment will also be the subject of this commitment. Only the best equipment will do: that which has all the attributes required to meet the output levels required in terms of speed, reliability, perfection, regularity and universality.

The maintenance of operations at a continuing high quality level is underpinned by both procedures and processes. The procedures include inspection, random sampling, testing and monitoring of products as they come off the line, and of the lines themselves during planned maintenance periods. The processes reflect the concept of continued improvement and must include work improvements and quality improvement groups addressing both product and production methods.

Dutton Engineering Ltd

Dutton Engineering Ltd employs 600 staff in the design, manufacturing and delivery of plastic and metal office furniture and equipment, specialist parts for the motor car industry, and components for the aircraft industry.

Some years ago, faced with ever-increasing staff, employment, manufacturing and energy costs, the company's majority shareholder and managing director, Ken Lewis, undertook a total restructuring.

He organized the production crews into autonomous work teams. As well as being responsible for the output of their particular products, production crews would now set their own targets, work schedules, and quality assurance processes. Production crews would be responsible for the attraction, recruitment and retention of new staff as and when they were required. Production crews would ensure that their own paperwork was accurate, answering directly to Mr Lewis and the board of directors in case of errors and omissions.

Production would be scaled back so as to manufacture only in response to orders. Orders were still required to be turned around within timescales demanded by customers.

The emphasis here was to ensure that sales teams concentrated on existing customers, with the purpose of generating repeat business, and on potential customers who were reassessed as being very likely or strongly likely to place orders.

Payroll was outsourced to a specialist firm. This cost the company a small monthly sum and prevented the need for employing up to four clerical staff to process time sheets, shift and productivity payments. These responsibilities were additionally handed to the production crews and sales teams.

Staff were shifted from regular daily patterns of work to a system of 'annualized hours' in which staff were responsible for attending at work, and being able and willing to do so at times of heavy workload pressures. This was to ensure that the priority of meeting deadlines was absolute.

Over the next four years, business volumes doubled. Over the four years after that, business volumes doubled again. Staff productivity bonuses averaged 50% of total salary over the period. Additionally, faults and rejects fell by 85%.

All of this was achieved in response to the increases in costs and market constraints, as above. By concentrating on quality, value and expectations – and in particular ensuring that staff expectations were addressed – product quality, service levels and customer satisfaction were assured.

Current managerial issues

Those responsible for managing within the constraints of a changing environment have to be able to deal with the following.

Technological advance

Technological advance brings possibilities in terms of increased opportunities for production, quality and durability; speed and flexibility of response to customer demands; and the capability to organize and develop workforces in ways that were simply not possible beforehand.

Additionally, organizations have been under both operational and cultural pressures to develop e-business and internet activities wherever they can. There is a widely held perception that not to have a website or internet activity is demeaning to the particular organization.

Investment

The best organizations are increasingly taking the view that much greater attention to investment is required. Investment in technology is viewed as a continued commitment, together with the need to change technology, overnight almost, if and when radically new approaches are invented. Investment in the production and maintenance of high quality staff is a prerequisite to long-term and continued customer service and satisfaction, and therefore, to long-term organizational well-being.

Investment

The apocryphal tale is told of two groups of managers, one British and one Japanese, who each ran a production line employing 20 people.

A machine was invented that could do the work of this line but which needed only one person to operate it. The British managers went home with heavy hearts because they knew they would have to make 19 people redundant.

The Japanese managers went home with glad hearts because they were going to get 20 new machines; they were going to expand output by a factor of 20; all the staff were going to get retraining and a fresh place of work; and they would not be adding to the wage bill.

The lesson for managers is that, however an opportunity is exploited, is very much a matter of individual choice. Neither of the above approaches is right or wrong except in the capability of the particular organizations to recognize investment as an opportunity and ensure that it is maximized, whichever line is taken.

Culture, attitudes and values

The best organizations and their managers are increasingly taking advantage of the changing environment to ensure their staff adopt distinctive ways of doing things that:

- support the organization's own distinctive and considered view of how it should conduct its affairs;
- are capable of accommodating the differing, and often conflicting, interests of the employees;
- transcend local cultural pressures, meaning that both products and the ways in which they are produced and offered must be of a fundamental integrity so that they are acceptable wherever business is conducted;
- create a basis of long-term mutual commitment serving the interests of the organization, its customers, the wider community and its staff;
- generate experience and expertise in managing across cultures, sectors, markets and locations.

This is all supported by continuous and effective communication, staff involvement and development activities. It is pointless to expect staff to do things in particular ways if they are not supported. Additionally, effective support and communication feed organizational activities and practices, and performance effectiveness, so that the whole becomes an ever-upward spiral of improvement and development.

Strategy

The Dutton Engineering example (see above) ought to give an indication of the opportunity to use change to develop greater clarity, awareness and understanding in the strategic aspects of business and management. This in turn makes it easier for all staff to acquire the following capabilities and expertise:

- reconciling a range of conflicting pressures;
- learning global and general lessons from successes and failures;
- investment and commitment to the long term in terms of technology, markets, customers and employees;
- flexibility and responsiveness in the immediate term in the face of changing customer demands;
- generating staff loyalty and commitment through a determination to invest in their long-term future. This above all, means attention to training and development. It constitutes a mutual and continuous obligation. The view is also increasingly taken that long-term customer satisfaction can only be achieved through a commitment to staff excellence.

Flexible patterns and methods of work

This is based on a combination of the demand to maximize and optimize investment in production and other technology, together with changing patterns of customer requirements. This has led, for example, to longer factory, shop, office, public and private facility opening hours, based in turn on the recognition that customers will use organization services when it suits them. As organizations have extended their activity times, so they have found that extra customers have come to them and also that there is a great demand for short hours and other forms of part-time working and job opportunities on the part of employees and potential employees.

> Those working on flexible and non-standard patterns of work need effective supervision and so management and supervisory patterns and priorities need to be adjusted and changed. Those on flexible and non-standard patterns of work also need to have their own clear and positive identity with the organization if there is to be any chance of getting effective work out of them.

Ethics

There is a realization that there is a much greater propensity for consumers to use organizations in which they have confidence and which they can trust. This is based on the expectation of a long-term and continuously satisfactory relationship; and on the knowledge that, if this is not forthcoming with one organization, it can be found with many others. There is also a much greater demand for work and staff relationships based on honesty and integrity rather than bureaucracy, barriers, procedures – and in many cases duplicity. If an organization promises lifetime job security, then its first duty is to remain in being for that lifetime – and to do this, it must take a view of itself based on integrity rather than expediency.

Concern for the environment

This is a matter of universal, political, economic and social priority at present; and is likely to become more extreme in the future. It has direct implications for business and managers. It is also plainly related to the investment concept detailed above. It affects ultimately all aspects of the business sphere. Globally, there is a balance that must be struck between developing economic and business activities in order to support the short-term needs of a world population that is expanding at a great rate (the population of the city of Cairo goes up by 1 million every seven months, for example) and preserving the world so that it may support life and a quality of life further into the future.

At an organization level there is a necessity to consider the effect of operations on the environment in relation to all business aspects. Marketing policies and activities, for example, may demand levels of packaging to preserve the product, to demonstrate it to its best possible advantage and to meet public and sectoral expectations. On the other hand, both the packaging itself and the technology used to produce it may be consumptive of resources themselves and also create high levels of pollution or waste. Production and operations and the technology related to this also create drains on the world's resources. They create waste and effluent that also have to be managed and disposed of. Human resource policies in certain parts of the business sphere (for example the UK) provide high quality, prestige cars to go with particular occupations; these cars are very often resource-intensive in production and highly consumptive of fuel.

The net result is that strategies and policies for managing the environment have to be devised globally, sectorally and organizationally. This requires organizations and their managers to place the environment at, or near, the top of their list of priorities. It requires them to take a much wider view of the true cost of operations. Related activities may therefore include reorientation of marketing and product presentation and a parallel re-education along these lines as part of the total strategy aimed at changing customer expectations in this way (and reconciling this with the positive, persuasive wider marketing activities). It also requires organizations to take a longer-term view of production processes. The approach required is that which relates both to responsibility for, and the adoption of, procedures and practices that truly address the problems of the disposal of waste and effluent and for which organization provision must be made in strategic, operational and investment terms.

The changing nature of public services

The restructuring of municipal, public and health services requires a mention here, as do the related concepts and realities of service level agreements and arrangements (we have made reference above to the privatization which often accompanies these). The strategic conception relates to the stated need to revitalize and regenerate these services, to restructure them, to improve the quality and effectiveness of their management and to make them more efficient. This is all based on the premise that it can be achieved only if the organizations responsible are freed from bureaucratic, state or other authority control. Managers will in turn be free to conduct, provide and order these services in the ways in which their expertise directs. This is of especial importance when the nature of these services is considered – they are the primary, critical, health, social and education activities that are evermore in demand, ever-expanding and the object of ever-higher social and public expectations. The same thinking has been applied to public utilities and strategic state industries. In the UK, gas, electricity, water, transport and telecommunications and some research have all been privatized or transferred from government to shareholder ownership. Others, especially postal services, are set to follow in the near future.

Conclusions

All the factors and issues raised in this chapter concentrate on the drive for business and organizational quality, effectiveness and excellence. They reflect the fact that these constitute the major concerns of the business sphere in the last decade of the 20th century; and moving forward into the 21st century. They are further underlined by the relationship that is drawn between the existence of these qualities in organizations and the success, effectiveness, growth and profitability of them, which are considered to arise from the fact that either they operate in these ways or that they exhibit these qualities.

The greatest mistake that anyone could make however, is to believe that they constitute an end in themselves; that, once achieved, an organization is guaranteed permanence and eternal profitability. This is not so. At their highest level (and if one is offering or preaching perfection) these concepts represent threads and strands that ought to run through the core of any organization or undertaking; they constitute a standard of ethic, aura, belief and pride in the organization that are increasingly recognized as the sound foundations on which business success must be built. They also represent the obsession with top quality of products and services, the central position of the customer in the activities of any undertaking and the critical importance of this. Such foundations require constant attention and maintenance as do the organizations, their structures, cultures and practices which are built on them. This is also the basis from which the next developments of the business and management sphere, and of managerial expertise, are to come. It has taken the composition of the expertise and reality of management that is currently recognized thousands of years to develop this far; and this includes the globalization of experience and practice.

The ability to operate effectively, and respond to pressures within the changing environment is a critical part of management expertise (see also above, Chapter 1). Products and services have to be capable of effective delivery whatever the present and envisaged constraints of the environment, and, as well as maintaining a steady-state, opportunities for business development and advancement have also to be created.

The processes, qualities and expertise of business and management outlined here and their interaction and interrelationship both among themselves and with the wider business sphere and environment are having great and lasting effects on business practices. The transformation effected is to generate the creative and energetic aspect in the business sphere and to develop the nature and level of expertise in as many ways as possible. Management is thus no longer a straitjacketed or bureaucratic process; above all, it is not the equivalent of administration. Both business and management are ever-developing concepts, phenomena and realities. Their progress and transformation are limited only by the capacities and capabilities of those who work in them in whatever sector or aspect.

Finally, these constitute global and universal activities and it follows from this that good practice is good practice wherever it is found. It is evermore evident that this is so and that any true expertise, whenever it is found and from wherever it is drawn, provides an increase both in understanding and in the fund of knowledge, skills and capabilities of the expert manager. Above all, the professional and expert manager has to bring to his chosen profession a willingness, openness and capacity to learn and develop; a preparedness to draw lessons from wherever they may become apparent and to assimilate these lessons in regard to his own expertise. This covers the whole spectrum of business and managerial activity with opportunities afforded in all sectors across the whole world. This is the scale and scope of the range and potential offered to the truly expert manager. The whole field therefore opens up opportunities that are truly exciting, challenging and adventurous for anybody who wishes to take advantage of them and who has the qualities, capacities and personal attributes to do so.

in brief

- Always remember that change is a process; and the summary 'change – from what – to what – when – where – how – why?' needs always to be kept at the forefront of everyone's mind.
- Change processes and activities need to address the needs of everyone. Even where some people are to be disadvantaged as the result, they still need to know and understand (and hopefully accept, if not always agree with) why things are being done.

- The use of change agents and catalysts, including bringing in outsiders, is valuable in many sets of circumstances. However, it is essential that they stick to their brief; and where this needs to be broadened, full consultation with everyone involved is required.
- Where technological change is envisaged, it is essential to know and understand the benefits that the new technology is to bring. The driving force of all technological change needs to be enhanced operational effectiveness and efficiency.
- It is essential that all change keeps organizational priorities and operational issues at the forefront. Clear aims and objectives are required when proposing change and these must be kept at the forefront of everything that subsequently occurs.

Further reading

Burnes, B. (2007) *Managing Change*. FTPitman.

Drennan, D. (1992) *Transforming Company Culture*. McGraw Hill.

Gratton, L. (2000) *Living Strategy*. FTPitman.

Harvey, D. (2010) *A Companion to Marx's Capital*. Verso.

Lewin, K. (1951) *Field Theory in Social Science*. Harper and Row.

Williams, A., Dobson, P. and Walters, M. (2000) *Managing Change Successfully*. Thomson.

Ethics and corporate governance

4

'The best organizations and managers deal continuously and openly with all stakeholders.'

In this chapter

- the nature and content of business and management ethics
- the relationship between ethics and profitability, viability and effectiveness
- setting and maintaining standards of conduct, behaviour and performance
- the nature of corporate governance and corporate social responsibility

Introduction

Ethics and corporate governance have come to prominence in business and management for a range of reasons. The result of the continuing professionalization of management, and aspiration to professional status, means that codes of conduct and practice are required in absolute terms. Organizational concentration on the short-term financial aspects of their performance, and refusal or inability to recognize the legitimacy and contribution of other interests and stakeholders have meant that resources have been wasted, investments failed, and initiatives have not delivered what was expected of them. High profile corporate scandals have brought into focus at least what top and senior managers ought not to be doing. The result of all this has been the establishment of an organizational leadership and managerial priority in attending to the wider context of what is being done, and how it is being done. In turn, this means that there is now sharp focus on:

- the ethics of business and management; and
- the governance of companies and organizations in all sectors.

Companies and organizations are required to establish clear policies and standards of practice in reporting how they conduct their affairs and arrive at summary financial performance. The salaries and remuneration packages of top, senior and key executives must now be published and justified. Statements of organization product, service, share and brand values must now be capable of justification. Specific activities, especially those that generate risk or hazard, must now be fully justified.

Ethics in management is concerned with those parts of organizational, operational, occupational and professional conduct that relate to absolute standards and moral principles. Corporate governance is concerned with establishing and implementing the principles and practices by which organizations are to be directed and operated; and this includes attention to culture, conduct, behaviour and performance, as well as to financial, operational and strategic substance and transparency. Establishing standards of conduct requires reference to questions of what is right and wrong in absolute terms; the desired ends and outcomes; and the ways and means by which the ends and outcomes are achieved.

expert view

'Business ethics applies ethical reasoning to business situations and activities. It is based on a combination of distributive justice – that is, the issuing of rewards for contribution to organization goals and values; and ordinary common decency – an absolute judgement that is placed on all activities.' **Sternberg** (1995)

In order to deliver all this, a full understanding of business and management ethics and corporate governance is required in the following areas:

- long-term organizational survival, profitability and prosperity; and an understanding of the strategic and operational elements necessary to deliver and assure this;
- enduring relationships with key stakeholders;
- attention to the external environment;
- the nature of working, professional and personal relationships;
- attention to the quality of working life;
- compliance with the law, and working with auditors, regulators and statutory bodies to ensure that compliance is active and positive;
- establishing the basis on which everyone is to be treated equally and fairly in the context of organizational practice and activities;
- establishing where specific responsibility and accountability lie;
- establishing where overall responsibility and accountability lie;
- establishing the basis on which staff are to be paid and rewarded;
- establishing the basis on which shareholders and backers are to receive returns on their investment;
- working effectively within the constraints of social, cultural and religious customs.

Understanding the nature of ethics and corporate governance is therefore a major management discipline. It is essential to know and understand these elements, both in absolute professional terms, and also as they relate to particular organizations in their environment.

Ethics and corporate governance

Taking what is written above as a basis for high and absolute standards of conduct, behaviour and performance, the basis of understanding can be further developed.

Adams, Hamil and Carruthers (2001): identify a series of factors and elements as measures against which the performance of organizations could be measured in ethical terms. These factors are:

- the nature of business (Adams, Hamil and Carruthers identify contentious industries such as tobacco, alcohol, chemicals, armaments);
- the quality, integrity, availability and use of information;
- participation, consultation, employment relationships, the recognition of trade unions, means and methods of representation;
- relationships with emerging economies and markets, and relations with developed economies and markets;
- marketing and selling initiatives – and again, with reference to contentious products and services as above;
- connections with governments – especially where these were considered to be undesirable or where the regime in question was considered to be unethical itself.

Connections with government of course change when regimes, political parties and individual leaders change. In practice, it is much easier to engage with regimes that are suddenly 'good', than to disengage with regimes and governments that suddenly become 'bad'. The opposite approach is to place the onus on individual managers.

According to **Drucker (1995):**

'The more successfully the manager does their work, the greater will be the integrity required. For under new technology the impact on the business of decisions, time span and risks will be so serious as to require that each manager put the common good of the enterprise above self-interest. Their impact on the people in the enterprise will be so decisive as to demand that the manager put genuine principles above expediency. And the impact on the economy will be so far reaching that society itself will hold managers responsible. Indeed, the new tasks demand that the manager of tomorrow root every action and decision in the bedrock of principles so that they lead, not only through knowledge, competence and skill, but also through vision, courage, responsibility and integrity.'

Payne and Pugh (2001): identified the relationship between the absolute standards of the organization and its 'climate'. They stated that: 'Climate is a total concept applying to the organization as a whole or some definable department or subsystem within it.' There are four main aspects:

- degrees of autonomy given to particular individuals, groups, departments, divisions and functions;
- the degree of structure or flexibility imposed on work positions;
- the reward orientation, in terms of both individual satisfaction and overall organizational achievement;
- the degree of consideration, warmth and support; the human aspects of staff–management relationships.

In particular organizations, locations and sets of circumstances there are additional specific issues to be considered:

- compliance with the law (as above), and compliance with specific local laws, habits, customs and ways of working;
- general approaches and attitudes to staff and customers;
- general approaches and attitudes to all stakeholders;
- establishment of attitudes to the communities in which they operate;
- establishment of attitudes to environmental issues;
- establishment of business relationships with suppliers and markets;
- being clear about approaches to product testing, especially where this involves the use of animals;
- being clear about product testing, especially where the outcomes are not fully known, understood or evaluated.

true story

Genetically modified (GM) crops

Scientists believe that they have found ways to improve the quality and durability of agricultural crops through modifying the genes of the particular plants. This has caused extensive political, social and media debate and argument – on the one hand, recognizing the need to enhance global food production; on the other, many concerns about long-term damage to the food, agricultural, and environmental infrastructure have been voiced.

The key problem here is lack of openness, quality and integrity of information. The companies responsible for producing genetically modified crops have found themselves under attack from powerful consumer and environmental lobbies, and have therefore retreated within themselves, concentrating on their existing markets and those that they are able to dominate, rather than opening up a higher quality of debate. Politicians, while recognizing the need to enhance quality and volume of food production, have equivocated on the environmental issues. Environmental lobbies have sought to simplify the debate into a single issue – the general rights and wrongs of 'tampering with nature'.

The net result is an entrenchment of position – resulting in a hysterical and ill-informed exchange of views, arguments and insults. The chief sufferers of this are the public at large, who to date have not been told the true merits and demerits of each part of the case.

There is clearly no common agreement on what constitutes an absolute body of knowledge and expertise in the area of business and managerial ethics. Some useful initial conclusions may however be drawn.

- It is essential to take a long-term view, as well as having to satisfy immediate interests and demands.
- Absolute standards are required relating to organizational policies, aims and objectives.
- Common standards of equity, equality, honesty and integrity are required; and if they are not established, they will, de facto, emerge anyway.
- There is a relationship between organization standards and integrity, the delivery of performance, and the distribution of rewards.
- There are key relationships between means and ends, and actions and motives.
- Identifying and establishing where conflicts of interest lie, and the reasons for their existence, is also an essential task.

It ought to be clear also that establishing particular standards of conduct, behaviour and performance is a critical function of organizational and managerial stability, integrity and assuredness, and a clear point of reference for stakeholders, the environment and markets served.

One of the key values of ethics and clear standards is that you help to remove people's uncertainties. In relation to the material covered above, for example, if you have set clear standards, then you will remove some of the uncertainties that you might have to face in dealing with contentious political regimes or controversial commercial activities such as genetically modified foods.

Survival

Survival therefore becomes the main ethical duty of the organization to its staff, customers, communities and other stakeholders. For this to happen over the long term, a long-term view must be taken of all that this means. For business and companies, profits must be made – over the long term; for public services, this means effectiveness – over the long term. This is the basis on which confidence and an enduring and continuous positive relationship with customers (or service users) is built and developed. This is also the only ground on which an effective and satisfactory organization for the staff is to be created.

Short-term views, expediency, the need for triumphs – all detract from this. Especially, there is a serious problem in this area with some public services. For example, the output of education can take 15–20 years to become apparent. Health and social services have similar extreme long-term requirements and commitments. Yet those responsible for their direction (both service chiefs and cabinet ministers) need to be able to show instant results to be presented before the electorate or before the selection panel for their next job.

This is not wholly confined to services. For example, pressures from bankers and other financial backers in some sectors (especially loan makers) lead to companies being forced or strongly encouraged to sell assets during lean periods in order to keep up repayments or show a superficial cash surplus over the immediate period. This happens, for example, with the civil engineering and construction industries whenever there are declines in work brought on by recession and general loss of confidence. Pressure is placed on the companies to generate short-term cash through the sale of assets especially land banks. The consequence is that long-term survival is threatened because these assets will not be present when any upturn in confidence and activity comes about.

However, this again has to be balanced with matters of general confidence and expectation. If backers expect to see a series of short-term positive results then these have to be produced, especially if backing may be withdrawn if they are not forthcoming or do not meet expectations. This implies re-educating backers into the long-term view. It also means seeking out others who are disposed to take the long-term view.

The best organizations and managers deal continuously and openly with all stakeholders, meeting with them, discussing and debating priorities and other issues, identifying problems, and providing comprehensive and clear information.

Relationships with employees

This refers to the nature of participation and involvement, and the point of view from which this is approached. Basic integrity in employee relations (ER) stems from the view taken of the employees, their reasons for working in the organization, their reasons for being hired to work in the organization and the absolute levels of esteem in which they are held.

Confrontational or adversarial styles of ER are always founded on mistrust and reinforced by offensive and defensive positions adopted by the two sides concerning particular issues. The phrase 'the two sides' confirms and underlines this! Resources are consumed in this way to the detriment both of organization performance and also of resource utilization – those used in these ways cannot be put to better use elsewhere.

Employee relations and problem-solvers

Many large industrial, commercial and public sector organizations have extensive human resource management departments and functions. In this context, an especial problem concerns those that have responsibility for ER.

These companies and organizations hire ER specialists to devise policies for the effective management of staff and resolution of conflict, and to resolve problems when they arise.

Serious organizational problems can, and do, arise when these ER specialists are rewarded on the basis of the problems that they solve. If emphasis is placed on the ability of ER specialists to solve problems, then they will find problems to solve.

For example, a large London radio station was going through a period of extensive restructuring. Two programme-producing departments were required to restructure their workforce, terms and conditions of employment and hours of work. The manager of one of these departments saw the problem early and, by engaging in extensive consultation and discussion with the staff, all problems were avoided, and the matter was resolved smoothly and without any disputes.

The manager of the other department did nothing about the matter until the weekend before the changes were due to take place. In the period immediately preceding this weekend, staff morale plummeted, and there was an increase in the number of disputes and grievances. Accordingly, the manager commanded all of the staff to attend a weekend briefing, consultation, and crisis resolution session immediately before the changes were due to take place. The matters were resolved at this weekend meeting.

The radio station's senior management, who were well familiar with the situation and the mounting crisis, looked on with admiration as, at the end of the weekend, all of the staff trooped out and announced themselves satisfied with the new arrangement. Because of his crisis management skills, the particular manager was rewarded. The manager who had tackled the problems early received no reward or recognition for the ways in which she had managed the situation. Not only was the approach of the radio station unethical, it was also inadequate – failing to recognize how members of staff were conducting themselves, and how they ought to be recognized and rewarded.

Adversarial ER is therefore normally unethical. On the other hand, greater or full participation and involvement is only ethical if the point of view adopted is itself honest – if a genuine view of respect and identity is taken. This is apparent – or not – in the continuity and enduring nature of this relationship. It is underlined by the volume, quality and relevance of information made available to staff, the means by which problems are addressed and resolved, the prevalence of equality of treatment and opportunity, and the development of staff. It also refers to the level of attention paid to setting standards to which employees are to conform and the reasoning and logic behind this process. It covers all aspects of the traditional personnel area – recruitment and selection, induction, performance appraisal, pay and reward, promotion and other opportunities for development and advancement. Above all, at its core, lies equality of treatment for everyone; and this is a legal as well as an ethical and human demand.

> The development of effective ER needs to be directly related to enduring business efficiency and effectiveness. Those responsible for organization management need to continuously evaluate ER from this point of view.

Means and ends

Crimes are not annulled by altruistic motives even though they may arouse human sympathy. For example, where a hungry person robs a rich person just so that they can eat, a crime is still committed. Robin Hood was a robber, whether or not he gave the proceeds of his robberies to the poor. The sale of cocaine on the urban streets of Europe and North America is wrong even if it provides the means of economic survival to the people of South America.

This applies to organization practices also. If a manager dismisses an employee to make an example of him, and if the employee did not deserve dismissal, then a wrong act is committed even if it brings the remaining staff into line. If the organization secures its long-term future through gaining a contract by offering a bribe to a major customer, then a wrong act is committed. In each of these cases in practice, stated ends are very unlikely to be secured anyway because there is no integrity in the relationship. In the first case, the staff will look for other ways of falling out of line (but without risking further dismissals); in the second case, the corruption may come to light and the relationship be called into question or cancelled as the result.

Organizations must recognize and resolve conflicts of interest. The first step lies in acknowledging their legitimacy and certainty. From this, measures can be taken to ensure their resolution, which benefits the long-term future of all concerned. Conflicts of interest arise between all organization stakeholders; and between individuals within, and between, departments and divisions. These conflicts may be based on divergence of aims and objectives, as well as on general professional and expertise disagreements as to the best interests of the organization (as well as matters of infighting and operational and personality clashes).

The ethical approach is bound up in an integrity and visibility of management style and working relationships, and the early recognition of operational, professional and personal problems. These are then addressed when they arise and before they are allowed to fester and become a part of organization folklore. What is to happen as the result of these matters arising can then be transmitted early, and it can be demonstrated why this is in the best interests of the organization.

Good ethics is good business

Although ethical conduct is not sufficient to assure business success, and business success is no guarantee of ethical conduct, distributive justice and ordinary common decency do typically enhance long-term owner value. They do so in many ways. Chief of these is obviating the difficulties of operating without them. Stakeholders who doubt the good faith of companies and organizations, or of their colleagues, are more likely to spend time in protecting their own backs than in performing their functions. Time, resources and energy that could be spent more productively and rewardingly are consequently diverted to basic self-preservation with a direct opportunity cost to the business. Decent treatment, in contrast, permits and encourages stakeholders to get on with the job, and to conduct business effectively and profitably.

The costs of disregarding ordinary decency and distributive justice are far-reaching. In a business characterized by lying, cheating and stealing, this illusion of low morale typically replaces initiative and enthusiasm; teamwork becomes difficult at best, and long-term commitments counterproductive. When exertions on behalf of a business are rejected or penalized, rather than encouraged and rewarded, they are unlikely to be repeated. Distributive justice and a modicum of decency are therefore essential for any business to operate. Without them, the best business is unlikely to attract the best people or their best efforts. But when they are respected, the business will normally be characterized, not only by responsibility and integrity, but by maximum long-term owner value.

Source: Sternberg (1995).

Standards of conduct and behaviour

Top and senior managers set the standards for the conduct and behaviour of the organization as a whole; and functional managers, section heads and supervisors do the same for their own people. The immediate issues are that:

- if top management set lax standards, there is ultimately little point in those lower down the organization trying to set high standards;
- if top management set high standards, then the extent to which these are absolute in practice is a direct reflection of what happens when those lower down the organization allow standards to slip.

Managing shareholders' interests

The priority in managing shareholders' interests is communication. Shareholders and their representatives need to know and understand the nature of returns on offer; the conditions under which returns are possible; and the changes in conditions likely to affect these returns. This is so that shareholders, and their representatives, know and understand where top management are taking the organization, and why, in terms of financial returns. It also provides shareholders, and their representatives, with a key point of reference in their dealings with top management; and ultimately, if they do not like what top management are doing, shareholders' representatives will replace them.

> The best organizations recognize that the shareholder's interest is not the only one that has to be addressed. As stated elsewhere, even if there is a stakeholder priority order, all interests need actively managing.

Managing staff interests

EU and other regulations on equality of treatment, working time, wage levels and consultation have caused all organizations to take a much broader view of their responsibilities to their staff. The overall effect has been to demand a much greater knowledge and transparency about pay, and terms and conditions of employment; and this has led in turn to a greatly increased propensity to make claims to courts and tribunals when collective and individual pay, and terms and conditions are known or believed to be wrong for some reason. Defending claims is expensive, stressful and time consuming. This can, and does, lead to wider adverse publicity; and this can, and does, lead to loss of confidence in the integrity of the organization as a whole.

Managing other stakeholder interests

Top and senior managers have a clear commitment to all those who come into contact with the organization, especially those whose immediate and future well-being is at stake.

Suppliers and contractors, especially those whose existence depends on large, understood and regular volumes of work from the particular organization, have a moral, as well as commercial, right to be told of immediate and potential plans for the future. In particular, they are entitled to know of any plans to restructure the supply side, or take key or critical orders elsewhere.

Top and senior management have a responsibility to ensure that products and services produced and delivered are of value to the particular markets and communities served. This responsibility is a combination of providing work for people; keeping the environment clean and tidy; and managing waste and effluent.

Managing waste and effluent itself is a specific corporate responsibility and falls into the following categories:

- ensuring safe dispersal of everyday rubbish, for example paper, packaging, food and canteen waste;

- ensuring safe management of production processes that produce particular hazards, toxins and otherwise dangerous effluent;
- ensuring in so far as is reasonably practicable that noise, heat, light and dust pollution, and fumes from transport fleets are kept to a minimum;
- ensuring that confidential waste in the form of staff, customer and supply records is disposed of with absolute security.

Probity and integrity

It follows directly from all of the above points that setting, and maintaining, absolute standards of probity and integrity comes from the top of the organization. Probity and integrity in corporate governance are concerned with the ways in which responsibilities and obligations are identified, accepted, met and discharged.

There is again a clear choice open to top and senior managers; and again, whichever is chosen, this becomes de facto an active choice with direct consequences for the future conduct of the organization. The choices are as follows.

- Setting standards which are fully transparent, open and honest, and which can stand detailed scrutiny from any quarter. In theory, this is the ideal position. In practice, the culture, behaviour patterns, norms, values and past history of the organization may simply not allow for this to happen. It may also not be acceptable to powerful and influential groups and individuals, shareholders and other stakeholders.
- Full and active compliance with the law and wider sets of responsibilities and obligations. This involves using the full range of communication and consultation processes to deal with all stakeholder groups in answering questions about conduct and performance as accurately and comprehensively as possible.
- Passive compliance, in which standards are set to comply with the law and other regulations and statutory instruments.
- Sectoral compliance, in which top managers discharge their obligations to the perceived and understood standards of openness, or otherwise, that prevail in the rest of the sector.
- Stretching the rules, which may be necessary from the point of view of meeting shareholder and stakeholder expectations in responses to crises and emergencies; or which, again, may reflect the norms and cultural perceptions of how matters are conducted in the given sector.
- Criminal intent, in which top and senior managers conspire among themselves to break the rules in order to gain advantages, either for themselves or for a particular group of stakeholders or, rarely, for the organization as a whole.

Managing dishonesty

In theory, the standards of probity and integrity chosen reflect the fact, belief and perception that 'either the organization is honest or it is not'. In practice, within the cultural constraints and the nature of organization conduct indicated above, it is rarely that simple. However, the active choice of a position and the consequences are absolutes.

A key test of the strength and integrity of corporate governance, and of the top and senior managers responsible, is the response to dishonesty. Dishonesty potentially exists in all areas of human activity, and organizational and managerial practices are no different.

Dishonesty in organizations is potentially present everywhere. This potential covers macro-organizational issues relating to misrepresentation of assets, finances, performance and profitability; through to micro issues concerning the fiddling of time sheets, expenses and the use of the phone and internet access for private matters, to petty pilfering.

Again, there is a clear absolute; and again, there are certain to be cultural issues and practices. For example:

- if an organization truly reports the absolute volatility of markets, this may cause total collapse in confidence, leading to loss of shareholder backing and customer bases;
- if an organization is fully open about staffing difficulties, this may lead to the best staff seeking jobs elsewhere, thereby compounding the problem;
- if an organization fully admits to flaws in production, service and information technology, then this again leads to questions about confidence and security.

At the micro level, if organizations spend time and resources on petty pilfering and fiddles, this too has to be conducted in such ways so as not to be counterproductive, while at the same time ensuring that the required standards are upheld. For example:

- most organizations take an absolute view of their staff who download internet material on political extremism, pornography, incitement to terrorism and violence;
- pilfering and fiddles can be managed out by ensuring that expenses are reimbursed on the production of receipts only.

At the micro level, the largest single issue arises from known, believed and perceived inequalities of treatment when seeking to enforce individual and collective honesty and conformity; and these problems occur when staff in some departments, divisions and functions, and above all, different ranks and status, are seen to get away with things that would not be tolerated elsewhere.

best practice

The best organizations and managers recognize that it is impossible to be 'a little bit dishonest'. You need to understand also that immediately you are 'a little bit dishonest', other people will invariably know this straight away.

Rewards for top and senior management

Wilkinson (1996) stated that the greater the divide in rewards between those at the top and bottom of particular societies, the greater the instability of those societies. This applies equally to organizations: the greater the divide between the highest and lowest salaries, the greater the likelihood that the organization is underperforming, unstable or at risk in terms of its ability to sell products and services on a long-term and enduring basis.

The issue of pay and rewards for top and senior managers again centres on the combination of perception and transparency referred to above. The law concerning the publication of annual reports demands that the salaries and rewards of directors are published; this does not, however, apply to those in top and senior executive and general management positions. It is therefore entirely at the organization's discretion as to whether it chooses to publish further information in this area.

There is the question of what top managers, directors and senior executives ought to be paid, and are being rewarded for; and again, this becomes a de facto acceptance and discharge of responsibility in practice. The options are:

- integrative rewards based on the ability to satisfy the demands of all stakeholders;
- distributive rewards based on the ability to satisfy one group of stakeholders but not all. This relates invariably to the ability to satisfy the financial interest delivering enhanced share values, earnings per share and assured dividend values.

Each position is in turn a reflection of why the top and senior management were appointed, and the extent to which they have any discretion in varying their brief. There are additional questions of timescales, outcomes and results to be factored in.

true story

Executive rewards in action

A chief executive officer (CEO) was brought in to complete the restructuring of a giant multinational pharmaceutical company. This company was one of the largest pharmaceutical companies in the world. However, following a spate of mergers and acquisitions, productivity, profit margins and turnover were now being affected by virtue of the fact that there existed no common standards for producing and delivering products and services.

The new CEO was appointed on a salary of £900,000 per annum. In addition he was given share options to the value of £2 million; and was promised a bonus of £1 million each year that productivity, turnover and profit rose by more than 10%.

Recognizing the difficulties, the new CEO managed to negotiate for himself a severance payment of £22 million should things not work out, and the Board dismiss him. At no stage did the Board of Directors of this company ever give a rationale for the structuring of the salary package, or for the high volume of the severance package. It also appeared that they had not considered that the new CEO would be much better rewarded for failure than for success.

This case emphasizes the need for specific expertise, understanding and involvement on the part of everyone concerned with the ordering and direction of all organizations.

It is not enough simply to 'pay the market rate'; indeed, the use of the phrase 'the market rate' is seldom backed up with hard data, comparisons or rationale. In the most extreme of cases, this general and insubstantial approach reinforces any perceptions that those at the top of organizations are being overpaid for passive rather than active involvement.

The structure of rewards is also critical. The pay of top and senior managers is normally based on a combination of salary, bonuses and share options; and it is increasingly usual to provide a pension and a severance payment. Severance payments are often controversial. As well as paying rewards for failure, there is also the issue of change in status or ownership of the organization. The severance payment may be so high as to make it in the overriding interests of top managers to engineer a takeover or change of status in order to work themselves out of a job. If payments are made for results, there is the question of standpoints to be addressed: what results, who decides on the achievements, and how much is to be paid?

At the core are the needs and wants of the organization's stakeholders, customers and staff; and there is again the issue of how the results are delivered, as well as the results themselves. For example:

- Short-term share advantages can normally be bought by outsourcing or contracting out specific functions, thereby reducing the ratio of payroll as a percentage of capital employed.
- Short-term market advantages can be bought or indicated as the result of product and service flooding and dumping.
- Short-term stock market interest can be bought as the result of engaging top brand consultants such as McKinsey or Bain.

Each of these eventualities has to be considered in terms of what is right for the long-term future of the organization, as well as addressing the immediate financial concern. Each has a critical bearing on the ways in which top and senior managers are going to conduct themselves, and the objectives that they are going to pursue.

Conclusions

The ethical approach is not altruistic or charitable, but rather a key concept of effective long-term organizational and business performance. The commitment to the staff is absolutely positive. This does not mean any guarantee of lifetime employment. It does mean recognizing obligations and ensuring that staff, in turn, acknowledge their obligations. These obligations are to develop, participate and be involved; to be flexible, dynamic and responsive. The commitment of the staff to organization, and organization to staff, is mutual and based on high levels of involvement and participation. A genuinely open approach to the establishment, development and implementation of absolute ethical standards, and transparency in corporate governance, requires the full involvement in all aspects of organizational development, and extensive and open consultations with all those affected when looking at the strategy and operations (see Figure 4.1).

This also extends to problem areas – especially the handling of discipline, grievance and dismissal issues, and redundancy and redeployment – and the continuity of this commitment when these matters have to be addressed.

Organizations must structure decision-making processes in ways that consider the range and legitimacy of ethical pressures. This also means understanding where the greater good and the true interests of the organization lie, and adopting realistic steps in the pursuit of this. An ethical assessment will consider the position of staff, the nature and interrelationship of activities, product and service ranges, mixes and balances, relationships with the community and the environment.

Organizations are not families, friendly societies or clubs. By setting their own values and standards and relating these to long-term effectiveness, they become distinctive. They are almost certain to be at variance from those that are, and would be, held by natural families and clubs. Problems that arise are clouded therefore, where the organization does indeed perceive itself to be 'a big happy family'. Families are able to forgive prodigal children; organizations may not be able to afford to do so, however, if they are to maintain long-term standards, or if substantial damage has been done to customer relations for example. Organizations exist to provide effective products and services for customers, while families and clubs exist to provide comfort, society and warmth. These elements are by-products, they are not the core.

Organizations are not obliged to provide employment at all except in so far as they need the work carrying out. They will select and hire people for this on the basis of capabilities and qualities. They have no obligation to take staff from the ranks of the unemployed (though they may choose to do so). They have no obligation to locate for all eternity in particular areas (though again they may choose to do so).

Organizations that pursue high ethical standards are not religious institutions, nor do they have any obligation to reflect any prevailing local traditions, values, customs, prejudices – or religion.

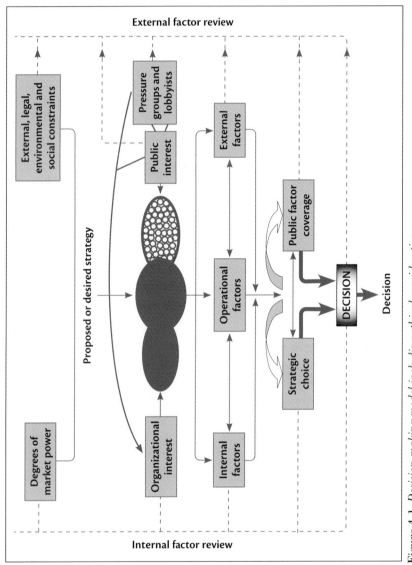

Figure 4.1 *Decision-making model including ethical considerations*

Japanese organizations setting up in the UK were, and remain, successful precisely because of this. Rather than trying to integrate their activities with the traditions of their locations, they brought very distinctive and positive values with which people who came to work for them were required to identify.

Organizations must distinguish between right and wrong. Lying, cheating, stealing, bribery and corruption are always wrong and can never be ethically justified.

This has to be set in the context of the ways in which business is conducted in certain sectors and parts of the world. If a contract is only to be secured by offering a bribe, the relationship is corrupted and based on contempt. If and when prevailing views change, the total relationship between organization and customer is likely to be called into question and any scandal or adverse publicity that emerges invariably affects confidence. It is in any case extremely stressful for individuals to have to work in this way or indeed to connive or conspire to any overt wrongdoing (though this may clearly be accommodated if the organization institutionalizes such matters, protects individuals who are caught or accepts responsibility for every outcome).

The ethical approach to organization and managerial activities is adult and assertive; it is not soft, religious or moral. It takes the view that continuous and long-term existence is the main duty of organizations to their staff, customers, suppliers, community and environment.

Above all, this requires a fundamental shift in corporate attitudes away from the short term or expedient, from the instant approach to returns, from the needs of the influential figures, and from wasteful and inefficient budgeting control and production systems. This is to be replaced by active participation and involvement by all in each of the areas indicated in the pursuit of effectiveness and success. It requires placing a value on everyone with whom the organization comes into contact – above all, staff, customers, backers, suppliers and communities. Organizations are only sustainable in the long term if adequate and continuous investment is made in technology, staff and staff development; research and development into new products and services; and in constantly improving and updating products, services, processes, systems and practices. This in turn is made most effective where everything is done with clearly stated aims, objectives, priorities, opportunities and consequences, and where these are understood, adopted and valued by everyone concerned.

There is a direct relationship between organization success and organizational and managerial attitudes to the elements indicated in this chapter. High profile and notorious organizational failures – for example BCCI and Maxwell – have demonstrated the consequences of this lack of basic integrity. Inefficiencies of some public services – for example health, education and social services – arise from a combination of imposing short-term and expedient priorities on long-term, enduring and socially valuable services which chiefly arise through the dominant pressures of key players and political drives. Conversely, the results achieved by organizations that do adopt high absolute standards clearly indicate the levels of sustainable achievement possible, whatever the industrial, commercial or public sector considered.

- It is essential to set, maintain and develop clear and absolute standards of integrity, conduct, behaviour and performance, not only because it is right to do so, but also because it is wrong not to do so. Organizations that set clear and absolute standards have a much greater clarity about other things, including strategy and operational effectiveness.
- Whenever information is offered, it needs to be as complete and transparent as possible. You should never say: 'We cannot disclose that' without going on to explain why.
- Organizations and managers that do work in contentious and controversial circumstances and industries need to be able to justify why they do so. This justification needs to be based in a fully ethical and transparent approach.
- Formal reporting mechanisms need to be suitable for the organization and its purposes. Within that constraint, the data and information produced must be transparent and complete.
- In terms of ethics, conduct, behaviour, performance and standards, it is essential to relate 'perfection' to the reality of what exists and occurs at the moment; and to use the ideal standards as a vehicle for driving improvements.

Further reading

Adams, R., Hamil, S. and Carruthers, J. (2001) *Changing Corporate Values.* Sage.

Crane, A. and Matten, D. (2010) *Business Ethics: Managing Corporate Citizenship in the Age of Globalisation.* Oxford University Press.

Drucker, P. (1995) *The Frontiers of Management.* Sage.

Griseri, P. and Seppala, N. (2010) *Business Ethics and Corporate Social Responsibility.* Cengage.

Harvard Business Review (2002) *HBR on Ethics.* Harvard.

Johnson, G., Scholes, K. and Whittington, R. (2009) *Exploring Corporate Strategy.* Prentice Hall.

Payne, D. and Pugh, D. (2001) *Managing in a Corporate Environment.* Penguin.

Sternberg, E. (1995) *Just Business.* Warner.

Wilkinson, R. (1996) *Unhealthy Societies.* Routledge.

The practice of management

5

'All managers need to have a creative faculty, bringing their skills, knowledge and expertise to new situations.'

In this chapter

- translating knowledge and understanding into effective practice and expertise
- working with pressures and under pressure
- working with scarce, finite and limited resources
- delivering performance in practice

Introduction

The final key foundation of effective management is the ability to put into practice, and relate to practice, every aspect of the skills, knowledge, understanding and experience that any professional and committed manager must have. This means that it is necessary to be able to apply whatever is required according to the demands of the particular situation and organization; and this in turn, reinforces and underlines the need for a full professional commitment to gaining as much skill, knowledge, understanding and expertise as possible so that effective actions are always taken.

Ernest Turley

Ernest Turley used to run Bynoe Construction Ltd, a medium-sized building company in southeast England. He started work at the company at the age of 16 as a labourer, and subsequently took an apprenticeship and qualified as a carpenter. He worked his way up through the company, becoming chief executive and chairman at the age of 47. For the next 35 years he ran the company, growing it from revenues of £2 million to £95 million over the period.

true story

For the whole of his period as chief executive and chairman, there were never any layoffs or redundancies, despite going through three major building and construction recessions.

For the 35-year period also, Mr Turley used to attend a professional, managerial, trade or general gathering or meeting at least once a week. He stated the reason for this as follows:

'All I ever wanted from any of these meetings was one idea that I could take back to Bynoe and use. If I could do this, my time was well spent. I would listen to people from any, and all, walks of life – they didn't have to be in building. I listened to how people from retail, hospitals, haulage and local government organized their work, managed their people, controlled their stocks and schedules. Some of the stories horrified me – and then I realized of course that I and some of our managers could easily behave and act like this. So – both good and bad – I got knowledge and ideas from each meeting that I went to.

And I always made sure that everyone else got to things whenever they could – not once a week, but certainly regularly.'

Mr Turley retired at the age of 82, leaving a full order book for the company, and an average profit margin of 15% achieved over his period as chief executive.

The practice of effective and successful management is founded on always looking for new ideas, knowledge and understanding that can be learned and applied. Additionally, with this approach comes a wider knowledge and understanding of how people think and behave, as well as knowing what it takes to run and develop an effective organization that is capable of performing in any, and all, sets of circumstances.

Pressures on organizations and managers

Any manager who aspires to be an effective practitioner has to know and understand the pressures under which they have to be able to operate. At the core of this is knowing and understanding the nature of the organization and where its priorities lie; and once this is understood, managers must have sufficient knowledge and understanding to be able to deliver their expertise in the ways required in order to meet the demands placed upon them. It is vital also to be able to reconcile the pressures from different sources. It is essential that managers are able to evaluate the true strength and nature of the pressures they face, and to establish the particular source. In all cases, managers must be able to respond to pressures; in many cases, the best managers, having evaluated the pressures, either resist or defy them. For example:

- if you can complete a project on time but only if you overspend – if you stick to your budget you will be late completing;

- if you have to lose a member of staff, and you have a known troublemaker or slacker;
- if your budget is suddenly cut meaning that you cannot do everything that is demanded of you;
- if one of your suppliers or distributors goes bankrupt;

what do you do?

The answers, of course, vary between organizations and situations. However, if you have a full professional and expert knowledge and understanding, you are much more likely to be able to propose, get agreement on, and implement the solutions that the particular situation actually demands. This is much better than guessing at the answer, or else imposing a solution that someone else has proposed or demanded.

British Airways

During one of its periods of difficulties, British Airways (BA) found itself facing declining passenger numbers, uncertainties in the fuel markets, and rising premises' costs and charges. BA called in McKinsey's, the management consultants, who proposed:

- a 10% cut in staff;
- a reduction in services offered from Gatwick;
- promotion of the premium-rate, first-class and business-class services.

BA duly and uncritically implemented all of this. However, there were consequences. The reduction in services from Gatwick led to a further decline in ticket sales, though these did pick up subsequently when the flights were re-established at London Heathrow.

Sales of first and business-class tickets continued to decline except on long-haul routes where they remained steady (but did not increase). The company took a one-off charge of £150 million in order to pay for the costs associated with the staff reductions; the staff were offered three years' salary by way of a severance payment and many took this offer.

None of this directly addressed the problems of declining sales and rising fuel costs. It was not until two years later that the company engaged in a major sales drive, targeted at customers that were likely to use BA, and revenues started to rise.

The company also at this stage finally negotiated and agreed flexible fuel contracts in order to drive this cost down and keep it manageable and more or less controllable.

While BA did finally take control of the situation, it could have done so much earlier had it concentrated on the core issues rather than coming belatedly to them. It could also have engaged in staff reductions alongside addressing these core problems. Finally, had BA taken a critical rather than responsive approach to the proposals from McKinsey's, it would have had its own rationale rather than somebody else's for doing the things that it did.

Sustainability

Sustainability in management has a variety of meanings, referring to the ability to:

- sustain the organization for the long term;
- sustain and develop successful and effective product and service ranges;
- sustain and develop an organization that people are committed to and want to work for;
- sustain and maintain the confidence of backers, suppliers, customers and markets served;
- sustain effective resource usage both immediately and also for the long term.

So this part of sustainability depends heavily on knowing and understanding the nature and effectiveness of the organization as an entity, and where the pressures exist, and what to do to ensure that these pressures remain capable of being accommodated.

This part of sustainability also depends on ensuring that product and service quality remains acceptable and valuable to markets, customers and clients, and knowing what steps to take when problems do become apparent.

Sustainability also means keeping a regular dialogue with backers and share-holders to ensure that they remain supportive of, and confident in, what is being done. Sustainability also has an environmental management connotation as follows:

- keeping waste and effluent to a minimum;
- disposing of waste and effluent in ways that are not simply moving the problem elsewhere;
- sustaining and improving energy and resource usage so that the best possible returns are generated from these factors;
- developing new facilities and practices that contribute to resource maximization and optimization;
- using and developing energy-efficient technologies and manufacturing and service delivery processes that, again, optimize and maximize the use of resources.

The approach to sustaining the organization as an entity, and developing activities that are known, believed and perceived to be environmentally friendly, as well as effective in business terms, ought to be complementary to each other. Effective resource management ought to complement the demands placed on the environment; and the demands of the environment ought to drive managers towards using resources effectively. To do this from both points of view is certain to become a major factor in the control and management of costs.

The best organizations make absolutely plain the relationship between effective resource management, the demands placed on the environment and business effectiveness. It is a simple lesson, and it ought to be clear to everyone that if you do reduce waste then you become more cost-effective, improving performance as well as reducing environmental impact.

Environmental pressures

As with sustainability, 'environmental pressures' has a diverse set of meanings.

On the one hand, 'environmental pressures' refers to the capability to understand and operate within all the pressures and forces considered in Chapter 2. Effective managerial practice requires that managers fully know and understand the pressures, drives and constraints that exist in their particular situation, and can operate effectively within them.

On the other hand, 'environmental pressures' refers to those factors concerned with:

- waste and effluent management and dispersal as above;
- fuel and energy usage;
- the use of materials that are known, believed and perceived to be damaging to the environment, for example plastics, polystyrene, some chemicals and oil and fossil fuels;
- the nature and value of the transport used;
- the energy that is consumed by technology;
- the energy that is consumed through production, manufacturing and service delivery processes.

As stated above, concentrating on these issues is a strong commercial as well as altruistic drive. It ought to be that organizations and managers concentrate on these aspects because it is cost-effective, even if they are not persuaded of the more altruistic issues. Additionally, a key part of sustainability, managing the 'environmental pressures' and resource management needs in any case to be driven by getting the most out of every part of organizational practice. This in turn is much more likely to ensure that organizations can sustain themselves for the long term rather than having to keep a constant eye on resource costs on a daily basis, and based on unit and individual consumption. Organizations need to have systems and processes that they know and understand to be as efficient and effective as possible in order to build the firmest possible foundation for resource management (see also below). There is also a wide perception that being 'environmentally friendly' carries a primary commercial advantage in marketing and customer relations terms – people prefer to do business with environmentally friendly companies. This position is attractive to some organizations and managers, consisting of producing, packing and delivering products in ways deemed to be environmentally friendly; or producing and delivering products and services that are deemed to be environmentally friendly in themselves. There are also assumptions that such products and services can carry higher prices, as customers are willing to pay more for something that somehow benefits the environment. Much of this is nebulous and subjective, depending on the definition of 'environmentally friendly' that is used. It is also essential that any specific claims of environmental-friendliness are evidence-based and can be sustained.

Resource and resourcing issues

As indicated above, the questions of sustaining and managing within environmental pressures and constraints are heavily driven by the nature of the resources used and the effectiveness of resource management. Resource usage varies between, and within, organizations. However, there are some key questions to address:

- energy usage;
- product and service delivery;
- transport costs;
- production, manufacturing and technological issues;
- the creation and disposal of waste and effluent.

Effective management practice in each of these areas is driven by a combination of managerial knowledge and understanding of what is needed to ensure sustainable and profitable activities. It also ought to be driven by attention to costs. However, neither is enough in isolation from the other: it is not possible to have production limited by over-attention to cost; nor can resources be used effectively, however rich an organization may be, without some kind of attention to cost.

Plush carpets

There is some evidence that a lack of sufficient attention to resource usage is actually detrimental to organization performance. For example, one national retail bank fitted out its London offices with top quality furniture, luxury carpets, the very best in canteen and other staff facilities. The staff were extremely well paid and enjoyed a large range of fringe benefits.

And yet the performance of the company was mediocre in terms of the norms of the sector; and it was one of the first and worst to suffer in the banking crisis of 2008 and onwards, recording massive losses and requiring an extensive government bailout.

When asked what went wrong, there were the usual rational answers from staff and management about investing in the wrong markets, and spending too much on assets that turned out to be toxic. However, many members of staff additionally referred to the luxury and opulence of the surroundings; they were simply unable to believe that anything could possibly go wrong in any organization that was equipped and fitted out in this way. Others referred to the clear extravagance of the office facilities and fittings as corporate self-indulgence; while others still, stated that of course this had to be paid for out of commercial activities. None of these responses gives any indication of a positive attitude or commitment to performance driven by the opulence of the surroundings; indeed, as stated above, there is a clear indication of a detrimental effect on performance.

The effectiveness of resource management practice depends on the capability of individual managers to assess what they need and how it is to be used. There are clear priorities in ensuring that the balance between adequacy and profligacy (an inadequacy) is reached, and that in so far as is reasonably practicable, the organization's people and processes are given everything that they need to do the work demanded, to the quality and volume required. Special attention is needed in terms of sustainability and environment management without compromising the effectiveness and efficiency of operations and activities. Special attention is also required when investing in technology.

Technology

Technology here refers to any, or all, of the following:

- production, manufacturing and service delivery technology;
- computer systems and information technology;
- mobile technology that may be used by staff;
- internet access;
- hardware and software;
- transport and distribution requirements.

Effective managerial practice demands a full knowledge and understanding of:

- what technology is required, and why;
- how much it will cost to install, what the returns on this ought to be, and what they are envisaged to be;
- how long its useful life is likely to be;
- whether to replace it or upgrade it when the time comes;
- how user-friendly it is;
- staff training implications;
- where overall value is added and lost to the business as the result of using it.

It is essential that all managers are technologically knowledgeable. Managers do not need to be technological experts or technologically proficient; they do need to know and understand how technology works, its impact on the organization overall, the different activities and processes that are carried out, and the costs incurred.

Technology has also to be examined and approved for quality assurance, security and reliability, and for the ease (or otherwise) of getting maintenance, upgrades and servicing. Technology needs to be examined for:

- compatibility with existing operating systems and the ability to integrate different technologies with each other;
- compatibility with other key systems, especially those of suppliers and distributors, partners in joint ventures, outsource providers, and remote organization locations and staff.

Managing technology effectively is one of those activities that is (or ought to be) not noticed all the time that everything is running smoothly. The only times that anyone notices or comments on technology are when it crashes, breaks down or fails to operate for some reason.

However, part of the practice of managing technology effectively is to keep an eye on how it does work, whether or not it is delivering what it promised, how much it costs, and its speed and effectiveness of operations. For this part of managerial practice to be effective, it is essential to have as above:

- clear costs and benefits known and understood;
- clear purpose in installing and operating it;
- clear targets for production, service delivery and data processing that it is supposed to deliver;
- clearly indicated maintenance, replacement and upgrade schedules.

Additionally, it is essential to have in place a write-off schedule. No technology lasts forever, and while no organization should be constantly disrupting things by changing technology too often, the time comes when everything becomes uncompetitive and needs replacing.

Finally, the technology itself ought always to be seen in the light of its contribution to the organization; it should never be seen in terms purely of its prestige, fashionability, isolated capacity, 'flash', or in isolation from the contribution that it needs to make.

For example:

- An airline spent £30 million installing alleged state-of-the-art baggage handling technology at one of its locations only to find that the new system could only cope with luggage under laboratory conditions; it could not cope with real flight arrivals and the peaks and troughs in activity.
- The UK NHS spent £14 billion on trying to create a national patient database only to find that while the data could indeed be stored, it could not be retrieved safely or securely.
- A university spent £6 million on re-equipping all its staff and laboratories with branded and fashionable Perspex PCs only to find that the operating systems installed in the new PCs were not compatible with existing databases, e-mail systems or file stores.
- A multinational manufacturer installed revolutionary production technology for a new line of soaps and detergents only to find that this had to be operated in isolation from everything else in the organization. The new system had to be loaded manually as existing automated operational systems were incompatible.

Clearly, to get the practice of technology management wrong is expensive and very damaging to the organization and its processes and activities. So it is essential that all managers know and understand fully the systems and equipment that exist in their domain, and that any technology is examined from these points of view in advance of it being installed.

Performance management

Performance management is dealt with in full detail in Chapter 15. At this stage however, it is essential to be clear about the following.

It is only possible to manage and assess performance against specific targets, aims and objectives. It is no use stating performance measures in terms of such phrases as: 'as much as possible', 'as soon as possible', or 'as quickly as possible'. Of course, everyone will want to do this; but the target needs to be expressed precisely; so that these phrases need to be translated as for example: 'a hundred items per hour', 'by Friday night', or 'by 12 o'clock'. This gives everyone involved a clear point of reference to work to, and also a measure of success and achievement – or failure.

Performance management is therefore a key management discipline as well as being an essential part of effective managerial practice. The practice of effective performance management demands that managers get to know and understand:

- their staff, their hopes, fears and aspirations;
- the nature of work, what it is that is required and how it is to be done;
- the demands and priorities placed on their own domain and how and why these integrate with other organization activities;
- the absolute standards of conduct, behaviour and performance required;
- how performance can be improved and developed;
- the financial aspects and targets, and how these are to be delivered.

In practice, performance management cannot be seen in isolation from everything else; it has to be integrated. Everything about the organization ought to be designed and implemented in order to create the conditions in which the desired levels of conduct, behaviour and performance are possible and achievable. So, for example:

- there is no use in requiring that staff are fully engaged if there is a distant or adversarial management style;
- there is no use in asking staff to work as hard as possible if managers clearly do not;
- it is bad practice to ask staff to work in ways that managers do not;
- it is also bad practice to sanction and punish staff for poor performance if the criteria by which performance is assessed are not made clear and agreed with everyone.

In order to achieve all this, it is therefore essential that managers are visible and accessible. It is very difficult to manage performance effectively unless individual managers are themselves fully engaged and involved. Visibility and involvement additionally help greatly to create the conditions in which high levels of performance are achievable. Managers and staff know each other. Managers see for themselves (rather than hear or perceive) what is going on. Problems and issues can be raised and addressed early rather than being left until they are serious. Mutual confidence between staff and managers is therefore built and enhanced all the time that this visibility, accessibility and engagement are present. On the other hand, mutual confidence is diluted as managers become less visible, accessible and apparently engaged.

expert view

Managing by walking about

Peters and Waterman (1982) stated that the basis of active engagement was based on what they called 'Managing By Walking About (MBWA)'. Peters and Waterman used the example of the Walton family, the founders and owners of Walmart (Asda in the UK), the largest supermarket chain in the world, and their practice of visiting every store at least once a year. While the company was growing, the Walton family stated that this was critical to success and achievement, and a key condition for keeping the staff fully engaged. Peters and Waterman tell the story that on one occasion, Walmart staff at a regional depot were loading up lorries for deliveries late at night, when someone approached them with coffee and doughnuts. When one member of staff asked the individual who he was, he replied: 'I am Sam, Sam Walton. I own the company, and I do my best to get around to see as many of our people as I possibly can'.

Of course, if you are going to take this kind of approach then it has to be followed through by all managers. It therefore becomes an obligation to ensure that other levels of management follow this practice becoming as fully engaged as they possibly can. Some companies and organizations now write this into managerial tasks, duties and priorities, and managers are assessed on this part of their practice as well as their ability to deliver the performance required.

Source: Peters and Waterman (1982).

Effective management in practice and the ability of 'management', as well as managers, to be visible, accessible and engaged therefore clearly depends on adopting expertise to the nature of present day organizations. This means creating management structures and priorities, and developing the practical expertise required, to be effective in:

- managing across cultures, national boundaries and timescales;
- managing remote and flexible workers and activities;
- addressing the issues raised by virtual organizations;
- addressing and managing diversity.

Managing across cultures

The advance of globalization and internationalization of organizations, business and activities has produced the need for a reappraisal of much that has hitherto been regarded as standard and effective management practice. To the expertise involved in strategic, operational and functional management must now be added knowledge, understanding and acceptance of cultural differences – how people think, believe, behave, act and react in different parts of the world. This in turn involves knowing and understanding the habits, norms, customs and patterns of behaviour in different places, and recognizing that these have to be accommodated and worked with when seeking to open up new ventures and activities elsewhere in the world.

The demand for this managerial approach and practical expertise is not new. Countries have been investing in, and creating, national and political empires for thousands of years; and companies and organizations have followed suit, working across cultures for at least the past three centuries. This aspect was however brought into sharp and enduring present day focus when Japanese manufacturing companies started to open up overseas operations, first in the US and Europe, and subsequently elsewhere in the world. They brought with them:

- standards of staff management;
- assurance of employment;
- high levels of pay in return for high levels and quality of work;
- staff training and development for all;
- investment in communities as well as work facilities that transcended the local standards and expectations of these places, wherever they chose to locate.

What was being offered was a set of standards, practices and attention to both performance and also the locality, that were absolute enough to meet the demands of any community or workforce anywhere in the world.

Not all organizations can (or probably should) behave like this. However, the need for a clarity of purpose, together with a clearly stated and agreed attitude to different locations in the world is absolute.

best practice

Wherever you locate in the world, it is essential always to be clear about why you have gone there. If you have gone simply to exploit cheap labour and technology, and fully deregulated working conditions, then the least that you can do is be honest about this.

Managing across boundaries and timescales

Alongside the need for cultural knowledge and understanding is the need to address logistical problems created by time and distance. Without adding too much to the expense and overhead of the organization overall, managerial structures (and managers) are required as follows:

- to enable quick and efficient decision-making processes wherever in the world decisions are required;
- problem-solving capabilities wherever in the world problems occur;
- the ability to access remote and distant locations when required;
- the ability to engage in profitable and effective activity wherever the organization establishes itself.

Beyond this, the organization and its managers need to take a continuous and business-oriented view of why they are involved in particular locations. As long as activities contribute to overall organizational and business performance and profitability, there is no problem of course. Additionally organizations engage in peripheral ventures in remote locations (for example buying up supply and distribution companies) to ensure the strength of the core business; and they engage in project work and joint ventures in order to gain footholds in particular locations, or to test the water for future prospects. The key is that when all this happens in practice, it is driven by business performance and can be justified in these terms.

Managing remote workers

Alongside managing organizations in remote locations exists the need to manage remote workers. 'Remote workers' are those who work on standard or flexible patterns of work spent wholly or partly away from the organization's premises.

People working in these ways need the same adequacy and effectiveness of management and supervision as those who turn up to a given location each day. The means of engaging with remote workers (and also ensuring that they stay engaged) has therefore to be found and this is so that they:

- do not become detached or alienated from the organization during extended periods of absence;
- are kept informed of the strengths and weaknesses of their own performance and contribution;
- can have problems and issues addressed whenever and wherever necessary;
- get the same opportunities for promotion, development, enhancement and advancement as everyone else.

One part of practical management in these circumstances therefore demands that channels of communication and opportunities to meet are kept open and flexible. Clearly the ability to use mobile phone, computer, laptop and blackberry technology is critical. Clearly also, these tools are effective but limited and this reinforces the need for face-to-face contact wherever possible. Wherever face-to-face contact can take place, time needs to be set aside for gossip and general chatter as well as addressing substantial organizational and operational priorities. It is also essential (whether managing remote workers or remote locations) that when crises and emergencies do occur, the organization and its managers have the means to get someone in authority to the spot as soon as possible so as to be able to address what has happened with full contextual knowledge and understanding.

Virtual organizations

Virtual organizations are those that exist wholly or mainly by virtue of the capability of computer technology and IT to support them and give them life. Virtual organizations therefore exist in every aspect of standard organizations, except for the size and structure of the physical premises that would otherwise be necessary.

Some virtual organizations are de facto a form of federation in which parts of existing organizations come together for projects, ventures and steady-state activities.

In all forms, virtual organizations exist for a particular venture and may then be disbanded; or they may continue for the very long term, delivering products, services and service exactly like any other.

In practice, management and supervision of activities in virtual organizations and federations have to be repositioned so as to be able to:

- maintain an active involvement in performance issues;
- ensure that finances, resources and other assets are used to best advantage and kept under control;
- ensure that cost, income and profit control are maintained;
- ensure that problems and issues can be addressed wherever they arise;
- ensure that crises and emergencies are notified early and tackled quickly and effectively.

The virtual organization has therefore to be supported by management practice that is suitable. Engagement and involvement have to be maintained, and this has to include regular physical meetings of everyone involved, as well as the continued use of mobile communication technology. Resources have to be committed therefore to ensure that people can get to face-to-face meetings, and that they have whatever technology is necessary to ensure that the virtual relationship remains effective.

best practice

If you create a virtual organization, then it is essential to ensure that this is done for the benefit of the whole business and all its stakeholders. Virtual organizations look attractive because they imply that there is no need for expensive premises. However, as with everything, if you go in purely for the purposes of cost-cutting, you will inevitably gain unlooked for expenses elsewhere.

Managing diversity

Managing diversity is about recognizing and addressing the sheer range of individuals and their differences, and creating standards and patterns of management that can accommodate these differences. This has to take place at the same time as creating, developing and maintaining a cohesive workforce, work ethic, and standards of conduct, behaviour and performance that deliver everything expected of the organization and its staff.

Diversity is normally understood to be a human resource (HR) term, and is referred to in Chapter 9 in that context. The practice of management, however, demands that full account is taken of the influence of technology, training, development, present experience, locations, patterns of work and the nature of work in addition to the more HR-oriented aspects of cultural and social background, language and dialect, gender, disability and age.

Effective management in this area must also refer to the nature and use of technology, the qualifications needed to use it, and how this affects both jobs and occupations themselves, and also patterns and locations of work and organizations.

Creativity

The effective practice of management demands creativity. The body of skills, knowledge, attitudes, behaviour and expertise that is increasingly coming to be recognized as the foundations of professional managerial practice has to be learned and applied. From this, it has to be developed so as to be capable of being used effectively in any situation that arises. Creativity in management is demanded in many different activities as follows:

- product design and development;
- the creation of expert and high quality service delivery;
- marketing, advertising and promotional activities;
- problem-solving and addressing staffing issues;
- motivating and engaging staff;
- building and developing excellent and effective work teams.

Creativity therefore permeates all the best organizations and is a key feature of effective expert and professional management practice. In order to be fully creative (and effective) in each of the above areas, a body of skills, knowledge, expertise and understanding is required so that the creative aspect that is brought to bear on any, or all, of the above areas, comes from a very strong basis of professional assurance. Indeed, in many cases, the creativity required arises directly from this expertise. At its lowest common denominator, creativity simply means ensuring that each issue is addressed effectively with a view to resolving or developing whatever is demanded.

All managers need to have a creative faculty, bringing their skills, knowledge and expertise to new situations, and positioning it so that whatever is necessary is addressed effectively. However, just because something is creative does not mean that it is good; creativity itself needs to be harnessed to the purposes of the organization and situation.

Conclusions

The purpose of this chapter has been to introduce and explain the major areas for the development of expert management practice, and to address as concisely as possible the key features that have to be taken into account. These areas and features are themselves diverse and complex; and at first sight do not necessarily appear connected in any way. However, there are three key connections.

- It is impossible to be an expert practising manager unless all of these elements and features are known, understood and recognized for their influence both within the organization, and also elsewhere.
- Staff and organizations expect managers to know and understand the effects of all these features and elements in their own domain.
- These features do not in fact exist in isolation from each other. For example, a virtual organization may make something sustainable due to the capability to reduce premises' costs to an absolute minimum; managing across cultures and the need for further knowledge and understanding of what happens elsewhere in the world may enhance standards of management, conduct, behaviour and performance in existing organization locations; creating a sustainable and environmentally friendly organization may cause managers to fundamentally reappraise how resources are sourced and used across all activities.

There are therefore elements to be learned and applied. As these elements are studied, anyone taking a professional approach will see the need to learn more about them, recognizing that they form the basis of critical areas of skills, knowledge and expertise that anyone who aspires to be an effective and expert manager must have. In broad terms, these areas can be broken down into:

- how things are done, and the learning and application of the behavioural aspects of organizations: culture, values and attitudes; team, group and individual behaviour; politics and conflict in organizations; human resource management (HRM); and leadership; and these areas form the basis of coverage of Part Two of this book;
- why things are done and the learning and application of how to formulate and implement strategy, policy, direction and priorities; marketing; managing

operations and projects; finance; and organizational and collective and individual performance; and these areas form the basis of coverage of Part Three of the book;

- the enduring managerial priorities of: risk; motivation; managing and reconciling the daily issues and pressures; and developing effective managerial practice and expertise; and these form the areas of coverage of Part Four of the book.

- The drive of putting skills, knowledge, understanding and expertise into practice and delivering performance ought to be at the core of all managerial practice.
- The ability to know and understand external and internal pressures in particular situations and respond effectively to these is a key management priority and expertise.
- The need to know and understand technology and its capabilities in terms of what it can do for the organization and particular functions is (or ought to be) the driving force for all technological development and installation.
- Knowledge and understanding of a variety of organizational forms is essential in terms of what it takes to be effective in different situations.
- It is essential to recognize that managerial practice can always be improved; nothing will remain adequate or effective forever.

Further reading

Gröschl, S. (2011) *Diversity in the Workplace.* Gower.

Hancock, M. and Zahawi, N. (2011) *Masters of Nothing.* Biteback Publishers.

Lessem, R. (1987) *Intrapreneurship.* Wildwood.

Peters, T. (1989) *Thriving on Chaos.* Pan.

Peters, T. and Waterman, R. (1982) *In Search of Excellence.* Harper and Row.

Ross Sorkin, A. (2009) *Too Big to Fail.* Penguin.

Management and people

If organizations are composed of people, then it is essential that all those in managerial positions know and understand how people behave. Managers need to know and understand the influences that cause behaviour to be modified and changed; and how people, think, behave and react when faced with the variety and complexity of situations present, or potentially present, in organized business and managerial settings.

The context for knowing and understanding collective and individual behaviour is capable of simple introduction. For example:

- if you prefer to work in a positive, cheerful and productive setting, then it is likely that most people will want to do so also;
- if you prefer to be treated with honesty and integrity, then it is likely that most people prefer this also;
- if you prefer an interesting and varied working life and career, then it is likely that most people prefer this also;
- if you expect to be treated fairly and equally, free from discrimination and harassment, then it is likely that most people will expect this also.

A key to learning and developing an understanding of collective and individual behaviour is therefore empathy. A lack of empathy or humanity is always present when top and senior managers find themselves having to explain why organizations have wasted resources on ill-considered ventures; when they have to make layoffs; or when they have to explain a fundamental organizational ineptitude or failure. This lack of empathy arises from a fundamental inability or willingness to recognize the legitimate concerns that everyone has when particular situations arise.

Understanding collective and individual behaviour from the point of view of everyone involved is essential. Understanding behaviour from the point of view of personal, professional and occupational commitment additionally requires giving a clear reference point for the range of likely, possible and potential outcomes when dealing with any situation in which people are involved.

Understanding collective and individual behaviour is not easy. However, it is possible to gain a good understanding of how most people behave in most situations; and this then forms the foundations of expertise in this particular area of management.

Part Two breaks down the nature of collective and individual behaviour so as to be able to provide points of reference in developing expertise in this field. Chapter 6 covers the basis of organization culture and the patterns of behaviour and attitudes that exist, and that have to be modified and developed. Chapter 7 deals with the critical nature of communication and, especially, the barriers and blockages that prevent effective communications from taking place, leading inevitably to conflict and dysfunction.

Organizational politics and the positive and negative effects of the ways in which people behave, either when standards are not set, or because of emergent behavioural patterns, are dealt with in Chapter 8.

The specific aspects of human resource management, and the professional and managerial knowledge and understanding required are covered in Chapter 9. Chapter 10 examines the critical nature of leadership expertise, and the extent to which it is required by all those in managerial positions. This chapter identifies specific traits, qualities, styles and expertise, and how these are applied in practice.

6

'The culture of an organization is the basis for its management style.'

Culture

In this chapter

- understanding the patterns of behaviour that underpin corporate life and activities
- developing the required organization culture
- making the culture work in relation to the nature of activities carried out
- establishing the basis for setting the required standards of behaviour and performance

Introduction

The culture of an organization is the basis for its management style, and the individual and collective attitudes, values, patterns of behaviour, customs, norms and habits. It is therefore essential that the required ways in which people are expected to behave are clearly established and accepted by all concerned. Distinctive standards of attitudes, behaviour and performance must be established and agreed, rather than allowed to emerge; and where attitudes and behaviour are legally, socially and morally unacceptable, they need to be stamped out.

All organizations have different collective and individual attitudes, values and patterns of behaviour. It is essential to recognize the influence of size, structure and location of the organization as a major influence on its culture. The following issues also influence culture, attitudes, values and behaviour.

- Technology influences work arrangements and groupings, physical layout and the nature of the people employed.

- Structure and hierarchy influence personal and professional interactions, personal and professional ambitions and aspirations.
- Status, and how it is accorded and recognized, especially in terms of rank, position in hierarchy, personality, achievements.
- Trappings and badges, especially cars, healthcare, fashionable computers and technology.
- Rules, regulations and systems influence attitudes and behaviour (positive or negative) depending on how they are drawn up.
- Leadership provides the key point of identity for everyone else, and from which people establish their own perceptions of the organization's general standards.
- Management style influences the general feelings of well-being (positive or negative) of everyone else, and sets standards of attitudes and behaviour as well as performance.
- Managerial demands and the ways in which these are made, and their influence on attitudes, behaviour and performance.
- Hierarchical and divisional relations and interactions influence the nature of performance, attention to achievement and the value placed on achievements; this also applies to functional activities.

'I cannot necessarily define organization culture. But I know it, feel it, and begin to understand it, every time I visit a company or institution' – **Tom Peters** (1986) *The World Turned Upside Down*. Channel 4.

Definitions of culture

Organization culture and the patterns of collective and individual behaviour that arise are not easy to define. Nevertheless, there have been many studies that have attempted to evaluate the collective attitudes, values, behaviour and performance of organizations, and how people interact with each other in their working lives. The major studies are:

- Handy and Harrison, and cultural definitions;
- Deal and Kennedy, and culture profiles;
- Hofstede, and cultural dimensions.

Handy and Harrison

Handy and Harrison (Handy, 1993; Harrison, 1995) defined organization culture in terms of the dominant force, factor or personality present as follows.

- **Power culture:** power culture exists where the one key relationship is between each member of staff and the individual who wields power and influence. Power cultures depend upon the figure at the centre – the source of power – for their well-being. Everyone else draws their strength, influence and confidence from the relationship with this person. The relationship is normally terminated when there is a loss of confidence in the person who holds power.

The main problem with power cultures is growth. As the organization grows and diversifies, it becomes difficult for the person at the centre to sustain continued high levels of influence. There is also the problem of permanence, of what happens when the person at the centre of power passes out of the organization. Where this individual has been totally dominant, a void is normally left when they leave.

- **People/person culture:** people/person culture exists for the people who work in it. Examples include research groups, university departments, family firms, and companies started by groups of friends where the first coming together is generated by those involved rather than the production of products and services. The key relationship is therefore between the people involved and what binds them is their common interest. Hierarchies may subsequently evolve, but these too will be driven by the common interest, at least in the first place.
- **Task cultures:** task cultures are to be found in project teams, marketing groups and service-oriented organizations. In task cultures, the emphases are on getting the job completed, keeping customers and clients satisfied and responding to, and identifying, new market opportunities. Such cultures are flexible, adaptable and dynamic. Problems arise, however, when the rules, regulations and norms are not drawn tightly enough; and this leads to duplication of effort, and staff and individual conflict even though this may be as the result of professional rather than personal disagreement.
- **Role cultures:** role cultures are found where organizations have gained a combination of size, permanence and departmentalization, and where the ordering of activities and the preservation of knowledge, experience and stability are essential.

The key relationships are based on authority, rank and status. Role cultures operate most effectively where the wider environment is steady and a degree of certainty can be envisaged. In times of great change, the best role cultures develop through the use of their own rule books; for others it may be more difficult.

Deal and Kennedy

Deal and Kennedy (2000) defined organization culture in terms of risk taking; individual and collective behaviour; and collective and individual habits. The classifications were as follows.

- **Tough guy/macho:** tough guy/macho cultures operate in fast moving industries and sectors. Examples of tough guy/macho cultures include banking and finance, stock market trading and commodities and other brokerages. The collective propensity to take risks is very high. Collectively also, the staff are very fashionable. Staff tend to be individualistic, concentrating on their own performance as a contributor to that of the collective good, rather than on the collective good in the first place. Tough guy cultures are particularly effective when crises occur, or when products and services have to be delivered in the very short term. Tough guy cultures tend not to learn from past mistakes.

- **Work hard/play hard:** work hard/play hard cultures operate in fast moving industries also. Work hard/play hard cultures exist in high technology and cutting edge design and development work (Google is widely perceived to have a 'work hard/play hard' culture). The overwhelming positive element of work hard/play hard cultures is the positive attitude. Those in work hard/play hard cultures expect short-term results and continued recognition for a steady stream of successes. Work hard/play hard cultures are present where there is an enduring commitment to hard work and continuous collective achievement. In work hard/play hard cultures, staff members will tend to socialize as a group, as well as work together.

- **Bet your company:** bet your company cultures tend to be found in expert, professional and top quality organizations; and also in industries such as oil and aerospace. Bet your company cultures tend towards high levels of risk taking, partly on the basis that they have been successful over long periods of time; and partly also on the basis that this success can induce a perception of complacency. Bet your company cultures have a strong respect for authority, and tend to be ordered in terms of rank, hierarchy and departmentalization. Older members of a bet your company culture serve as mentors for the younger ones so that the culture is preserved.

- **Process cultures:** process cultures are to be found in banks, insurance companies, pharmaceuticals, financial services, and government departments. Those working in process cultures tend to be cautious and protective of their own position. Risk taking is low and never undertaken without first establishing that there is a procedure to be followed. The great advantage of process cultures is their attention to detail and their willingness to follow procedures, and to bring order and systems to the place of work.

Hofstede

Hofstede (1980, 2004) studied the workforce of IBM in its operations in over 40 different countries. This work enabled Hofstede to identify both national cultures that were present, and also how the presence of national characteristics affected the organization culture of IBM. Hofstede identified five dimensions of national cultures as follows.

- **Power/distance:** the extent to which power and influence is distributed across the society; the unevenness of power and influence depending on organizational position; the extent to which this distribution was acceptable to the members of the society. Hofstede also referred to the physical and psychological distance that exists between people, and the sources of power and influence.

- **Uncertainty avoidance:** this reflects the extent to which people prefer order and certainty, or can cope with uncertainty and ambiguity. It also reflects the extent to which they feel comfortable or threatened by the presence or absence of uncertainty, both in the short term and also as an enduring factor of working life and wider social aspects of the particular location.
- **Individualism/collectivism:** this reflects the extent to which individuals are expected to take care of themselves; or the extent to which individuals expect to take care of themselves. Individualism/collectivism also reflects the extent to which a common good, clearly defined set of goals and organizational direction can be accepted.
- **Masculinity/femininity:** this reflects the distinction between masculine values – the acquisition of money, wealth, fortune, success, ambition, possessions, reputation and recognition – and the 'feminine' values of sensitivity, care, concern, attention to the needs of others, quality of life; the value, importance and mix, and the prevalence of each.
- **Long-term orientation/short-term orientation:** this is a reflection of the values held in particular societies, professions and occupational groups. Values associated with long-term orientation include thrift, perseverance and career development; values associated with short-term orientation include respecting traditions and habits, fulfilling social, as well as workplace, obligations, and protecting and developing one's reputation.

The great contribution of these, and other, studies of organizational, national and social culture is to begin to classify and present points of reference that give everyone a start in understanding the components and content of organization culture.

The weakness of each of the approaches is that they necessarily tend to generalize. For each of the definitions, it is possible to find a counter-argument. For those who work in anything but the smallest of organizations, it is possible to find elements of many, if not all, of the above statements and classifications. Within bureaucratic organizations, it is commonplace to find people who are very task and customer driven; within dynamic and go-ahead organizations, it is nevertheless possible to find people who do everything by the rule book.

Additionally, and most crucially, many would argue that there is no such thing as national culture. For example, people living in the west of England would regard themselves as being very different to those from the north, south or east; and people living in the west of London perceive themselves to have very different customs and habits to those living in the east. Without a doubt, these differences exist in every part of the world.

The key contribution that these studies and definitions of organization and national culture make is to begin developing an expert understanding of organizational, collective and individual behaviour. It is only a start; it needs to be the basis for further study and evaluation. Adopting these approaches to organizational and collective culture and behaviour should never become the basis for stereotyping.

Developing an understanding of organization culture

As stated above, using the Handy and Harrison, Deal and Kennedy, and Hofstede studies is a useful point of reference and a basis on which to build knowledge, understanding and expertise. In order to develop this knowledge, understanding and expertise within particular organizations, locations and situations, the following have to be understood and evaluated.

- **History and tradition:** the origins of the organization; the aims and objectives of the first owners and managers, and their philosophy and values; the value in which these are currently held; the ways in which they have developed.
- **Nature of activities:** historical and traditional, and also current and envisaged; this includes reference to the general state of success and effectiveness; the balance of activities – steady-state, innovative, crisis.
- **Technology:** the relationship between technology and the workforce, work design, organization and structure; levels of technological stability and change; levels of expertise, stability and change.
- **Alienative factors:** those factors that cause a form of psychological distance or alienation to develop between organizations and their staff. Psychological barriers include: rank, status, hierarchy, dress codes; and they all influence the ways in which those working at the company behave and perform. Alienation occurs as the result of technology usage in a variety of ways, including:
  - remote workers do not meet with other colleagues and co-workers on a regular basis;
  - e-mail rather than face-to-face communications become the norm and the basis for establishing patterns of behaviour and activity;
  - mobile and computer technology means that people are able to work according to their own individual schedules rather than those that are uniform or imposed by the organization.
- **Past, present and future:** the importance of the past in relation to current and proposed activities; special pressures (especially struggles and glories) of the past; the extent to which the organization 'is living' in the past, present or future, and the pressures and constraints that are brought about as the result.

- **Purposes, priorities and attention:** in relation to performance, staff, customers, the community and environment; and to progress and development.
- **Size:** and the degrees of formalization and structure that this brings. Larger organizations are much more likely to have a proliferation of divisions, supervisory structures, reporting relationships, rules, processes and procedures tending to cause communication difficulties, interdepartmental rivalries and problems with coordination and control.
- **Location:** geographical location, the constraints and opportunities afforded through choosing to be in, for example, urban centres, edge of town or rural areas. Location has to be considered also from the point of view of the impact of multi-site locations, geographical spread, and the physical distances that exist between the different locations; and the physical distances that exist between different activities and the head offices. The question of location also includes recognizing and considering prevailing local, national and sectoral traditions and values. Location has also to be seen from the twin points of view of:
  - needing to have a point of reference for summarizing and understanding and evaluating the culture of a locality;
  - recognizing that it is impossible to make sweeping generalizations about culture.
- **Leadership and management style:** the stance adopted by the organization in managing and supervising its people; the stance people require of their managers and supervisors; the general relationships between people and organization and the nature of superior–subordinate relations.

When all these factors are combined together then the elements of organization culture are in place; and the result may be that organization culture is:

- designed or emergent;
- strong or weak;
- positive or negative;
- cohesive or fragmented.

It is especially important that culture is designed, shaped and reinforced by those in top and senior positions. This involves setting standards of attitudes, values, behaviour and performance to which everyone is required to subscribe as a condition of employment. Policies and procedures are produced so that everyone knows where they stand; and these are enforced when attitudes, behaviour, commitment and performance fall short in any way. Organizations with strong, positive and designed cultures are not all things to all people; and this needs to be made clear at recruitment and selection processes.

A designed culture is essential if organizational conduct, behaviour and performance are to be optimized over the long term. This means that managers have to take active steps to ensure that they determine and implement the required standards, conduct, patterns of behaviour and human and professional/occupational interactions. If organization culture is allowed to emerge, the result is that people think, believe, behave and act according to their own priorities, and the pressures of their peers; and this leads to the tendency to pursue their own agenda.

Organizations that allow this to happen succeed only if the aims and objectives of the staff, and interest groups, coincide absolutely with their own. When this happens, staff set their own informal procedures and sanctions; and it is a short step from this to bullying and victimization. Organizations faced with emergent cultures invariably have staffing problems of some kind. When this happens, the characteristics of culture have to be identified and tackled.

Characteristics of culture

Both in designing culture, and also in response to remedying the problems of emergent cultures, attention needs to be paid to each of the following areas to ensure that culture becomes strong, cohesive, positive, inclusive and designed. Culture has the following characteristics, and is:

- **Learned** – rather than genetic or biological.
- **Shared** – members of groups and organization share culture.
- **Continuous** – cumulative in its development and passed on from one generation to the next.
- **Symbolic** – based on the human capacity to symbolize, to use one thing to represent another.
- **Integrated** – a change in one area will lead to a change in another.
- **Adaptive** – based on human qualities of adaptability, creativity, innovation and imagination.
- **Regular** – when participants interact with each other, they use common language terminology and recognized and accepted forms of behaviour.
- **Norms** – distinctive standards of behaviour; the ways in which people interact with each other; relationships between, and within, ranks and hierarchies; the general patterns of behaviour, familiarity, habits, dress and speech.
- **Dominant values** – advocated by the organization and expected by participants.
- **Philosophy** – policies concerning beliefs and standards of performance, attitude, behaviour and conduct. Organizational philosophy gives the cornerstone for establishing what is rewarded, punished and sanctioned.
- **Rules** – the formal rules that underline the constitution of the organization; the informal rules that govern the interaction of individuals on a daily basis. The rules and procedures enforce what is rewarded; and especially, what is punished and sanctioned.

- **Organizational climate** – conveyed by the physical appearance and layout of the organization, and reinforced through the ways in which staff interact with each other and with the outside world.

Each of these characteristics is additionally a point of inquiry and potential influence when managers seek to change, develop and enhance organization culture overall.

Pressures on organization culture

Pressures on organization culture exist both inside and also outside the organization. Organizations must respect the attitudes, values and ethics of the places where business is to be conducted; and this includes reference to social and religious customs. External social and cultural prejudices may also have to be taken into account.

Human prejudices

It is important to recognize that 'prejudice' – the subjective and unfounded attitudes adopted towards particular people, products and services – is a fact of human existence and behaviour. Most prejudices are harmless. For example, people who choose only to wear blue clothing are exhibiting a form of prejudice, as are those who always vote for a particular political party. Supporting a football club is a form of prejudice, as is always using the same supermarket for grocery shopping.

However, prejudices against particular members of the community are abhorrent and unacceptable in organizations. As well as being illegal, it is repugnant to treat people with less respect on the grounds of: gender; race; disability; membership of a trade union/non-membership of a trade union; spent convictions from a previous criminal conviction. It is ethically and morally abhorrent to treat people differently and with less respect on the grounds of: age; sexual orientation; marital status; physical appearance; the way they speak; the place in which they live. It is both abhorrent and also illegal to allow bullying, victimization, harassment, and physical and verbal assaults.

Organizations that allow repugnant forms of prejudice invariably suffer from low morale, and declining levels of output. Organization cultures become weak and divided as people gang up on the particular oppressed individual or group; and as those who are being oppressed seek the means to fight back.

Local working practices and customs, expectations of hours of work and ways of working all have to be considered. In some places, activities close down for several hours during the day; in others people expect to start and finish work early. In some cases also, people are expected to socialize outside working hours as a condition of their employment.

Nissan UK

Headquarters' staff at Nissan UK in north-east England used to meet regularly on Thursday and Friday evenings. This was expected by the company on the basis that: meeting in a social atmosphere encouraged personal and professional understanding; and it additionally gave the opportunity to sort out organizational problems away from the pressures of work.

One member of staff objected to this. This person, a woman in her early thirties, considered that her work commitment ended when she left the office. She had other priorities in her life, and especially had to return home early in the evening in order to feed her children.

Nissan first encouraged her to participate; then when this did not work, she was disciplined. The woman complained to ACAS and then to the UK employment tribunal system. Nissan initially defended the case; however, at the point at which the case was to be heard, the company proposed a settlement which was acceptable to all.

Physical distance affects culture and cohesion. The inability to see and meet with others, for example when work is being carried out in a foreign or remote location from the main organization leading to the structuring and ordering of tasks and activities, affects relationships between the staff at the location, and relationships between the location and head office. It also affects decision-making processes, and the attitudes and approaches to local problems and issues. Those in remote locations, and especially the person with overall responsibility and control, are likely to experience feelings of isolation from time to time and this may need to be supported if overall effectiveness of that part of the organization is to be sustained.

Flexible working

Maintaining a collective corporate identity is an enduring problem for those managers responsible for flexible and non-standard patterns of work. Whether these are related to irregular hours, working in remote locations or telecommuting, the core need is to ensure that everybody is instilled with collective, cohesive and positive attitudes and values in their relationship with the organization.

It is therefore a priority for managers faced with these issues to ensure that they visit and meet with their staff as often as possible; and where this is not possible, to ensure that they speak to them on the telephone. This is preferable to regular e-mails; and where e-mails are used, important and urgent issues must always be followed up with telephone calls, and meetings where possible.

Additionally, where flexible staff do attend at the organization's headquarters or premises, they must be given the opportunity to meet and socialize with their colleagues so that a personal, as well as occupational, identity is developed.

Psychological distance has also to be managed. Psychological distance is likely to exist as a feature of physical distance even if there is a full range of electronic and telecommunications available. Psychological distance is also present to a greater or lesser extent between the organization and the communities in which it works; and the interaction of organizational attitudes, standards and values with those of the localities must also be considered. The relationship with the community has also to be considered from the point of view of the economic contribution made by the organization in the provision of work. This is a responsibility for all organizations; it is a critical responsibility when the organization is the largest single or dominant employer in the area.

Legal and ethical pressures

All organizations have to work within the laws of their locations. Laws exert pressure on production methods, waste disposal, health and safety, marketing and selling, contractual arrangement, staff management, human resources, industrial relations and equality (or otherwise) of opportunity and access, community relations, organizational and professional insurance, and the reporting of results; and each of these in turn affects the behaviour and priority of the organization.

Pressures are compounded when the organization operates in many countries and under diverse legal codes. Balances have to be found in these cases to ensure that, as far as possible, everyone who works for the organization does so on terms that transcend the varying legal constraints. Organizations are therefore obliged to set absolute standards that more than meet particular legal minima. Moreover, the phrase 'we comply with the law' invariably gives the message that 'the only reason that we set these standards is because we have to' and that the organization has therefore been pressured into these standards rather than achieving them because it believes that they are right. It calls into question not just the organization's attitude to the law, but also its wider general attitudes, values and standards.

Ethical pressures arise from the nature of work carried out and from the standards and customs of the communities in which the organization operates. There are also general ethical pressures on many activities concerned that are covered by the law.

Again, the ideal response of any organization is to put itself beyond reproach so that these pressures are accommodated, leaving the way clear for developing productive and harmonious relationships with all concerned.

Internal pressures

The internal pressures on organization culture and collective attitudes and behaviour are as follows.

- The interaction between the desired culture and the organization's structures and systems. Serious misfit between these leads to stress and frustration and also to customer dissatisfaction and staff demotivation.

- The expectations and aspirations of staff, and the extent to which these are realistic and can be satisfied within the organization. This becomes a serious issue when the nature of organization changes and prevailing expectations can no longer be accommodated. Problems also arise when the organization makes promises that it cannot keep.
- Management and supervisory style, and the extent to which this is supportive, suitable to the purpose and generally acceptable to the staff.
- The qualities and expertise of the staff, and the extent to which this divides their loyalties. Many staff groups have professional and trade union memberships, continuous professional development requirements and career expectations, as well as holding down positions and carrying out tasks within organizations. In many cases – and especially when general dissatisfaction is present – people tend to take refuge in their profession or occupation, or their trade union.
- Technology and the extent to which it impacts on the ways in which work is designed, structured and carried out.
- Working customs, traditions and practices including restrictive practices, work divisions, specialization and allocation, unionization and other means of representation; and the attitudes and approaches adopted by both organization and staff towards each other – flexible and cooperative, adversarial, degrees of openness.
- The extent to which continuity of employment is feasible; or conversely, uncertainties around future prospects for work and employment. This includes degrees of flexibility, the extent and prevalence of employee and skills development, learning subcultures and the wider attitude of both staff and organization to this. It also affects reward packages.
- Internal approaches and attitudes to the legal and ethical issues indicated; the extent of genuine commitment to equality of opportunity and access for all staff, whether or not different grades have different values placed on them; standards of dealings with staff, customers, communities, suppliers and distributors.
- The presence of pride and commitment in the organization, its work and its reputation; standards of general well-being; the extent of mutual respect.
- Communication methods and systems, the nature of language used, the presence/absence of hidden agenda.
- Physical and psychological distance between functions, departments, divisions and positions in the organization and its hierarchies.

Joint ventures

Organizations involved in joint ventures normally create a company or entity with its own distinctive identity for the duration of the project. This is to generate positive feelings of commitment towards the matter in hand and override the view that would otherwise remain on the part of those involved that they continue to be a part of their old organization. A fragmented and disordered – and negative – approach and identity would thus otherwise ensue. By creating the separate and new identity, the negative is overcome and a distinctive focal point for the work in hand is established.

Mergers and takeovers

Mergers and takeovers are normally extremely attractive from the point of view of generating short-term share price advantages. Almost invariably however, less attention is paid to how the newly merged organization is to operate in the future. In particular, staff coming from the previously independent organizations have to be steered and guided through the transition period in which the culture, values, attitudes and identity with the previous organization are translated into a new and positive identity with what now exists. This is not always easy to achieve; and it is rarely considered by those steering mergers and takeovers. Failure to do so however, means that people will constantly hark back to the good old days before the merger or takeover; and they become even slower to accept and internalize new ways of working, colleagues from other organizations involved, and new patterns of behaviour and ways of working that now have to be followed.

Other aspects of organizational culture

Other features of organizational culture may be distinguished. One way of looking at these features is as a web in which each strand or loop both feeds off, and also strengthens, all the others (see Figure 6.1).

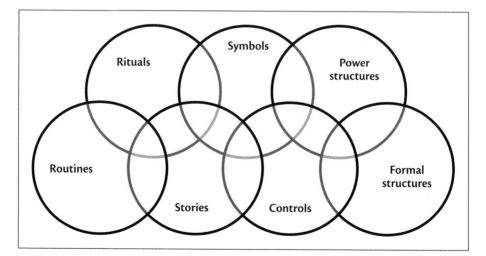

Figure 6.1 *The cultural web*

- **Relationships with the environment:** including the ways in which the organization copes with uncertainty and turbulence; the ways by which the organization seeks to influence the environment; the extent to which it behaves proactively or reactively.
- **History and tradition:** the extent to which the organization's histories and traditions are a barrier or a facilitator of progress; the extent to which the organization values and worships its past histories and traditions; key influences on current activities and beliefs; the position of key interest groups – for example trade unions.
- **Power structures and the internal relationship balance:** the mixture and effectiveness of power, status, hierarchy, authority, responsibility, individualism, group cohesion; the general relationship mixture of task and social development.
- **Control mechanisms:** and how control is exercised over particular groups, and over the organization as a whole; the extent to which some groups have preferred status and the reasons for this; how resources are controlled and allocated.

best practice

It is essential to look at the inherent strength and integrity of each aspect of organization culture in order to assess it for integrity; and also to assess it for effectiveness.

For those in managerial positions where there is a lack of integrity or effectiveness, these ought to be points of attention in the development of the individual and collective behaviour required.

- **Rites and rituals:** these are the punctuation marks of organization operations. They include: pay negotiations; internal and external job application means and methods; disciplinary, grievance and dismissal procedures; rewards; individual, group, departmental and divisional publicity; training and development activities; parties and celebrations; key appointments and dismissals; socialization and integration of people into new roles, activities and responsibilities.

just a minute

It is essential to recognize the effects on people's comfort when rites, rituals, routines and habits are disrupted. If people are asked to change their times or location of work, they are also being asked to change patterns of behaviour with which they have come to be extremely comfortable. Whenever you ask people to change their location or hours of work, remember to ensure that, in so far as is reasonably practicable, you are able to accommodate their existing routines and habits.

- **Routines and habits:** these are the formal, semi-formal and informal ways of working and interaction that people generate for themselves (or which the organization generates for them) to make comfortable the non-operational aspects of working life. They develop around the absolutes – attendance times, work requirements, authority and reporting relationships – and include regular meetings, regular tasks, forms of address between members of the organization and groups, pay days, holidays and some trainee development activities.

- **Badges and status symbols**: these are the marks of esteem conferred by organizations on their people. They are a combination of location – near to or away from the corridors of power for example; possessions – cars, technology, personal departments; job titles – reflecting a combination of ability, influence and occupation; and position in the hierarchy pecking order.

The effects of rites, rituals, routines, habits, badges and status symbols all lie in the value that the organization places on them and the value in which they are held by the members of staff. There is no point in offering anything, or in undertaking any form of cultural activity, if a negligible or negative response is received. In general therefore, these forms of culture development both anticipate people's expectations and seek to reinforce them and to meet them.

Stories, myths and legends

All organizations have their fund of stories, myths and legends. The nature and content of these represents and reflects the current state of organizational culture and well-being.

Stories, myths and legends: Examples

- 'I knew I'd made a mistake, and I knew that the senior consultant was in a towering rage. I could hear him coming. So I borrowed a patient's dressing gown, wrapped it around me so that my uniform was not showing, and sat on a commode next to one of the beds until he had gone.' **Staff Nurse**, south-eastern general hospital (2000), on inter-professional relations.

- 'We took an incredible risk going into the airline business.' **Richard Branson** (1998), keeping up the adventurous image of the Virgin Group; in fact the venture was meticulously planned and the subject of extensive investment before Virgin Atlantic ever flew.

- 'McKinsey consultants used to be brilliant, creative and interesting – they were eccentrics. Now they all look the same, say the same, and have the same thing to offer – whether or not this is what the client requires.' **Tom Peters** (2000) *Masters of the Universe*, Channel 4, on the development of McKinsey Management Consultants since his departure.

- 'Everybody is harking back to the good old days. They speak and reminisce fondly of bygone times, a golden era – in fact, an era that never was.' **John Major** (1998).

Culture management and attention to culture

Both the actual culture and the perceived ideal are subject to constant development. With this in mind, the best organizations therefore pay this constant attention. There are some basic assumptions here.

People can, and do, change if it is in their interests to do so. People resist when they perceive or understand that it is not in their interests to do so. All changes in standards and behaviour therefore need to be presented as being in the best interests of those affected; and where this is not the case, people still need to know and understand clearly what is to be expected of them so that they can then choose whether or not to remain with the organization.

Culture can be changed and developed. There are too many examples where this has happened to think otherwise. Nissan UK transformed a population of ex-miners, shipbuilders and steelworkers into the most productive and effective car company in the UK. Toyota at Derby is following suit with former railway staff. British Airways transformed a bureaucratic nationalized monopoly into a customer-oriented multinational corporation. British Steel transformed itself from a loss-making national corporation, riddled with demarcation and restrictive practices, to a profitable, effective and flexible operator before being sold on to the Dutch Chorus Group.

Culture should be changed and developed. The constant development of operations, technology, markets, customer bases and the capabilities of the human resource make this inevitable also. Current ways of working and equipment; and current skills, knowledge and qualities serve current needs only. The future is based around the developments and innovations that are to take place in each of these areas. Therefore, the culture must itself develop in order that these can be accommodated.

Culture change can be long and costly, especially where people resist. It is certainly true that where stability has existed for a long while, it is traumatic at first – and therefore costly in terms of people's feelings and possibly also in terms of current morale. It is made easier for the future if new qualities and attitudes of flexibility, dynamism and responsiveness are included in the new form and if this is reinforced through ensuring that people understand that the old ways are now neither effective nor viable.

Culture change need not take forever. Indeed, people who are told that there are to be lengthy periods of turbulence lose interest and motivation. The reality of change and development can be quickly conveyed through critical incidents – for example the gain or loss of a major order; the collapse of a large firm in the sector; the entry of a new player into the sector; radical technological advances; and so on. Once this is understood, the attitudes, behaviour and orientation of the staff are given emphases in particular direction, and the general positioning of their aspirations, hopes and fears is changed.

Conclusions

Effective organization cultures are positive and designed rather than emergent. They must be capable of gaining commitment to purpose, to the ways in which this is pursued and to the standards adopted by everyone. Cultures are a summary and reflection of the aims, objectives, and values held. Where neither is apparent, different groups and individuals form their own aims and objectives and adopt their own values; and where these are at variance with overall purpose, or negative in some way, they are dysfunctional and may become destructive.

Excellence and culture

In the view of Peters and Waterman (1982):

'Without exception the dominance and coherence of culture proved to be an essential quality of the "excellent" companies [the 62 American companies studied by Peters and Waterman]. Moreover, the stronger the culture, and the more it was directed to the market place, the less need there was for policy manuals, organization charts or detailed procedures and rules. In these companies, people way down the line know what they are supposed to do in most situations because the handful of guiding values is crystal clear.'

For this to be effective, a strong mutual sense of loyalty and acceptance between organization and people is essential. Employees exert positive effort on behalf of the organization, making a personal as well as professional or occupational commitment. The reverse of this – the organization's commitment to its people – is also essential. A strong sense of identity towards the organization and its purposes and values is required; and this happens when these purposes and values are clear and positive. Any commitment made by people to organizations (or anything else) is voluntary and personal – and can be changed or withdrawn. The best organizations produce cultures that are capable of generating this. They create the desire among their people to join, remain with and progress, recognizing their mutuality of interest and the benefits available to everyone.

The conclusion of this is an organization culture that has the following elements.

- A positive aura, one to which people can subscribe and identify with confidence, pride, feelings of well-being; which in turn encourages positive views of the organization and its work; and positive and harmonious working relationships.
- Shared values and standards, capable of being adopted and followed by all concerned; this includes attention to high standards of integrity and morality; mutual concern and interest; and equity and equality.
- High levels of individuality, identity, motivation and commitment; high levels of group identity and mutual respect and regard.
- Organization and management style that is supportive of everyone involved (whatever the style, whether autocratic or participative) and that concentrates on

results and output, effectiveness and quality of performance, and also on the development and improvement of the people.

- Regular flows of high quality information that reflect high levels of respect and esteem for the people on the part of the organization.

Again, these can provide a useful point of reference for those concerned with the general well-being of the organization when it becomes apparent that things are going wrong.

Much of this is clearly concerned with setting high standards and creating a positive general environment and background. This is to be seen in the context that where these elements are either not present or not attended to, or where the converse is present – negative aura, one to which people do not subscribe, lack of shared values, unsupported management style, for example – there is no identity or common purpose. People seek refuge in groups or in their profession or technical expertise. Absenteeism and turnover increases, performance declines. There becomes an ever-greater concentration on self, on individual performance, often at the expense of the performance of the organization. Interpersonal and inter-group relationships also suffer.

Both the positive and the negative feed from each other. Striving for a positive and ideal culture tends to reinforce the high levels of value placed on the staff and the more general matters of honesty and integrity. Similarly, allowing the negative to persist tends to mean that relationships will get worse, aims and objectives become evermore fragmented or clouded, organization purpose evermore obscured.

in brief

- Organization culture reflects the desired standards of conduct, behaviour and performance required. It is essential therefore to understand culture from the point of view of ensuring that the standards are as required.
- Organization culture is deeply embedded in collective and individual behaviour.
- Studies of organization and national culture are a useful starting point for understanding the complexities. However, it is essential that all managers use this knowledge as the basis on which to build their own expert understanding of collective and individual behaviour.
- Culture can be changed and developed (and in many cases, needs to be changed and developed). It is essential to ensure that, as with all change, people will only change if they understand that it is in their own best interests to do so.

Further reading

Deal, T. and Kennedy, A. (2000) *Corporate Cultures*. Perseus.
Handy, C. (1993) *Understanding Organizations* (4th edn). Penguin.
Harrison, R. (1995) *Collected Papers*. McGraw Hill.
Hofstede, G. (1980, 2004) *Culture's Consequences*. Sage.
Hofstede, G. (2005) *Cultures and Organizations*. Sage.
Peters, T. and Waterman, R. (1982) *In Search of Excellence*. Harper and Row.
Williams, A., Dobson, P. and Walters, M. (1990) *Changing Culture*. CIPD.

7

Communication

> 'Effective communication is vital for the successful functioning of any organization.'

In this chapter

- the value of excellent and effective communications; and the cost of bad communications
- tools and techniques for the management and implementation of effective communications
- the specific concern of communication toxicity and its effects on the viability of organizations
- delivering effective interpersonal communications and negotiations

Introduction

Effective communication is vital for the successful functioning of any organization. All organizations normally establish formal mechanisms and processes of vertical and lateral lines or channels of communication to provide the means by which information – facts, ideas, proposals, emotions, feelings, opinions and problems – can be exchanged. They also normally create integrating activities such as groups, committees and other meetings, and the means of consultation and participation to improve the all-round quality and understanding of this information.

Effective communication is based on: volumes, quality and integrity of information; the integrity of information systems; the ways in which information is exchanged, presented and delivered; and the overall integrity of the wider situation.

Communications and information feed the quality of all human and operational relations in organizations. Good communications underline good relations and enhance the general quality of working life, motivation and morale. Bad and inadequate communications lead to frustration, loss of trust, alienation, fragmentation, and lack of identity and unity.

Communication structuring

Communications may be:

- **One-way:** information presented to particular target audiences that does not seek, or allow for, responses. General information may be presented on websites or in the media. Advertising is also generally one-way communication, although it does seek to build and reinforce product, service and brand awareness and identity.
- **Two-way:** two-way communication is the ability to engage in active and productive discussion, consultation, participation and involvement. Two-way communication is the basis of all effective staff management and employee relations, as well as customer, client and supplier liaison, and dealings with shareholders and backers.
- **Downward:** some downward communication is essential because overall standards and direction have to be communicated from those responsible, to those who have to carry things out. Written rules, procedures and handbooks also require the backing and support of top managers. To be effective, downward communication requires active participation and consultation.
- **Upward:** upward channels of communications are those that provide access to top management for the rest of staff. Their effectiveness is enhanced or limited by:
  - organization culture that sets the boundaries of openness, integrity and honesty;
  - physical and psychological distance between top managers and the rest of the organization;
  - attitudes of top managers to the rest of the staff.
- **Lateral:** between different professional and occupational groups and locations, departments, divisions and functions. In many cases, this is especially hard to manage because of in-built and historic barriers that exist between:
  - primary functions and head office staff;
  - professional staff and their managers;
  - organizational managers and backers;
  - senior and junior staff;
  - different departments, divisions and functions.
- **Spoken:** effective spoken communication exists everywhere. The effectiveness or otherwise is driven by fundamental organization integrity, the nature of working relationships, and the openness, or otherwise, with which people deal with each other. Problems arise with spoken communication when people know, believe or perceive that they have been told that something is to happen, only to find out

subsequently that what was stated (or understood to have been stated) is not in fact going to happen.

- **Written:** effective communication is underpinned by written documents, and by policies, procedures and practices governing standards of attitudes, behaviour and performance; the management of conflict and specific issues such as customer, client and supplier management, public relations and other aspects of organization presentation.

Channels of communications

Channels of communication may be formal, institutional or informal:

- **Formal:** the hierarchies, systems, procedures and committee structures established to underpin management style and organization effectiveness (see Figure 7.1).
- **Institutional:** less formal channels that nevertheless carry both validity and influence – for example professional, occupational and managerial cluster groups, work improvement groups, quality circles. Institutional communications include consultation, participation and involvement activities; committee work; and meetings (see below).
- **Informal:** ad hoc gatherings, scribbled notes and the grapevine.

The cascade effect

Cascades are attractive to hierarchies. Those at the top delude themselves that cascades work as effective communication mechanisms. Cascades take their name from the appearance caused by pouring champagne into the top glass of a pyramid of glasses. The pouring is continued until the wine overflows and eventually fills all the glasses of the pyramid (see Figure 7.1). The effect of this – both for champagne and for communication – is the same. The quality of both is lost and there is a good measure of wastage by the time the bottom of the pyramid is reached.

Grapevine

All organizations have a grapevine – consisting of gossip, half-formed opinions and general chatter about the present state of affairs.

It is an important indicator of general organizational well-being. If the grapevine is concerned with personal gossip and the mythical activities of individuals, all is more likely to be well than if the primary topic of conversation is the future state of the organization, uncertainty over job and work security, and spreading of rumours about redundancies.

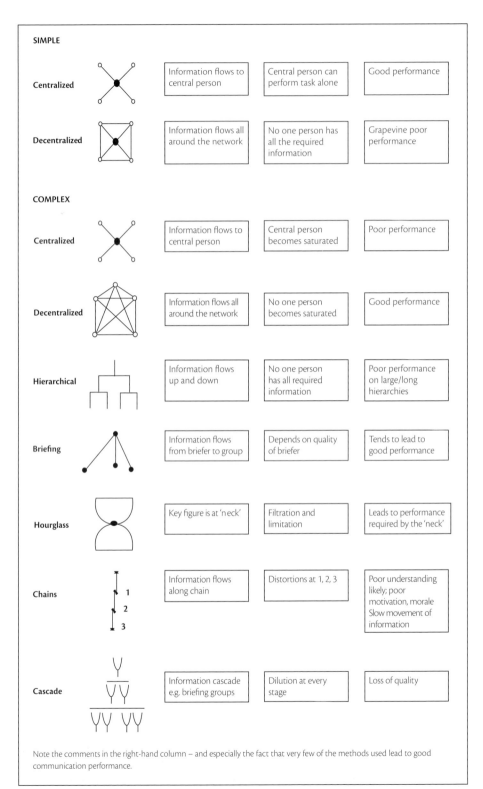

SIMPLE

| Centralized | | Information flows to central person | Central person can perform task alone | Good performance |
| Decentralized | | Information flows all around the network | No one person has all the required information | Grapevine poor performance |

COMPLEX

Centralized		Information flows to central person	Central person becomes saturated	Poor performance
Decentralized		Information flows all around the network	No one person becomes saturated	Good performance
Hierarchical		Information flows up and down	No one person has all required information	Poor performance on large/long hierarchies
Briefing		Information flows from briefer to group	Depends on quality of briefer	Tends to lead to good performance
Hourglass		Key figure is at 'neck'	Filtration and limitation	Leads to performance required by the 'neck'
Chains	1 2 3	Information flows along chain	Distortions at 1, 2, 3	Poor understanding likely; poor motivation, morale Slow movement of information
Cascade		Information cascade e.g. briefing groups	Dilution at every stage	Loss of quality

Note the comments in the right-hand column – and especially the fact that very few of the methods used lead to good communication performance.

Figure 7.1 *Channels of communication*

Communication policies and priorities

Communication policies are based on the extent to which organizations and their managers are prepared to engage in consultation, participation and effective committee work.

Consultation, participation and involvement

Organizations consult with their staff on the implementation of decisions and policies. The purpose is to ensure that everyone understands what is required of them, and why, and to give them a full understanding of a particular situation. It also reflects the need for mutual confidence and unity of purpose among everyone in the organization. Effective consultation, participation and involvement also help to ensure that what is proposed has been well thought out and tested, as well as providing a means for information exchange and staff input (see Figure 7.2).

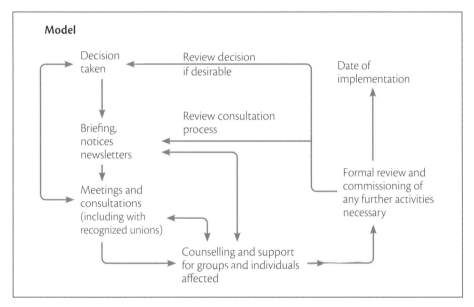

Figure 7.2 *Consultation process following a decision*

Genuine consultation also helps to ensure that any flaws in decision-making processes or the implementation of particular proposals may be raised. However well or thoroughly an issue has been overtly thought through, it must be capable of wide general scrutiny and examination.

Committees

Committees are constituted for a variety of reasons. From the point of view of communication, it is essential that they enhance both the quality and value rather than act as a blockage. To ensure this, the purpose, scheduling, size, composition, agenda, control and recording must be managed. The ultimate test of the value of any committee is its output. If this is not forthcoming, then alternative means should be found to tackle the issues that the committee or committee system is supposed to face.

Committees may be used to render inert something that is threatening to a particular vested interest. They are used to filter and edit information. They are used to draw the teeth of lobbies or pressure groups – and to advance particular desired points of view. In many cases, there is a pecking order. Committee membership may be subject to patronage or favour. Membership of certain committees is often the mark of status or achievement.

Committees should therefore be constituted for a purpose, and when this purpose is satisfied, they should be disbanded. They satisfy human needs of association, belonging, participating and contributing; and it is important that they do this in the context of advancing the total quality and effectiveness of the organization.

Meetings

Meetings are constituted for a variety of reasons. From the point of view of communication, it is essential that they have clearly stated agenda and time schedules; and in many cases, people are required to attend fully informed and with a direct and expected contribution in mind.

Meetings become ineffective when there is a lack of agenda or clearly stated purpose. When this happens, people find excuses for not attending, or else send one of their junior staff instead. The overall effect is to lose the opportunity for information exchange; and in many cases, this leads also to a lack of value placed on those activities that the meetings are supposed to address.

Principles of effective communication

Communication is at its most effective when it is delivered face to face, allowing for discussions and questions. Effective communication is underpinned by written documents, rules and procedures as above. It is additionally normally the case that core messages at least have to be repeated many times (this is a key lesson from brand building, and product and service awareness from the advertising industry).

If you are unsure of the need to repeat messages many times, try to imagine going for a week without seeing a Coca-Cola or McDonald's logo, advertisement or product. These, and of course many other companies, are global icons universally recognized. And yet – they continue to broadcast and advertise themselves. Repeating messages universally and regularly is a major lesson in communication for everyone.

just a minute

- **Language:** of sender, receiver, and anyone else who may read or listen to it. The greater the clarity of language, the greater the likelihood that what is transmitted will be received and understood; and the reverse – when language is not clear – always dilutes effectiveness. It also leads to feelings that things are being hidden or not stated fully.
- **Conciseness:** in which everything that needs saying is done so simply and directly. This is not to be confused with lack of full coverage or leaving things out.
- **Precision:** language that addresses points directly reinforces total confidence in the communication. Language that is not direct tends to reinforce any feelings that may be present of dishonesty or mistrust.

Language barriers

Forms of words and phraseology are used extensively to give off coded messages and to reinforce the real agenda that is being followed. Examples include:

- *With greatest respect, I respect your views, I am sure that you/he/she is a person of great integrity* = you are wrong, you are talking rubbish, I don't value you at all.
- *We will take all steps, we are doing everything possible, we are complying with the law, we are complying with specific regulations* = we are doing as little as possible in the circumstances, we are doing the least we can get away with in the circumstances, you cannot touch us.
- *We do not have the resources/money/staff/equipment* = we do not want to do it, we are not going to do it.

- **The positive/negative balance:** people respond much more actively to positive communications. Where negative messages have to be transmitted, these should be done with the same clarity and precision; at least then bad news is quickly, clearly and completely understood.

The selection of the correct media is essential and many communications go wrong because the wrong choice is made. The basic rules are:

- Say what needs to be said; write what needs to be written; make best use of all the senses of those affected and media available.
- Say what needs to be said and confirm this in writing.
- Operate on a fundamental basis of openness, honesty, integrity and trust in terms of access to, and provision of, information.
- Use e-mails and written documentation as far as possible only for giving and exchanging general information, or to reinforce what has already been said.

Non-verbal communication

Non-verbal communication gives an impression of people to others without saying or writing anything. It additionally reinforces what is being said or written. It also tends to give the real message – the non-verbal message is usually much stronger. The main components that must be understood are as follows.

- **Appearance:** this includes age, gender, hair, face, body shape and size, height, bearing, national and racial characteristics, clothing and accessories. Each of these items, and their combined effect, has great implications for: interviewing, public images, creating impressions, advertising public relations, salesmanship, presentation, design, brand, marque, layout, comfort and familiarity.
- **Manner:** indicating behaviour, emotion, stress, comfort formality/informality, acceptability/unacceptability, respect/disrespect.
- **Expression:** expression, especially facial expression, becomes the focus of attention and that is where people concentrate most of their attention.
- **Eye contact:** regular eye contact demonstrates interest, trust, concern, affection and sympathy. The depth of expression in the eyes generates deeper perception of feelings – anger, sorrow, love, hatred, joy.
- **Pose:** this is either static or active, relaxed, calm, agitated, nervous or stressful. It reinforces the overall impression conveyed. Different parts of the body, especially arms and legs – are used for expression, emphasis, protection and shield.
- **Clothing:** especially in work situations, clothing provides an instant summary of people. A technician is instantly recognized by their overalls; the police and traffic wardens by their distinctive uniforms; and so on. Many organizations whose staff deal regularly and consistently with the public insist either on a dress code or the wearing of a uniform – it helps to reinforce organizational image and the trust and confidence of the public.
- **Touch:** touch reinforces a wide range of perceptions. For example, consider the difference between different people's handshakes and the impressions that these convey. Touching also reinforces role and sex stereotypes – the chairman/chairwoman banging their fist on the desk; the woman meticulously arranging her clothes.
- **Body movement:** this may be purely functional and fulfilling certain requirements – for example cleaning the car. Movements may be exaggerated, conveying anger or high emotions; languid, conveying comfort, ease or indolence; or sharp and staccato, conveying forcefulness and emphasis.

point of view

Body movement is extremely hard to control. Whatever you are saying, and however you may be saying it, your body movement will invariably give away your true feelings.

In particular, if you are not telling the truth, or not telling the full truth, or have a fundamentally unpleasant or negative message to deliver, you will almost invariably start moving your feet. If you are standing, you shift your weight from foot to foot; if you sitting, your feet will also move.

Those responsible for presidential briefings at the White House learned this while Ronald Reagan was president. Even Reagan, a trained actor, could not prevent this from happening. The White House advisers therefore made sure that, unless the message being delivered was truly straightforward, all briefings took place from behind a full-length lectern so that the effects of body movement on the message were minimized.

- **Position:** this reinforces formality/informality; dominance/dependency; superiority/ subordination. People use position to enhance feelings of control and influence. For example, people may face each other across a large desk – this conveys a sense of security and defence to the person whose desk it is and a barrier to be crossed by the other.
- **Props and settings:** props and settings are used to reinforce impressions of status, position, dominance and formality. They are designed to ensure that whatever happens does so to the greatest possible advantage of the instigator. They either reinforce or complement perceptions and expectations; or else they contrast perceptions and expectations so that the person coming into the situation is impressed for whatever reason.
- **Discrepancy:** this occurs where the body conveys one message while the spoken or written conveys others.
- **Social factors:** people are conditioned into having preconceived ideas and general expectations of particular situations. For example, people do not generally attend promotion panels or job interviews unshaven or dressed informally. There is no rationale for this other than the expectations of society and the general requirement to conform.
- **The other senses:** other aspects of non-verbal communication include: the use of scent and fragrance; the use of colour and coordination of colours; matters of social and ethical importance and expectation; design and use of materials.
- **Listening:** listening is both active and passive. Passive listening may be no more than awareness of background noise; it may also be limited to a general awareness of what is going on. Active listening requires taking a dynamic interest in what is being received. While the message is received through the ears, it is reinforced through eye contact, body movement, and pose and through the reception of any non-verbal signals that are given by the speaker.
- **Reinforcement:** non-verbal communication tends to reinforce: relative and absolute measures of status, value, importance and achievement; relative and absolute measures of authority, power and influence; confidence and well-being; and psychological barriers.

Barriers and blockages

Communication barriers and blockages arise through accident, negligence or design. Barriers arise by accident where the choice of language, timing or method of communication is wrong despite the best of intentions. In these cases, those involved ought simply to step back from the situation and rectify it as quickly as possible.

Negligence is where barriers and blockages are allowed to arise by default. In such cases, communication dysfunctions are either not acknowledged; or if they are acknowledged, are nevertheless not tackled.

It is very much the case, however, that people within organizations create barriers and blockages in order to further their own ends.

In the worst cases, information becomes a commodity to be bought and sold, to be corrupted, skewed and filtered in the pursuit of the sectoral interest in question. This is endemic throughout the mid to upper echelons of the military, civil and public service institutions, multinational companies and other multi-site organizations with large and complex head office institutions where an active and negative form of real-politik exists.

Within this context the following barriers are identified.

- **Departmental, divisional, hierarchical** and **functional boundaries**: the problem is compounded when expertise or information held by people in one department is used as a bargaining chip, or else filtered out in their own interests.
- **Language**: use of bureaucratic and imprecise phrases acts both as a barrier to effective communication, and also as fuel to the fires of any inherent discontent.
- **Distance**, both physical and psychological: physical distance acts as a barrier when people working away from particular locations simply do not receive information. The filtering, editing and presentation of information also reinforces any other psychological barriers (for example status, hierarchy, modes of address) that may be present. Also some managers put up physical barriers between themselves and the rest of the world in the form of secretaries, switchboards, and information filtering systems.
- **Trappings**: trappings reinforce rank, status and position; and they also reinforce (positively and negatively) behaviour. For example, the manager who has a genuinely open-door policy always props the door open unless otherwise occupied (and so the open door is the trapping). Trappings that put up barriers or give off a negative or even fearful message include: expensive furniture; office location (for example top managers are always on the top floor). Some people also cultivate aggression and temper as trappings in order to manage their own position within the organization.
- **Control mechanisms**: where requests for specific information (for example output figures and costs) are requested in forms that are either inappropriate or which may be taken and used for purposes other than that for which they were

originally produced. The problem is compounded when those who are required to produce such information do not fully understand the purposes or standpoint from which it is being requested.

The need to know

'The need to know' barrier occurs where organizations decide that information is to be issued in different ways or different information is to be issued to different groups and individuals. It is a process of limiting the availability of information. On the face of it, there is some sense in this – most organizations have far too much information to issue for any one person to understand, analyse and internalize.

The barrier arises from the reasoning behind 'the need to know'. As long as this is for operational reasons, it is sound. Otherwise, the message given is one of:

- a lack of capability to understand what is being said and especially that the organization (or an individual superior) does not think or believe that the subordinate has this capability;
- lack of value or different levels of value placed on different groups of staff, especially those who are excluded from the 'need to know' list;
- access: in order to be privy to certain information it is necessary to have reached a particular level of the organization. Communication therefore becomes a trapping of personal status and importance;
- general disrespect: operation of this form of approach to the giving of information gives off an overall view of lack of respect to those affected;
- psychological distance: again, this emphasizes the differences and divisions that exist in organizations and between its functions, departments, divisions and individuals.

Operating a 'need to know' approach also leads to distortions in the presentational style and use of information media. What is issued is for the purposes of the issuer rather than the receiver, emphasizing their distance and supremacy rather than imparting valuable and useful information.

More generally, any restriction on information leads to reductions in the capabilities of those who need to take decisions and make judgements. Even if operated from the highest and most positive standpoint, this approach is restricting in this way.

- **Confidentiality:** which becomes a barrier when it is used as a means of attracting or acquiring status rather than for operational effectiveness. Confidentiality should normally be limited to people's personnel files, technological advances, marketing initiatives and research, development and pioneering inventions.
- **Lack of visibility or access:** which leads to feelings and perceptions that problems and issues cannot quickly be resolved.

- **Information systems:** combinations of communications, people and technology all have imperfections and therefore the potential to be a blockage or barrier. Information technology especially acts as a barrier where there is a lack of training for the staff, a lack of full understanding of the system's capabilities, where there are different and incompatible systems and formats present, and where not all staff have access.
- **E-mail:** e-mail is now more or less universally used as a means of information exchange – and communication. E-mail acts as a barrier to communication when it is the only means used. It is essential that e-mail exchanges do not become a substitute for face-to-face communication or telephone discussions.

All barriers and blockages to effective communications should be seen in terms of the nature of work and activities within the organization. The greater the intrinsic interest in the work, the greater the volume of reasons that the staff have for being there, and thus the greater the likelihood that effective communications will exist. Where work is boring and alienating there is normally a more general background of lack of respect and trust. Problems are compounded where there are extensive and complex rule and regulation books and committee management structures; where meetings are structured and undisciplined; and where those with influence, power and authority choose the communication media that suits them best rather than the organization as whole.

Use of media

Those with influence, power and authority choose the communication media that they believe they can use to best advantage, regardless of whether that is what the situation requires.

This is especially true of political debate. For example, one party persists with the view that 'not enough resources or priority is being given to a particular area' (for example roads, education, health, social services and social security). The other party counters this by saying that 'more resources are being spent in the given area than ever before'.

This is reinforced by the production of statistics, again for the individual ends being pursued. On the question of health, for example, one party will say that 'waiting lists for treatment are longer than ever'. The other counters with 'we are treating more patients than ever before'. Each produces statistics to back up its point of view.

The result is a stalemate. It is compounded by the overwhelming impression given that:

- there are only two possible points of view to hold – the one or the other indicated; and
- aligning others to either point of view is dependent upon their own vested interest, personal and political preference and conviction.

These distorted forms of debate and discussion take place in all organizations from time to time. The protagonists either take refuge in their own vested interest, seeking statistics to underpin it; or else produce counter-arguments to the opposing point of view. No productive debate and discussion takes place. This dissipates any feelings of shared commitment and involvement, reinforcing the differences between various departments, divisions, functions, groups and individuals. It is compounded where one view is seen to be that of the organization as a whole; or where the protagonist gains advantage or favour as the result of holding or presenting a particular point of view.

Organizational toxicity

Organizational toxicity and toxic communications exist in organizations that have themselves become dishonest or corrupted for some reason. Essentially, all organizations have communication agenda as follows:

- stated and primary, where what is said is precisely what happens;
- secondary and hidden, in which messages are given out dishonestly, using lack of clarity to distort and undermine what is being said.

Secondary and hidden agenda are forms of organizational toxicity. Toxic communications demotivate and demoralize staff, and ultimately dissipate the volume and quality of organizational effort and effectiveness. In these cases, clusters of staff debate endlessly the general state of the organization. High levels of disciplinary problems and grievances exist. There are complicated and duplicated sets of rules and procedures. The problem is reinforced by physical and psychological distance, and remoteness between managers and their staff.

The results are as follows:

- **Blame and scapegoat:** the organization finds individuals to carry the can for its corporate failings. Sales departments get the blame for falling profits. Personnel get the blame for disputes and grievances. Individuals are blamed for specific failures (for example the failure of a particular promotion campaign; the failure of work restructuring). They are often also named in this respect and their failure publicized around the organization. A more insidious version exists whereby the scapegoating is not official but is allowed to get around the grapevine and the organization does nothing to deny the rumours or rehabilitate any individuals that are so named.
- **Communication as a weapon:** communications are targeted so as to cause maximum damage to particular individuals, groups, departments and divisions. This reinforces any culture or perception of blame and scapegoating that may be present. Information is fed, both officially and unofficially, into the hands of

powerful and influential groups and individuals in the hope and expectation that this will be used to the detriment of the departments or individuals targeted.

- **Secrets:** secrets are used as bargaining chips, and as forms of corporate or institutional blackmail, again with the purposes of getting powerful and influential groups and individuals to come round to a particular way of thinking.
- **Elites:** elites and specialist groups use the means and methods of communication at their disposal to reinforce the fact, belief and perception of their excellence and infallibility.

The result of this is that those who wish to wield any influence have to become toxic communicators. Toxic communicators take active responsibility for, and become actively involved in, corrupting communications and information for their own ends.

It is clear from the above, that once an organization and its practices are corrupted in these ways, this quickly becomes the organization's way of life. It is a short step from this to concentrating the whole of collective and individual efforts on fighting internal battles rather than tending to products and services.

Assertiveness

Assertiveness and assertive communications arise from the point of view that anything can only be effective if it is well thought out, its effects understood in advance, and that the message is delivered clearly and directly to the recipients.

Assertiveness and assertive communications seek to deliver honest, complete, clear and direct messages as follows:

- **Language:** clear, simple and direct; easy to understand and respond to on the part of the hearer or receiver; the words used are unambiguous and straightforward; request and demands are made in a clear and precise manner and with sound reasons.
- **Aims and objectives:** precise and clear; considered in advance; recognizing the effect that the message is likely to have on the recipient.
- **Delivery:** in a clear and steady tone of voice, or where written, in a well presented and easy to read format. The use of voice is always even, neither too loud nor too soft, and does not involve shouting, threatening or abuse.
- **Persistence and determination:** where problems or issues are raised by the recipient, the sender sticks to their message, aims and objectives; they do not become side-tracked; they answer any problems that are raised without diverting from the main purpose.
- **Positive and negative:** the general thrust of the message is always clear and apparent; this does not vary, whether the overall tone is positive or negative. This approach is especially important in handling general staff problems – especially matters concerning grievances and discipline.

- **Face and eyes:** the head is held up. There is plenty of eye contact and steadiness of gaze. The delivery is reinforced with positive movements that relate to what is being said (for example smiles, laughter, nodding, encouragement; or a straight face when something has gone wrong).
- **Other non-verbal aspects:** the body is upright; hands and arms are open (in order to encourage positive response and productive transaction; there is no fidgeting or shuffling; there are no threatening gestures or table thumping; or displays of other forms of behaviour.

point of view

Use and value of assertive communications

Assertive communications are designed to ensure clarity and integrity of message, as stated in the text above. Assertive communications are additionally designed to neutralize the following behaviour.

- **Aggressive:** characterized by shouting, swearing, table thumping, arguments (cross transaction). The matter in hand is lost as the aggressor strives to impose their point of view. Winning the argument becomes everything.
- **Hostile:** where the main emphasis is on the personalization of the matters in hand. Often also characterized by shouting and table thumping, the outcome is normally a personal attack (sometimes in public) on an individual or group.
- **Submissive:** characterized by saying or doing anything that the other party wants so that they will finish the argument or transaction and remove themselves.
- **Inconsistent:** characterized by according people different levels of quality and value, having different standards for individuals and groups. This also extends to treating the same individual or group in different ways according to mood or the environment for example.
- **Non-assertive:** characterized by the inability of the individual to put their message across. This is either because they are not sure what to put across, or else have not used the correct words or media.

best practice

If you have the capability and expertise to be an expert assertive communicator, it gives you a huge advantage in all your dealings with everyone. It is essential however, that you go into every situation knowing and understanding what you are talking about, what the intended outcomes are, and the kinds of questions that you are likely to be asked.

Negotiations

Effective negotiation requires the application of communication skills in addressing and resolving individual and collective problems. It requires undertaking discussions with a view to establishing agreements; and arranging and delivering those terms of agreement. All managers should be able to do this. The keys initially are:

- knowing what you want from the situation, and the requirements of the others involved;
- knowing what you do not want from the situation, and what others involved also do not want;
- knowing what is acceptable and unacceptable, both to yourself, and also to the other parties.

The elements of successful negotiations are based on having the authority to make and deliver the agreements; paying attention to detail; having the resources to deliver and implement the agreements; attention to the ability of everyone concerned to make sure that it continues to work. It is also to consider:

- the question of setting precedents – implications for future dealings along similar lines;
- internal and external pressures – especially pressures from subordinates, superiors and backers;
- the opportunities and consequences of agreeing to something; and the opportunities and consequences of not making an agreement;
- what is open to negotiation and what is not.

The negotiating process has three key elements:

- **Substance**: the matter in hand.
- **Process**: how it is to be addressed and resolved.
- **Presentation**: how the end result is to be perceived and received.

Negotiations may be conducted from two points of view:

- that those involved trust each other to do their best by the particular situation and to resolve a particular matter in ways acceptable to all concerned;
- a basic lack of trust – managers do not trust staff members or their representatives; and staff and their representatives do not trust their managers or the organization's owners.

In many situations therefore, negotiations are an integral part of the process of the management of conflict. It is essential therefore that both negotiating expertise and understanding of the demands of the environment are present.

Where there is a basis of mutual trust, matters can be discussed openly and honestly with a view to resolving them. Where this basis does not exist, the following approaches have to be taken:

- the opening position is always stated on the basis that it will be rejected;

- there then follows a process of counter-offer and counter-claim with each party working its way gradually towards the other;
- the content of the final agreement is usually clearly signalled before it is made as is the basis of what is genuinely acceptable or otherwise;
- serious disputes occur when one side is determined not to settle or where there is genuine misunderstanding or misreading of the signals;
- settlements are normally couched in positive terms in relation to all concerned to avoid the use of words such as 'loss', 'loser', 'climb down' and 'defeat', which have negative connotations, and which tend to store up resentment for the future and polarize attitudes.

Behavioural aspects of negotiation

The following must be understood.

- **The distributive effect:** opportunities and consequences of settling with one group at the expense of others.
- **Integrative drives:** opportunities and constraints of settling everything to the satisfaction of all involved.
- **Influencing attitudes:** in which attitudes are formed, modified and developed as follows:
  - confrontational – whereby the parties are motivated to defeat the other or win them over to their own point of view;
  - individualistic – in which the parties concerned pursue their own self-interests without any regard for the positions of others;
  - cooperative – whereby each party is concerned about the other, as well as its own position;
  - collusion – whereby the parties concerned form a coalition in which they pursue a common purpose, possibly to the detriment of other groups within the organization, or else to the organization as a whole;
  - use of language – which may be confrontational or cooperative;
  - the formality–informality balance – especially the need for informal systems of communication between the parties involved where the formalized are presenting barriers.

best practice

Expert negotiators always know, understand and respect the positions of the others involved. They never treat others with contempt or disdain. They also know and understand that any agreement that is reached has to be capable of implementation at the end of the negotiation.

- **Individual and collective expectations:** based on what people know, understand, believe and perceive that they are likely to gain from a particular situation. Serious misunderstandings occur when individuals and groups have either been misinformed, or else have failed to read the fact that substantial changes in a particular situation have led to radically altered expectations.

These processes must then be understood and engaged according to the demands of the particular situation (see Figure 7.3).

(a) Steps in the negotiating process

	Substance and process	Other factors
→	Initial offer and response claim	Strategic nature of offer
→	Adoption of postures	Strength and validity of cases
→	Ritual: movements and processes	Strengths of each party Morale of each party Attitudes of each party
→ ←	**Negotiations** Further offers/responsibilities	Public sympathy and support Government sympathy and support
→	**Basis of agreement** Final offer/response	Media coverage

Each of these activities must be undertaken in these circles.
Each of the other factors must be acknowledged and understood.

(b) Process operation

- - → Offer	**Area of agreement**	← - - Claim
A B Low Management	C	D High Staff/union

The collective bargaining process: offers between A and B rejected by staff; between C and D instantly accepted by staff; claims between A and B instantly accepted by management; between C and D rejected by management; B–C is basis for negotiated settlement; normal first offer is around A, which leads to instant rejection; normal first claim is around D, but engages the process.

Figure 7.3 *The negotiating process*

issues concerning the following.

t, in the pursuit of individual and collective
rises and improvements in terms and
nal UK organizations, this process is known

heir customers.
, managing and resolving misunderstandings,

grievance, disputes and dismissals; resolving

ng and managing complaints.
d output sides; in the engagement of
ted staff.

- Gathering resources, especially where this is known, believed or perceived to be a competitive or distributive issue.
- Managing barriers and blockages, especially resolving crises and hold-ups on the supply and distribution sides.
- Managing the concerns of stakeholders and influential figures.

Conclusions

Effective communication is vital for the successful functioning of any organization. It follows from this that all managers must be effective communicators, and all organizations must have effective formal methods, mechanisms and processes of communication as well as suitable and effective means of making sure that what they wish to say is transmitted effectively.

Effective communication is dependent on the volume, quality and accessibility of information; the means and media by which it is transmitted and received; the use to which it is put; its integrity; and the level of integrity of the wider situation.

Understanding and being able to apply the rules, principles, skills and techniques indicated are core and universal managerial skills. They result in the ability to produce effective communication capable of being received, accepted and acted upon or responded to. All levels of communication should be monitored. Remedial action where communication is poor or ineffective should always be taken. Concentration on barriers and blockages to effective communication should be designed to reinforce the need for clarity of purpose and language. As many channels of communication as possible should also be used, each giving the same message, so that the message received is complete and not subject to editing, interpretation or distortion. Wherever toxic, expedient or dishonest communications take place, these are always instantly recognized by those on the receiving end.

Organizations and their managers are therefore responsible for creating the conditions in which effective communications can take place, and ensuring that their managers understand the full effects of what they say, write and present. It is essential to understand the broad context, as well as being able to apply specific skills and techniques.

- All managers need to be expert communicators. Communication in all its forms is a key area to practice.
- Understanding organizational communications requires constant observation. It is especially essential to observe where and why things go wrong, and the contribution that is made by bad or inadequate communications.
- Technology is not a substitute for communication. Technology should be used in conjunction with all other communication media. E-mail especially, should never become the dominant form of communication.
- All communications need to have clearly stated aims and objectives. This is especially true of written documentation, meetings, committees and negotiations.
- All communication media need to be carefully chosen, recognizing the effects that particular media have on the receivers.
- In all communications, it is essential to make sure that you know, understand and respect the position, needs, wants and expectations of everyone else involved.

Further reading

Adair, J. (2009) *Effective Communication: The Most Important Skill of All.* Arrow.
Barker, A. (2010) *Improve Your Communication Skills (and create success).* Kogan Page.
Cornelissen, J. (2008) *Corporate Communication: A Guide to Theory and Practice.* Wiley.
Hargie, O. (2006) *The Handbook of Communication Skills.* McGraw Hill.
Quirke, W. (2008) *Making the Connections.* Kogan Page.
Stanton, N. (2009) *Mastering Communication.* Palgrave Macmillan.

Management influence, power and conflict

8

'A key factor in the presence of conflict and its resolution is the level of honesty and integrity present.'

In this chapter

- the nature of power and influence in organizations
- managing those with powerful personalities and agenda
- identifying and managing the sources and causes of conflict
- creating the conditions in which power and influence and conflict work for the good of all

Introduction

Influence, power and authority are present in all organizations; and all managers have measures of influence, power and authority.

- **Influence** is where a person, group or organization changes the attitudes, values, behaviour, priorities and activities of others.
- **Power** is the capability to exercise influence in these ways.
- **Authority** is the legitimization of the capability to exercise influence and the relationship by which this is exercised.

There are responsibilities attached to influence, power and authority; and those who wield influence, power and authority are normally accountable for their actions and results.

Power and influence are to be seen as positive and negative. The positive occurs where power and influence are used to energize, enhance and develop productive and profitable activities. The negative is where power and influence are used to block or diminish activities; to limit the ability of others to succeed through the capability to restrict resources, money or information for example; or to bully, victimize and harass.

Influence, power and authority are all themselves limited and modified by organizational structures and methods of behaviour. Authority is normally given out for a limited range of activities or people only, and the extent of influence and the ability to wield power are therefore also limited. Authority also normally impersonalizes: when someone acts with authority, they do so in the name of the organization and not in a personal capacity. The need to exercise authority will be founded on both personal and professional judgement; the actions carried out are in ways prescribed by the organization.

Sources of power and influence

There is a range of sources of power and influence present in all organizations. These are as follows.

- **Physical and coercive power:** the power exerted by individuals because of their physical size and strength, the force of their personality, and their appearance. Physical and coercive power is used to dominate situations, and influence the outcome of meetings and decisions. Large and dominant organizations exert their own equivalent of physical power in the pursuit of market or sector domination and in the ability to select their own preferred range of prices to determine the ways in which markets will operate, and in the ability to command staff expertise and resources.

  Physical power is also used by individuals to intimidate, bully and victimize others; for example:
  - managers lose their temper or become aggressive and strident in meetings in order to get their own way;
  - people use loud and strident voices, and angry tones in order to enhance their physical presence;
  - people become aggressive when forced to defend a point of view that they know they have mistaken or which is wrong;
  - people threaten and sometimes use physical force against colleagues when disagreements and disputes get out of hand;

- people use aggression and the threat of physical force when personal issues are allowed to extend into the workplace.
- **Traditional power:** whereby the ability to command influence derives from accepted customs and norms. Traditional power is present in the hereditary principle whereby the office or position is handed down from parent to child – for example kings and queens and the aristocracy; family businesses; and (less frequently at present than in previous times) in areas such as dock working where the child took the parent's job.
- **Expert power:** based on the expertise held by an individual or group, its relative availability, and the demand for this. The power and influence exerted by those with scarce expertise can, and does, cause its price and cost to rise; and those with this expertise can then take their own steps to control and limit its availability.
- **Charismatic power:** charisma is the effect of one personality on others, the ability to exert influence based on force of personality. Charisma is the ability to inspire high levels of confidence and identity among other people. Those with charisma are found in all parts of society, and all departments, divisions and functions in organizations. Hitler, Napoleon and John F. Kennedy all had charisma; and all went to a lot of trouble to manufacture the kind of personality and identity that they knew would be well received by those who followed them.

Charismatic power and influence normally has to be manufactured. Those who have the power of personality normally know and understand this, and go to a lot of trouble to ensure that their appearance, powers of speech, communication, public appearances and media coverage are all carefully structured and manufactured so as to give the lasting desired impression.

- **Resource power:** is the ability to influence others based on the command of resources. This may be beneficial and positive – the giving and allocating of resources to enable someone else to succeed, the result of which is a feeling of well-being towards the resource giver.

  It may be negative, threatening or coercive, based on the ability to limit or cut off particular resources if the receiver does not behave in certain ways. Resource power is closely related to reward power, which is the ability to influence behaviour and activities by holding out and offering rewards for compliance and acceptance. The extent of influence exerted in this way is dependent upon the nature and volume of rewards and the extent to which these meet the needs of those over whom influence is sought. The other side of this is the power to punish. Again, the extent of the influence exerted depends upon the nature of the punishment being threatened and whether this is felt to be important by those affected.

- **Legal, rational and position power:** the limitation, ordering and direction of power and influence in the name of organizations. Legal, rational and position power is based on the setting of rules, procedures, regulations and norms for each job, role, department, division and sector, and for the individuals who carry out the work. It is based on certain principles:
  - the right and duty of organizations to establish what they consider to be the best ways of working;
  - the managerial prerogative – the establishment of persons in positions of command, responsibility and accountability to ensure that these are put into practice;
  - the willingness of subordinates to accept direction and the right of superiors to expect this;
  - duties of care placed on organizations by legal, social and ethical pressures which means that they will seek to operate in efficient, effective and profitable ways without being punitive or coercive.

Responsibility, authority and accountability are based on the legitimacy of the position held, and the specific duties and obligations that have to be carried out.

Centres of power in organizations

Every organization, department, division, function and group always has its own power bases and centres of power. These power bases are both structured, and also limited, by a range of organizational and environmental circumstances.

All departments, divisions, functions, groups and individuals have legitimate areas of influence that they need to exert in the pursuit of their working activities. Problems arise when this legitimacy is either not made clear or where particular groups and individuals are allowed to extend their power and influence without proper authorization from the organization.

As well as this extension, organizations and their managers additionally have to be aware of the existence of: vested interests, pressure groups and lobbies; overmighty and over-influential individuals and departments; the structures of relationships, and the spheres of influence that they develop.

Vested interests, pressure groups and lobbies, both internal and external, bring their own point of view to bear on particular proposals and activities. For example, work groups may lobby for improved facilities for themselves, citing as reasons for this that many people have already left the group, and that they are difficult to replace. Pressure is then exerted on the organization to consider the request and if necessary reallocate and re-prioritize resources in order to comply.

Externally, organizations are subject to public pressure groups wherever they contemplate engaging in activities that are, or are perceived to be, detrimental to the environment (for example, construction, infrastructure projects and waste disposal always have to cope with this).

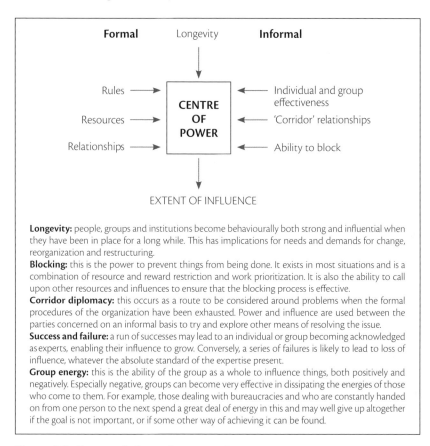

Figure 8.1 *Factors relating to the centres of power*

Pressure groups may also arise among shareholders and other stakeholders as the result of, or in response to, proposed sets of activities; or conversely, they may propose or attempt to influence these sets of activities themselves. They may also consist of cluster groups of managers, supervisors, technical and professional experts; specialist groups; trade unions and employee representatives.

Overmighty and over-influential staff and groups exist to an extent in all but the smallest organizations. Organizations need to be able to devolve and delegate particular activities to groups and individuals and this is normal practice. Problems arise when, as the result, the individual or group becomes too powerful for the interests of the organization. Especially where there is a regional, federal organizational structure, or where the individual or group has a distinctive or scarce expertise, staff in these positions become very influential and can exert influence that serves their own interests on the organization as a whole. Examples are:

- traders in the investment banking sector who continue to do things in their own preferred ways regardless of the risks inherent as the result of the banking crisis;
- top and senior managers in central and local government departments who form cartels to preserve salary and reward levels;
- regional managers in global and international organizations who need to be able to act without having to refer everything back to head office;
- top brand consultancies such as Bain and McKinsey who are very often engaged simply to push up short-term stock and share prices; and whose proposals and recommendations have then to be uncritically accepted and implemented.

Examples of personality types within organizations that gain influence are:

- managers and others who lose their temper, as above, or who adopt unpleasant and prickly personalities so as to be able to get their own way;
- people with distinctive expertise (for example maintenance, IT) who use their position to regulate, prioritize and limit the flow of their expertise;
- key figures such as personal assistants to top managers who use their position to attract favours from others, who seek in turn favours and preferential treatment from the top manager.

Relationship structures and spheres of influence are created by individuals, groups and departments, both to serve themselves and also to act in the name of the organization as a whole, as follows.

- **Mutual interest groups and alliances** occur between individuals, groups and functions to try and exert wider pressures on their organizations. This occurs, for example, where one of these has failed and where there is nevertheless a widely perceived need for particular changes or activities to be undertaken.
- **The extent and prevalence of other means of interaction, participation and involvement.** This includes departmental and group staff meetings, work improvement groups, quality circles and project groups. It may also include pioneering activities, research and development functions where those involved are drawn from across the organization.
- **External consultancies, agencies and statutory bodies** may be called in or cited in support of particular points of view. For example, consultants carry great influence when engaging in restructuring operations; changes in working practices may lead to health and safety experts being called in; in some cases, trade unions exert influence when the restructuring of work and changes to working practice are being considered.
- **Isolation and inclusion**; and both isolation and inclusion may be physical, as well as psychological. Inclusion may be used to ensure that specific individuals and groups support (or oppose) particular ideas, proposals and initiatives.

Isolation is used to ensure that specific groups and individuals have as little influence on proposals as possible.

Organizational politics

Politics exists in all organizations; and organizational politics influences the relationships between groups, divisions, departments and functions, and individuals.

Those involved seek initially to ensure that their position is legitimized within the organization both in terms of functional outputs, and also in terms of influence on direction. In practice, this is then developed, in many cases, to try and influence the orders of priority; and to try and influence any position of dominance and dependency to the advantage of the particular group or individual. If this is not possible, then individuals and departments use other means (for example personality, resource control) to assure their position and influence, and to try and move themselves up the organizational order of priority.

Orders of priority

Orders of priority refer to the position each individual, group or department has in relation to the organization as a whole. This is the organizational pecking order; and it is established as the result of a combination of factors – the respect and regard held for the group or individuals by the organization's top management; demands for resources and the ability to command these; the extent of the group's influence on organization output; the extent of its influence on internal ways of working; the size of the group and the nature of the expertise that it wields; its physical location; and the nature and quality of its leadership, output and results both in absolute terms and also in those required and valued by the organization.

In establishing the integrity or otherwise of the organizational pecking order, the following need to be considered:

- the use, value and influence of think-tanks and project groups, especially those constituted by top and senior management;
- attendance at particular groups, committees and other meetings where there is a status rather than operational drive to attend;
- the relative value placed in fact by organizations on their primary and frontline activities relative to those that operate processes and support functions;
- the relative value and position accorded to those who are working on new projects, ventures and initiatives relative to those who are delivering the steady-state activities of the organization;
- physical distance from head office; in which the fact, belief or perception (truth or untruth) of those who work in distant and remote locations, away from centres of

power, is that their contribution is less valued because they are not seen on a daily basis.

Dominance and dependency

Dominance and dependency is the summary of the extent to which some groups are able to influence, direct and dominate the courses of action of others, and the benefits and consequences that arise as the result. How organizations, managers and particular groups work within positions of dominance and dependency is a mark of overall organizational integrity. It is necessary to distinguish between external dominance and dependency and internal dominance and dependency.

External dominance and dependency

The key areas of external dominance and dependency are as follows:

- Captive markets are dominated by their suppliers and providers and this brings responsibility in terms of level, volume, quality and frequency of supplies and service, and the prices that *can* be charged – and the prices that *should* be charged.

point of view

High levels of prices and charges

There is a great pressure exerted on organizations and their managers to charge the highest possible levels of price that they can reasonably get away with. While the customer base is self-evidently being exploited (and in many cases, wronged), the drives for this are:

- maximizing short-term shareholder and backer returns;
- maximizing staff and managerial bonuses;
- creating funds that can then be used as the organization sees fit, at least for the short-term future.

In many cases of course, exploiting captive markets in these ways is only sustainable in the very short term. Eventually, someone comes in with a different business model enabling them to provide alternative supplies for a much lower price. Knowing and understanding this of course increases the pressure to maximize the prices and charges. It does not alter the fact that, unless a justification can be clearly made on business and operational grounds, the approach is morally wrong and commercially unsustainable except in the very short term, as above.

- Locations may be dominated by a single employer or industrial, commercial or public service group and this brings with it responsibilities in terms of corporate citizenship, as well as the local dependency for employment.
- Individuals may dominate an organization or work group through the combination of their expertise and their force and strength of personality and charisma.

- Experts may dominate in particular situations, especially when their expertise is urgently or highly required, or prized. This leads to the ability to charge at very high levels (economic rent); and experts may also choose to limit or filter their expertise, or else to prioritize those with whom they have dealings.
- Owners and controllers of rare supplies, raw materials and specialist information may, from time to time, exert undue influence at specific points during the relationship. This includes putting up prices and charges, reducing or limiting the supply, and restricting supplies to preferred or otherwise useful customers and users.

Internal dominance and dependency

The key areas of internal dominance and dependency are as follows:

- Resources, especially finance, command and control, are, in many cases, a dominance–dependency issue. This especially occurs where organizations require their staff, managers, departments, divisions and functions to bid against each other as part of the allocation process. This is always morally questionable and operationally inefficient. Those involved nevertheless have to engage in bidding activities in the particular environment and context. For some groups, this requires the need for alliances and other forms of support.
- Staff and workforces are dominated by their employers; the potential for this increases at times of increasing unemployment, causing some organizations to take a more expedient view of the working relationships.
- Organizations can find themselves dominated by powerful professional and occupational groups. They can also find themselves having to do things according to the priorities of particular stakeholder groups (especially shareholders and other financial interests), regardless of whether this is indeed the best thing for the organization or for others directly involved.

Dominance–dependency also exists as a consequence of physical and psychological distance. Those in remote locations find themselves powerless to influence the course of events; and this is compounded when organizations have preconceptions about particular locations based on prejudice rather than strategic and operational assessment. Those in positions of real and perceived lesser status find themselves marginalized when decisions about future activities and initiatives are being taken and implemented.

The ways in which organizations and their managers address their responsibilities is critical for long-term success and well-being. In the short term it is possible for organizations and groups to use a dominant position to drive home advantages; in the longer term, people and organizations that find themselves in a dependent position will strive to ensure that they remove themselves from this as soon as the opportunity arises. When this happens, those in hitherto dominant positions have to completely reposition themselves in order to regenerate the advantages that they had before.

Hierarchy

Organizational hierarchies are normally based on a combination of rank and function and this is reflected in job titles (marketing director, quality manager, production supervisor, personnel assistant). This is normally well understood by those in particular organizations. The process is clouded by job titles such as secretary, officer, executive and controller, and again these have to be understood by those involved.

The hierarchy is a feature of organization design and is composed of structure, job and work allocation, and rules and procedures. It indicates the extent of collective and individual power and influence; and it indicates spans of control, areas of responsibility and accountability, chains of command (the scalar chain) and reporting relationships.

Status

Status influences the perceptions of power relationships in organizations. It is also a reflection of general perceptions of influence. Status is a reflection of the rank or position of someone (or something) in a particular group. Relative status is based on the interrelationship of each position. Status is based on the importance and value ascribed to the rank by the organization and individuals concerned, and by the esteem and respect that accrue as the result of holding the given rank. Status is also based on the ambition, self-esteem and self-worth of the rank holder – the ability to say with pride 'I hold job x' or 'I work for organization y'.

Status is reinforced by the trappings that go with the rank held – personal office, expensive furniture, car, top brand computer, blackberry and mobile phone technology, expense account; and by the volume and quality of items such as these.

Status is also reinforced by the responsibilities of the rank held – size of budget, numbers of staff, performance requirements. It is also often reinforced by the physical location of those concerned; for example whether their office is in the 'corridors of power' (that is, the same as that of the top managers). In wider social circles it may also be reinforced by perceptions of glamour or excitement that are assumed to exist in certain occupations – for example show business, publishing, travel.

Status and rank are closely related; and it is additionally essential to note that both status and rank can be used both with and without responsibility.

Friendships

Friendships influence power relationships in organizations where people who have positive feelings for each other also work together. A part of the way of working then becomes the desire to support the friend to ensure that they derive some of the benefits that are to accrue from particular courses of action. The use of friendships, of personal contacts to resolve problems and address issues is a general feature of the informal organization.

It represents the ability to use personal influence (referent power) to the organization's advantage; and it also represents the ability to use personal influence to the individual's advantage. Ambitious individuals cultivate friendships that they know are going to be useful to them as they make their way up the career ladder. These friendships are built on mutual use and value within the organization, as well as (or instead of) genuine liking and respect.

Dislike

The converse of friendship is where dislike and antagonism exist between people. Dislike and antagonism are nearly always barriers to effective organizational activities. This form of power and influence is used to block or hinder the progress of the other individual or group, and is compounded where operational reasons are given for the purpose of satisfying a personal grudge or grievance.

This is influenced by other personal emotions – of envy, jealousy, hatred and resentment. It is also influenced by organizational and operational matters of expediency, especially where there is the need to find a scapegoat for a failure.

Delegation

Delegation is the allocation of work to subordinates accompanied by the handing down of:

- authority in the given area to carry out the work and to make requests for equipment, materials and information; to act in the name of department, group or superior in the given area;
- control over the process by which the work is to be carried out. This normally involves, in turn, relaxing a part of the process of work supervision. Activities taken in pursuit of the task are normally left entirely to the subordinate.

There is an effect on the wider issues of responsibility and accountability. Overall responsibility, especially to the wider organization, normally remains with the superior. Any problems arising, especially questions of failure or ineffectiveness, therefore remain a matter between the superior and the rest of the organization. However, this is invariably accompanied by discussions between the superior and subordinate. Where such problems do arise, to apportion blame to the subordinate in dealings with the wider organization, leads to loss of morale and accusations of scapegoating.

Effectiveness

For effective delegation to take place, strong mutual trust, respect and confidence must exist. On the part of the superior, this is based on respect for the capabilities, motivation and commitment of the subordinates and the fact that they are interested in the work and wish to pursue it to a successful conclusion. On the part of the subordinates, this is based on an understanding that they will receive support and backing in their efforts to get the work done, help with any problems and a proper assessment of the end results. This is always enhanced where a strong and effective reporting relationship is already established and mutual trust and confidence are already in place. This is in turn influenced by the relationship between the tasks to be delegated and the staff available to carry them out. The greater the control the superior has over this, the more likely that confidence and trust are present and the greater the willingness of the superior to cede the required measure of control.

For both, work is likely to be successful only if expectations are clearly set out at its commencement. This is reinforced wherever possible with the establishment of proper, measurable, deadlined objectives. The subordinates can then be given enough autonomy over the process to see that the work is done.

Misuses of power and influence

It remains the case that in practice, both individuals and groups misuse the power and influence that they have. The main areas of misuse are:

- **Favouritism:** the ability to influence an individual's career, prospects and advancement by virtue of a personal liking and at the expense of others.
- **Victimization:** the converse of favouritism; the blocking or reduction of career prospects and advancement.
- **Lack of manners:** calling out rudely to people, abusing and humiliating subordinates in public.
- **Lack of respect:** treating subordinates with contempt; giving individuals dressing-downs in public; conducting discipline in public.
- **Bullying and harassment:** overwhelmingly by superiors of subordinates. This is usually found in the following forms: racial prejudice; sexual harassment (especially of female staff by males); bullying of the disabled by the able-bodied; religious manias and persecutions (for example, where a Catholic company bullies the elements of its workforce that are of other religions); personal likes and dislikes – especially where the dislike is based on a perceived threat to the security of the senior's position.
- **Scapegoating:** the need to find someone to blame for the superior's errors.
- **Inequality of opportunity:** the setting of a priority order for the advancement of staff based on gender, race or disability elements.

just a minute

Each of these misuses can, if not checked, lead to serious problems. For example, in HR and ER terms, about 150,000 individual cases arising from the misuse of power are referred to ACAS and the employment tribunal system of the UK each year.

The problem is compounded by the fact that many managers and supervisors often do not see that they are acting improperly. In many cases, managers and supervisors state that they act in these ways because this is how they were treated when they were in more junior positions. Other managers state that they only act in these ways because they thought that it would help to get the job done. It is, however, clear that many managers and supervisors do indeed know that they are doing wrong. Whether by accident or design, this is an organizational problem and needs to be stamped out wherever and whenever it is found.

Organizational integrity and toxicity

Organizational integrity and toxicity are reflections of the fundamental wholesomeness (or lack of) that exists within the organization, the working and interpersonal relationships, the communication systems and networks, and the dealings with the staff, the markets, communities and other stakeholders.

At the core of organizational integrity are the purposes and interests that are genuinely served. Of course, no company ever states overtly that it serves anything other than its markets, customers and clients, and the shareholder and staff interests, as priorities. For many organizations, this is indeed the case; and the result is to form the basis for ensuring long-term effectiveness, viability and profitability.

Elsewhere however, this is not always the case. For example:

- RBS and Lloyd's banking groups continued to pay out standard levels of staff bonuses after they had gone bankrupt and had been bailed out by the government;
- when Nike and Gap were caught by journalists using child and slave labour in their manufacturing activities, they first denied all knowledge and then restructured, separating off the factories as independent companies so that they were no longer responsible for work practices;
- Glasgow Rangers football club continued to pay salaries that they simply could not afford, collectively denying that there was any problem at all, until called to account by the tax authorities;
- when faced with budget cuts in local authorities, the top and senior managers of 30 UK councils took themselves off to Nice in the South of France to 5-star hotels to discuss the problems.

The overall extent of organizational integrity or toxicity can be seen in the speed at which top management salaries rise relative to the rest of the organization. The overall spread between top and bottom salaries and pay levels is another indicator; the greater the spread, the greater the fundamental lack of integrity.

Within organizations, integrity and toxicity is evaluated through reflections on the overall culture, climate and collective well-being. Signs to look out for include the overall conduct of interpersonal, inter-professional and inter-group relations. If these relations are fundamentally open, honest, productive and inclusive, then there are fewer problems than if they are based on competition and jockeying for position and influence, or if professional and occupational groups know, believe and perceive that they have to protect their position and influence.

University administration

Two university administrators were talking over the differences and difficulties that they had in booking accommodation for lectures, classes and other meetings. One of them, Jane, constantly found problems in getting accommodation with matters often only being resolved at the last minute; and this meant that both staff and students very often did not know where to go for particular events. This in turn meant that the students missed classes, staff missed meetings, leading to extra work, tutorials and follow-up activities and gatherings.

The other administrator, Jill, had no such problems; and the two tried to work out why. It transpired that Jane's approach was always formal and through the required channels. Jill also used the formalities and required channels; however, she had also taken the time and trouble to get to know the room booking's people, to find out what their pressures were, and to find out also essential facts like league times and how bookings could be integrated best within the booking environment.

On the one hand, it is clear that the purely formal system had to be followed. However, it was either not working effectively or at the very least, it could only resolve problems and deliver what it promised at the very last minute. On the other hand, it is a part of the humanity of any organization and working relationship that people respond better to the human touch as well as following operational processes. In this case, Jane was doing nothing wrong; Jill was doing more things right more often.

So organizational integrity has to be seen in terms of how things actually work, as well as how they ought to work.

The balance of integrity and toxicity can also be observed in terms of:

- the sources, causes and nature of conflict within the organization;
- the nature of interpersonal relationships especially in terms of the regularity, frequency and content of disputes and grievances;
- fundamentally unacceptable staff management practices, including the frequency of bullying, victimization, discrimination and harassment cases;
- the nature of rewards on offer and how they are distributed and allocated;
- the nature of opportunities on offer and how these are distributed and allocated.

One of the greatest influences that any manager can make on their overall staff perform-ance is to be completely transparent in the distribution of rewards and opportunities. If rewards and opportunities can be clearly demonstrated to be distributed from a funda-mentally wholesome and open position, then in this critical field, staff have nothing to complain about.

Where there is a fundamental integrity, those responsible must never allow their standards to slip. Where there is toxicity, this needs to be addressed; and the lead in remedying this has to come from the top, addressing the basis of all relationships, and taking whatever steps are required in order to clean up this part of organizational practice. If the existing leadership and management cannot do this, then others need to be brought in.

Conflict

Conflict, or the potential for conflict, exists everywhere where two or more people are gathered together. It is inevitable that people will have differences and disagree-ments. The nature of differences and disagreements is enhanced and sharpened by the nature of organizational settings where departments, divisions, functions, groups and individuals pursue their own agenda, activities and priorities, as well as those of the organization.

Conflict may be positive and beneficial, capable of being harnessed for the greater good, and contributing to organizational effectiveness, performance and development. Conflict is also clearly negative and destructive in many forms.

The following levels of organizational conflict may be distinguished.

- Argument, discussion and debate, which are essential if any progress is to be made at all; they do however need to be structured and ordered so that everything is concentrated on the matter in hand rather than becoming a competition between the personalities involved.
- Competition, which may be positive and beneficial, capable of being harnessed for the greater good of everyone and contributing to enduring organizational effectiveness. Competition becomes negative where it is used as a form of 'divide and rule' by top managers in the fond (and mistaken) belief that, for example, having different departments, groups and individuals competing for resources at the expense of each other is 'a good thing'.
- Conflict as 'warfare', which exists where inter-group relations have got out of hand, where the main aims and objectives of activities have been lost and where energies and resources are therefore taken up with fighting a particular position whether or not this is in the interests of the organization as a whole.

Sources and causes of conflict

The main sources and causes of conflict are:

- real and perceived unfairness and inequality of treatment;
- real and perceived unfairness in the allocation of resources;
- real and perceived unfairness in the overall treatment, favour, patronage and victimization of different groups and individuals;
- where people and individuals are publicly denigrated or shown to have lost a particular position, leading to humiliation and wounded pride.

just a minute

It is essential for all managers to know and understand that the greatest injury that they can do to anyone is to humiliate them or injure their pride. Even where somebody has to be demonstrated or proved wrong, this should still be done with professionalism in order to avoid the kind of resentment that builds up from public humiliation.

Conflict is also caused where the attitudes, values, belief and priority of the organization in general are not the same as those of the individuals who carry out the work. People can, and are, from time to time asked to do things that are counter to their own personal beliefs. For example, they may be asked to lie on the part of the organization (such as give a false excuse for the failure of a delivery), and then to sustain this in public at least. They may be asked to dismiss or discipline someone because those at the top of the organization say so rather than because they want to or see the professional and occupational need to do so. The result is that, from within, the organization's fundamental integrity is questioned.

Forms of conflict

The main forms of conflict in organizations are as follows.

- Differences between corporate, group and individual aims and objectives, and the inability of the organization to devise systems, practices and activities in which these can be reconciled.
- Interdepartmental and inter-group wrangles overwhelmingly concerned with:
  - territory – where one group feels that another is treading in an area that is legitimately its own;
  - prestige – where one group feels that another is gaining recognition for efforts and successes that are legitimately its own;
  - agenda – where one group feels that it is being marginalized by the activities of others;
  - poaching and theft – where one group attracts away the staff, resources, reputation and prestige of others.

- Conflict also arises from changes in the status quo both where people seek to alter their own positions, and also from changes that the organization is making. For example, when an individual or group suddenly loses power, then there is certain to be resentment. Conversely, individuals or groups may suddenly find themselves in favour for some reason and so the others rush to do it down.

- The relative status awarded by an organization to its different departments, divisions, functions, groups and individuals is also a source and cause of conflict. Again, especially where it is clear that some groups have favoured status and others have unfavoured status, there is resentment in terms of: the means by which these differentials in status are arrived at; what it means to those concerned; and what the consequences are for everyone.

- Conflict is also caused by the emergence of secondary and hidden agenda. This is where individuals and groups become involved in particular activities for a stated set of reasons and then other reasons – the true reasons – subsequently become apparent. For example, if a group or individual has been engaged on a particular venture because of its own expertise, and yet this venture is seen to carry little prestige or recognition, then they may nevertheless do their best to ignore it or only carry it out to the barely minimum acceptable standards.

best practice

A key factor in the presence of conflict and its resolution is the level of honesty and integrity present. The greater the fundamental integrity of the situation, the greater the likelihood of the effective management of conflict.

Conflict management

As well as the operational issues indicated above, human emotions, especially those of envy, jealousy, anger and greed, are brought into being when people are confronted with a situation in which they perceive themselves to be losing out. Resentment flourishes if the nature of the situation is such that those involved feel threatened by the ways in which conflict is developing and progressing.

The first step towards reconciling and resolving conflict therefore lies in a true understanding of the sources and causes, and the extent of human emotions present. Once this is assessed, then the relative positions of: the parties to the conflict; the issues in dispute; and their causes and sources can be fully evaluated.

The outcomes of conflict

Everyone who enters into conflict needs to know and understand what they need and want to get out of it; and the minimum conditions under which a settlement can be made. This involves knowing the aims and objectives of all parties involved; and within this context, the ideal is to get to: **win–win**, in which everyone is content.

Other outcomes – **win–lose** or **lose–win** – mean that resentment is generated and the matter is certain to arise in some form at a future date. The position **lose–lose** simply means that the conflict escalates.

Whatever the approach, it is always essential to remember that people do not like to be defeated and neither do they like to have been seen by others to have been defeated. It is essential in the management of conflict that people are not humiliated even when they do lose a dispute, otherwise again, resentment is generated.

Workplace power and influence: Strikes and disputes

Strikes and disputes are used as part of the mechanism for addressing the grievances in staff and employee relations. Strikes and disputes are also used as each of the following:

- enhancement of charisma, authority and influence by the strike leaders;
- rites and rituals in pay bargaining processes;
- trials of strength between staff and managers;
- trials of strength between organizations and strike leaders;
- safety valves;
- additional holidays;
- catalysts for change, as well as for the resolution of grievances.

Individuals and groups engage in strikes and disputes to serve their own ends as well as addressing the problems that exist. Everyone involved is invariably seeking to gain influence and be taken more seriously as well as (or alongside) addressing the particular matters in hand. Those involved also understand that taking these forms of action may cause attitudinal changes on the part of those with whom they have the dispute. This is clearly an extremely fragile position:

- from the point of view of management involvement, it is always possible that staff members (or key members of staff) will simply leave the organization;
- from the staff point of view, there is always the possibility that senior mangers will simply close things down altogether.

Conclusions

In all organizations, everyone involved recognizes to some extent the nature and prevalence of particular forms of power, authority and influence within organizations, and the ways in which these are wielded. They also recognize the presence or absence of integrity in organizational approaches to the management of the different power and influence bases that are present. Above all, they understand the extent of their influence in the given situations; and become especially disillusioned when they know that the management of influence is based on expediency rather than integrity.

The integrity of the organization as a whole and its managerial practices, in particular, form the basis of the effective management of the different sources of power and influence. It is essential therefore that a full understanding of the true extent and nature of power and influence is established by those responsible for the strategy and direction of the particular organization. This can then be translated into managerial authority so that this part of organization management and activity is addressed effectively. In particular, when addressing either organizational toxicity or serious conflicts, this authority has to be exercised with a clear set of aims and objectives in mind; and it is also essential that the sources and causes of toxicity and conflict are tackled effectively.

This is especially a problem when authority is devolved to those working in remote locations, or as a result of their distinctive expertise. It is, for example, very difficult for some health authority managers to confront expert surgeons and other medical practitioners, especially where this expertise is linked to an extremely powerful and dominant personality. It is very difficult for head office managers to exercise full authority over those who work in remote locations or in the operational field, and this is often compounded by the lack of a full understanding of what the exact nature of this authority should be. The result, in each case, is that there is great potential for the particular individuals to run their part of activities as their own *monarchy*, and for effective accountability and responsibility to be diluted or lost. Once problems such as these arise, they become extremely difficult to retrieve. Indeed, in some cases the situation may only be brought under control as the result of a scandal or disaster.

- Power, authority and influence are present in all organizations, groups and individuals; and everyone seeks to exert their influence and authority (such as it may be) in order to assert their position within the organization.
- Power, influence and authority may be exercised positively and with integrity; or they may be exercised with negativity and ulterior motives, leading to organizational toxicity.
- The use of power, influence and authority by managers comes with the need to accept responsibility and accountability for particular decisions and actions.
- Conflict is present in all organizations; the potential for, and extent of, internal organizational conflict has to be recognized in each situation.
- In order to resolve conflict effectively, it is essential to know the ideal and intended outcomes of everyone involved.
- In order to resolve conflict effectively, it is essential to know what processes and approaches are going to work in given situations and in response to particular issues; it is not possible to prescribe a standard or foolproof approach to everything.

Further reading

Etzioni, A. (1964) *Power in Organizations.* Free Press.

McAlpine, A. (2000) *The New Machiavelli.* Wiley.

Pettinger, R. (2010) *Organizational Behaviour.* Routledge.

Shapiro, D. (2004) *Conflict and Communication.* Kogan Page.

Stanley, A. (2009) *Leadership and Conflict Management Styles.* Sage.

Wheeler, D. and Sillanpaa, A. (2000) *The Stakeholder Corporation.* FTPitman.

Human resource management

9

> 'The principles of equality, fairness and diversity must be embedded within the organization culture.'

In this chapter

- the purpose of human resource management (HRM) in providing the basis for effective and sustainable levels of work and performance
- the need for strategic approaches to HRM
- the relationship between the HR strategies defined and the nature of HR practices
- developing HR strategies and operations in line with overall organization demands

Introduction

The purpose of human resource management (HRM) is to provide the basis for staff management, employee relations (ER), and personnel practices required by the organization. This is so as to be able to fit work to people, and fit people to technology, producing effective and profitable products and services. This in turn enables maximization and optimization of return on return in what is normally the largest single fixed cost incurred – the staff.

Strategic HR – Nissan UK: The art of the possible

true story

When Nissan UK opened its factories in Sunderland, north-east England, it was entering what had become an industrial wasteland. The docks, steelworks and shipyards had all been closed down or greatly reduced. There was a commonly held view that, because of social and historic industrial problems, it was impossible to conduct effective and profitable business in the area.

Nissan knew and understood this in advance, and went ahead nevertheless. Nissan started by clearly setting out the basis on which the staff were to be engaged and managed, and the conditions under which they would work. These were:

- Nissan would pay up to 130% of the average wage for those working in the car industry in the UK;
- there would be full flexibility of working, and Nissan would spend as much time and resource as necessary in training the staff;
- there would be a no-strike deal, replaced by a speedy and substantial arbitration mechanism to resolve disputes;
- attendance would be monitored, and those off work would always be interviewed when they came back;
- promotion and development opportunities would always be offered to the existing workforce before being advertised externally.

Nissan used this strategic approach to HRM as the basis for attracting and retaining its workforce, and developing its capabilities. By 2007, Nissan UK was the most productive car production plant in the world – producing 135 cars, per annum, per employee. Staff absenteeism runs at 0.5% per annum. The company has had no collective industrial action; and only two disputes that have gone to employment tribunal. During the car production crisis of 2008–2009, Nissan UK weathered the storm with no compulsory redundancies. In the industrial and economic crisis of 2010 onwards, the company continued to produce cars for export all over the world, as well as the domestic market; and continues to set production and output records for the entire industry.

HR strategies

Organizations require clear and understood HR strategies. HR strategies are set in the overall context of core foundation or generic positions adopted; and this then forms the basis for the structure, composition and expertise of the workforce. HR strategy is then implemented and delivered through the adoption of one of the following positions in relation to the staff:

- **Unitarism:** which assumes that the objectives of all involved are the same or compatible and concerned only with the well-being of the organization and its products, services, clients and customers.
- **Pluralism:** admitting a variety of objectives, not all compatible, among the staff. Recognizing that conflict is therefore present, rules, procedures and systems are established to manage it and limit its influence as far as possible. This is the approach taken especially in public services, local government and many

industrial and commercial activities, where diverse interests have to be reconciled in order that productive work may take place.

- **Radicalism:** the view that commercial and industrial harmony is impossible until the staff control the means of production, and benefit from the generation of wealth. Until very recently, this was a cornerstone of the philosophy of many trade unions and socialist activists in industry, commerce and public services.

- **Conflict:** the basis on which staff are to be dealt with is one of mistrust, divergence, irreconcilable aims and objectives; disparity of location; divergence and complexity of patterns of employment and occupations; this includes professional, technical, skilled and unskilled staff. In such cases as this, the HR strategy will be devised to contain the conflicts; to reconcile differences; and to promote levels of harmony as far as possible.

- **Conformity:** where the diversity of staff and technology may be (and often is) as great as in the above scenario, but where the HR strategy rather sets standards of behavioural and operational aims and objectives that in turn require the different groups to rise above their inherent differences.

- **Consensus:** where the way of working is devised as a genuine partnership between the organization, its staff and their representatives; the consensus position in HR is rare in all but the simplest and smallest of organizations (and may not exist even in these).

- **Paternalism:** in which the organization accepts responsibilities for providing staff comfort and support in return for known, understood and assured ways of working, including flexible responses when pressures on the organization are heavy.

Whichever approach is adopted must be known, agreed and implemented by all managers whatever their department, division or function. This then forms the foundation of leadership and management style (see Chapter 2); and it also forms the foundation and standpoint for the conduct of all staff management, as well as HR and personnel activities. Whatever the approach adopted, the role and function of strategic and operational HRM is:

- to produce, deliver and implement policies;
- to support line managers and staff;
- to establish standards of best practice, and reinforce absolute standards of conduct, behaviour and performance.

best practice

Whichever the HR strategy in place, it is essential that you are able to make it work for you to best advantage. While it is clearly indicated that consensus, conformist and participative approaches are 'the best', in practice you may have to work with conflict or pluralist approaches because these are the only things that can be done in the given set of circumstances. So you need to understand where the opportunities for development and intervention are, and take full advantage of these when they occur.

HR and employment law

HRM and employment practice are governed by the law and statutory instruments and regulations as follows:

- laws and statutes relating to equality and fairness of treatment, discrimination, bullying, victimization, and harassment;
- health and safety at work;
- the conduct of recruitment, selection and remuneration activities and policies;
- the management of ER, disputes, grievances, dismissals, strikes and other industrial action;
- stress and occupational health management;
- working hours;
- protection from hazardous substances; and protection when carrying out hazardous activities;
- the production and implementation of internal policies and procedures, especially those related to collective and individual discipline, conduct, behaviour and performance.

The principle of equality and fairness

Whatever the size, location or activities, all staff must be treated equally and fairly. As well as being a legal requirement, this is a fundamental prerequisite to the creation of organization and operation effectiveness. Managers and organizations must first over-come the tendency to compartmentalize people by race, gender, religion, marital status, disability, age, location, postal address, non-essential qualification, school background, club membership, hobby and interest. They must take the opposite standpoint of isolating the qualities essential and desirable to carry out a job. They must view people in terms of their potential as staff members, as contributors to the success and pros-perity of the organization. Without this, true equality of opportunity cannot exist.

There is also a question of basic human decency, which requires that all people be treated the same. This is a social as well as organizational concern. For organizations, all activities, management style, policies, practices and procedures, publications, advertisements, job and work descriptions, and person specifications are written in ways that reinforce this. This emphasizes, formulates and underlines the required attitudes and beliefs.

These standards are based on operational capabilities alone. Anyone, including managers, adopting a negative approach or attitude to equality of opportunity, or who victimizes, harasses or bullies members of their staff, must be subject to organization discipline.

Offering equality of opportunity to all sectors of the workforce is both cost-effective and profitable. By concentrating on (discriminating against) certain sectors of the population on operational grounds, organizations greatly limit their prospects either of making effective appointments or of maximizing the human resource.

The lead therefore, comes from the top of organizations and the attitudes filtered down to all the staff. Organizational equal opportunities policies must be clear, unequivocal and easily understood by all concerned. They must be valued and adopted at all levels and in all sectors and departments. A genuine adoption of the principle of equality for all constitutes excellent marketing to the human resource of the organization – staff are known to be valued for their capabilities. It also underlines any high moral or ethical stance taken in other business and organizational activities.

Managing diversity

The management of diversity is concerned with ensuring that people from a wide range of backgrounds, ethnic origins, social groups and occupational disciplines are brought together and harmonized into an effective and productive workforce. Effective diversity management seeks to bond and maximize the strengths inherent in the absolute standards set by the organization, and the different knowledge, understanding and expectations brought by those from a variety of different backgrounds.

Diversity management takes the fundamental premise of equality of treatment and opportunity a stage further. Diversity management concentrates on ensuring that everyone gets the same treatment and opportunities, rather than identifying and separating out those whose career paths and opportunities may be hindered, and then removing the obstacles faced by the particular groups.

Overall workforce cohesion is then further reinforced by the business opportunities that this form of employment practice brings.

expert view

Equality and diversity management

The CIPD (Chartered Institute of Personnel and Development) states:

'Managing diversity is based on the concept that people should be valued as individuals for reasons related to business interests, as well as for moral and social reasons. It recognised that people from different backgrounds can bring fresh ideas and perceptions which may make the way work is done more efficient, and products and services better.'

The business benefits identified are:

- improved customer satisfaction and market penetration by employing and supporting a diverse workforce whose composition reflects that of the local population;
- a diverse workforce brings a range of skills and approaches to generic problems and issues;
- effective diversity management improves the supply of staff, confidence between staff and organization, and reduces costly discrimination cases.

For example, HBOS invited members of Manchester's Chinese community to apply for work within the bank. In the past, the company had few customers and staff from this community. Bilingual posters were placed in the main Chinatown advice centre in the city asking whether people were interested in working for the bank. This eventually led to the employment of six Chinese people by the bank in the Manchester area. A consequence of the policy has been increased business from the Chinese community at large, because of both cultural recognition, and also language capability.

Over the period since 1998, HBOS has increased the proportion of employees from ethnic minorities from 4% to 6.4% nationally. Increases in some localities are even higher, for example from 9% to 27% in Keighley, West Yorkshire.

The bank's diversity programme is also about women, older workers and people with disabilities. The company uses a diversity team, and this team includes a disability manager and an equal opportunities adviser.

Sources: CIPD (1999); Merrick (2001); Marchington and Wilkinson (2009).

To be fully effective however, diversity management requires fully institutionalizing as a corporate commitment and priority in strategic HRM. Diversity is an investment on which both immediate and also enduring returns are sought and demanded. Once the decision is taken to go down this route, this then becomes a key factor in organization development and the creation of an effective positive and cohesive culture and set of values.

Equality and diversity ought to be a fundamental element of all HR practices. Apart from anything else, a genuine respect for equality and diversity promotes the overall humanity and inclusiveness of the organization. Failure to do so means that inequality and a lack of diversity are being accommodated; and this is certain to lead to pressures and conflicts at some point.

Pay and reward

All staff need to be paid adequately and effectively for their work, expertise, commitment and contribution. Pay and reward packages consist of:

- **Payment:** annual, quarterly, monthly, four-weekly, weekly, daily. Commission, bonus, increments, fees. Profit, performance and merit-related payments.
- **Allowances:** attendance, disturbance, shift, weekend, unsocial hours, training and development, location and relocation, absence from home.
- **Benefits:** loans (for example for season tickets), pension (contributory or non-contributory), subsidies (on company products, canteen, travel), car, telephone/car phone, private healthcare, training and development, luncheon vouchers.

- **Chains of gold or super benefits:** school holidays (teachers); cheap loans (banks); free/cheap travel (railway, shipping, airlines); pension arrangements (for older or longer-serving staff).
- **Economic rent:** high rates of pay for particular expertise (especially scarce expertise or that which is required at short notice).
- **Work/life and rewards:** in which people who have to balance work demands with outside pressures, accept a given level of pay in return for flexible working arrangements.
- **Performance and profit-related pay:** in which bonuses are delivered in return for meeting performance criteria, particular targets, and collective and individual profit and output levels.
- **Specific incentives:** related to particular occupations, partly reflecting people's expectations, and partly reflecting performance.

Always think about what you are rewarding, and what you want to reward. It is essential to remember that, in practice, what gets rewarded gets done.

This is very complex, and the mixes adopted by organizations in the devising and implementation of reward strategies for different staff categories cover a variety of aims and purposes in response to particular situations. The overall general objective is, however, to address the following.

- **Expectations:** all systems must meet the expectations of the job holder to a greater or lesser extent if they are to be effective at attracting and retaining staff in the required occupations.
- **Motivation:** within the constraints illustrated above, all payment and reward motivates to a greater or lesser extent; the levels of reward offered to particular job holders also carry implications for the nature, complexity and commitment to the work in hand that is required on their part.
- **Mixes of pay with other aspects:** much of this relates to expectations also – for example, in the UK, the offer of a company car to professional and managerial staff is still very attractive, in spite of the diminishing tax advantage.
- **Occupational aspects:** part of the reward package may include the provision of specialist or expert training and equipment.
- **Training and development, and career development:** which has assumptions of leading to higher levels of pay and reward and further opportunities for the future.
- **Other prospects and opportunities:** again, providing potential for higher levels of pay and salary, and further career development.
- **International variations:** organizations operating in different parts of the world offer different reward packages including pay, opportunities and career development potential.

Always remember the difference between motivation and incentives. Motivation is a process based on the relationship between organization and staff; incentives are specific financial and material rewards delivered in return for short-term effort.

Attraction, recruitment and retention

The ability to attract, recruit and retain staff is based on a variety of factors:

- the relative attraction of the organization, the work offered, its wider reputation, together with perceptions of more general contacts with the organization, for example through media coverage, or as a customer;
- the location of the organization; and this refers both to the place of work, and also in relation to ease and convenience of transport and access;
- the relative value and worth of the occupation, both to the individual and also to the organization;
- the relative perception in which the organization and the work are held.

Assessment of these factors indicates the overall attractiveness or otherwise of the organization and the work. This has then to be related to the rewards on offer:

- material rewards – salary/pay/wages, and other benefits;
- intrinsic rewards, including responsibility, autonomy, opportunities for progress and development;
- reflections of personal value, including status, esteem, rank and job title, each of which is important to some people in particular sets of circumstances;
- recognition factors on the part of the individual, the organization and society at large;
- the fit between the particular occupation and the management style with which the work is directed.

Attraction, recruitment and retention of staff are based on good levels of expert knowledge of each of the factors indicated above. Full assessment of these factors indicates why people want to carry out their occupation for the particular organization, and the advantages and barriers relative to this.

It is additionally necessary to see the nature of the rewards on offer relative to people's professional and occupational demands and expectations.

Sources of staff

Potential staff exist everywhere, limited only by qualifications, capability and willingness to work in the organization. Organizations use: recruitment advertising in newspapers and trade press; agencies and specialists; and local and professional word of mouth. Recruiting people with specialist or scarce expertise may additionally require such approaches as 'executive search'. Advances in international education, together with the opportunities afforded by technology, have additionally led organizations either to establish specialist services overseas, or to recruit staff from overseas to come and work in the UK.

Ideally, a mix and diversity of sources of staff will be used; and this is to ensure the maximum possible opportunity of gaining the best people for the job, and gaining a wide range of approaches and perspectives.

Some posts within organizations will attract both internal and external candidates. The priority here is to reconcile the issues relating to:

- the need to offer opportunities for development to staff already working within the organization; and reconciling this with preventing becoming too inward looking;
- attracting fresh talent and energy as above; and reconciling this with the fact that external expertise has to be capable of being harnessed and delivered within the culture and operational constraints of the particular organization;
- attracting and retaining key staff, and filling skills shortages, for which it may be necessary to vary standard terms and conditions of employment, and especially pay and remuneration packages.

Wherever staff come from, they need to be given the best possible opportunity to demonstrate their capability and willingness to do the job in the ways demanded by the organization. Where there is a field of candidates for particular positions, everyone must be given the same fair and equal opportunity to demonstrate their capabilities. Consequently, recruitment interviewing, selection testing, personality tests and other specific requirements must be structured in order to be fair to everyone involved.

The attraction, recruitment and retention of staff is, from time to time, a competitive process. Competitive pressures arise when:

- new employers open up in the particular locality;
- existing employers move from the particular locality, resulting in spouses and dependants of particular groups of staff having to go with them;
- wages and salaries increase within organizations in the same sector;
- wages and salaries increase within professional and occupational groups in the same sector;
- changes in transport affect access and egress availability.

Induction

The purpose of induction is to get the new member of staff as productive as possible, as quickly as possible. This consists of matching the organization's needs with those of the individual as follows.

- Setting the attitudes and standards of behaviour required, ensuring that new employees know what is expected of them, and that they conform to these expectations and requirements. It is most important that the organization assumes absolute responsibility for this, rather than allowing employees to set their own standards, or for these to emerge by default.

- Job training and familiarization, mainly to do with the ways of working required by the organization, and ensuring that these are matched with the new employee's expertise; and establishing the required standards and methods of work.
- Introductions to the new team, work colleagues, and other key contacts as part of the process of gaining confidence, understanding and mutuality of objectives required for the development of effective working relationships and environment.
- Familiarization with the environment, premises, ways of working, and particular obligations on the part of the employer; ensuring that the new employee understands their position in this environment; emergency procedures and health and safety.

The induction process will have been started in general terms by any vague impression that new employees have picked up of the organization; it will have been further reinforced if, for example, they have been customers or clients in the past. Any correction of these impressions must also be addressed as part of the induction process, which will also be reinforced by the ways in which the selection process is conducted.

Performance measurement and appraisal

Performance measurement is conducted for the organization, departments, divisions, groups and individuals. To be effective and successful, it must be conducted as follows.

- Pre-set and pre-agreed aims and objectives, priorities, performance targets, and deadlines for achievement.
- A process of regularized formal reviews, combined with a continuous and participative working relationship.
- Fully participative between appraiser and appraisee.
- Concentration on a combination of measuring and evaluating achievements, together with establishing what is to be done for the future.

Within this framework, particular organizational appraisal schemes may seek to: provide merit pay awards; identify potential; identify training and development needs; identify job–person mismatch; identify organization development prospects; identify poor and substandard performance; be a vehicle for other remedial action.

Appraisal schemes fall into disrepute for the following reasons: that they are not believed in or valued; they do not contribute to the wider success of the organization; they are bureaucratic or mechanistic; that it is the scheme and its paperwork that are important, and not the process that should be completed; that the reviews are too infrequent, or (in practice) missed altogether; that what is promised in them (for example pay awards, training, promotion) is not delivered in practice.

Maintenance factors in human resource management

Like every other resource, the staff require maintenance if their value is to be maximized and optimized. Attention is therefore required to:

- job and work development;
- training and development;
- career management;
- discipline and grievance;
- creative approaches to employment;
- stress;
- occupational health.

Job and work development

Job and work development are designed both in terms of the formation of attitudes and standards at the workplace to which employees are required to subscribe, and also in the division, regulation and allocation of the work itself. They are undertaken with the intention of generating a greater measure of positive commitment and a reduction of workplace alienation. This may involve job rotation and progression schemes; and project work, secondments, and fixed-term action learning type placements also. Related to this is the ever-increasing obligation on employees to maintain and improve their skills, knowledge and technical expertise in the interests of continuing organization effectiveness, profitability and prosperity. On the other hand, the expectations of those at work have also changed, and part of the job design process increasingly includes improving the quality of working life.

Training and development

All staff require training and development – initial and continuing job training, identification of potential, and as the result of performance appraisal. Organizations have to strike a balance between ensuring that employees maximize and optimize their potential relative to the opportunities that are genuinely on offer. It is essential that organizations do not raise people's expectations unrealistically; on the other hand, staff should never be restricted from pursuing their ambitions as long as the organization can accommodate these.

Career management

Whatever their occupation, most people require some kind of a career based on progression, development and enhancement. Career management and progression therefore becomes a partnership between organization and individual. The priority, as above, is to make clear what the organization can offer and then be realistic about whether individual ambitions can be satisfied by the organization, or whether the organization's demands fit in with the capabilities and potential of particular individuals. Once this context has been established, opportunities should be clearly stated and then, all things being equal, when these arise, individuals should be given the first opportunity to apply for them and to see if they can work within them. It is usual also to ensure that individuals have training and development prior to accepting career progression opportunities so that they are at least familiar with what they will be doing in the future.

Discipline and grievance management

All organizations require disciplinary and grievance policies; and these must be clearly stated and published to everyone concerned.

Discipline, and the procedures that underpin it, exists in order to ensure that people conduct themselves to the required standards of behaviour and performance. Clearly stated sanctions must be published indicating what is to happen when particular transgressions occur; and especially what is to happen when serious or gross misconduct takes place. It is essential to remember that all organizational approaches to discipline and grievance are bounded by the law. Especially, procedures must be followed and rights of representation, response and appeal must be allowed; otherwise any sanction, including dismissal, will normally automatically be found to be unfair.

Grievance management exists to ensure that any problems or issues are raised as early as possible and dealt with quickly and effectively. Individuals have the right to raise a grievance against any member of staff about any matter at all, including: interpersonal, inter-professional and inter-occupational relations; attitudes and behaviour of management; pay, remuneration and reward policies; equality and fairness of treatment. When issues are raised, again individuals have statutory rights; they must be allowed to state their case, have their case heard and answered, and then appeal against the findings if they are still not satisfied.

Creative approaches to employment

Creative approaches to employment involve a much greater awareness and willingness on the part of organizations to relate the hours of work that they offer to the non-work commitment and aspirations of potential staff members. This means having regard to the use of flexitime, annual hours and other flexible work patterns; job sharing; working away from the organization and especially allowing staff to work at home and providing them with the means and workstations to do so; and the devising of shift patterns especially to fit around those with primary responsibility for looking after young children. More widely, organizations may offer career breaks – extended periods of time off for employees in which they may go to do other things.

Organizations may offer 'returner schemes' pitched primarily at those who have had lengthy periods of time out of work, usually for the purpose of bringing up a family; the returner scheme tackles the issues of familiarization, confidence building and personal and professional comfort that are the concerns of anyone coming into any job after a lengthy break. Such schemes also provide specific job training and retraining as necessary and desirable. Organizations may also underline their commitment to these creative approaches, through the provision of nursery facilities for very young children; canteen facilities that are open all day so that all work patterns are accommodated; and through the adoption of general ways of working and general attitudes at the workplace that place the same intrinsic value on all members of staff regardless of their own particular pattern of work.

Stress

Stress may be either positive or negative. It essentially consists of the amount of pressure present in a given situation in which the individual finds himself. The sources of stress are occupational, role, organizational, hierarchical, social and personal; and pressures arising on the individual result from an imbalance of these. There is, in particular, a growing awareness of the links between work and stress and other illnesses such as nervous exhaustion, executive and professional burnout, heart conditions and high blood pressure. The manager's role in this is therefore threefold: to recognize it as an issue; to prevent stress among staff; and to recognize it in himself and take steps to limit it.

Good occupational health schemes thus have stress recognition and the ability to treat the symptoms and manifestations of it as a central part of them. The ability of organizations to accept and recognize the condition, to treat it where it occurs and, above all, to engage in practices and a style of management that prevent it from arising as far as possible is an essential contribution to the maintenance of the human resource.

best practice

It is essential to remember that 'stress' means different things to different people: one person's stress may be something that others can cope with easily. When questions of stress are raised with managers, a full investigation should always be carried out, and findings made available to those who have raised the issues.

Occupational health

Organizations are increasingly assuming responsibility for the good health of their staff, and taking positive steps and making interventions that are designed to ensure this. This consists of determining that the employee is fit and healthy when he or she first starts work and that this continues throughout the period of employment. For those who have persistent or regular time away from work, there may be included assessments by company medical staff as well as the employee's own doctor. Moreover, this may require the employee to take medical treatment at the behest of the organization as a precondition of continuing to work for it. Occupational health schemes at the workplace are, in the best cases, particularly strong and valuable in the early diagnosis of job-specific illnesses and injuries. They also provide a valuable general source of medical knowledge by which the organization may assess the overall state of its workforce's health.

Particular matters related to the workplace have come to the fore and gained recognition and currency. Major issues of which any manager should be aware are:

- stress, its causes and effects and techniques for its management, as above;
- repetitive strain injuries (RSI) which are caused by continuous use of certain muscles or the carrying out of certain activities – for example continuous keyboard working and process work;
- provision of protective clothing, equipment and training;
- back injuries caused either by bad lifting practices or by a continuous bad back posture;
- the effects of VDU screens on eyesight;
- industrial and commercial heating, lighting and working conditions; and the relationship between these and eye strain, coughs, colds and other minor but recurrent ailments;
- smoking, both active and passive, and the effects of it on all staff, both in relation to health and also more general concerns of its offensive odour;
- alcohol abuse;
- HIV and AIDS, and other serious illnesses and diseases; and the implications for particular workplaces and occupations.

Employee relations

Employee relations (ER) – or industrial relations, employment relations, staff relations – is the system by which workplace activities are regulated, the arrangement by which the owners, managers and staff of organizations come together to engage in productive activity. In practice, ER is concerned with setting standards, promoting agreement between staff and management, addressing and resolving staff problems and managing conflict.

It is usual to define a broad framework for ER as a relationship between:

- government, which legislates for ER and workplace practice in many areas; and which influences all organizational ER in its role as dominant employer and in the management of public services;

- employers, in discharging their enduring responsibilities to staff; and in conducting and developing their relationships with the staff in accordance with the provisions of the law;
- employees, and their representatives (including trade unions) in ensuring that required standards of behaviour, probity and performance are carried out within the constraints of the particular situation.

The Donovan Commission

A key part of the review of the Royal Commission on Trade Unions and Employers' Associations (the Donovan Commission of 1965–1967) was to define for the first time what the real roles of unions were. In summary, the findings were that unions:

- bargain for best possible wages, terms and conditions for members;
- lobby for improved share in national wealth for members;
- influence government policy, legal framework on behalf of members;
- lobby for social security for all;
- lobby for full employment, job security, wage levels, cheap housing for the poor;
- bargain nationally, regionally, locally, industrially, for organizations and individuals;
- represent members at disputes and grievances and for any other reason according to need.

In recent years, the collective and political influence of trade unions has declined partly as the result of legislation, and partly also because of the collapse of those industries where trade unions were traditionally strong.

The main work of trade unions at present is to represent individual employees in individual disputes and grievances.

Source: Donovan (1968).

ER developments

In recent years, many organizations have actively redrawn the relationship between staff management practices and ER in terms of integration with, and contribution to, overall organizational performance. As well as being concerned with employee terms and conditions, and the state of the working environment, many organizations now negotiate and consult with staff representatives and recognized trade unions on a much wider range of issues including:

- productivity and service delivery issues, including attention to quality and customer satisfaction;
- organizational operating expenses, engaging consensus and cooperation in how best to manage these;

- the design and implementation of technology changes and upgrades;
- the opening up of new markets, products, services and locations.

This represents a shift away from adversarial and conflict-based approaches to ER, towards consensus and cooperation; and this in turn has led to much greater levels of participation and involvement on the part of the staff in many organizations.

Problem-solving

It remains true that a substantial part of organizational ER practice is concerned with resolving problems, disputes, grievances and disciplinary issues. These issues arise as the result of:

- genuine misunderstandings;
- negligence;
- personality, professional and occupational clashes;
- determination to engage in conflict.

Historically, these matters used to be resolved through reference to lengthy and complicated procedures. The provision of procedures, together with ensuring adequate representation, remains a statutory duty. However, many organizations and their managers have come to know and understand that, if matters can be resolved without recourse to formal procedures, this is more productive and less stressful for everyone concerned. This in turn has led to a much greater emphasis on management development and training in the field of ER, with specific reference to:

- problem-solving and resolution;
- disputes and grievance management;
- correct ways to conduct disciplinary hearings.

This is underpinned by organizations producing comprehensive staff handbooks in which all duties and obligations are clearly set out. Such staff handbooks ensure that everyone knows and understands what constitutes: minor misdemeanours; major problems; and serious and gross misconduct (the penalty for which will normally be dismissal).

The onus is therefore shifted on to managers to resolve problems when they do arise; and to create the conditions and relationships in which matters are raised early and resolved quickly without the need to resort to formal procedures.

It does however remain true that many organizations do still conduct ER in more traditional ways. It is not always easy to shift managerial or collective staff attitudes; and not always possible without more extensive organizational restructuring. It remains the case, however, that where adversarial ER does exist, there is a much greater organizational expense inherent in its management and conduct, leading to a much greater proliferation of disputes, grievances and disciplinary matters.

ER – and disputes and conflicts

A strategic approach to ER matters will be adopted by organizations and their managers. As well as briefings for staff, and training for managers in ER skills and knowledge, organizations will take an approach to the management of workplace conflicts based on answers to questions in the following six areas.

1 What is the likelihood of a dispute occurring? If it does, how long might it last? What are the wider consequences to ourselves, and to our staff?

2 If it does occur, can we win it? What are the consequences of winning it? What are the consequences of losing it?

3 If it does occur, what costs are we going to incur? As well as financial cost, what of the questions of PR, media coverage and local feelings in our community? Is this a price worth paying?

4 What happens when it all settles down? How will we interact and work with the staff afterwards? How long will any bad feeling last? What are the wider implications of this?

5 What other ways are there around the matter or dispute in hand? Are we able to use these? What are the pros and cons of going down these alternatives, vis-à-vis a dispute?

6 What are the behavioural and psychological aspects that surround this issue? If we win, what will be the effects on the workforce? And on managers? Are there questions of morale to be considered? If we lose, would loss of face be important? How could we save face if that were to arise? What would be the response of the workforce and its representatives?

From consideration of the matter in hand this way, and by establishing the answer to these issues, the answer to the critical question emerges: **Why are we seeking, entering, or preparing to enter, into this dispute?**

This approach will form the basis of any strategic consideration of any conflict, or potential conflict, whether global, organizational, departmental, or divisional; or at team, group or individual level.

Conclusions

Staff management, human resource management, and ER strategies and policies must be designed to work in harmony and in the interests of the organization, rather than those of HRM and ER specialist functions. Many organizations are coming increasingly to the view that HRM is a strategic rather than operational issue; and that this, in turn, means that day-to-day HRM issues are tackled and resolved by the particular line managers and supervisors involved, rather than referring them to specialist functions. It is therefore necessary that all managers are expert in HR and staff management operational issues at least.

Especially, failure in each of these areas normally leads to staff disputes and grievances, or staff problems, and these invariably turn out to be expensive. In detail, the areas of knowledge and understanding required are as follows (see Table 9.1).

Table 9.1 *Human resource management summary*

Area of work	Strategy and direction	Personnel operations
Work design and structuring	Principles, approaches, departmentalization, organization structure	Job descriptions, work patterns, work structuring
Staff planning	Systems appraisal, design commissioning	Systems usage
Recruitment and selection	Standpoint (grow your own, buy in from outside)	Training of recruiters and selectors, recruitment and selection activities
Induction	Policy, content, priority	Delivery
Use of agencies and external sources of staff	Principles, circumstances	Contacts and commissions
Performance appraisal	Purpose, systems, design, principles, aims and objectives	Systems implementation, training of appraisers and appraisees
Pay and rewards	Policy, levels, mix of pay and benefits, package design	Assimilate individual staff to policy
Occupational health and stress management	Policy, content, design of package	Operation of package in conjunction with functional departments
Equality and diversity	Standards, policy, content, context, ethics	Policy operation, monitoring of standards, remedial actions
Employee relations	Standpoints (conflict, conformist), representation	Negotiations, consultation, participation, staff communications
Discipline	Policy, procedure, practice, design, standpoint	Implementation of policy and procedure, support for staff, training of all staff
Grievance	Policy, procedure	Implementation of policy and procedure, training of all staff
Training and development	Priority and resources	Activities, opportunities, accessibility
Dismissal	Standards of conduct, examples of gross misconduct	Operation of disciplinary procedures, operation of dismissal procedures, support and advice

Human Resource Management is divided into strategic and directional activities, and personnel activities. The role and function is:

- policy, advisory, consultative, supporting, a point of reference;
- personnel practitioner;
- establisher of policy content;
- establishing standards of best practice;
- creator of personnel activities;
- monitor/evaluator of personnel activities.

There is clearly a pressure for this strategic approach to be developed and enhanced. With the increased complexity of organizational structure, uncertainties of market, and continuing need for the development of expertise, a strategic approach to HRM is much more likely to make a long-term and enduring contribution to organizational effectiveness through following this agenda than by concentrating on specific issues and minutiae in functional departments and divisions. The strategic HR role also requires specific attention to establishing, maintaining and developing the required organizational management style and culture, and of engaging management development programmes in support of this. Staff development, expertise and technological training are also much better managed from a strategic point of view. Finally, the procedures that underwrite the required and desired HRM style and strategy are much more likely to be effective if they are written from a strategic, rather than operational, point of view.

- Knowing and understanding the legal and operational boundaries of HRM is essential, whether an HR expert and practitioner or not.
- It is essential to know and understand the legal, statutory and operational framework of HRM; and essential also to recognize that these frameworks give specific rights, duties and obligations to employers and employees.
- If organizational staff are indeed recognized as 'the human resource', then it is essential to ensure that their value and well-being are maximized and optimized as far as possible.
- There are specific interventions – staffing policies, training and development, and the management of ER – that, if conducted effectively, go a long way towards ensuring organization well-being, profitability, viability and long-term effectiveness and stability.
- The principles of equality, fairness and diversity must be embedded within the organization culture.

Further reading

Bratton, J. and Gold, J. (2007) *Human Resource Management.* Palgrave Macmillan.

Cheatle, K. (2001) *Mastering Human Resource Management.* Palgrave Macmillan.

CIPD (1999) *Managing Diversity.* Chartered Institute of Personnel and Development.

Donovan, T. (1968) *Report of the Royal Commission on Trade Unions and Employers Associations.* The Stationery Office.

Marchington, M. and Wilkinson, A. (2009) *People Management and Development.* CIPD.

Merrick, N. (2001) *People Management.* CIPD.

Pettinger, R. (2002) *The Future of Industrial Relations.* Cassell.

Storey, J. (2001) *Human Resource Management: A Critical Text.* Routledge.

Leadership and management

10

'Leadership is a key part of management that has its own distinctive expertise and set of demands.'

In this chapter

- the nature of organization leadership, and its critical importance and value as a part of managerial expertise
- leadership traits, styles and types
- the critical position of confidence that is required of all those in leadership positions
- identifying and developing leadership expertise

Introduction

The context in which leadership expertise is required of managers is as follows.

- It is becoming increasingly essential to be able to legitimately assign responsibility, authority and accountability to those in charge of organizations, and those who head individual departments, divisions and functions.
- It is increasingly difficult, and in some cases impossible, to sustain the expense incurred through having large and complex hierarchical and bureaucratic systems for the coordination and control of organizations.

Employing and assigning those with expertise in leadership, and developing the traits, characteristics and qualities required, is therefore a clear alternative. Employing people with leadership expertise in key and critical positions and functions therefore reduces expense; and it additionally leads to clearer lines of authority and accountability, resulting in increased output, delivered more quickly, and with fewer problems and barriers.

Leadership is therefore the core of all managerial and supervisory activities. This is more clearly observable in some areas than others – political leaders and chief executives officers are self-evidently 'in charge'. However, all those in managerial positions have a leadership function; and all those in leadership positions have managerial responsibilities. These are:

- to give vision and direction;
- to energize;
- to set and enforce absolute standards of behaviour, attitude, presentation and performance;
- to determine, implement and develop strategy, operations and performance (and this applies whatever the levels of management undertaken);
- to allocate and prioritize resources and activities.

In this context, the key role and function is having the combination of expertise, commitment and personality required to see things through to completion. It is additionally essential that leaders surround themselves with expertise that they themselves do not have so that any gaps in their own shortcomings are filled.

Winston Churchill

Winston Churchill, the UK prime minister during the period 1940–1945 of the Second World War, provided identity and inspiration to the British population at a time of enduring national crisis.

Many of Churchill's military commanders, however, complained of his constant meddling and interference in both the strategy and tactics used. The commanders took the view that they were employed as experts in the particular field, and so should be allowed to get on with the job.

Those employed in key and critical positions need to be sufficiently expert themselves in order to be able to respond to detailed questioning. From the leader's point of view, it is therefore much better to be accused of interference, meddling and over-attention to detail, and having the character and capacity to 'back off', than it is to be accused of remoteness, distance and inapproachability.

Leadership in practice

Leaders are expected to deliver and achieve what they set out to do; or else to provide a clear explanation as to why this was not possible, and what they now intend to do as the result. Leaders have specific responsibilities and accountability in the following areas.

- **Organizational expertise, knowledge and understanding.** Especially when appointed to a top, senior or key position, this means becoming actively involved and immersed in the organization at the earliest possible stage. Leaders are expected (and required) to have a full grasp of where the organization's strengths, weaknesses and priorities lie with a view to taking things on to the next stage.

- **Results.** Results are measured in terms of what was intended, and the actual outcomes; how and why these were achieved; how they were viewed at the time and subsequently by posterity; and whether this represented a good, bad or indifferent return on the resources and energy expended in their pursuit.

- **Inspiration.** In order to achieve success, leaders must be able to motivate, inspire and energize. In order that people follow, and resources are attracted to their cause, this is normally translated into a simple, direct and positive statement of where the leader is going and how and why this is to be achieved and the benefits that this is to bring to others as the result. Leaders must be capable of inspiring others – it is no use having a good idea if people do not recognize it as such.

- **Hard work.** For all of this to occur, leaders must have great stores of energy, enthusiasm, dedication, zeal and commitment. They have to inspire and energize people and resources in pursuit of the desired ends. They also set the standards for their followers – in normal circumstances, hard work cannot be expected of others if the leader is not also prepared to put this in.

- **Honesty.** People follow leaders, either because they believe in them or because it is in their interest to do so (or for a combination of the two). Leaders who fail to deliver are normally rejected or supplanted. Leaders who say one thing and mean another will not be trusted and people continue to work for them only until they can find something else.

- **Cheerleading and advocacy.** Those in leadership positions are expected to be fully enthusiastic about the organization and its future, and to demonstrate their enthusiasm and commitment in public whenever required. It is no use expecting enthusiasm and commitment from everyone else, if those in top and key positions do not have it.

- **Strategy and direction.** Leaders are expected to know and understand what the organization strategy is, how it is expected to work, and what demands will be placed on the people and resources concerned.

- **Combined long-term and short-term view.** Those in leadership positions must know in detail what is to happen over the short term, and to have a detailed grasp of everything that is required. Leaders must also have a long-term view of the organization, be able to project ahead how the organization ought to (or might) look in, for example, five years' time.

- **Focus.** Leaders are the focal point and point of identity for everybody who works in the organization. This does not mean necessarily that the top and senior managers of organizations need to be public figures; it does mean that they have to have sufficient identity within the organization to provide this focal point and the confidence that goes with it.

- **Crises and emergencies.** Leaders are expected to be able to respond adequately and effectively to crises and emergencies. A part of this requires leadership expertise in understanding where crises and emergencies might occur, and taking steps to ensure that these are kept to a minimum. When they do happen, leaders need to have a clear understanding of what has gone wrong and why, and quick and effective – and expert – responses designed to put things right.
- **Responsibility, authority and accountability.** It is additionally essential that leaders accept responsibility, authority and accountability in the context required. When things go well, it is essential that everyone knows and understands that this was a collective effort, and not purely down to the actions of the person at the top. On the other hand, when things go wrong, the leader is always accountable.

The practice of leadership also requires that those in top positions are able to create and develop senior management teams in order to ensure that the direction of the organization is as sound, clear and effective as possible. Leaders act additionally as energizers and coaches of these teams.

This short summary of the practice of leadership and what it entails indicates the range of expertise and personal traits and qualities of all those who go into any leadership or management position.

Traits and characteristics

There have been a great many studies of leaders, directors and managers from all walks of life and all parts of history. By studying a range of leaders and managers from a variety of situations and backgrounds – for example sport, politics, the military, exploration, religion and business – it is possible to infer and draw conclusions as to what the basis for their success or otherwise was and what the reasons and causes of this were. Their contribution can be assessed and analysed together with the other elements and factors present.

Attempts to identify the traits and characteristics present in successful leaders are largely inconclusive, in that none identify all the attributes necessary to lead, direct or manage in all situations. However, the following are more or less universal.

- **Communication:** the ability to communicate with all people with whom the leader comes into contact regularly, continuously and in ways and language that those on the receiving end will be able to both understand and respond to.
- **Decision-making:** the ability to take the right decisions in given situations, to take responsibility and be accountable for them, and to understand the consequences of particular courses of action. Part of this involves being able to take an overview or strategic view of particular situations, to see the longer term and to take a wider general perspective. This is sometimes called 'the helicopter view'.

- **Commitment:** to both matters in hand and also the wider aspects of the organization as a whole. This includes an inherent willingness to draw on personal, as well as professional, energies and to bring qualities of enthusiasm, drive and ambition to the particular situation.

- **Concern for staff:** respecting, trusting and committing oneself to them; developing them, understanding them and their aspirations and reconciling these with the matters in hand. Staff should be treated on a basis of equality and confidence.

- **Concern for teams and individuals:** making sure that teams remain effective, energized, resourced and suitable for purpose; and taking steps to ensure that resources and expertise are made available as and when required. When teams need reconstituting or re-energizing, this also is a leadership priority. It is also essential that leaders pay attention to the demands, drives, hopes and ambitions of individuals within the team.

- **Concern for, and commitment to, tasks and activities:** ensuring that the 'people' part of leadership is as closely related as possible to the work in hand; and again, taking steps to ensure that the work is adequately staffed and resourced.

- **Quality:** a commitment to the quality of product or service such that, whatever the matter in hand, customers receive high value and high satisfaction, and the staff involved receive recognition for their effort.

- **Values:** leaders bring a given set of values with which others will identify, and to which they will commit themselves. These values are founded in personal integrity, and the establishment of high absolute standards of conduct and performance required and demanded. Values are then additionally developed and enhanced through levels of respect accorded to all members of staff.

just a minute

It is always useful to reflect on the extent to which the possession of these traits means that individuals are seen as good leaders. It is invariably possible to identify those who are known, believed or perceived to be good leaders but who do not have all these traits; conversely, it is possible to identify individuals in leadership positions who do have all of these traits – but are perceived to be bad leaders.

Leadership styles

The rationale for studying management styles is that employees will work better for managers who use particular styles of leadership than they will for others who employ different styles (see Table 10.1 and Figure 10.1).

In practice, there is always a question of appropriateness of a management style in relation to the organization, work or situation. Very often there is an assumption or perception that more participative management styles are 'good'; in practice this is not always the case. In some industries, companies, organizations and locations, people expect to be told what to do (and in some cases, how to do it), so in these cases effective management styles have to be able to respond to this.

Table 10.1 *Leadership and management styles*

Autocratic (benevolent or tyrannical)	Consultative/participative	Democratic/participative
Leader makes all final decisions for the group.	Leader makes decisions after consultation with group.	Decisions made by the group – by consultation or vote. Voting based on the principles of one person, one vote; majority rules.
Close supervision.	Total communication between leader and members.	All members bound by the group decision and support it.
Individual members' interests subordinate to those of the organization.	Leader is supportive and developmental.	All members may contribute to discussion.
Subordinates treated without regard for their views.	Leader is accessible and discursive.	Development of coalitions and cliques.
Great demands placed on staff.	Questioning approach encouraged.	Leadership role is assumed by Chair.
Questioning discouraged.	Ways of working largely unspecified.	
Conformist/coercive environment.	Leader retains responsibility and accountability for results.	

It is also the case that where things are truly democratic, the leader has to be prepared to go along with the majority, however small that may be. The fact that the majority of people want to do something or have a preferred direction in mind does not necessarily make that right for the organization as a whole. Additionally, where there is a 51%–49% split, the preferred direction is effectively being chosen by one half of the organization only.

The use and value of the leadership continuum and spectrum is the ability to recognize how leadership is carried out; and again, once this is recognized, it can be related to what is appropriate to the situation. Again also, it is essential to recognize that in many cases, people do prefer to know and understand where they stand with the leader regardless of whether this is democratic or participative, or not.

Any management style must therefore be supported by mutual trust, respect and confidence existing between manager and subordinates. If these qualities are not present then no style is effective. There must be a clarity of purpose and direction in the first place – and this must come from the organization. Participation can only genuinely exist if this clarity exists also – it cannot exist in a void. Leadership and management styles must also be suitable and effective in terms of cultural and environmental pressures, as well as personal, professional and occupational acceptability.

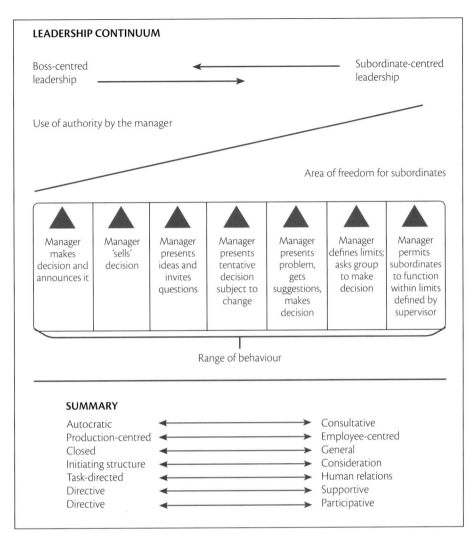

Figure 10.1 *Leadership spectrum*

These factors are interrelated. Account must also be taken of the fact that where leadership style is to be truly democratic, the decisions and wishes of the group must be accommodated, whatever is decided and whether this is 'right' or 'wrong' in terms of the demands of the work and the pressures of the wider environment.

best practice

As well as identifying the leadership style preferred by the organization and its staff, it is essential to recognize the demands of the situation. What people are used to and can respond to may or may not be appropriate; and where this is clearly not the case, the situation can be changed. However, especially in times of crisis and emergency, or extensive pioneering activity, a more prescriptive and directive form of leadership is normally appropriate.

Blake and Mouton: The managerial grid

Blake and Mouton's (2004) managerial grid is a configuration of management styles based on the matching of two dimensions of managerial concern – those of 'concern for people' and 'concern for production/output'. Each of these dimensions is plotted on a 9 point graph scale and an assessment made of the managerial style according to where they come out on each (see Figure 10.2). Thus, a low score (1–1) on each axis reflects poverty in managerial style; a high score (9–9) on each reflects a high degree of balance, concern and commitment in each area. The implication from this is that an adequate, effective and successful managerial style is in place (Figure 10.2).

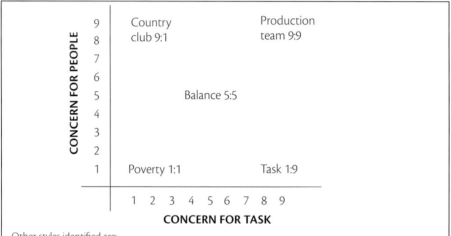

Other styles identified are:

9–1: the country club – production is incidental; concern for the staff and people is everything; the group exists largely to support itself.

1–9: task orientation – production is everything; concern for the staff is subordinated to production and effectiveness. Staff management mainly takes the form of planning and control activities in support of production and output. Organizational activity and priority is concerned only with ouput.

5–5: balance – a medium degree of expertise, commitment and concern in both areas; this is likely to produce adequate or satisfactory performance from groups that are reasonably well satisfied with working relations.

Figure 10.2 *The managerial grid*

The 9–9 score is indicated as the ideal by Blake and Mouton; and this reflects a desired position of equal concern for people and task, and the need for continuous improvement.

The managerial grid also implies that the best fit is along the diagonal line – concern for the task and concern for the people should be grown alongside each other rather than the one emphasized at the expense of the other.

The information on which the position on the grid is based is drawn from structured questionnaires that are issued to all managers and supervisors in the organization section, unit or department to be assessed, and also to all their staff. Once this is recognized, changes and improvements can be made as necessary. Especially where the task is being neglected, it becomes apparent that this must now be attended to; and where the staff are being neglected, this too can be remedied.

Best practice demands that the leadership style in particular situations and organizations is identified and then assessed for effectiveness. It is essential to recognize that leaders have to be able to call on a range of styles to fit particular situations, and that a style or approach that is ideal for one situation (for example the need to engage staff in change processes) may not be appropriate for others (for example response to crisis or emergency). It is therefore essential that those in leadership positions can change and vary their style according to the demands of the situation – and without losing their credibility, respect or integrity. The key test of any form of leadership in any situation always must be: **does it work? if so, why? if not, why not?**

Contingency approaches

Contingency and 'best fit' theories of leadership take account of the interaction and interrelation between the organization and its environment. This includes the recognition, and accommodation of, those elements that cannot be controlled. It also includes recognizing that those elements that can be controlled and influenced must be addressed in ways that vary in different situations – that the correct approach in one case is not a prescription to be applied to others. There is a constant interaction between the leader's job and the work to be done; and between this and the general operations of the organization in question. There is also the requirement to vary the leadership style according to the changing nature of the situation.

Fiedler (1967) used the contingency approach to identify situations where directive and prescriptive styles of leadership and management worked effectively. Directive and prescriptive styles could be engaged where the overall situation was very favourable to the leader; where the leader was liked, respected and trusted by the group. Tasks needed to be clearly understood, easy to follow and well defined. The leader needed to have a high degree of influence over group members in terms of reward and punishment. Additionally, the leader enjoyed unqualified support from the organization.

Directive and prescriptive styles of leadership and management were also effective from the point of view of achieving results where the situation was unfavourable to the leader. Where leaders were disliked, distrusted and disrespected by the group, where they had low degrees of influence over rewards and punishments, and where the leader did not always enjoy the full backing of the organization, concentration on tasks and outputs, together with a knowledge and understanding of the nature of leadership, meant that standard and understood levels of achievement were possible.

Reddin (1970) developed the contingency approach by identifying dimensions of:

- appropriateness and effectiveness;
- inappropriateness and ineffectiveness;

in relation to the organization, nature and composition of work groups, products and services, and environmental pressures. Reddin presented a spectrum of leadership and management behaviour as follows (see Figure 10.3).

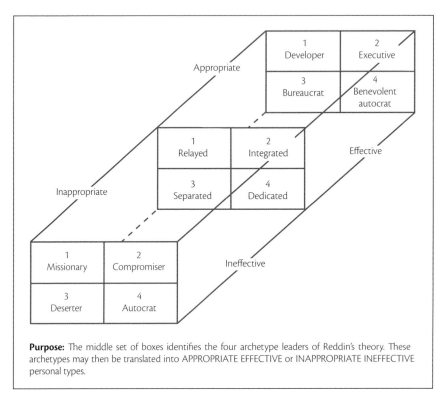

Purpose: The middle set of boxes identifies the four archetype leaders of Reddin's theory. These archetypes may then be translated into APPROPRIATE EFFECTIVE or INAPPROPRIATE INEFFECTIVE personal types.

Figure 10.3 *W.J. Reddin: Leadership and management behaviour*

Appropriate, effective

- **Bureaucrat:** low concern for both task and relationships; appropriate in situations where rules and procedures are important.
- **Benevolent autocrat:** high concern for task, low concern for relationships; appropriate in task cultures.
- **Developer:** high concern for relationships and low concern for tasks; appropriate where the acquiescence, cooperation and commitment of the people are paramount.
- **Executive:** high concern for task, high concern for relationships; appropriate where the achievement of high standards is dependent on high levels of motivation and commitment.

Inappropriate, ineffective

- **Deserter:** low concern for both task and relationships; the manager lacks involvement and is either passive or negative.
- **Autocrat:** high concern for task, low concern for relationships; the manager is coercive, confrontational, adversarial, lacking confidence in others.
- **Missionary:** high concern for relationships, low concern for task; the manager's position is dependent on preserving harmony and there is often a high potential for conflict.
- **Compromiser:** high concern for both tasks and relationships; manager is a poor decision maker, expedient, concerned only with the short term.

The contingency and best fit approaches to leadership draw attention to the specific requirement and priority to be effective in the given organization, environment, and present and evolving set of circumstances, as well as drawing attention to the critical need for an effective style. The question therefore arises as to whether or not individual leaders are capable of varying their style in response to demands; or whether it is necessary to have leaders with particular styles at which they are expert according to the precise nature of circumstances and demands.

The consequence is that leadership is in turn itself becoming more specialized and compartmentalized. In this context, it is usual to identify different types of leader, and the balance of their expertise and effectiveness, as follows.

- **Pioneer:** pioneers and pioneering leaders establish and create new products, services, brands, ventures and markets. Pioneers have a clear vision of what is possible, and through their commitment, energy, enthusiasm and ambition, they use their expertise to create and energize whatever is proposed, and see it into existence, effectiveness and profitability. Pioneers may however become ineffective once a particular venture is established, secured and viable.
- **Transformational:** transformational leaders undertake major initiatives and ventures on behalf of organizations that require 'transforming' in some way. Often appointed purely to see the particular initiative through, transformational leaders must be able to assimilate and become authoritative, comfortable and familiar in a new organizational setting very quickly and effectively.
- **Second in command:** all organizations need a 'second in command', a deputy CEO; someone to take the place of the overall leader whenever they are not present for any reason, and someone to act as a sounding board, confidant, reflector and analyst at top organizational levels. The second in command has to have their own strength of character and expertise in order to be able to debate, argue – and disagree when necessary – with persons more senior than themselves; and additionally to deliver their own expertise in ways credible and acceptable to powerful and expert personalities.

From number two to number one

There are sufficient examples of where an excellent deputy has not made the transition successfully to the top job to draw attention to the differences between the two.

The person in charge is ultimately accountable to all stakeholders, and responsible for delivering the results desired and demanded. This is very different to acting as a sounding board during the process of ensuring that the results are delivered; or ensuring that conditions are being met for entering into a specific venture or range of products and services.

The person in charge is the figurehead and point of identity of the company or organization; and the deputy is not. Anyone who moves up from second to first has to create an identity and focus for themselves in exactly the same way as someone who would have been appointed from outside the organization.

Many deputies use their elevation and new position to introduce pet schemes, projects and ventures that they have nurtured under the previous regime, but which have so far been rejected. Such schemes and ventures require the same degree of rigour and evaluation as under the previous regime.

Many former deputies fail to appoint their own adequate deputy; and this results in not having the capabilities and character close by, as confidant, sounding board and evaluator, that the new number one used to provide so effectively.

Many former deputies know, believe or perceive that they are themselves on trial, under pressure to deliver early and high profile results. Everything then becomes concentrated on producing a triumph, whether or not this is in the longer-term best interests of the organization and its stakeholders.

- **Corporate:** corporate leaders are appointed to serve the interests of primary and dominant stakeholders; and this normally means the shareholders and their representatives. Problems arise when the returns to shareholders are not made for some reason. Problems additionally arise when someone who has been successful in one industry or company and is engaged on that basis, subsequently encounters problems in the new organization.
- **Strategic leader:** strategic leaders are engaged because of their capability in seeing and envisioning the direction that a company or organization ought to take over the medium to long term. The key need for strategic leaders is the ability to engage the quality and standing of expertise required to translate the vision and strategy into action and achievement.
- **Operational leader:** operational leaders are those who provide clear leadership and direction to those who work for them when they themselves are working to a clear remit given to them by the organization. The best operational leaders do not normally make fully effective pioneers or creators. Indeed, to be effective in a chair or CEO role, corporate leaders normally have to have been given a clear remit or set of targets or directions by those who appointed them, especially shareholders.

- **Team leader:** leadership is required of all those in any position of responsibility; and team members will look to (and look up to) their leader or supervisor to address and resolve problems when these arise, and in times of crisis or difficulty, as well as for assistance with general and operational matters and issues that rise during the course of the normal working day and pattern.
- **Problem-solver and crisis leader:** problem-solvers and crisis leaders are appointed to get an organization out of a mess. Problems and crises may relate to stock market, product or service performance; or to scandals, negligence or incompetence. The key here is the ability to master the brief; and additionally to be able to address and resolve the particular problem, while at the same time restoring morale and reputation. The organization has to be left strengthened by the actions of the leader in this context; it is no use solving one problem but leaving others.

best practice

It ought to be clear from the points above that there is a great range and complexity of demands placed on leaders in different positions and situations. Sometimes, all of this is within one person's capability; sometimes, and completely legitimately, the leadership needs to change in order to respond to different problems, issues and circumstances. There is no hard and fast rule for this; each situation needs to be considered on its own merits.

point of view

The leader as servant

When Winston Churchill was appointed prime minister of Great Britain in 1940, his immediate response was: 'I am now the leader. Therefore I must serve'.

It is an often neglected part of the understanding of leadership that part of the role is to serve and support the rest of the organization, and ultimately its suppliers, customers and clients (see Figure 10.4).

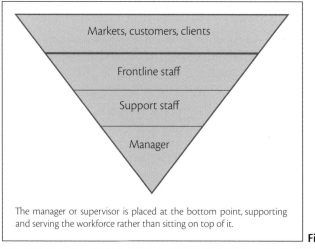

The manager or supervisor is placed at the bottom point, supporting and serving the workforce rather than sitting on top of it.

Figure 10.4 *The inverse pyramid*

As well as emphasizing one key position that all leaders ought to be able to operate in and respond to, it also relates directly to the expectations of those working in operational and other functions. They will expect that the leader will provide resources, technology and equipment; and they will expect also that when crises and emergencies do occur, they can turn to the leader to get them out of whatever mess there may be.

Measures of success and failure

The performance of those in leadership positions is assessed in simple terms against whether they delivered what they set out to achieve, or not, and the reasons for their success or failure. The broader approach to the assessment of performance of those in leadership positions relates to the key questions of confidence and complexity.

Confidence

Those who appoint others to leadership and managerial positions are normally confident at the outset that they have got the right person for the job; and following appointment, the development of mutual confidence is essential. Once those in leadership and managerial positions have lost the confidence of the people who appointed them, they normally leave.

For example, the chair of a publicly quoted company must maintain the confidence of the world's stock markets. If they do not, the share price falls. If the share price continues to fall, whatever the activities and directions proposed, the leader will normally have to leave. The need to go may also occur as the result of a bad set of company figures, either for a period or on a more continuous and long-term basis.

Confidence can also be lost among backers and stakeholders, the markets in which business is conducted, and the communities in which activities are carried out.

Confidence may also be lost where a high profile leader who is identified fully with the company suddenly leaves for some reason. This leads to a void being created; and so confidence in the company is lost as the result of the leader's departure. Where this is likely to happen, it is essential that key stakeholders, including backers and financial interests, take active steps to ensure that the person in question is replaced as quickly as possible.

Finally, confidence is only maintained through honesty and integrity. Where the leader (of anything) is caught lying, the clear, instant and unambiguous message given out is that 'he/she is a liar'. Any subsequent dealing or transaction with this particular individual is therefore invariably prefixed by questions of the extent to which they may be trusted. It is in turn exacerbated during briefings for those who are to be involved with them along the lines of 'don't believe a word they say' and 'get something in writing and get their signature'.

> The relationship between leadership and confidence is heavily dependent on perception. In many cases, the judgements placed on leaders arise out of whether others think that they are doing a good job (whether in fact they are or not).

Complexity

Measures of success and failure will also address the question of what else was achieved during the particular period of office. The direction taken may have opened up a great range of subsequent opportunities and a part of this measurement will relate to the extent to which these were exploited.

This is also to be seen in the complexity indicated. The hard targets may be achieved, for example, but only at the expense of the soft – the destruction of staff relations, motivation and morale. Conversely, a superbly integrated and supportive group may be built but one that never actually produces anything of substance. The targets that were set may turn out to have been unmeasurable, hopelessly optimistic or, conversely, far too easy. In the latter case in particular, it is both easy and dangerous to indulge in an entirely false sense of success.

The legitimacy of the objectives and performance targets must also be generally and constantly questioned. To return to the hard examples quoted above – increases in output, profit and cost effectiveness by $x\%$ should always be treated with scepticism. They assume that the basis on which the percentage is calculated is legitimate and valid. They assume that this constitutes the best use of organization resources. They assume (this especially applies to public services) that adequate and effective activity levels can be maintained.

It should be clear from this that the setting of organization performance targets is a process capable of rationalization and founded on the understanding of general organization requirements. In the particular context of leadership, it should be clear also that ultimate responsibility for the success/failure in achieving these targets rests with the leader.

It is also clear that leaders are made and not born. People can be trained in each of the qualities and elements indicated so that (as with anything else) they may first understand, then apply, then reinforce and finally become expert in these activities indicated. This is understood to be on the same basis as aptitude for anything else however. Not everyone has the qualities or potential necessary in the first place. There is nothing contentious in this – not everyone has the qualities or potential to be a great chef, racing driver, nurse or labourer, and in this respect leadership is no different.

Peters and Austin on leadership

Peters and Austin (1985) identified a comprehensive list of factors, attributes and priorities present in a 'leader'; and these they contrasted with those of the 'non-leader', as follows:

Leader	Non-Leader
• Carries water for people	• Presides over the mess
• Open door problem-solver, advice giver, cheerleader	• Invisible, gives orders to staff, expects them to be carried out
• Comfortable with people in their workplaces	• Uncomfortable with people
• No reserved parking place, dining room or lift	• Reserved parking place and dining table
• Manages by walking about	• Invisible
• Arrives early, stays late	• In late, usually leaves on time
• Common touch	• Strained with 'inferior' groups of staff
• Good listener	• Good talker
• Available	• Hard to reach
• Fair	• Unfair
• Decisive	• Uses committees
• Humble	• Arrogant
• Tough, confronts nasty problems	• Elusive, the 'artful dodger'
• Persistent	• Vacillates
• Simplifies	• Complicates
• Tolerant	• Intolerant
• Knows people's names	• Doesn't know people's names
• Has strong convictions	• Sways with the wind
• Trusts people	• Trusts only words and numbers on paper
• Delegates whole important jobs	• Keeps all final decisions
• Spends as little time as possible with outside directors	• Spends a lot of time massaging outside directors
• Wants anonymity for him/herself, publicity for the company	• Wants publicity for him/herself
• Often takes the blame	• Looks for scapegoats
• Gives credit to others	• Takes credit
• Gives honest, frequent feedback	• Amasses information
• Knows when and how to discipline people	• Ducks unpleasant tasks
• Has respect for all people	• Has contempt for all people
• Knows the business and the kind of people who make it tick	• Knows the business only in terms of what it can do for him/her
• Honest under pressure	• Equivocation
• Looks for controls to abolish	• Looks for new controls and procedures
• Prefers discussion rather than written reports	• Prefers long reports
• Straightforward	• Tricky, manipulative
• Openness	• Secrecy
• As little paperwork as possible	• As much paperwork as possible
• Promotes from within	• Looks outside the organization
• Keeps his/her promises	• Doesn't keep his/her promises
• Plain office and facilities	• Lavish office, expensive facilities
• Organization is top of the agenda	• Self is top of the agenda
• Sees mistakes as learning opportunities and the opportunity to develop	• Sees mistakes as punishable offences and the means of scapegoating

Source: adapted from Peters and Austin (1985) *A Passion for Excellence: The Leadership Difference.* Harper and Row.

Conclusions

In business, commercial and public service sector organizations, leadership is that part of management that provides the vision, direction and energy that gives life to policy, strategy and operations. It provides everyone involved – above all, the staff, but this also applies to suppliers, customers and community groups – a point of identity and focus, a personification of the organization with which they themselves are involved, and with which they are dealing. Problems always occur when the leader, for whatever reason, is either unwilling or else unable to accept the full responsibilities of the position. These problems are compounded when it becomes known, believed or perceived that the leader is acting without integrity, and is seeking to blame either circumstances or else other people for organizational, strategic and operational shortcomings. In these cases, staff only remain in employment so long as they believe it in their interests to do so; and this invariably leads to the early loss of good and high quality staff. Problems also arise when leaders accept their responsibilities to one group of stakeholders in preference to others – this is a serious problem in large public and multinational corporations when senior managers discharge their responsibilities to shareholders, political interests, and the drives of boards of directors and governors, at the expense of staff, suppliers, customers and clients.

Those who aspire to leadership positions must therefore be prepared to accept that there are certain qualities that go with the job – above all, enthusiasm, ambition, clarity of purpose, energy and direction – and must be prepared to develop these as the condition of employment in these positions. It is also important to recognize that this part of management development cannot be achieved except through a period of long-term prioritized intensive and demanding training, supported with periods of further education either at a university or conducted through the private sector. It is impossible to develop leaders purely on the basis of single or isolated short periods of training, unsupported by activities at the workplace. Moreover, it must be stressed again, that the best practitioners of a particular trade, profession or occupation do not necessarily make the best leaders and managers of groups of these staff. Assessment for leadership and management potential must be carried out on the basis of the ability to observe the fledgling qualities required, rather than existing professional and technical expertise.

It ought to be clear from the content of this chapter that leadership can be taught, learned and developed. The qualities, traits, styles and approaches indicated can all be learned; there is nothing magical or mystical about them. Organizations requiring the development of the next generation of their top and senior figures ought therefore to concentrate on these aspects, and identify members of staff who have them and who are capable of, and willing to be, developed for the future.

It is clear therefore that leadership development is going to become very much more important in the future. Organizations are certain to value much more highly the all-round capabilities and willingness to accept responsibility of those whom they place in top positions. In the medium to long term, the ability to satisfy dominant shareholder or political interests is certain not to be enough.

- Leadership is a key part of management that has its own distinctive expertise and set of demands.
- There is no 'one right way' of leading and directing organizations or activities within them; different companies, staff groups and situations require different types and styles of and approaches to leadership.
- The range of situations faced by leaders means that in some cases, a single leader will be capable, adequate and able to deal with everything; in other cases, a change in leadership is required.
- All those in leadership positions must be prepared to act as a focal point and point of identity for all the staff groups and stakeholders that they serve.
- The development of leadership expertise is certain to be much more important and critical in the future. Leadership expertise is becoming evermore sought after and prized by all organizations.

Further reading

Adair, J. (2004) *Inspirational Leadership.* Arrow.
Anderson, M. (2010) *The Leadership Book: How to Deliver Outstanding Results.* Pearson (FT series).
Blanchard, K. et al. (2010) *Leadership by the Book.* Sage.
Kotter, J. (2009) *What Leaders Really Do.* Harvard Press.
Peters, T. and Austin, N. (1985) *A Passion for Excellence: The Leadership Difference.* Harper and Row.
Ratcliffe, S. (2009) *Leadership Plain and Simple.* FTPitman (FT series).
Reddin, W.J. (1970) *Leadership and Management Behaviour.* McGraw Hill.
Schein, E. (2010) *Organizational Culture and Leadership.* Jossey Bass.

Strategy, policy, direction and priorities

The best, most profitable and most effective organizations are those clear about what they are doing; how, when, where and why they are doing it; for whom they are doing it; and what they intend the results to be. This can only be achieved, however, if a clear core or foundation for activities is established, and this is because everything else emerges and is developed from the core or foundation position.

For the sake of this clarity, organizations and their managers therefore need to establish and agree this foundation. This is because if those who are responsible for the direction of organizations are not themselves clear about this, they cannot expect anyone else to be either.

Once the core is in place, everything else can then be developed in support of this position. Marketing strategies and operations present the quality and benefits of the products and services on offer, in alignment with the overall intentions of the organization. The financial position can be clearly established, and the financial returns and rewards anticipated.

For this to be successful and effective, it is usual to recognize the core position as depending on one of the following.

- Cost leadership and advantage, in which products and services are produced to the maximum/optimum cost-effective position. Investment is driven by the need for production and service delivery technology that can deliver products and services to a sustainable position of cost advantage.
- Brand leadership and brand advantage, in which everything is driven by the need to secure a set of brand values and the real and perceived product and service quality as the result. Marketing and promotion are therefore a priority, and so

investment is required in driving, building and developing brand identities, again reinforcing the core position and giving clarity and consistency.

If it is not possible to secure either a cost advantage or brand leadership, the organization needs a distinctive alternative core position on which customer and client confidence can be secured and built, and on which the foundations of enduringly profitable and successful operations can be developed.

Part Three therefore deals with everything necessary to ensure a full understanding of the establishment of a core position, and the integration of all the other aspects into enduringly effective and productive activities. Chapter 11 covers the establishment of strategy, policy, direction and priorities. Chapter 12 covers marketing, both from a strategic and also an operational point of view, indicating how all marketing activities reinforce the development of enduringly profitable business activities.

Chapter 13 covers the different aspects of the management of projects and operations, recognizing that there are organizational and managerial aspects that have to be present if viable activities are to take place. Chapter 14 covers the nature of financial management, including how to analyse financial performance and manage finances effectively. Chapter 15 covers the nature of organizational performance, and all the different aspects and factors that have to be addressed.

Strategy, policy and direction

'All organizations have an absolute need for clear strategy.'

11

In this chapter

- what business and organization strategy are, and what they are not
- the need for a clear core and foundation position as the basis for effective activities and the ability to compete
- developing an effective and enduring strategy process using different approaches
- integrating organization sub-strategies with the main drives and priorities

Introduction

No organization is ever going to be fully effective unless it has a clear reason for existence and clearly defined direction, purpose and priorities. In other words, a strategy is needed. The overall purpose of strategy is to guide and direct the inception, growth and change of organizations as they conduct their activities. The purpose of this chapter is an introduction to the essentials of corporate policy and strategy; the form that it takes in different types of companies; the variations in strategy between companies, public services and other sectors; the issues involved in devising policy and strategy; and the development, implementation and evaluation of policy and strategy.

point of view

What strategy is not

The aim of all industrial, commercial and public service sector organizational strategies, policies, purposes and directions should be: **long-term existence in a competitive and turbulent world**.

Anything that does not contribute to this should not be contemplated. Strategy therefore is not:

- a product of focus groups contemplating what would happen in a hypothetical or imperfectly modelled set of circumstances;
- a statement of blandness or general intention that binds nobody to anything;
- about prestige, triumphalism, vanity or image – except where these factors can also be translated into successful, profitable and enduring activities;
- about growth, expansion, pioneering or exciting adventures into new and unknown territories unless underpinned by a clear rationale.

These approaches invariably lead to the avoidance of the real issues of: matching opportunities with resources; accepting the consequences of particular choices; concentration on one group of stakeholders at the expense of others; determining to satisfy all groups of stakeholders as far as possible; and above all, ensuring that everything is driven by the required and desired volumes and quality of product and service delivery.

A clearly articulated, accurate and understood strategy is at the hub of all successful commercial and public activities. Where success is not forthcoming, it is often where this clarity of purpose is also not present. This clarity additionally gives a standpoint for the need and capability to manage resources effectively and efficiently; and this continues to be intensified by requirements for greater accountability in both public and private sectors.

If you are not clear about the purpose and priorities of your organization, nobody else will be either. So it is essential to make sure that you do get this clear before you do anything else.

Core foundation and generic strategies

In order for this clarity to exist, all organizations need a core foundation or a generic strategic position on which to base all the rest of their activities. Porter (1980, 1985) identifies three generic positions from which all effective and profitable activities arise:

- **Cost leadership:** the drive to be the lowest cost operator in the field. This enables the absolute ability to compete on price where necessary. Where this is not necessary, higher levels of profit are achieved in both absolute terms and also in relation to competitors. To be a cost leader, investment is required in 'state-of-the-art' production technology and high quality staff. Cost leadership organizations are lean form with small hierarchies, large spans of control, operative autonomy, simple procedures, and excellent salaries and terms and conditions of employment. The drive for cost leadership and cost advantage is essential in any strategic approach that seeks: mass market/mass volume products and services for which price is the overriding benefit to customers; and public services and utilities delivery.

- **Focus:** concentrating on a niche and taking steps to be indispensable. The purpose is to establish a long-term and concentrated business relationship with distinctive customers based on product confidence, high levels of quality, utter reliability and the ability to produce and deliver the volumes of products required by customers when required. Investment is necessary in product technology and staff expertise. It is necessary to understand the nature of the market and its perceptions and expectations. It is also necessary to recognize the duration of the market, where developments are likely to come from and the extent to which these can continue to be satisfied.

- **Differentiation:** offering homogeneous products on the basis of creating a strong image or identity. Investment is required in marketing; advertising; brand development, strength and loyalty; and outlets and distribution. Returns are generated over the medium to long term as the result of cost awareness, identity, loyalty and repeat purchase.

Porter argues that the common factor in all successful strategies is clarity and that this stems from adopting **one** of these positions. Organizations that fail to do this do not necessarily fail themselves; they do however fail to maximize and optimize resources. Having said that, it is clearly possible to engage in long-term and profitable activities for organizations that are not the cost or brand leader; for example, there are four major supermarket chains in the UK (and many other smaller providers); and there are up to 20 very profitable and effective car manufacturers and suppliers. However, long-term, secure and profitable existence and viability are only possible for those organizations and their managers that are prepared to accept the constraints of these positions and develop a market share and products and services that are neither cost leaders nor brand leaders. It is also essential to recognize that, especially in difficult times, people will tend to gravitate towards what they know, believe, perceive and understand to be the cost or brand leader.

best practice

In simple terms, from the point of view of defining a core foundation or generic strategic position, you need to have cost leadership or advantage, brand leadership or advantage, or something else of known and understood value to particular customer and client bases.

The development of strategy, policy and direction

Corporate strategy is the outcome of a series and pattern of decisions that determine the organization's aims, objectives and goals; that produce the plans and policies required to ensure that these are achieved; that define the business in which the organization is to operate; and how it intends to conduct this business and what its relations with its markets, customers, staff, stakeholders and environment will be.

The internet revolution

The inability to attract, retain and serve customers on an enduringly commercial basis is a fundamental, invariably fatal, weakness of the vast majority of internet companies at present. Overwhelmingly, the vast amount of capital drawn into internet company start-ups was driven by:

- fashionability and faddishness, based on extensive media coverage and public relations activity surrounding what was perceived to be *a new generation* of entrepreneurs;
- the perceived technological supremacy of the internet and its infallibility as a commercial medium;
- environmental pull – in which those who were known, believed or perceived not to be at *the cutting edge* of technology were deemed to be obsolete or boring;

unfortunately:

- nobody considered the customer, consumer, client or end-user aspect in any detail;
- nobody considered how the levels of investment made in internet organizations were to generate returns, or where and when these would arrive.

The problem was also compounded by the attitude adopted by many of the new venturers and entrepreneurs when their companies ceased to trade. One virtual shoe retailer stated: 'It was a lovely place to work, and we still can't think of anything we have done wrong.'

Another, a virtual cookery and recipe production company, stated: 'We assumed that further investment funds would be forthcoming on exactly the same basis as they had been before.'

The organizations that have succeeded using the internet as their hub of activities are those that have concentrated on the enduring commercial drives in this context. Amazon, the online retailer, continues to sustain business viability through high volume, low profit margin approaches to sales. Google, the search engine company, makes its profits through its ability to sell advertising space alongside search results. Supermarket and department store chains generate internet sales largely as the result of customer familiarity with their products and services, gained over many years of traditional retail shopping.

Operational policies are based on the choices made within the overall strategic view. They are based upon a continuous appraisal of current and potential markets and spheres of activity; the ability to acquire, mobilize and harmonize resources for the attainment of the given aims, objectives and goals; and the actual means of conduct, including philosophical and ethical standpoints, and the meeting of wider social expectations (see Figure 11.1).

Effective strategy development requires that the following are understood and assessed in detail.

- The level of finance and capital required in order for the operation to be established and maintained successfully.
- The levels of income, surplus and profit that the organization needs to make and wishes to make.
- The structure of the organization that is appropriate for those operations to be carried out.
- The management style that is to be adopted and the style of leadership, direction and supervision.

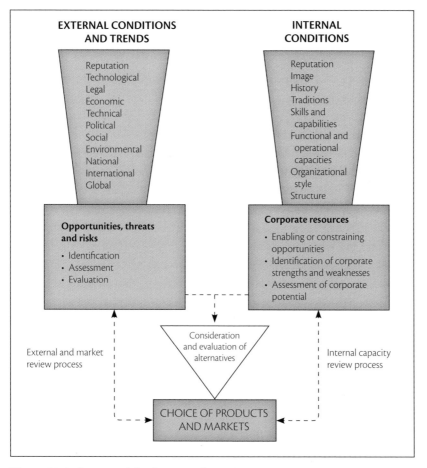

Figure 11.1 *Source and development of organization strategy*

Whatever you decide to do, you have to relate your own expertise and ambitions to what is (and is potentially) available in the market in terms of customer and client bases, and willingness to come to you for the particular products and services.

- The priorities that are to be placed on each of the operations; the markets and sectors in which business is to be conducted.
- The timescales involved, especially where these are long term, and therefore difficult to predict.

Strategic development and timescales: Examples

The long-term nature of strategic development, essential if the overriding aim of long-term viability and existence is to be contemplated, is often in direct conflict with financial, competitive and other stakeholder drives for short-term, indeed immediate, financial results and advantages. Timescale issues have to be known and understood, however, if strategy development is to be successful. For example:

- **The airline industry:** it was not until the 1930s, a generation after the first manned flight took place, that anyone was able to produce a sustainable, commercially profitable airline, operating on a regular schedule of routes. The concept of flight as a means of mass travel took 35 years to develop into something that was commercially viable. The airline industry has time constraints around each one of its core operations. It is only possible to change route networks and destinations during periods when landing and take-off slots are made available. It then takes time to build a customer base, familiarity and confidence in the viability and permanence of the new routes. There are timescale issues at departure and arrival points (the need to check in early for security reasons; the need to wait for baggage to be delivered to the arrival halls).
- **The airliner industry:** it is additionally the case that new generations of airliners take many years to develop. The Airbus A380, the largest plane ever built and capable of carrying up to 800 passengers, took 10 years from conception to delivery. Demand for medium-size airliners capable of travelling long distances without refuelling has also led to commitments of between 5 and 10 years on the part of both Boeing and Airbus, which remain the world's dominant suppliers of commercial planes. These constraints go directly against the short-term pressures for financial results. It is true that both Boeing and Airbus deliver continuing financial results in the form of continuing sales of existing products. The need to commit to the level of resources required over the long term to ensure that the industry and companies are able to sustain themselves and produce the next generation of products remains, however, an essential feature of the industry; and those responsible for backing strategic development have to know, understand and accept this, or else move their funds elsewhere.

The foundations of organization strategy

It is usual, having defined the core position, to establish:

- a grand strategy, which is a clear statement of the vision and direction of the organization, customer bases served, and the quality and value of the products and services on offer;
- sub-strategies, which define the internal strategies and policies required to ensure long-term organizational effectiveness and viability, relating activities to the grand strategy.

Internal strategies and policies

Effective and successful organization strategy is dependent upon integrated and complementary internal policies as follows.

- **Financial, investment, budgeting and resourcing** strategies, concerned with both the underwriting and stability of the organization, and also the maintenance of its daily activities.
- **Human resource** strategies designed to match the workforce and its capabilities with the operational requirements of the organization; and related policies on ensuring the supply of labour; effective labour relations; and the maintenance and development of the resource overall.
- **Organizational design and development** so that the required size, scope, structure, technology and expertise are in place.
- **Marketing** strategies, designed to ensure that the organization's products and services are presented in such ways as to give them the best possible impact and prospects of success on the chosen markets.
- **Capital resource and equipment** strategies, to ensure the continued ability to produce the required value and quality of output to the standards required by the markets; and to be able to replace and update these resources in a planned and ordered fashion (that is, including research and development and commissioning of new products and offerings).
- **Communication and information** strategies, both for the organization's staff and its customers/clients, designed to disseminate the right quantity and quality of information in ways acceptable to all.
- **Organization, maintenance, development and change** strategies, for the purpose of ensuring that a dynamic and proactive environment is fostered; a flexible and responsive workforce; and an environment of continuous improvement and innovation.
- **Ethical factors** including establishing overall standards of attitude and behaviour; absolute standards in dealings with customers, suppliers and the

community; specific approaches to the environment, corporate citizenship; the nature and quality of leadership.

- **Subjective elements** – a recognition that strategy is a process, requiring particular clarity and direction, ought also to ensure that subjective elements, reflecting collective and individual preferences and priorities, are examined in order to establish that they deliver value to the organization and contribution to its long-term viability. If this cannot be proved or demonstrated, then subjective elements need to be removed.

The outcome of all of this ought to be a business model – a fully integrated direction and purpose for the organization. The business model then needs to be translated into:

- a clarity of overall purpose which is capable of being conveyed to what customers, clients, staff and backers expect to see;
- a reflection of the organization size, structure, location and standing;
- a product and service portfolio which the organization can produce to the quality and volume demanded by customers and clients;
- a clear knowledge and understanding of where value is being added and lost;
- a clear knowledge and understanding of the value placed on products and services by particular groups of customers and clients;
- a clear knowledge and understanding of the regularity and frequency with which purchases will be made.

Additionally and crucially, the outcome is a clearly defined position for future development, as well as present activities. It therefore ought to be clear that strategy is a process and not an activity.

Core and peripheral activities

Core activities

Core activities reflect primary purpose and may be assessed in terms of:

- **volume of activity**: what most people do, or what most resources are tied up in;
- **profit and income**: where most of the money comes in from;
- **image and identity**: that which gives the organization its position, status and prominence in the sphere in which it operates;
- **perceptions**: what people, especially customers, clients and backers, think your core business is, and what they are prepared to get involved with.

Peripheral activities

These are the other activities in which the undertaking gets involved. They must not be at the expense of the main or core activities, nor should they be a drain on resources. Rather they should enhance the core activities, or reflect niche or segment opportunities that exist as the result of the core business. Such activities will nevertheless be essential, expected, and extremely profitable. A hospital is not 'in business' to sell food, sweets, newspapers, books, cards, fruit and flowers; nevertheless, it is essential for a variety of operational and social reasons that these activities are undertaken. Similarly, a car company will invariably make additional parts for the replacement, service and spares sectors; these simply require some form of repackaging or 'differentiation' to generate additional business in an obvious and profitable area of activity.

Strategies for failure

While it is impossible to predict with absolute accuracy where success and failure are likely to occur – especially if a rigorous approach is not taken – it is possible to indicate likely causes of failure. These are:

- **Increased price/standard value:** risks loss of market share, especially where lower price, undifferentiated alternatives are available to the same quality and value.
- **High and increasing prices/low value:** this is unlikely to be sustainable in the long term in anything but a monopoly situation. Where perceived quality and value for money are not forthcoming, customers and clients will change from using such organizations if they have any choice in the matter at all.
- **Standard price/declining value:** this occurs where people continue to pay the same price for products and services, but where the volume and/or quality are decreased. This position is only sustainable as long as the declining value nevertheless continues to meet customers' expectations. When this ceases to be so, customers will look elsewhere for satisfaction.
- **Low value/standard price:** in these cases, customers and clients perceive that they are over-paying for a reduced or basic level of benefits and satisfaction. Especially where there is no cost advantage possible, organizations finding themselves in this position are at immediate risk either from others who improve quality and value levels, or from those who reduce prices in order to reflect existing levels of quality and value.
- **Present activities, products and services/unknown markets and sectors:** this occurs where assumptions are made that, because the organization is successful in its existing markets, other markets will also value the products and services. It is essential that new markets are tested before commitment is made so as to be sure that there is indeed space in the sectors targeted.

Any strategic approach that is based on each of these is sustainable only as long as there is a relatively captive medium to long-term customer and client base. For example, petrol retailing manages to secure medium to long-term advantages under the heading of **increased price/ standard value** simply because their product is such a fundamental commodity of the present state of civilization. Some privatized health and social care organizations are able to sustain themselves under **increased price/low value** and **low value/standard price** because of the political drive to place clients of these organizations; and the activities are underwritten to some extent by government policy and willingness to pay. Nevertheless, serious disadvantage is certain to be reached if there is ever a political drive to improve the quality and value aspects, or if new organizations come into the sector able to deliver the quality and value required at a price that is acceptable to the sector.

In recent years, as the result of the internet revolution, a further indicator of likely failure has become apparent:

- **Standard price/low convenience:** in which customers and clients are required to search for products and services on the internet. Even assuming that the correct company website can be found, problems are often compounded by the fact that while the site is technologically brilliant, it is customer and end-user unfriendly. It is also increasingly apparent that, at least in commercial–consumer transactions, it is essential for the virtual presence to be reinforced by helplines, or increasingly, an access to a physical presence alongside.

Strategic approaches

All effective organization strategies must have the following components.

- **Performance targets,** in whatever terms these are to be measured (for example income, volume, quality, but set against measurable, understandable and achievable targets).
- **Deadlines that are achievable,** that have been worked out in advance, and that represent a balance between commitment, resources and contingencies.
- **Contingencies** built in, to cover the unlikely, and the emergency.
- Consideration of the **long-term effectiveness** of the organization, as well as short-term results.
- Consideration of the organization's **products and services** in terms of value and quality, and utility to customers, clients, consumers and end-users.

Outcomes

Outcomes should be pre-evaluated in terms of the following (see Figure 11.2). In particular, the level of bare acceptability of the outcome of a particular strategy should be assessed at the stage of devising strategy.

Outcomes should be extrapolated from each of these positions to try and envisage the following stage of the organization's activities and the wider implications for the short, medium and long term.

Having established the need for a core foundation or generic position, the main approaches to strategy, development and implementation are as follows.

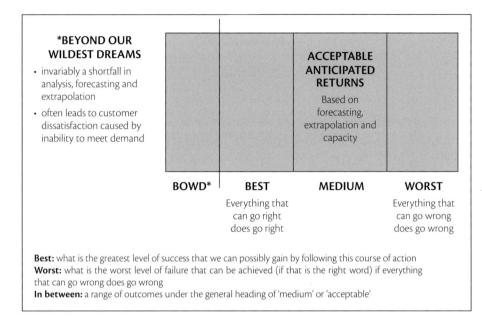

Figure 11.2 *Pre-evaluation of strategy, policy and direction*

You need then to decide whether everything that is posed is acceptable in terms of return on investment, reputation development and enhancement, and customer and client service.

Growth strategies

Growth is measured against preset objectives, whether in terms of income, profit margins, shareholder value, reputation enhancement, income per customer, income per location, income per product, market share, sales volume and new products and services. Required, expected or anticipated measures of growth, and the reasons and timescales for these, must be stated in advance. How such strategies are to be supported, financed and resourced, and the implications of this, must also be clearly stated and understood. The staff concerned must know this and the implications involved.

Acquisitions, mergers and takeovers are all variations on the theme of growth. Again, these approaches must be set against preset objectives, and with the overall view to enhancing the profitability and/or quality of the business. In support of this, what may actually happen is to introduce the organization into new geographical areas to increase the sectoral position; it may also help to defend and protect the organization's own position.

Such activities may also include the acquisition of suppliers and distributors and sources of raw materials; this is known as 'vertical integration'.

They may additionally represent niche opportunities, the ability to get into new and profitable market sectors, to purchase the client list, resource or base of a competitor, or parallel operator.

just a minute

Whenever proposals for growth are being considered, you always need to ask yourself: 'Is growth a good thing; and if so, why?' It is very easy to be led down the path that 'all growth is good'. Growth has to be sustainable and capable of being accommodated either by the resources that are presently available or by those that can be made available on a cost-effective basis.

Retrenchment

Retrenchment is usually the withdrawal from niche or peripheral activities; the sale of assets; the concentration on the core activity. It need not have negative connotations; for example, an organization may sell off its lorry fleet and lease lorries at a time of credit squeezes and high interest rates. On the other hand, where there are negative connotations, effective retrenchment will have the overall purpose of protecting the core business and the certain markets (in so far as there are any) at the expense of the niches in which the organization has been operating.

Retrenchment in relation to core activities may need to occur as the result of changes in market demands, and customer needs and wants. Retrenchment from core activities becomes serious when it calls into question the overall viability of the organization's primary ranges of products and services; and if this is truly necessary, organizations normally need to have something with which to replace them.

Retrenchment activities in public services are very often the cause of operational crisis because there has to be every attempt to maintain the level of service against a declining budget provision.

Diversification

This is where organizations take the conscious decision to move into new markets and activities, very often in spite of the fact that there is no particular expertise in the new chosen field. Expertise in the new field, and the assimilation of its modus operandi, must be acquired by the organization if it is to be successful.

In practice, most effective and successful diversification strategies follow the vertical integration patterns, moving into new sectors that are clearly indicated by the current core business. For example, the Murdoch organization moved into satellite television; it had no particular expertise in television or satellite technology but, looked at from a different standpoint, was a major player in mass media and communications.

The Virgin Group

The move by the Virgin Group into the business of airline operation, financial services and railways from music, video and record distribution was, and remains, successful; but to do it required extensive research, projections, expertise acquisition, and market understanding on the part of what was hitherto essentially a chain of shops. There were certain assets perceived by the group of which it could take advantage as it moved into other areas – a large customer base, strong UK image, reputation for quality, and public confidence; however, these were qualities that had, in practice, to be refashioned by the new airline for itself. Moreover, any failure on the part of the new venture would have had serious consequences for continuing and future confidence in the rest of the group's activities.

The Virgin Group's approach to involvement in new ventures is based on:

- the proposed new sector of activities is already well established and served by other providers;
- the service provided by other organizations falls short in some way – especially perceived customer satisfaction;
- there must be commercial and profitable potential for engagement in 'the Virgin way';
- there must be potential for developing the sector using the existing Virgin customer base;
- there must be a sense of fun and adventure.

Provided that any proposal meets at least four of these points, the company will consider it seriously.

Price leadership

The organization in this case sets out to gain the reality and the reputation of being the market player with the lowest prices, and to ensure that everyone who purchases from the organization knows this. This will not be entirely at the expense of quality: products and services still have to be good enough to attract people to purchase in the first place.

Some price leadership activities are spectacularly successful such as the sale of petrol by British and European supermarket chains. Supermarkets in Europe and North America do adopt 'pile it high, sell it cheap' strategies, but this is generally limited to certain products. 'Do-It-Yourself' chains will generally have some products at good prices for the consumer. The concept is most widely developed as 'loss leadership', rather than as price leadership. The IKEA furniture chain, however, is making attempts at present to expand across the countries of the EU, on the premise and image that all its prices are low and represent better value than the indigenous competition.

Branding strategies

Branding strategies concentrate on using a combination of marketing, operational, technological and professional activities in order that an instant perception of the company product or service in question is fixed in the mind of the customer or client (and also the community at large) immediately they see the brand name. A strategic approach to branding usually considers one or more of the following points of view.

- **Global branding**: examples are McDonald's and Coca-Cola, whereby a set of core business drives – in the case of McDonald's, quality, value, cleanliness and convenience – are presented in ways that will generate the maximum response from the particular location in question.
- **National**: in which particular marketing strategies are devised to generate the required responses among particular nations of the world.
- **Organizational**: in which the organization seeks to attach organizational values to any line of business or activity into which it chooses to go. For example, Virgin attaches a single name – its own – to its airline, music, bridal wear, publishing, and high-tech activities; Heinz attaches a single name to its food products, whether they are for babies, children or adults, and whether they are standard, good value, healthy option or high value. Supermarkets also offer extensive ranges of their own brand products, though with very few exceptions sell these alongside other branded goods thus offering the maximum range of consumer choice.
- **Organizational diversity**: in which organizations adopt different brand names according to different product lines and/or different markets served. For example, Sony offers high quality, high value, premium price ranges of electrical goods under its own name; it offers medium quality and medium priced goods under the name AIWA; and it offers computer products under the name VAIO. Similarly, Matsushita offers commercial electrical goods under its own name, and consumer electrical goods under the name Panasonic.
- **Local**: in which smaller organizations seek to gain a local presence and reputation through being good corporate citizens, model employers, or high quality, high value servants of local markets. The ability to brand locally is very often the driving force for niche or focus strategies.

Market domination

Strategies aimed at market domination normally adopt and adapt components from each of the above to ensure a dominant position. Domination may be by sales volume, assets, derived income, largest number of outlets, or outlets in the most places (or a combination of some or all of these). It may also arise as the result of being the majority supplier (that is, holding more than 50% of the market); the largest single player, though with less than 50%; or one of an oligopoly of operators (in some countries and sectors, this may be organized into a cartel, though this is illegal in many sectors and many countries).

It is still quite rare to find massive majority dominators of sectors, though there are exceptions. For example, Ryanair handles about 40% of UK short and medium-haul air traffic; EasyJet about 30%; and British Airways about 23%. Tesco handles about 30% of food and grocery sales; Sainsbury's about 18%; Asda about 16%; and Morrisons about 12%. Organization domination is otherwise limited to gas, electricity, water, telecommunications and public road and rail transport. Commercial oligopolies are also found in media, newspapers, cars, and oil and petrol sales.

Incremental strategies

The view of strategy as being incremental is popular with those who argue a rational approach to long-term business and public service sustenance. The reasoning is that a genuine long-term strategy is actually impossible to achieve given the sophisticated structure of organizations, and the turbulence and instability of markets and sector activities, without paying constant attention to direction and purpose. A successful approach to long-term viability has therefore to be seen as being constantly influenced by changing environmental, social, political and economic circumstances.

The starting point for future strategies is therefore the position of the organization today. From this, the organization moves forwards in small steps or increments. As each of these steps is successful, the next becomes apparent. If a mistake is made, it is easy to retrace the step and seek other directions from the previous position. The status quo and present levels of performance are both taken as correct. If costs are reduced or if profits have gone up in relation to last year, this is a good general measure of performance. If costs have risen or profit has declined in relation to the previous period, this becomes a cause for concern.

Opportunities arise from the fact that the organization is moving slowly enough to recognize and evaluate those situations that present themselves before rushing in headlong, or rejecting out of hand.

Measurement and evaluation

Measurement and evaluation are carried out against the preset aims and objectives of the particular strategy; quantifiable where possible, areas of particular success or shortfall will be apparent, contributing to the organization's expertise in the field and ensuring further improvement in the strategic and planning processes for the future.

Beyond this, evaluation is both a continuous process and the subject of more formalized regular reviews at required and appropriate intervals, thus setting a framework against which the strategy is to be judged.

The following can then be assessed.

- The extent to which the strategy is **identifiable**, clearly understood by all concerned, in specific and positive terms; the extent to which it is unique and specifically designed for its given purpose.
- Its **consistency** with the organization's capabilities, resources and aspirations; and the aspirations of those who work in it.
- The levels of **risk** and **uncertainty** being undertaken, in relation to the opportunities identified.
- The **contribution** that the proposed strategy is to make to the organization as a whole over the long term.
- Market **responses** and **responsiveness**; degrees of market captivity or choice.
- The effects – **positive and adverse** – of dominant stakeholders, driving and restraining forces, and product, service and project champions.

These questions can be answered as part of both the continuous evaluation and the regular review process.

Implementation of strategy

The determination of strategy is therefore a combination of: the identification of the opportunities and risks afforded by the environment; the capabilities, actual and potential, of the organization, its leaders and top management; and issues of ethical and social responsibility. Turning this into reality requires that the following are addressed.

- **Key tasks** must be established and prioritized, effective decision-making processes drawn up, and systems for monitoring and evaluation of strategic process devised.
- **Work and workforce** must be divided and structured to a combination of functional and hierarchical aspects, designed to ensure the effective completion of the tasks in hand; this must include relevant and necessary committee, project coordination, working party, and steering group activities (see Figure 11.3).
- **Information** and other management systems must be designed and installed; control and constraint systems must be a part of this and include financial, human resource, production, output and sales reporting data.
- Tasks and actions to be carried out must be **scheduled** and **prioritized** in such a way as to be achieved to given deadlines. As well as establishing a background for precise work methods and ways of working, scheduling provides the basis for setting standards against which short and medium-term performance can be measured.
- The **required technology** must be made available, and staff trained to use it.
- **Maintenance** and **repair** schedules must be agreed and integrated with other activities.
- **Research** and **development**, improvement and enhancement schedules must be incorporated with the rest of activities. This includes making financial,

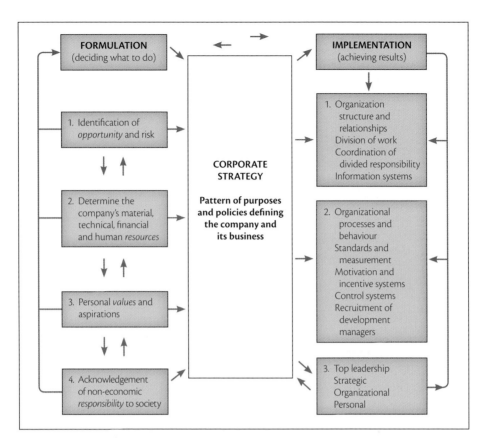

Figure 11.3 *The implementation of strategy*

technological and staff resources available as a key part of organization product
and service development.

- **Monitoring, review** and **evaluation mechanisms** and **procedures**, attending to
  hard aspects of market responses, sales figures and product and service usage;
  and *soft* aspects of meeting customer, client, consumer and end-user satisfaction
  and expectations.
- The **measurement** of **actual performance** against forecasted, projected or
  budgeted activities.
- **Staff management** and **human resource** polices must be assessed for
  effectiveness and quality; the extent and prevalence of conflict, communication
  blockages, disputes and grievances; the effectiveness of pay and reward systems;
  the application of rule books and specific procedures.
- **Financial returns** must be assessed in line with projections and forecasts. A key
  feature of strategy implementation is the ability to compare overall returns, costs
  of sales, product and service delivery with projections; and to gauge the effects of
  unforeseen circumstances on particular activities.

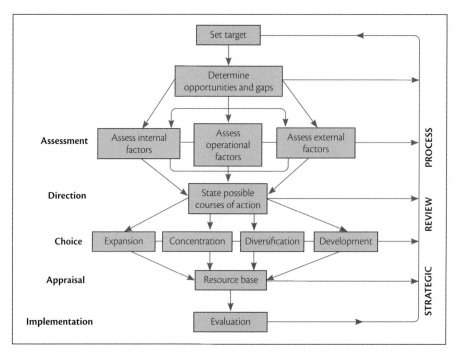

Figure 11.4 *The monitoring, review and evaluation of strategy and direction*

Each of these aspects provides a critical element for effective monitoring, review and evaluation activities (see Figure 11.4).

Conclusions

A successful strategic approach can only be achieved if the ways in which the particular sector operates are fully understood and analysed. This analysis must also depend on gaining as full an understanding as possible of customer and client behaviour, demands, wants and needs.

Ideally, the main outcome of these analyses is an informed base for those responsible for organizational direction. This should consist of a full understanding of the wider environment and general pressures that exist, as well as the more specific aspects indicated.

It is important in the process of educating and informing all managers, and especially top managers, to think strategically, as well as operationally, and to relate the two directly. All the approaches and models indicated should cause managers to look beyond their operations, activities and areas of responsibility to the wider context, and from the short to the long term. They also act as initial indicators of opportunities and threats. Areas of risk and uncertainty should start to become apparent and points of stress and strain that may be created by following certain directions should also be indicated, especially if the full environment has not been analysed.

These activities are not ends in themselves. The key to successful strategic management lies in how the information gained is evaluated and used; how accurately the particular position of the organization is assessed. Organizations must be able to translate this into effective activity based on their own strengths of flexibility, dynamism, responsiveness and commitment. They must also be able to recognize potential weaknesses and pitfalls, and take whatever steps are necessary to address these.

- All organizations have an absolute need for clear strategy as this informs clarity of purpose and priorities, and what customers and clients can expect from their dealings with the organization.
- In support of this clarity, there is an overriding need for a clear core foundation or generic position which must be based either in seeking cost advantage, brand advantage, or something else that is of value to the markets served.
- Strategy is a process, driven by a need to integrate all activities in the pursuit of the stated organizational purpose and priorities.
- Strategy must always be monitored, reviewed and evaluated for effectiveness. Where problems are likely to arise, or where present position is becoming unsustainable, strategic, as well as operational, decisions need to be taken.
- Strategy is a continuous process requiring attention to the long term as well as to immediate results. The strategy process is a critical aspect of developing opportunities and activities for the future, as well as ensuring what is done at present remains effective.

Further reading

Campbell, D., Edgar, D. and Stonehouse, G. (2011) *Business Strategy: An Introduction.* Palgrave Macmillan.
Johnson, G., Scholes, K. and Whittington, R. (2009) *Exploring Corporate Strategy.* PHI.
Pettinger, R. (2004) *Contemporary Strategic Management.* Palgrave Macmillan.
Porter, M. (1980) *Competitive Strategy.* Free Press.
Porter, M. (1985) *Competitive Advantage.* Free Press.
Whittington, R. (2009) *What is Strategy and Does it Matter.* Thomson.

Marketing

'Marketing strategies should always relate to core foundation and generic organization and business strategies.'

In this chapter

- the nature of marketing and its position in developing effective business and organizational activities
- knowing and understanding the components of effective marketing strategies, processes and activities
- managing the development of products and services
- identifying, managing and developing customer bases

Introduction

The purpose of this chapter is to introduce and illustrate the priorities and principles required for a full understanding of marketing.

Marketing is the competitive process by which goods and services are offered for consumption at a profit. Marketing combines product and service substance with effective presentation, convenience, value and acceptability to engage the interest and commitment of customers, consumers and clients, and the public at large.

Marketing processes and activities are normally classified as follows.

- **Consumer marketing:** which comes in two basic forms:
  - unconsidered purchases, leading to instant satisfaction (or dissatisfaction);
  - considered, high value purchases, leading to enduring satisfaction (or dissatisfaction).

- **Industrial and business-to-business marketing**: unconsidered purchases (for example the office coffee) and considered purchases (for example capital goods, databases); and based on the development of relationships so that considered purchases carry trust and confidence, as well as enduring utility.
- **Public services marketing**: an area in which substantial development is required, particularly in response to political drives to engage commercial interests in these activities.
- **The not-for-profit sector**: advantages gained by engaging interest, sympathy and, above all, action from those targeted.
- **Internal marketing**: activities designed to build mutuality of interest and confidence, and enduring workplace relations, across organizations.
- **General marketing**: including communications, television advertisements, posters, internet straplines, all designed to reinforce general impressions of products and services.
- **Internet and digital marketing**: considered as a marketing process and activity in its own right because all companies and organizations now have an internet presence (whether for commercial purposes and sales or not), and this approach and presentation is therefore a key part of marketing. As more and more data is known about consumers, this also enables products and services to be directed very much more precisely.
- **Viral marketing**, in which keys are found for products and services, presented to the first wave of consumers, who then spread the benefits through social media and websites.
- **Direct marketing**: targeting individuals, and customer and client groups with specific products and services known, believed and perceived to be of direct interest to them.

A core outcome of the marketing process is the development of relationships between the organization and its customers and clients. Every interaction between the organization, its staff and customers makes a contribution to the development of these relationships. This is a function of generating customer loyalty, and in getting customers to relate that loyalty to purchasing and consumption activities.

Marketing processes and activities have the immediate goal of:

- attracting customers and drawing attention to the products and services on offer;
- gaining the potential customer's interests, and encouraging them to find out more;
- generating the desire to purchase the products and services;
- making it easy and convenient for the customers to actually purchase the products and services.

Relationships and loyalties are built, maintained and developed through the combination of product and service quality on offer; immediate and after-sales activities; and the continued ability of the customers to buy, use and consume the products and services in ways that are of value to them.

All marketing activities need to be seen as building relationships between organization products, services, customers and clients. A key part of marketing is therefore ensuring that these relationships are based on trust and confidence. Overwhelmingly, given any choice in the matter, people buy products and services from companies and organizations they trust, and with whom they perceive they have a positive and productive relationship.

Customer needs and wants: The Packard approach

Packard (1957) sought to define the relationship between product, presentation and image, and customer and consumer motivation. The conclusions were that the most successful marketing of products and services arose when both the product and also its presentation engaged one or more of the following responses among customers, clients, consumers and end-users.

- **Emotional security, comfort and confidence:** related to bulk purchases of food; safety features in cars; domestic security; and insurance.
- **Reinsurance of worth:** purchases must make customers feel good. This means that customers have to be satisfied with the products and services on offer; and their use of the products and services must also be respected and valued by others around them.
- **Ego gratification:** anything that is sold to gratify the ego must meet the subjective demands of luxury, exclusivity and immortality. Products and services sold to gratify the ego include expensive luxury cars, exclusive holidays, and vanity publishing.
- **Creativity:** products and services sold to feed the creativity need put a critical value on the contribution of the customer or end-user to make the product effective. For example, cake mixes that required the addition of eggs were found to be more successful than those that simply required the addition of water, because there was a greater input on the part of the user or consumer.
- **Love objects:** this aspect may be summarized as: 'cuddly toy', 'dear little child', or 'sweet/cute little animal'. Andrex, the major suppliers of toilet tissue to the UK retail sector, has used labrador puppies as the central feature of its commercials since the 1970s. Children are used extensively in television commercials in the pursuit of engendering this sense of love and warmth; and this extends to the marketing of washing powder, grocery shopping, fast food, cars, holidays, central heating and double-glazing.
- **Power:** the power of the product or offering is reflected in the user of it. Nearly all automobile advertising and marketing is on the basis of power, performance and speed as well as security. Power and strength are also strongly related to cigarette marketing,

especially in Formula 1 motor racing, and also the sponsorship of cricket, rugby league, sailing and powerboat racing.

- **Traditions and roots:** this is relating 'the good old days' to the modern era. For example, food promotions use phrases such as: 'just as good as mother used to make'; Rolls-Royce cars maintain the traditions of fittings and furnishings, and reliability and exclusivity on which their original reputation was built. Politicians exploit perceptions and visions of golden ages with calls for returns to 'traditional values' and 'back to basics' because there is a very strong perception of 'the good old days' and association with historic success, order, stability and prosperity.
- **Immortality:** this is related to security, ego gratification and traditions and roots. Maintaining the illusion of immortality is an essential prerequisite to the effective marketing of housing, life assurance, other insurances, loans and other financial products.

People buy products and services for the value, benefits and satisfaction delivered; and the work of Packard sought to indicate that maximizing the chances of delivering benefits and satisfaction required targeting at least one of the above points.

It is additionally the case, that by using a managerial approach to marketing and product and service presentation using the above criteria, it was much easier to target the subjective (rather than perceived or pseudo-rational) needs of customers, consumers, clients and end-users.

Source: Packard (1957).

Marketing strategies

As stated in Chapter 11, all organizations require a core foundation or generic strategic position; and all effective marketing strategies consequently need to reflect the core foundation or generic position chosen. Marketing strategies are then used to build on the core foundation or generic position as follows.

- **Pioneering or 'first in the field'**: opening up new markets or new outlets for existing products, and new products for existing outlets; taking an original and distinctive view of the marketing process and devising new methods and campaigns.
- **'Follow the leader'**: the great benefit of being second in the field is to learn from the mistakes and experience of the pioneer, and make informed judgements about the nature of the involvement to be taken based on their experience. Or it may be that the second organization can see opportunities that were not exploited by the first.
- **'Me too' or 'all-comers'**: where the market is wide open, entry to, and exit from, it are relatively easy when the products and services in question are universal or general, and when there are many suppliers, provided there are more buyers than suppliers.

- **Supply led:** where the product is produced because the organization has complete faith in it and knows that once made, it will be able to be sold at a profit.
- **Technology led:** whereby the organization finds itself in a particular line of business because it has at its disposal a particular type of technology which can be turned to productive and profitable advantage in a variety of sectors.
- **Staff led:** because of the skills, qualities and preferences of the staff of an organization that happen to be gathered together, and where the products or offerings reflect these (very prevalent in the small business sphere).
- **Market led:** where the organization looks first at a range of markets, then assesses their requirements, and finally decides which of these it can most valuably and profitably operate in and fill.
- **Moral or ethical marketing:** creating and developing a high value reputation as the result of a distinctive moral or ethical stance, such as using Fairtrade ingredients (for example Starbucks); or using trading practices as a presentational feature (for example Waitrose).

In relation to each of the above, marketing strategies may be either offensive or defensive. Offensive marketing activities seek to make inroads into the competitive position and customer and client bases of others. Defensive and responsive marketing activities are undertaken with the object of preserving the present position in response to the offensives of others.

just a minute

You need to recognize that in practice, all marketing is a combination of offensive, defensive and responsive activities. Concentrating purely on the offensive means that you are running the risk of neglecting your existing customer base. Concentration purely on the defensive means that you are likely to be missing opportunities elsewhere.

Segmentation

Effective marketing demands that the needs and wants of customers and clients are defined as precisely as possible. It is therefore essential to be able to 'segment' or classify the population in some way. The normal approaches are: social segmentation; market and social segmentation; and customer definition.

Social segmentation

Social segmentation breaks down the population according to the occupation of the head of household as follows.

A   Aristocrats and upper middle class, directors, senior managers, senior civil and public servants

B   Middle class, lawyers, doctors, senior managers

C1 Lower middle class, teachers, nurses, doctors, engineers, technologists, managers

C2 Skilled working class, including some engineering and technology activities

D   Working class

E   Subsistence, including the underclass and unemployed

Market and social segmentation

Market and social segmentation has existed in the UK since 1998, when the UK national Office of Population Censuses and Surveys produced the following framework.

- **Class 1A**: large employers, higher managers, company directors, senior police, fire, prison, military officers, newspaper editors. The structure also included top football managers and restaurateurs in this section.
- **Class 1B**: professionals – doctors, solicitors, engineers, teachers. This section also included airline pilots.
- **Class 2**: associate professionals, journalists, nurses, midwives, actors, musicians, military NCOs, junior police, fire, prison officers. This section also includes lower managers (with fewer than 25 staff).
- **Class 3**: intermediate occupations – secretary, air stewards and stewardesses, driving instructors, telephone operators. This section also includes 'employee sports players', for example footballers and cricketers.
- **Class 4**: small employers, managers of small departments, non-professional self-employed, publicans, plumbers, farm owners and managers. This section also includes self-employed sports players – for example golfers and tennis players.
- **Class 5**: lower supervisors, crafts and related workers, electricians, mechanics, train drivers, bus inspectors.
- **Class 6**: semi-routine occupations, traffic wardens, caretakers, gardeners, shelf stackers, assembly line workers.
- **Class 7**: routine occupations, cleaners, waiter/waitress/bar staff, messenger/courier, road worker, docker.
- **Class 8**: the excluded. This includes the long-term unemployed, those who have never worked, the long-term sick, and prison populations.

Clearly, social segmentation is subjective and imprecise. However, it is essential to start somewhere in order to begin to define the nature, habits and behaviour of the customer bases desired. When customer bases have been classified, it should never be forgotten that this has been done with a lack of precision and a measure of subjectivity. Once the customer base has been defined in this way however, there is in turn a basis for much greater and more precise customer analysis (see Chapter 2).

Whatever the customer base defined, it is essential to recognize the difference between:

- 'Would buy'
- 'Will buy'

You are looking at all times for customer bases that will buy products and services from you in the volumes and regularity that you need. Getting a 'generally favourable response' to your products, services and activities is very comforting but it does not generate business volumes.

Customer definition

Customer and segment definition is defined according to one of the classifications above; and then this is further refined by identifying in detail the customers required by: age, sex/gender, status, aspiration, values, location, occupation and expectations. Marketing then concentrates on defining products and services in terms of the benefits of value to the given and precisely defined segments.

Additional approaches to customer definition produce the following information:

- types and class of buyers;
- size of customer bases in given locations and niches;
- the balance of quality, volume and price that customers expect;
- the value of the product or service relative to other items available for consumption;
- the value of the product or service relative to other items that the customer base either needs or wants to purchase;
- patterns of spending among members of the niche or customer base, and the extent to which they use credit, credit cards, cash or cheque books;
- the need for access to product and service after-sales;
- the ease of access to facilities and services;
- the frequency with which a given product or service is to be used.

Social segmentation and customer definition are not exact sciences. They are however useful means of defining and classifying society for the purpose of targeting products and services as effectively as possible; and as a focus for understanding better the needs and wants of the particular segment targeted so as to refine and improve both product and service quality and performance, and also the marketing effort in terms of the benefits that are of value to the given customer base.

Ethical marketing

'Ethical marketing' has been developed in recent years by companies and organizations providing particular products and services. As shown below, the ethical marketing approach is complex. The ways companies go about it include:

- emphasizing the 'green' (and perceived 'green') nature of their products and services, and developing niche markets in: organic produce; energy efficient electrical goods and cars; products that have been produced under 'Fairtrade' (whereby the people, companies and organizations sourcing the products get paid 'adequately' for their efforts);
- making sure that products and services are only sourced in countries and regions that are being developed rather than exploited;
- refusing to use unwholesome images in advertising, sales and PR campaigns;
- making a virtue of precise product and service performance;
- making a virtue of the fact that a percentage of purchase prices will always be donated to charity.

Clearly, much of this is subjective also! However, by targeting triggers of value to particular market sectors and segments, companies and organizations have developed significant and very profitable niches in these areas.

The complexities of ethical marketing: Examples

Friends Provident

Friends Provident, the mutual life insurer and financial services company, launched its first ethical financial services lobbying unit some years ago. The purpose of this unit was to put pressure on FTSE companies to amend their environmental policies, including investments in:

- 'wholesome industries', rather than safe and assured sectors including defence, oil, energy, gas and chemicals;
- companies that took active responsibility for waste and effluent management and disposal;
- companies that engaged in 'fair trading policies' with Developing World governments and organizations;
- companies that took active responsibility for infrastructure development in developing countries in order to provide social, as well as economic, benefits.

BSkyB

BSkyB, the broadcasting and news reporting arm of NewsCorp, runs wildlife campaigns to raise funds in order to save endangered species. BSkyB states that every time someone takes out a subscription to its campaigns, it will match the donation with funds of its own. To date, BSkyB has put over £40 million into helping endangered species, conservation and environmental management projects.

Charities marketing

There is no question that at the core of the activities of all major charities is the fundamental drive to alleviate problems that exist in different parts of society, and different parts of the world. However, the drive for ever-greater access to source of funds, as well as overall increases in funding, has led to questionable marketing and promotional activities on behalf of these charities.

Many charities now 'blitz' town and city centres with teams of subcontracted public relations staff. These teams stop passers by in the street, engage them in conversation, and then ask for covenanted or credit card donations in support of the particular cause. This is a clear direct sales approach, and would probably be unacceptable if it were for consumer or capital goods and services. However, the large charities point to the financial results of this approach – for example, in one year, donations to 'War on Want' rose by 27%.

Each of these examples illustrates the complexities that have to be considered when adopting an ethical approach to marketing, and marketing for ethical reasons. In the above cases:

- Friends Provident is using the approach to enter new markets, examine new products and product ranges, and evaluate the extent to which these are profitable;
- BSkyB continues to expand its broadcasting activities, and again is seeking to explore and define potential new market segments;
- charities marketing is taking core marketing and direct sales activities and targeting potential groups in exactly the same way as all commercial marketing activities.

Marketing mixes

Marketing activities are based on mixes of the following elements. Each is present to a greater or lesser extent in all marketing activities; though the balance of each clearly varies between different products and services.

The 4Ps

- **Product:** variety, branding quality, packaging, appearance and design. There is also a presumption that all products are capable of being developed, improved and enhanced. For example:
  - the first mobile phone was the size of a loaf of bread and cost £2,000; today the product has been revolutionized and completely repositioned as a data management, information processing, entertainment and media product, as well as a telephone;

- motor car engines are being developed so that their dependence on oil is reduced.
- **Promotion:** advertising, sponsorship, selling, publicity, mailshots, internet presentations, television product placement, and branded clothing.
- **Price:** basic, discounting, credit, payment method, appearance. Price is also used as a form of promotion where it is so different (usually lower) to what has hitherto existed in the sector that the public is forced to take notice. For example:
  - Lidl, the supermarket chain, offers a core range of grocery products at prices very much lower than Sainsbury's, Tesco and Asda so people are forced to take notice;
  - the original Ryanair ticket prices were so much lower than the major airlines that people were more or less forced to consider them as an alternative to the existing services provided.
- **Place:** coverage, outlets, transport, distribution and accessibility.

The internet as location

The use of the internet as a marketing and organizational location has to be seen from a variety of, often conflicting, points of view, as follows.

- From the organization's point of view, it means it has a presence – a location – on every computer screen in the world.
- From the point of view of customers and clients, the particular organization has a general presence on every computer screen in the country. However, this location is convenient to customers and clients *only if* the organization website is easily accessible, and then customer-friendly once accessed. This has especially to be borne in mind when it is remembered that speed and convenience of access (and also perceived speed and convenience of access) are a key marketing function.
- If the great strength of the internet as location is its potential presence on every computer screen, the great weakness of the internet as location is the lack of physical or human presence. This has to be seen in the context that the enduring success of all marketing activities is built on the expectations of customers and clients. This in turn is universally reinforced by the human interaction that also takes place in every traditional transaction – whether consumer, industrial, commercial or public service.

The 4Cs

- **Customers:** directing marketing and presentational activities at the needs and wants of customers.
- **Convenience:** a combination of establishing the required and desired outlets; and of educating customers and clients to access the available outlets.

- **Cost**: the equivalent of price in the 4Ps; implicit in this is the additional management discipline that requires the balancing of cost and price with value and benefits.
- **Communication**: the production of advertising, sponsorship, selling, publicity, mail-shot and internet material that is customer, client and consumer friendly, rather than technically or visually brilliant per se.

Marketing mixes arise from combinations and interactions of each of these elements. Consumers of products and services – offerings – will normally hold one of the elements more important than the others. In turn, the forces and pressures of the markets in which the offerings are made also reflect their relative importance. For example:

- some markets will only sustain particular levels of price, and so therefore everything has to be produced at a cost that means that profitable activities are sustainable themselves;
- if the price of core commodities (for example gas, electricity, water) rises then disposable income is reduced elsewhere and price levels of non-core products and services have to fall;
- if a company leaves the market sector, it may be possible for those remaining to increase prices in the short term; however, it should always be recognized that prices may have to come down if others come into the market.

There are legal and ethical restraints placed on marketing activities in the Western world. In general, spurious or misleading claims may not be made for products, nor should misleading impressions be deliberately fostered – apart from anything else this is very bad for repeat business. Actual products must reflect the reality or impression given by both promotion and packaging. Products must also not be harmful or detrimental to their consumers; minimum standards of performance, manufacture, quality and safety have therefore to be met. Additionally, images used in marketing, advertising and promotion campaigns must reflect the demands and expectations of the locations in which they are delivered. At present in the UK, there is a backlash against the use of sexual images, the glamorization of smoking and drinking, and extravagance.

Products and services

The marketing of products and services requires a combination of the core substance on offer, together with the ways in which it is presented. The product and service mix is the range of products offered by an organization. This is determined by the matching of the organization's capabilities and capacities with the markets and niches to be serviced and by the scope and scale of its operations. People buy the benefits that they expect to accrue from a product or service as follows.

- **Quality and durability:** product and service quality and durability must be considered from the point of view of the balance required, and also in terms of customer demand (for example, there is no point in offering a highly durable product to the stated market sector if that is not what the customers want).
- **Branding:** which gives credence and confidence, especially where the brand is well known and the consumer is content with what is offered and comfortable with the appearance of the name on the product. Top brands have become household names; and some have even become verbs (for example hoover, google).
- **Packaging:** used to present the product to its best advantage and to protect it up to the point of consumption. The design and consistency of packaging reinforces the identity of all products and services – for example Barbie (toys); Persil (soap powders); brochure presentation (for example Thomson package tours).
- **Product and service benefits:** these should be seen in their widest context. The full offering often includes after-sales service, spare parts, help and emergency lines, call-out facilities, and product and service advice and familiarity sessions.
- **Product and service ranges and portfolios:** the confidence and reputation of each element of the product and service range and portfolio ought to reinforce the strength and value of all the others. When one product or service is perceived to be bad or unreliable, it is likely to have a knock-on effect to all of the others. There are various different ways of looking at product and service portfolios and ranges. Examples are:
  - those which are advertised; those which sell; those which make money;
  - yesterday's breadwinners; today's breadwinners; tomorrow's breadwinners; sparkles and twinkles; deadweights (see Figure 12.1).

Product and service classifications: Examples

Ford, the car manufacturer, uses the following approach:

- **Cars to advertise:** high performance (for example RS Turbo); high specification (for example top of the range Granada, off-road, Ford MPV, SUV).
- **Cars that sell:** Ka, Fiesta, Bonus, Xetec – especially the mid-range; both the high specification at one end of the scale, and also the basic model at the other end of the scale, sell less well than the mid-range.
- **Products and services that make money:** accessories, servicing packages, trade-in value, and finance plans.

Sony, the electrical goods manufacturer, classifies its product range as follows:

- **Yesterday's breadwinners:** the Walkman, sales of televisions, other electrical goods, video, audio and computer equipment and accessories.
- **Today's breadwinners:** music catalogues, the Walkman, DVD and other advanced computer, audio and video equipment, iPod-equivalent.

- **Tomorrow's breadwinners:** mini-disc, Playstation, Columbia-TriStar Pictures, music and video production, the VAIO range of computers.
- **Twinkles and sparkles:** Playstation developments, commercial computer software, VAIO and iPod-equivalent developments.
- **Deadweights:** very little – the company takes the view that even if something is a commercial failure, the knowledge and expertise gained as the result of its development should not be lost, but rather retained within the organization.

Ryanair, the low cost airline, classifies its product range as follows.

- **Plane tickets:** designed to ensure that all flights are as full as possible, as often as possible. Ryanair makes only a tiny fraction (if anything at all) on individual ticket sales; the viability of routes depends on enduring high volume ticket sales.
- **Add-ons:** partnerships with car hire companies, local airports, transport networks and hotels bring in assured revenue streams.
- **Catalogues:** including the sale of branded goods, duty free and other on-board sales is an additional revenue stream.
- **On-board sales of food and drink:** especially on flights of more than 2 hours' duration is a major revenue stream.

The Ryanair view is therefore that it is the total package that generates profits rather than the narrow attention to ticket sales.

Effective product and service classification clearly identifies:

- those products and services that make money;
- those products and services that lose money;
- those products and services that are declining in sales, profitability and effectiveness;
- those products and services that are increasing sales volumes and profitability;
- those products and services on which decisions (positive or negative) cannot yet be made;
- those products and services that are capable of development for the future.

One way of classifying products and services in this way is to use the 'Boston Matrix' (see Figure 12.1).

Product and service lifecycles

All products and services have a beginning, middle and an end (see Figure 12.2). The concept of product and service lifecycles defines more precisely these stages and identifies the points at which specific marketing initiatives and activities might usefully be generated.

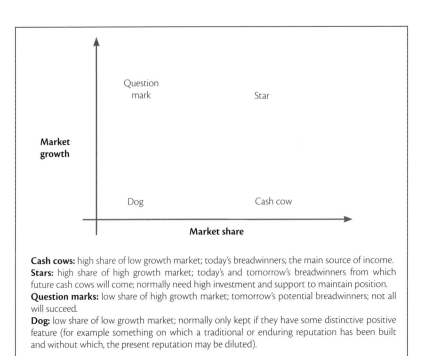

Figure 12.1 *The 'Boston Group' matrix*

There are four stages:

1 **Introduction:** the bringing in and bringing on of the new product or service following a period of extensive market research.

2 **Growth:** this is where the product or service takes off and its true potential (rather than that projected by research and modelling) begins to become apparent; sales and demand both rise where this is successful; unit costs decline.

3 **Maturity:** the product is now a familiar and well-loved feature on the market; people are both happy and confident with it, unit costs are low. The last part of the maturity stage is that of saturation; this is where the company seeks to squeeze the last remaining possible commercial benefits from the item before it loses its commercial value.

4 **Decline:** where the product is deemed to have run its course and no more value or profit is to be gained from it, it will then be withdrawn from the market. Marketing interventions are made at each stage to ensure that the product potential is maximized. The product must take off so that the full range of benefits to be gained from its consumers is realized by the sector at which it is aimed. Then, as it reaches maturity, initiatives are taken to breathe as much new life into it as possible using the whole range of promotional and advertising media; very often this means one advertising campaign too many before the product declines.

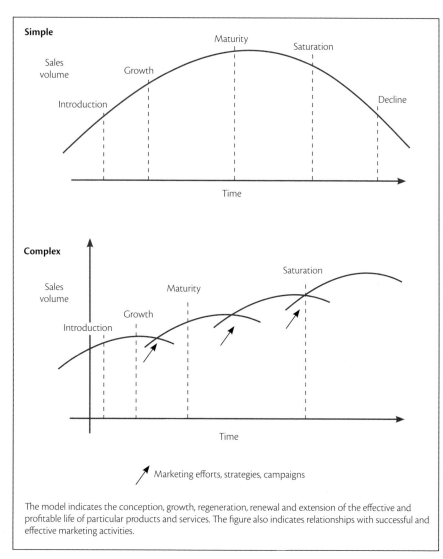

The model indicates the conception, growth, regeneration, renewal and extension of the effective and profitable life of particular products and services. The figure also indicates relationships with successful and effective marketing activities.

Figure 12.2 *Product lifecycles*

Products may also be rejuvenated through re-packaging, re-presentation and changing the quality or value emphases.

best practice

It is essential always to consider product and service mixes in full, even if one element is clearly declining. It is essential to understand any likely or potential effects of withdrawing a particular product or service from the full portfolio.

Marketing research and development

The purpose of such research is to identify and maximize opportunities that the product and marketing mix of the organization affords. Essentially, this combines the need to seek alternative outlets for products and the technology that the organization has at its disposal with that of finding out what customers' wants and needs are. Initiatives can then be proposed and generated with the view to satisfying these needs; and in the devising and initiating of further business opportunities. Properly structured, market research also addresses the 'generally favourable response'. Once a generally favourable response is engaged in, the customer or client group can be targeted. It then becomes essential that this is followed up in detail to establish exactly how often the product or service is to be bought, used and consumed; how much the particular segments are prepared to pay for this; and how often they are willing to pay it.

Customer perception

Research conducted by the tobacco industry demonstrated that brand loyalty was almost entirely based on image and identity rather than the taste of the product. Tests were conducted on those who stated categorically that they only liked their own brand. Smokers could not differentiate between their own brands and others of equivalent strength and similar tobacco when they were not given the packet from which to choose.

Research carried out by the Coca-Cola company on the blind tasting of both its own Cola products, and also those of competitors, gave initial cause for alarm. In the blind tasting sessions, Virgin Cola was found to carry what the testers perceived to be the best taste. At first alarmed by this finding, the company soon became comfortable with its products when it was realized that, whatever the results of blind taste, the customer-base at large would buy the Coca-Cola product anyway.

This applies to other soft drinks; tea and coffee; bread, cakes and biscuits; butter and margarine; beer, wine and spirits.

People are also more positively disposed towards any of these products if they are told that it is of their preferred brand, whether it is or not.

Source: Clark (1988).

The process undertaken is concerned mainly with an understanding of the capabilities and capacities of the organization on the one hand, and the requirements of the market and environment in which business is conducted on the other. This will address matters concerning general levels of confidence on the part of the market, customers' purchasing power, their needs and wants, their priorities and any other seasonal aspects, and relate these to the capabilities and capacities of the organization. Other factors to be taken into account will include a more general assessment of the market and the products in question; the extent to which these are in expansion, decline or stability. Research will include competitor analyses and the extent to which alternative and substitute products are available in the broadest sense. It will consider the reputation of the organization in question from a universal and general standpoint, as well as in the particular case of its own relationship with its own market sector. Customer assessments will also be conducted in order to gain a general understanding of their motives, desires, preferred images and identity with the particular product, or range of products, that is to be offered.

Finally, modelling activities will need to be commissioned or conducted by the organization with a view to assessing the extent of the profitability or effectiveness of the range of activities in question. Marketing research and development is thus an integral part of, and critical to, the success of wider strategic aspects; and critical also to the determination of the organization's future direction and instrumental in the determination of its success.

Having gone through an extensive and rigorous market research process, it is essential always to ensure that the questions asked have been as precisely targeted as possible at the needs, wants and demands of the market sector in question.

Public relations

The public relations or PR function is to ensure that the marketing wheels are kept oiled and that the organization's marketing machine works smoothly and positively in order to fulfil the purposes for which it was designed. It has a maintenance and development function that mirrors the operational equivalent. Planned PR concerns the identification in advance of suitable initiatives and items that will generate good publicity, and placing them in the media where they will have the greatest positive effects. There is also remedial PR, which is where the organization has to take responsive or other creative action to put right something that has gone wrong or to address a negative story concerning it that has appeared somewhere in the media.

Similarly, the handling of the press, television and radio must be conducted in ways that ensure an overall positivism is maintained, and that when problems arise, the last and most enduring note of the story is of the progress that is now to be made.

Organizations will also engage in the placement of stories favourable to themselves in the media, and in those parts of it where the greatest benefit to them will accrue. This is both as a counter to those occasions when problems do arise, and also as part of the more general process of building confidence, positive images, and an aura of 'good corporate citizenship'.

Organizations may also engage in more general customer and market liaison activities as part of their PR effort. This usually takes the form of sending staff on high profile and sectoral seminars and conferences, and taking stands at trade fairs and exhibitions.

Part of the effort of the sales force may also be simply to ensure that customers, and potential customers, are kept aware of the organization's continued existence and activities. The sponsorship of events also contributes to this general effort.

All aspects of company and organization communications and presentation contribute to the PR effort. For example, companies and organizations use positive media coverage that arises from such things as sectoral prizes, contributions to the community and recruitment advertising campaigns to build on their overall general image.

A key part of PR is the use of service as marketing. Customers contacting organizations in order to have questions, queries and problems addressed, expect that their queries will be taken seriously and resolved in full. To do this adequately will not necessarily enhance positive PR; to do this inadequately is certain to generate adverse PR.

Conclusions

Effective marketing management stems from the successful identification of a core or generic strategic position, and then relating this to the distinctive marketing strategic approach of first in field, me-too, all-comers, product or service-led, staff and expertise-led, or market-led.

From this, it is essential to develop effective marketing mixes of all products and services on offer, targeted at customer and client perceptions, expectations and connotations of quality, value, and convenience.

Alongside this, it is essential to develop images and impressions of the organization as being safe and steady, full of confidence and strength. This is both directly related to the current range of offerings, and also has implications for new products and future activities, and for the organizational culture and management style.

point of view

Cheap and good value

All those with responsibility for marketing should understand that very few customers or consumers (or for that matter commercial clients) buy anything purely on price alone. Even mercenaries (see customer analysis, Chapter 2) who state that they buy on price alone, very often spend a lot of other resources (especially time and energy) in finding the perceived, cheapest or best value option.

There is also the serious behavioural issue to address. Feelings of self-worth are affronted if consumers believe themselves to be forced into buying the cheapest option. Anything that is pitched at the low price market should carry enduring perceptions of 'good value' because this is a reinforcement of self-esteem and self-worth ('I am getting excellent value for money'), rather than cheap, which gives negative feelings ('I am forced to buy this because I haven't any money').

In the capital goods and major projects sectors, where competition is overtly on price, very often the cheapest tender carries with it all sorts of hidden extras. In construction and civil engineering, there is a long history of a claims process at the end of a contract. The companies that have successfully tendered for the work have offered a superficially attractive price up front to the client, and have then sought to build on this by seeking to claim for extras that were either not built in to the original tender, or else have become apparent as the contract has been completed.

Effective marketing depends on determining the sectors in which products are to be offered so that the benefit and satisfaction to be accrued through ownership and usage may be presented in ways that reflect customer and consumer needs. Activities created in support of this, including advertising campaigns, sales teams, brochures, information, help and support lines, websites, public relations activities, product placement and sponsorship, must reflect the hopes and aspirations of those targeted, as well as concentrating on the benefits of the specific products and services. Increasingly popular also are perceived and real relationships between organizations, their markets, and communities at large, and this includes support for local groups, clubs, and philanthropic and charitable activities, as well as precise attention to concerns about the particular products or services in question.

Market research and development are essential to ensure that high levels of mutual satisfaction and advantage continue to accrue. This is particularly critical in assessing likely and potential demand, opportunities to be gained and possible consequences of failure.

Product and service lifecycles have also to be continually assessed. This needs to be conducted for both individual items, and also for the total range.

It is also essential to consider the effects of general organizational and management practice on the confidence in which particular products and services are held. For example, Northern Rock, the UK regional bank, was extremely well regarded by customers and consumers with enduring high levels of confidence until it became clear that the company's asset base was heavily overvalued. This caused a loss of consumer confidence and ultimately became one of the triggers of the UK banking crisis of 2008–2009. Conversely, Gordon and Anita Roddick were able to maintain extensive confidence in the Body Shop by consistently drawing attention to the ways in which they conducted business and what their expectations of it were, in spite of the fact that the profit margins are much lower than those available elsewhere in the department store, cosmetics, and gift shop sectors.

Finally, the management of marketing requires continued attention to all aspects. Activities that are acceptable and effective today have to be maintained, developed and improved in order to ensure that their currency is retained into the future. The development of marketing strategies must be entwined with the wider aspects of organizational direction, purpose and priorities. Marketing, as with all functional activities, has to be directed and managed in support of this in order to ensure that the presentation of the organization, its products and services, remains as effective as the substance.

- Marketing relates the substance of products and services to their presentation. Marketing strategies should always relate to core foundation and generic organization and business strategies.
- People buy benefits and value. The purchase of these benefits and value depends on the confidence in which they hold the organization's products and services.
- It is essential that all organizations have core markets on which they can depend for future existence, viability and profitability provided that they continue to deliver products and services that have value to the customers.
- Product and service lifecycles, and continuous improvements and developments, mean that there is a constant need for the development of marketing activities.
- Marketing is all-pervasive. Every aspect of organizational conduct, behaviour, and performance, as well as product and service value, contributes to the overall marketing process.

Further reading

Baker, M. (2002) *The Marketing Book*. Wiley.
Brassington, F. and Pettit, S. (2006) *Essentials of Marketing*. Pearson.
Clark, E. (1988) *The Want Makers*. Corgi.
Kotler, P. (2009) *Marketing Management*. PHI.
Packard, V. (1957) *The Hidden Persuaders*. Penguin.
Ries, A. and Trout, J. (1997) *Marketing Warfare*. Wiley.

Managing operations and projects

13

In this chapter

- the complexities of operations and project management
- creating the conditions for effective operations and project management
- attending to the common elements of quality of working environment, health and safety management
- identifying the different approaches to managing the supply side of all activities

Introduction

Projects and operations management exists to ensure that the organization's primary functions and purposes are fulfilled. Projects and operations management is concerned with producing the organization's products and services in the volumes and quality required, to the deadlines and cost bases demanded, and in the locations and outlets suitable and convenient for purchase and usage. Projects and operations managers are therefore in turn concerned with organizing and scheduling production; gathering resources and expertise; designing and implementing work schedules; attending to problems and glitches; managing crises and emergencies; and ensuring that equipment and technology are cost-effective and fully operational.

just a minute

The priority here is therefore to recognize the complexity of the management task, and the obligations placed upon those responsible for project and operations management. It is also essential that all those in projects and operations management have an expert knowledge of everything that can possibly go wrong in each of these areas.

239

It is usual to define operations as steady-state activities relating to the day-to-day outputs and product and service delivery, and the processes and administrative and management systems that support this. Projects have a clearly stated beginning, middle and end resulting in: the production of something that did not previously exist; changes to product and service design; changes in business processes; new inventions; and the evaluation of new opportunities.

Large-scale operations and projects also have programmes, including:

- programmes of product and service delivery for operations;
- programmes of different projects, and programmes of sub-projects and contributory projects.

Everything in the project and operational environment has to be recognized, reconciled and structured in order to meet the demands placed on project and operations managers. In all project and operational work, there is a series of pressures and trade-offs that arise from:

- the need to reconcile time, cost, quality and safety issues (see Figure 13.1);

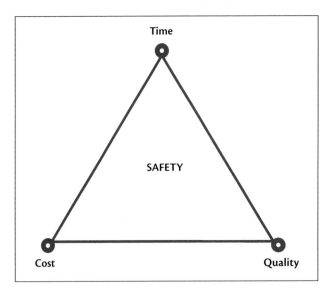

Figure 13.1 *Project and operational trade-offs*

- work schedules and demands to meet specific deadlines, product and service delivery targets, and project completion dates and times (and milestones for large and complex projects);
- the value of all activities, and their contribution to product, service and project quality, and overall effectiveness and viability;
- specific pressures arising from the availability of resources when required; for scarce resources, raw materials and expertise, this often means having to pay high charges in order to ensure their availability;

- time issues and critical paths, which need to be defined, understood and accepted by all as being the shortest timescale possible for the delivery of products, services and project work.

There is a Russian proverb that states: 'You cannot make a baby in one month by working nine times as hard.' Clearly, some timescales and schedules are fixed; however, all timescales and schedules should be evaluated on an individual basis to see if it is possible to speed things up.

However, there are fundamental differences in the overall approach to, and outcomes of, operations and projects work.

Operations and product and service delivery are the reasons for the existence of the organization in the first place, producing and delivering what customers and clients need, want and expect.

Project work exists to change things. The result of project work is to create, develop and bring about new systems, buildings, engineering and chemical inventions, and business processes. Project work is needed to design, develop and bring to production and market new products and services, and upgrades and improvements to those that already exist. Project work therefore changes things and moves them on, while operations deliver that which already exists and is either commercially viable or else (in terms of support activities and processes) supports the range of primary work carried out.

Primark

Designs for the clothing industry, and the fashionability of individual items, used always to be controlled by the major fashion houses and the annual shows in London, Paris, New York and Milan. This meant that the major fashion houses had a clear run of up to a year, able to sell their products at high prices, before the designs filtered through to the mass production and cheap/good value retail outlets.

Primark, the good value clothing company, commissioned a project that was designed to change all this. The purpose was to produce a computer programme that scanned the clothing when it was first displayed for materials, design and appearance. When the company produced the first viable version of this scanner, it took it along to one of the fashion shows.

The company was refused entry. The project now shifted its focus to concentrate on photographs and television images. A series of images was produced, translated into clothing patterns, and the first set of prototypes was delivered.

This approach was not only successful; it also transformed the fashion and clothing industries. Designs that took anything up to 12 months to come to the mass market could now be on the good value and mass market production lines within six hours of being scanned, either from moving images or photographs.

This illustrates the relationship between project work and operations. In this case, the project work transformed the nature and basis of operations, and also moved the company from being 'a late follower' into 'an early follower'.

Recognizing the fundamental difference of orientation between the nature and management of projects and operations, the core issues are:

- location of work;
- health and safety;
- working environment;
- scales of production;
- control.

Location

Location depends on the following.

- Sources, frequency and regularity of input deliveries, especially where this includes physically heavy or bulky resources. There must therefore be adequate access to transport and distribution infrastructures.
- Virtual location: this is less of a problem where the delivery of everything critical can be guaranteed through computer networks and via the internet. However again, it is necessary to ensure that the staff required do have access to places of work; where the 'place of work' is at home, at business centres, or on the road, the process is reversed because managers and supervisors require convenience and access to their staff working in these ways.
- Just in time inputs and deliveries effectively mean that a lot of physical storage takes place on the road; and again, the 'location' aspect has to ensure that there is sufficient infrastructure capacity for this to remain effective and profitable.

Location is also affected by political, social and cultural factors. For example, many transport, distribution and haulage companies, or multi-activity companies with transport, distribution and haulage fleets, are now looking at the best places to locate from the point of view of optimizing their corporation and capital taxation allowances as some countries load these elements much more heavily than others.

Location used always to be influenced by the nature of production processes. Traditionally, industry tended to locate near its markets, if the production process added weight to the product; and at the sources of materials, if the processes detracted weight from the products.

Location is affected by wider environmental support. For example, communities expect to have their own schools and social, health and hospital services, as well as commercial services, including supermarkets and banks.

For project work, location is dictated by where the work is required. The constraints of the environment have to be reconciled with demands of the project. Building and civil engineering require consideration of effective access and egress. Information technology projects have to reconcile the demands placed on the particular system with the constraints of their physical location and the size of the environment in which they are to be implemented.

Organizations must choose their location on the basis that there is a sufficient volume of staff available; where this is not possible directly, those employed must be able to get to work through the use of commuter routes and public transport.

Access to work

Access to work is becoming a serious problem for those responsible for the location, management and delivery of public services. Solutions have to be found to problems caused by the inability of those in public services to afford local property because of the high prices of homes in relation to salaries offered. It is also an enduring problem for those on career paths in public services. In the overwhelming majority of cases, frustration and stress are caused by strong and enduring levels of commitment to the service itself, and to the client groups in question, against the inability to afford to remain in the sector; or if doing so, then reconciling this with the high levels of fixed charges that accrue as a consequence and condition of remaining in the profession.

This has led to highly publicized, long-term and enduring shortages of teachers, nurses and social workers. However, this is not confined to the high commitment, low salary occupations; there is also long-term enduring shortage of those coming into the medical, legal and military professions, which enjoy high salaries, and high levels of job security. The location of these activities, together with the enduring levels of stress and social dysfunction faced as the result, mean that:

- a better quality of life can be enjoyed in other occupations for the same level of qualification, salary, and expertise;
- equivalent levels of personal, professional and occupational satisfaction can be gained without the locational dysfunction.

For example:

- A lawyer working within the military establishment found himself having to stay in London during the week for a period of two months. This was due to a combination of particular work pressures at the time, combined with the uncertainties of public transport. This meant that he was only able to return home at weekends, and this caused domestic stresses and strains, in spite of the fact that he had been married for over 15 years.

- A country GP in the south-west of England found himself working from any one of six locations. This was because he was required to cover his own surgery; a cottage hospital; two clinics; and two out-of-hours call centres and emergency surgeries. While this was a clearly stated and understood precondition of the job, it took nearly three years for the local health authority to agree to provide a mobile telephone, or a substantial medical emergency travelling kit.

Health and safety

> It is the duty of every organization, so far as is reasonably practicable, to provide a place of work that is both healthy and safe. (Health and Safety at Work Act, 1974 – Preamble)

Organizations are required to provide a place of work that is both healthy and safe; and to take an active responsibility for this, rather than to respond to a detailed set of legally stated criteria.

This responsibility is underpinned with specific legislation and regulations in particular areas. Both the EU and also the UK government have legislated to address particular operational issues, especially in the following areas:

- **Working time:** the establishment of a basic level of maximum hours that may be requested without the employee's further consent. In the UK, this is 48 hours per week. This may be varied in particular cases according to the nature of the work being carried out; where longer hours are required in some weeks, time off must be given in others to ensure that the average of 48 hours per week, over a reasonable period of time, is not exceeded.
- **Substances hazardous to health:** these must be registered, monitored, recorded and, when not in use, kept under lock and key. Such substances may normally only be used under supervision, or with the knowledge of someone else on the premises.
- **Protective clothing:** required for those working outdoors or on construction or engineering sites; and required also of those working with chemicals, and toxic and hazardous substances.
- **Training:** health and safety training is required for all employees; and basic health and safety training is required for those who come to work on particular premises as contractors.
- **Qualifications:** many professional, technical and managerial qualifications include specific attention to health and safety, both from the point of view of understanding and following the legislation, and also in relation to the sorts of hazards that are present in particular occupations.
- **Computers:** it is normal practice not to allow anyone to work for longer than 2.5 hours at a computer screen without giving them at least 15 minutes away from it.

- **Breaks:** it is usual to ensure that everyone who works for a continuous period of four hours is then given a break of at least 30 minutes. Anyone working longer than eight hours per day must be given a break of at least one hour.
- **Emergency procedures:** all organizations must have stated emergency procedures. These must be written and made available to all staff and visitors to the premises, regardless of size of the organization, or complexity of operations.
- **Road haulage and transport:** there are specific regulations that have to be followed by all those working in road haulage and transport; and organizations have an active responsibility to ensure that these regulations are followed.
- **Waste and effluent disposal:** all organizations are responsible for disposing of any waste or effluent that their operations and activities produce.

The effectiveness of these statutory approaches to the management of health and safety in operations activities lies in:

- the acceptance of corporate responsibility and accountability, as well as the one-dimensional duty to work within the law;
- the powers of statutory and regulatory bodies, and levels of fines, in order to act as deterrent to corporate malpractice;
- the relationship between being a known healthy and safe employer, and levels of positive operational activity; the effects of being a known unhealthy and unsafe employer, and the detrimental effects on business and service operations.

Overall responsibility for health and safety at the place of work rests at the top management level in terms of setting standards and producing formal policies. However, all individuals at every level have a joint degree of responsibility to ensure that their own aspect and work environment is kept as far as possible both safe and healthy. The policy will identify any instruments for monitoring and assessment – such as safety representatives and the election or appointment of safety committees. This may also include training for both managers and operative staff. Finally, particular hazards will be indicated, as will the requirements to wear particular types of clothing, use particular types of equipment and follow particular procedures in dealing with particular hazardous or potentially unsafe situations and practices at the place of work. This includes the storage, handling and usage of restricted or supervised goods, chemicals and other equipment.

Quality of working environment

The work environment must be organized in such a way as to be healthy and safe as far as possible, and to provide the required and acceptable standards of comfort and humanity. This includes:

- **Temperature** levels: appropriate training and clothing must be provided for those who have to work in extreme heat or cold.

- **Lighting,** which must be adequate to work without strains on the eyesight of the workforce.
- **Ventilation** of all work premises, where necessary through air-conditioning and filtration procedures.
- Suitable and sufficient **sanitary accommodation** for all, including separate conveniences for each gender and the disabled; and related provisions of washing and drinking water facilities.
- **Machinery** must have guards and cut-outs in-built, and training must be given in usage and operation; these guards must be maintained in an effective state, and not be removed during operations.
- **Offices** must also be **maintained** in a safe way: telephone and computer wires must not be left trailing; fire doors must not be propped open or locked shut; passages and corridors must be clear and unobstructed.
- **Floors, stairs and passages** must be soundly constructed and maintained, and railings put on stairs and raised walkways.
- Specific **training** must be provided for all those who are required to lift **heavy weights;** or to work with **toxic** or **dangerous fumes or substances** (for example laboratories, chemicals and radioactive substances).
- **Records of accidents** must be kept; all accidents that result in fatality, loss of limb, or absence from work of more than three days must be notified to the Health and Safety Inspectorate.
- **Technology** provided must be capable of safe, effective, productive and profitable use; where necessary, training must be provided, and this applies to upgrades as well as the installation of new equipment.

Project operations and technology

Rationally and logically, all technology should be provided on the basis that it is useful, valuable, effective, profitable and productive in the terms demanded by the organization as it produces products and services for the enduring satisfaction of its customers and clients. There are, however, other points to be considered:

- No technology is ever effective on its own. Its value to the organization is entirely dependent upon the capability of those operating it.
- The purchase of generic technologies – especially in production and information technology – must always be considered from the point of view of their precise suitability for the particular organization. In particular, many off-the-shelf personnel information management systems have been found to be less than effective because they do not address the precise questions required by the particular organizations that have purchased them. Many financial management information systems purchased by central government as an aid to the management of public services, and by

multinational corporations as an aid to the management of international purchasing and distribution, have been found not to address the substantial and priority questions required by these institutions.

- Many technologies are produced to demonstrate the technological brilliance of the inventors and designers, rather than the requirements of the end-users.
- Many technologies have insufficient capacity for upgrade, maximization, or changes in product and service specification.

Additionally, many *perceived* revolutionary technologies have failed to deliver the benefits promised or strongly indicated. Many companies are still struggling to maximize their commercial usage of the internet. Many organizations additionally have websites in order to ensure that they have a presence on the internet, rather than as a directly operational instrument.

Many individuals, groups, departments, divisions and functions are fitted out effectively with particular technology (especially computer technology) as part of the reward package. For example, for managers or other key staff not to have a personal computer in their office or individual place of work is seen to reflect a loss of status or face; or a perception that the reason why there is not one present is because the particular individual does not know how to use it; and, above all, the understanding that they are not important enough to have one.

The structure, design and presentation of any place of work needs to combine a good quality of comfort with the capability to carry out activities effectively. Additionally, it is expected that all organizations provide a modicum of human comfort and humanity, as well as attending to the technological, professional and occupational drives and priorities.

Scales of production and output

Woodward (1961) defined the following scales of production.

- **Jobbing or unit production:** the production of single, unique or specialist items; unique quality of service delivery; the ability to customize or make unique products and services according to customer and client demands.

Customized production at Levi Strauss

Levi Strauss conducted a project to test the feasibility of offering a customized service allowing customers to choose from a set of features enabling them to have, within these constraints, the jeans of their choice. Levi Strauss has created a website page offering the range of features – including colour mixes, measurements around the hips, waist, thighs and ankles, choice of waist fasteners, and belt buckle options. Customers simply log on to the website, choose their precise requirements from the range on offer, and arrange to collect their jeans or have them delivered at their convenience. For those wanting more precise made-to-measure, a body scanning service is available. This comes through one of the following:

- indicating precise measurements, where the individual customer knows these, on the website;
- attending a Levi Strauss outlet that has the body scanner facility;
- attending another outlet which has the scanner facility available by arrangement with Levi Strauss.

The pioneering work of Levi Strauss is now fully integrated into the company's mainstream operations and activities. Because of its commercial success, it has been examined closely by many other organizations, both from within the clothing sector and also elsewhere, to see how the customization of particular products can be developed in fully commercial ways.

Source: Pringipas (2001).

- **Mass production:** organizing work in order to produce high volumes of standard quality products and services. Traditionally, mass production is the cornerstone of all consumer goods; the same principles apply to the output of consumer services (for example holidays, travel and transport, banking and financial services).
- **Process and flow production:** traditionally applied to oil, petrol, chemicals, plastic extrusion, steel and paper manufacturing – the output of commodities in a continuous stream or flow. This approach also applies to commercial and public services.

Process and flow in commercial and public services

Problems in both commercial and public services become apparent when managerial attention is concentrated on operational efficiency rather than quality of service, and customer and client satisfaction. For example:

- **Banking:** one major clearing bank went through a process of closing hundreds of small branches. The defining criterion was simply the volume of money held in each account. Accordingly, a tiny rural branch in which one or two wealthy people held accounts was kept open; while branches with a larger volume of accounts were either closed down altogether, or opened on a part-time basis only, because the particular branch did not serve a sufficient number of more opulent customers. The programme was subsequently rescinded, costing the bank a total of £170 million. Paradoxically, the bank was the same one that greatly improved the effectiveness of service in the eyes of customers by introducing the single queue in place of individual queues at each desk. Just as effectively, this was copied by, among others, post offices, large estate agencies, and travel agents. Some banks are, however, diluting the effectiveness of this part of their operations by restricting the nature of services that can be provided through the cashier and customer service, and insisting that customers use machines for their particular service requirements, whether or not they wish to do so.

- **The National Health Service (NHS):** the single operational criterion in the provision of hospital services is frequency of bed usage. Extremely efficient in narrow terms, in that it is most unusual to find a bed unoccupied for more than an hour between patients, this has nevertheless led to ward closures, and reductions in hospital capacity. This in turn has led to increases in waiting lists for hospital treatment that is deemed to be non-emergency or non-urgent; increases in times between admission through casualty, accident and emergency departments, and being found a ward bed; and, in extreme cases, the stacking up of patients on trolleys in hospital corridors, canteens, and other non-operational areas. In some cases, it is possible to observe a queue at the entrance to wards where patients are waiting to go in before the previous bed occupant has actually been discharged.

- **Batch production:** the output of medium volumes of products and services; normally based on the ability to rejig production and service technology so that different inputs, processing and production methods can be accommodated, and different outputs produced. Batch production is the standard form used in the manufacture of drugs and pharmaceuticals; and in the package holiday sector, whereby companies buy up volumes of hotel bookings, airline seats and other facilities in advance that are then combined into distinctive batches of offerings.

- **Project production:** a combination of technology, expertise, information, resources and components for the purposes of producing substantial, unique, finished items. Project work is a major concern in all sectors, both internally (for example the installation of information systems), and externally where market testing and feasibility may be conducted on a project basis. This is quite apart from those sectors that do operate on a project basis – information systems; civil engineering and construction; defence; and electronics and robotics.

Whatever the scale of production and service delivery, production capacity and productivity have to be clearly understood. Whatever the set of circumstances, production capacity and productivity are a direct consequence of the nature of the available equipment and technology, and the quality of staff employed. Both the technology and staff have to be capable of meeting the demands for product and service output, and project delivery, on an immediate and enduring basis. This means ensuring that a realistic and practical view of the nature and volume of demands on the organization is undertaken. It is additionally necessary to reconcile the balance between getting adequate returns on technology and expertise, while retaining both the flexibility and the spare capacity to undertake special activities when required.

Measuring productivity: Examples

- **McDonald's:** McDonald's calculates that the average stay per customer in each of its restaurants is 12 minutes. This can lead the unwary into thinking that every seat in the restaurant can be filled five times an hour.
- **The NHS:** for many years now, the NHS has entered into extensive calculations designed to work out: costs per patient across the entire service; costs per patient in particular regions; costs per patient in particular hospitals; costs per patient in other activities – clinics, day care centres, doctors' surgeries, district nursing, and midwifery. This has led to a system of service budgeting that was flawed from the outset.
- **Further education:** a further education college calculated the costs of using its classrooms at £130 per hour. A nearby hotel offered conference facilities at £80 per hour. It was not until extensive discussions had been held between the college authorities and the hotel management concerning the feasibility of renting rooms on a regular basis from the hotel that the college realized the fundamental flaw in its comparisons – that the calculation of costs and the payment of charges are only tenuously related in complex activities.
- **Semco:** 'One sales manager sits in the reception area reading the newspaper hour after hour, not even making a pretence of looking busy. Most modern managers would not tolerate it. But when a Semco pump on an oil tanker on the other side of the world fails, and millions of gallons of oil are about to spill into the sea, he springs into action. He knows everything there is to know about our pumps and how to fix them. That's when he earns his salary. No-one cares if he does not look busy the rest of the time' (Semler, 1993).

Managing the supply side

The standpoint here is to ensure that all materials, resources, and information required are in place when necessary, while at the same time striking a balance against unnecessary storage costs and charges.

The main elements for consideration are:

- convenience of access, frequency and reliability of sources and deliveries, the flexibility or otherwise of production and project scheduling;
- speed of obsolescence of components and information;

- whether to bear the price of stockpiling as a comfort or necessity;
- any specific demands of the particular range of operations, or project requirements;
- the extent to which it is necessary to do things in accordance with the demands of suppliers;
- specific issues on the supply side, especially the scarcity of expertise or raw materials;
- storage costs and charges;
- the need for specific storage facilities: large storage facilities become expensive in terms of land and capital resource usage; information may require storage in specific formats.

Whatever the approach taken to managing the supply side, the priority must be the availability of component supplies, resources and expertise when required.

Just in time

The just in time (JIT) approach to purchasing is attractive because it removes the need to use expensive premises for the storage of components and supplies. JIT is based on the ability to engage in relationships with suppliers requiring regular (daily and in some cases, many times a day) deliveries to be made. This form of supply has always been the norm in the fresh foodstuffs industry. It has now been extended into many industrial and commercial areas, and public service activities.

When they are delivered, supplies go more or less straight into production areas. As long as it works well and supplies can be more or less guaranteed, JIT is both efficient and effective. Its success depends entirely on the reliability of the suppliers. In practice, it also depends on the ability and willingness of the supplier (or suppliers) to vary the volumes, normally at short notice, to cope with sudden up-flows and down-flows in production.

Further developments are as follows.

- Only when required – in which the supplier has the capacity and willingness to provide what is required, when required, at instant or very short notice, in response to individual requests from purchasers.
- Booking in advance – especially when critical supplies or expertise are needed for a particular operation, or in the delivery of project work. In many cases, 'booking in advance' means having to pay either a premium or a retainer to ensure that the supplies and expertise are delivered at precisely the time required.
- Only when provided – in which the supplier establishes a set pattern of frequent deliveries. This enables suppliers to schedule their own activities with a degree of certainty, and requires entering into relationships with purchasers to establish the enduring convenience of the 'only when provided' approach. From this it is possible to plan hourly, daily, or weekly schedules by arrangement.

'Just in Time': Examples

- **DHL:** DHL is a fully flexible, high quality, instant response mail, delivery and courier service provider. The company undertakes to take and deliver anything, anywhere in the world, within three hours (local), six hours (regional), ten hours (national) and twenty-four hours (international) – subject only to the vagaries of long-haul air flights. The only leeway that they allow themselves in setting their standards concerns long-haul air deliveries – in these cases, specific terms of business are drawn up with particular clients in order to establish reasonable parameters around scheduled air services. In return for this quality assurance, reliability and flexibility of delivery, the company charges extremely high prices.

- **Harrods:** Harrods and other perceived exclusive providers of goods and services insist on full flexibility of response when dealing with those who supply them with exclusive, unique or customized goods and services. Again, the charges incurred in such a relationship are very high; and again, this is reflected in the price paid by individual customers for this quality of service.

- **Sandals:** Sandals, the exclusive travel and tour operator, had to change its West Indies weddings package from 'only when provided' to 'only when required', and accept any increase in costs that this brought about. This was because, on some days, couples to be married found themselves being rushed through due to the numbers being married on the same day. While on other days it was impossible to provide the full range of services (for example video packages, priests of particular religious denominations) because the lack of volume demand meant that those subcontracted to provide these found it economically unviable to turn out.

It is important to recognize that each situation brings its own advantages, disadvantages, opportunities and consequences. If a durable and high quality working relationship is to be established between suppliers and purchasers, then any potential pressures brought about by instant demands, short-term changes in quality and volume, and changes to production and service specifications, are addressed by those managers responsible.

Control

Operational and project systems, procedures and processes must be both sufficiently well ordered, and also flexible enough to be improved where necessary. This is to ensure the effectiveness with which the task in hand is addressed and also gives the means of improving every aspect.

The following key questions have to be addressed.

- **The slowest part of the process:** where this occurs; why it occurs; what if anything should be done about it; how it might be speeded up; the consequences of this on other activities.

- **The quickest part of activities:** together with any consequences; this especially becomes a problem if it results in staff or equipment operating to less than full capability.
- **Blockages:** where, why and how these occur; how often these occur; and the range of possible responses. Blockages occur as the result of the nature of production, service, and output processes; shortage of specific facilities; and stockpiling at the input and output locations. It causes stresses and strains on other parts of the process.

Blockages in the NHS

Regular, enduring and frequent blockages occur in the provision of effective patient services in many parts of the NHS. Specific blockages occur in:

- casualty, accident and emergency departments, where patients often have to wait many hours for urgent and non-urgent treatment;
- patients often have to wait many hours for admission to the correct hospital ward; in extreme cases, where a patient's urgent condition becomes an emergency, this has resulted in the need for high speed transfers to other hospitals;
- bed-blocking occurs when it becomes difficult to pass patients on to the form of care required next, or back into the community. This is an especial problem with elderly patients.

Each of these has a compounding effect on activities in the immediate future.

These blockages are caused by a combination of staff, equipment and bed shortages that have resulted from a lack of full understanding or attention to the broader medical environment.

- **Volume, quality and time issues:** consideration of what is available, what is possible and what the customers, clients and consumers require.
- **Wastage rates:** these should always be attended to, and constantly assessed for acceptability or otherwise; the expense incurred requires calculation and evaluation; this may also increase concerns for, and volume of activities in, waste and effluent disposal.

It is essential to be able to respond effectively to customer complaints. This was not normally regarded as being a part of the sphere of operations or project management. However, it is essential to recognize that all customer complaints are founded in dissatisfaction with products and services; and so where questions do arise, production and service delivery functions ought to be involved. Indeed, many organizations now make their production functions responsible for managing customer complaints. Even where this is not the case, production and output processes require assessment for the potential for dissatisfaction and complaint.

There is a direct relationship between being able to operate in a good quality working environment, and sustained high and satisfactory levels of volume and quality output. Attention to the working environment requires:

- a full assessment of the working environment, its strengths, weaknesses and shortcomings;
- a full assessment of the expectations of individuals and groups, and what they require to do their jobs properly and effectively;
- prioritizing those areas that require attention;
- identifying those factors inside and outside the control of those involved;
- identifying accurately staff pressures brought about by the requirement to work, for example, in untidy, dirty, damp or draughty conditions; and recognizing that these conditions may exist in any form of activity;
- recognizing the particular health and safety constraints inherent, and taking all steps necessary to ensure that accidents, injuries, emergencies, and illnesses, are kept to an absolute minimum.

Finally, it is necessary to recognize and understand the particular constraints placed by engaging people on different patterns of work. Specific professional and occupational groups also require particular attention. Those with high degrees of specialization or expertise, or who work away from the organization, or to non-standard patterns of work, require full organizational and managerial support if they are to remain effective for the long term. This applies to many occupations, for example:

- professional health service staff working nights and weekends;
- sales staff working in the field for long periods of time; and in many cases, also working evenings and weekends;
- those who work twilight shifts, at times when senior management are likely not to be present;
- those on 'job and finish' activities;
- those working for agencies, subcontractors, consultancies and other distinctive specialisms that are only required for short periods of time.

The complexity of operations and project management

Project and operations managers must be able to address effectively the following as and when they arise:

- information flows must be worked out in advance and evaluated for effectiveness;
- establishing the means of dealing with crises and emergencies;
- the management of the financial aspects of the work based on accurate high quality information available to, and understood by, everyone involved;

- the management of the work and task schedules inherent in the work, including the establishment and acceptance of work methods, timescales, resource gathering, problem-solving, maintenance and development functions;
- managing communications between everyone involved with especial reference to organizational, occupational, professional, cultural and language difficulties;
- attention to the demands of key stakeholders;
- attention to all individuals involved, including making constructive use of talent and expertise of all those involved;
- the creation and adoption of a positive and dynamic management style, with especial concentration on the coordination and communication aspects; ensuring effective staff, supplier, customer and client liaison;
- agreement of common aims and objectives which are understood, valued and accepted by all those involved; or at least capable of being harmonized in pursuit of the ultimate outcome;
- the establishment of key and specific areas of responsibility and accountability with procedures established for the resolution of any conflict or dispute.

It is essential to understand all these factors. In the management of a computer or information systems project, for example, ultimate responsibility for its effectiveness lies with the client, and their ability to communicate their precise requirements to the contractor. For civil engineering and building projects, responsibility lies with the capability of the contractor to translate the project requirements into something that is acceptable using their design, building and environmental management expertise.

In certain public projects, it may be necessary to develop the liaison process into a non-executive but highly authoritative steering group because of the requirements or demands of the commissioning bodies; for example where these are municipal health authorities or instruments of national, regional and central government.

Conclusions

The effectiveness of the management of projects, operations and activities lies in the ability to understand and apply the extremely complex set of principles indicated in this chapter to particular situations. There is no absolute set of rules that applies to all circumstances, and the balance and mix of these principles varies between organizations (even those in the same industrial, commercial or public service sector) and projects (even those concerned with the same ultimate output, for example a new motorway, a new information system).

It is additionally apparent that all project and operations work is carried out within particular constraints and limitations. Nothing can ever be planned for or completed in isolation from the various pressures within the operating environment. All project and operations managers therefore need to be aware of the following.

- **Sectoral economics**: activities in every sector are limited by the rates of return available; and by the costs of technology and expertise required.
- **Schedules**: the speed at which operations and projects progress is, in part, dictated by the speed at which supplies, expertise and information can be made available.
- **Operational and project lifecycles**: relating to the length of useful life of the finished item (for example, fashionable and seasonal goods and services have to be provided at very short notice; project work often requires substantial redesign in order to meet changing social, economic and technological pressures).
- **Resources, expertise and technology**: project and operations work is always affected when resources, technology and expertise suddenly become unavailable due to matters outside the organization's control. For example, finance may suddenly become unavailable because of wider economic changes (especially downturns); expertise may no longer be available when required (for example, due to the UK recession in building and civil engineering in the early 1990s, much expertise was lost to these sectors altogether).

Operations and project managers therefore need as full an understanding of their particular environment as possible and as quickly as possible. Additionally, it is a mark of professional practice that those responsible for activities or projects become fully knowledgeable in the particular field in which they are working. For example, the project managers working on the 2012 Olympic project in London are completely committed to the success of the Olympic Games. Those managing the development of new products for Starbucks know and understand the contribution of each ingredient to the finished product.

Finally, it is essential to recognize the broader context of operations and project management. It is perfectly possible to create anything from the point of view of the satisfaction of narrow self-interest or key stakeholder drive. Anything that requires development in the long-term interests and enduring viability of the organization needs to be understood in terms of the sheer range and complexity of activities in which managers have to be expert.

in brief

- Managing operations and projects is complex. As well as a range of expertise, those responsible must have the ability to operate within the constraints of the given environment.
- The health and safety of all activities is paramount; and is bounded by law.
- Technology is to be seen as a resource that contributes to enduring viability and effectiveness of projects and operations. It has no intrinsic value.

- Projects and operations form the basis of the mainstream activities, and therefore profitability, of organizations; and this is the reason for paying prime attention to them.
- The fundamental difference between projects and operations is that projects exist in order to change products, services and processes, or in order to create, develop and produce new inventions, buildings, engineering and technology capabilities; operations exist to provide organizations with a steady stream of the products and services which they produce for customers and clients.

Further reading

Association for Project Management (2011) *Project Management: Body of Knowledge.* APM Publications.

Goldthorpe, J. et al. (1968) *The Affluent Worker: Industrial Attitudes and Behaviour.* Cambridge.

Johnson, R. and Clark, G. (2009) *Service Operations Management: Improving Service Delivery.* Pearson.

Lockyer, K. (1996) *Project Management.* Penguin.

Semler, R. (1993) *Maverick.* Century.

Slack, N. et al. (2009) *Operations and Process Management.* Pearson.

Thomsett, M. (2009) *The Little Black Book of Project Management.* Jossey Bass.

Woodward, J. (1961) *Industrial Organization: Behaviour and Control.* OUP.

Financial and quantitative aspects of management

14

'In many ways, the work of managers starts where that of the accountant and statistician finishes.'

In this chapter

- the critical need to understand all aspects of finance
- identifying and understanding different numbers and their presentation, and what the numbers mean and state
- using numbers and figures to support decision-making
- developing a managerial awareness of how figures are used by different professions (for example statisticians and accountants) for their own legitimate purposes

Introduction

Finance is the lifeblood of all organizations, and therefore at the core of all activities. Commercial organizations are required to make profits, generating over periods of time a surplus of income over expenditure that supports the continuation and viability of the business, and provides an adequate return to shareholders and backers. Public and government services, working to targets and budgets allocated by governments and other authorities, use their resources to best advantage to satisfy the sectors they serve.

It is therefore essential that managers know and understand financial structures and mechanisms, and the other sources of data that support decision-making.

The content of financial management

Financial management is concerned with all aspects of organization finances as follows.

- Producing accounts in accordance with statutory and regulatory demands; having these accounts audited, agreed and signed off by independent and expert auditors who must be allowed to take a detached view of the presentation, as well as knowing and understanding the context in which the accounts were produced.
- Accounting for the use of resources in all of the organizations activities. This in turn means:
  - accounting for capital expenditure on technology, capital goods, equipment and premises that the organization needs in order to conduct its business effectively;
  - accounting for revenue (or short-term) expenditure on daily activities and operations;
  - assessing where the balance of income, expenditure, costs, profits and losses occurr.
- Assessing performance from the point of view of immediate and enduring financial results; being able to evaluate the balance of activities for contribution to the effectiveness of financial performance; and from this evaluation, being able to recognize and address those areas where financial performance can, and should, be improved.

Financial management is additionally concerned with addressing investments, new products and services and new ventures from the point of view of the returns generated, whether this represents maximum value for all concerned, and whether these activities represent the best use of the organization's resources.

Financial management is concerned with value as well as cost, income and profit; and so has to provide structures and bases for valuing activities, the ways in which activities are carried out, and the total contribution to the organization's financial strength and integrity.

Financial management is concerned with ensuring that income and expenditure policies and priorities address the immediate demands of stakeholders (including the financial interests), as well as ensuring that adequate levels of resources are available to support the activities necessary for the long-term future of the organization.

best practice

Finance and financial management should never be allowed to stand alone, either as separate organization disciplines, or as the only driving forces of performance priorities. The best organizations and managers integrate financial performance and the data that they use with all other aspects of organization and management, and to inform and support decision-making, risk analyses and forecasting activities.

The context of financial management

The context of financial management needs to be known and understood fully by all managers in any situation. The context of financial management consists of:

- knowing and understanding the nature of the financial performance that ought to be achieved in a particular set of circumstances, and, in the context of market activities, costs of raw materials and energy, customer and client activity and trading conditions;
- knowing and understanding the balance of profitable and loss making activities in terms of which products and service activities and markets are profitable, which parts cover their own costs and which parts run at a loss;
- knowing and understanding the cost of primary activities which produce, deliver and sell the organization's products and services;
- knowing and understanding the balance between the costs involved in effective primary activities, and organization support and service functions.

It has become very fashionable to scrutinize organization support functions on the basis that they are less important and valuable than primary activities and can therefore be dispensed with. While knowing and understanding the balance of primary and support functions is clearly essential, the costs incurred in having these support functions do need addressing from the point of view of cost-effectiveness and contribution, as well as financial implications.

Within this context, financial management is concerned with:

- the production and verification of accounts as above;
- identification and management of costs;
- financial performance management;
- the apportionment of resources and budgets for departments and activities;
- asset and liability management;
- valuation of the organization and its activities and operations;
- managing investments;
- attending to the financial aspects of risk;
- developing management information systems that support and underpin the financial management effort.

Accounts

Accounts are produced by qualified professional accountants and other experts in accordance with legal requirements, and the existing rules, codes of conduct and conventions that govern the ways in which these activities are carried out. Explanations and support for how accounts are produced are given in organizational, annual and other public reports.

From a managerial point of view, the approach to accounts and financial aspects involved ought to be concerned with the use, evaluation, interpretation, analysis and judgement of the data, and how it is to be used. Accounts are one point of information used as the basis for effective decision-making. Organizational accounts ought to indicate the strengths and weaknesses of existing financial performance, and where the opportunities and problems for the future are likely to occur.

Profit and loss account		0001 £ million	0000 £ million
	INCOME	3188	3097
	OPERATING COSTS	(2736)	(2771)
	OPERATING PROFIT	452	326
	INTEREST	(27)	33
	PROFIT BEFORE TAX	425	359
	TAX	(140)	(117)
	PROFIT AFTER TAX	285	242
	DIVIDEND	(82)	(72)
	RETAINED PROFIT	203	170

(Brackets indicate subtraction)

Figures are then normally given for earnings per share and dividend per share

Balance sheet		31 December 0001 £ million	31 December 0000 £ million
	FIXED ASSETS	2106	1996
	Current Assets	1109	1043
	Short-term Creditors	(771)	(890)
	NET CURRENT ASSETS	338	153
	Total Assets	2444	2149
	Long-term Creditors	(475)	(325)
	Liabilities and Charges	(299)	(359)
	NET ASSETS	1670	1465
	CAPITAL AND RESERVES		
	Share Capital	1470	1000
	Capital Reserve	150	265
	Other Resources	50	200
	TOTAL EQUITY	1670	1465

(Brackets indicate subtraction)

Note: It is used to give current and previous year's figures for purposes of comparison. Thus, the overall performance can be compared, and also the line-by-line movements and charges.

Figure 14.1 *Profit and loss account and balance sheet example*

From a managerial point of view, the key points of assessment of accounts ought to be:

- **Gearing:** gearing is the relationship between bank loans and other capital sources of finance. In particular, dependence on very high volumes of loan capital ought to be a cause for concern. While this is not an absolute imperative, organizations that are wholly or mainly financed by share capital and retained profits are understood to have a much greater inherent financial strength than those that depend on loans.
- **Profit and loss accounts:** profit and loss accounts give a true and fair reflection of the amounts of income generated over particular periods, and the costs of generating this income. Again, conclusions can be drawn as to the relative strength of operations and the extent to which these are meeting expectations. Additionally, comparing profit and loss accounts from the present and recent periods indicates where movements are occurring, especially if costs are rising or profits are falling.
- **Balance sheet:** the balance sheet balances assets and liabilities on a given date. Assets and liabilities are valued; and the result is that the nature of assets and liabilities are presented. From a managerial point of view, the balance sheet gives a clear indication of the strength and nature of particular assets and the strength and balance of the financial capital supporting the activities (again, the balance of share and loan capital is clearly stated) – see Figure 14.1.

Identification and management of costs

It is usual to define:

- **Fixed costs** – are those that the organization has to bear as the result of its existence regardless of any business activities carried out.
- **Variable costs** – are incurred as the result of business activities. Variable costs vary according to the volumes of business and other activities carried out.

From a management point of view, it is additionally necessary to be aware of:

- **Sunk costs** – are those incurred by the organization on which there is no discernible or tangible return. Such costs include paying for errors and omissions; commissioning work, products and services that turn out to fail; developing and installing IT and other technology systems that turn out to be wrong and that have therefore to be junked; and engaging in ventures and new initiatives that turn out to have no prospects for the future.
- **Marginal costs** – are the costs of producing and delivering one extra item of product or service. It is essential to know where the margin lies; as soon as 100%

of capacity is reached, it then becomes necessary to invest in new product and service delivery technology and the staff to use it.

- **Consequential costs,** or the costs that arise as the consequence of being involved in particular activities. Examples include: the need for deficit finance when engaged in long-term and major project work; and the costs incurred in developing and evaluating the capacities and performance of new IT systems before they can be installed and used.

From a managerial point of view, it is essential to know and understand how the costs work out in particular situations. It is also essential to provide a clear and substantial rationale for how costs are considered.

Financial performance management

When assessing financial performance, managers need to know and understand the overall profitability, viability and enduring effectiveness of activities, and of the organization as a whole. As stated above, they therefore need to know the overall figures and structures produced in profit and loss accounts and balance sheets.

Managers additionally need to know the full detail that goes into these overall figures. Managers need to know, understand and be aware of income, profits and costs as follows:

- per product and service; per product and service group or cluster; per product or service range; per activity; in total;
- per employee; and this should be broken down into the contribution per member of frontline staff, and per member of support staff, as well as in total;
- per square metre; per outlet; per location; per region; per country;
- per customer or client; and this should be the starting point for assessing and evaluating customer spending habits and frequencies;
- per hour/day/week/month/season/year.

This approach to evaluating financial performance is essential so that where costs and income occur they can be assessed and evaluated. Judgements can then be made about the contribution of particular departments, divisions, functions and activities to the overall effectiveness and viability of performance. Decisions can then additionally be made about the effectiveness and viability of particular products and services, and of the entire range.

Budgets

Budgets are streams of money given to departments, divisions, groups and managers on the basis of their needs in order to be able to pay for activities. There are many ways of looking at budgets as follows:

- evaluating every cost and charge necessary to run a department, division or function and then apportioning this amount;
- carrying fixed costs centrally and creating budgets that cover variable costs only;
- giving over a single sum of money and then allowing managers to conduct their business as they see fit.

Budgeting

There are additionally organizational, behavioural and cultural factors to consider in budgeting processes as follows:

- whether budgeting processes are to be used as bidding wars playing different departments and functions off against each other;
- whether managers need to ask for 130% of what they need, hoping that they will get at least 100%;
- whether the organization operates on the basis of total budget usage, meaning that whatever resources are not used or consumed are lost by the department, division or manager; and this is worse when budgets are cut for the following year as a consequence.

Managers therefore need to understand the budgeting and apportionment processes in their particular situation. Budgeting is as much a contextual and organization cultural exercise as a financial one.

The other critical aspect of budget establishment and management is the period of time allocated. Many organizations set annual budgets and this is for a combination of practicality and expediency. The annual cycle is culturally and behaviourally easily recognizable and understood, and it gives managers time to make effective choices and decisions and then to make things work. Shorter time periods will enhance financial control; but the consequence would be to increase the cost of the budgeting process.

Whatever the budgeting process, it is essential that everyone knows and understands the core basis on which it operates. Problems indicated arise only if there is not full knowledge and understanding, or if the process is known, believed and perceived to be operated on a competitive, political, or otherwise unfair, basis.

The keys to effective budgeting are the ability to control resources, and to provide accurate financial and management information. In the pursuit of these elements, organizations tend towards one or other of the following:

- historic approaches, in which the previous year's budget is used as the basis for the present year, and it is then either increased by 'a bit' (often a percentage that reflects real and perceived inflation rates); or else it is frozen or cut so that the manager has to make savings and find efficiencies;

- zero-based approaches, in which the budget for the period is calculated from scratch with each element questioned so that as far as possible, a true as well as realistic amount is identified.

Assets and liabilities

In simple terms, assets are any resource that adds to and enhances organizational performance; liabilities are any item or obligation that places a drain on organizational resources.

Assets

Assets may be defined as:

- capital and tangible assets, consisting of premises, technology, equipment and expertise;
- intangible assets, consisting of reputation, goodwill, confidence, identity and expectation levels;
- business assets, including brand names and images, and customer and client bases;
- key figures and expertise, including top, senior and key individuals; and including also the expertise retained in work teams and departments, divisions and functions;
- perceived assets, including the historic reputation of the organization; and including also perceptions about present and enduring products, services, service levels and quality.

Liabilities

Liabilities are those factors that detract from, or place a drain on, organization resources. Liabilities are the obligations and charges that are incurred as the result of the organization's present activities. Liabilities are as follows:

- regular and continuing costs and obligations;
- activity-related charges, including maintenance charges, technology upgrades, research and development, and other pioneering and prospecting work;
- short-term liabilities, for example the need for consultants or specialist staff;
- intangible liabilities, including bad or declining reputation;
- sudden liabilities, including the sudden obsolescence of products and services, or sudden increases in the price of suppliers, technology, gas, electricity, water and premises' charges.

From an accounting point of view, assets and liabilities can be clearly stated. From a managerial point of view, the picture is more complex. In particular, something that is bought in as an asset can turn quickly into a liability. Production and information technology, bought in as long-term investment, may be rendered obsolete at any time by new inventions. Building companies that bought land banks at a particular price find that these become liabilities if the demand for building dries up, or if the price of land falls.

Depreciation

Depreciation is an accounting convention that shows the period of time over which an item is gradually paid for, paid for in instalments, and written off altogether. It is essential to remember that depreciation is purely an accounting convention, and not a managerial tool.

For example, an item of capital equipment may have cost £100,000. The organization's accounting function may then set out to depreciate it quite legitimately, at £20,000 for a period of five years. The accounting convention states therefore that the item has a useful life of five years before it is written off. However, from a managerial point of view, if it becomes obsolete after two years, then it will need to be scrapped and replaced, whatever the accounting convention may say.

Value and valuations

Organizations and their managers need to know and understand the value of everything: the organization overall; the staff and expertise employed; the products and services; property; technology; brands and identity. Organizations and managers also need to be able to place a value on their reputation, the ways in which they conduct their activities, and goodwill.

Valuing each of these items, and valuing the organization overall, is based on a combination of ascribing a monetary value to everything – and then coming to a combination of informed, objective and subjective judgement about what something is worth at a given time.

To look at value and valuation in more detail, it is necessary to ask the questions:

- What is this element worth to us?
- How much would it cost us to replace it?
- How long would it take us to replace it?
- How much is it worth to someone else?

Alongside the answers to these questions, the actual costs of acquiring, owning and using assets, equipment, expertise and brands are calculated. There is then a basis for beginning to arrive at a judgement. This judgement can then be related to:

- market values for property and expertise;
- the extent to which property and expertise is being sought after by others;

- the size and duration of commercial markets;
- the amount of business that customer and client bases bring in;
- the consequences of not having access to property, expertise, markets and locations.

Particular values can then be ascribed to each element as follows.

Staff expertise

Staff expertise includes the pay and rewards commanded; replacement costs; replacement duration (for example if someone leaves, how long it will take to replace them, and the consequences of not having the expertise for this period); any 'brand value' that the staff carry (for example iconic figures such as David Beckham; distinctive expertise such as specialist surgical skills for hospitals). Moreover, it includes any additional value that is known, believed and perceived to be added by the workforce to the organization as a whole.

Valuing Beckham

Over the years, David Beckham, the former England football captain, has been built into a brand. As well as his considerable professional expertise, he has succeeded in developing a combination of presence, personality and presentation that has enabled him, his employers (Manchester United, Real Madrid, AC Milan and LA Galaxy), and other commercial interests to benefit and profit from the association. For example:

- his period at Real Madrid resulted in sales of 3.5 million replica shirts;
- his period at LA Galaxy resulted in doubled television advertising revenues wherever he was playing.

With the exception of one or two alleged marriage infidelities, David Beckham's press, media and PR coverage has been overwhelmingly positive. The outcome is a brand which has value in terms of:

- the cost of his present and future employment and employability;
- value that he is understood to add to his employers, and also in terms of the television and merchandising issues indicated above.

Calculations can therefore be made on the basis of all this, and a view arrived at of:

- how much he is worth paying;
- how much he is going to bring in, and from where;
- whether present and future employers want him at that price.

Clearly, this is an extreme and iconic example! However, all organizations need to be able to value the real and perceived expertise that they have available. In particular, the contribution of all staff needs valuing from the point of view of the work that they bring in and carry out, and whether they are worth employing at that price. This is especially true where it is difficult to get hold of professional staff (for example nurses, teachers). The problem here is not whether you want them at the price, but in many cases, a clear understanding that the price (the salary) on offer is undervaluing their expertise.

Human asset valuation

As indicated above, the 'human assets' – the staff and their expertise – carry a value that is measured in terms of the performance that they deliver for the organization, and the organizational reputation and confidence that is developed as the result.

The basis of valuation is the cost of employment, which includes:

- the total payroll costs;
- payroll costs by staff category and expertise;
- the amounts that have to be paid in order to attract and retain high value or scarce expertise;
- any other factors, including sectoral and occupational norms, local factors, and the extent of sectoral or local competition for each.

As with other assets, the staff remain an asset only for as long as they continue to deliver the behaviour, performance and value required.

The issue of human liability has therefore to be addressed. Staff and their expertise become obsolete if they are not developed; and so from a general, as well as financial management point of view, continuous attention to training and development is required if the staff are to remain effective (in financial or any other terms).

Organizations additionally place value on top, senior and key figures. Questions of profitability, effectiveness and organization and market development have to be assessed in terms of the contribution of these individuals, as well as the activities of the staff who deliver performance. In particular, any question of economic rent (or very high value) placed on particular expertise has also to be assessed. Where individuals are known, believed or perceived to be overvalued, there is always a detrimental effect on collective performance; and this above all, should be a key driving force when assessing and delivering reward packages for top and senior managers and other key figures.

Property valuation

Valuing property is more straightforward in that there will always be known, believed and perceived 'going rates' for property and premises based on existing local markets, and the prices presently being achieved. To this is added the question of preferred location: when the property is in a capital city, industrial centre, or other sought after place, the value tends to go up. It is also necessary to be aware of the potential limitations on the property in terms of size, access and egress. It is also necessary to recognize that property prices and values can fall as well as rise. Situations to be particularly aware of are:

- where the property remains critically useful to the organization, and is tenable from every other point of view except the ability to pay for it;
- where the property has been valued as a capital asset, but this value has now fallen;
- where the property has been purchased for operational reasons, but has now risen in value so much that the organization has to consider whether or not to cash it in.

Technology

Technology has a value only in terms of what it can deliver for the organization; it is now more or less universally understood that there is little, if any, resale or residual value once it has fulfilled its anticipated useful life. Technology is therefore normally regarded as a sunk cost although the expertise required to use it, and maximize and optimize its output, does have a value.

Products and services

Products and services have wholesale and retail values based in the first instance on the prices charged and the volumes of business conducted. Products and services have additional value in terms of the overall customer and client bases attracted and served. For example, a company may buy up a product or service line from another wholly or mainly in order to gain access to the customer or client bases for its own purposes.

Brands

Brand values are ascribed to the brand of products and services; the reputation of the organization; and the organization itself. Valuing brands is a combination of the measurable, in terms of the amount of business generated, and the highly subjective, based on the questions: 'How much do we think the brand is worth?', 'How much do we want for it if we do decide to sell it?' or 'How much do we want to pay for it if we do decide to buy it?'

From an organizational point of view, all valuations are ultimately based on the relative value ascribed by buyers and sellers. If someone is determined to buy something, the price (and therefore the value) goes up. If someone is determined to sell something, or needs to sell it, then the price comes down. If two or more buyers are interested, then there is further upwards pressure. If nobody is interested in buying, then the price has to come down far enough to make it attractive to potential buyers.

This part of the managerial perspective on finance needs careful assessment and expert understanding. In many cases, company accounts and organizational and departmental budgets are the only financial points of reference available. It is essential that organizations and their managers have a much deeper understanding of assets and liabilities (and the differences between the two, and how they change from one to the other), and values and valuation, to ensure that they know where money is being made and lost and the contribution of each activity.

From a managerial point of view, the definition of assets and liabilities especially is a matter of expert and informed judgement. Assets are anything or anyone that adds to the productive effort and overall performance; liabilities are anything or anyone that detracts from the productive effort and places a drain or strain on resources. This fundamental approach ought to be the guiding principle in defining assets and liabilities from a managerial point of view.

Investment appraisal

The purpose of any investment is to gain returns and these are normally expressed in financial terms, as well as other desired outcomes.

Effective investment appraisal therefore requires that the desired and demanded levels of returns must be made explicit at the outset. Clear financial projections must be stated, as must related issues of returns on investment that concern market development, sales of products and services, and reputation enhancement.

The nature of returns on investment

As an example, if returns of 30% per annum are required, then investments have to be concentrated in areas and activities where these levels are possible. Conversely, if organizations are determined to be in specific activities even though these only normally deliver returns of 3% per annum, then this represents a particular consequence that has to be understood and managed. It is also essential to recognize that returns do change and vary over the lifetime of an investment, and returns that were envisaged at the outset may not be available when the investment comes to fruition or to be realized.

In practice, it is impossible to predict with absolute certainty or accuracy the outcome of specific investments and initiatives. It is therefore usual to define boundaries of acceptability or margins against the target that are agreed to represent success and achievement in context.

Investment appraisal and management additionally needs timescales and time frames in all circumstances. Timescales and time frames also require understanding and acceptance at the point at which resources are committed to particular initiatives. Timescales can in practice, be changed, extended or contracted as the result of changes in circumstances within the environment, changes to market, product and service demands, and as the result of changes in specific issues, especially the costs of finance, or the prices that can be charged for products and services.

In order to conduct effective investment activities, pre-investment groundwork is essential. This has the purpose of gaining full and comprehensive knowledge and understanding of the context in which investments, initiatives and ventures are being considered. The issues that normally have to be covered are:

- the range of returns possible, both positive and negative, expressed in financial terms;
- the range of returns possible, both positive and negative, expressed in non-financial terms;
- determination of priorities, aims and objectives for the particular initiative or proposal;
- determination of secondary or subsidiary aims and objectives for the particular initiative or proposal;
- assessment of the risks involved;
- definitions of success and failure, known, understood and accepted by everyone involved.

It becomes clear that investment appraisal is a process rather than an activity. At the core of all investment appraisal activities are the financial considerations. However, much of the complexity involved is non-financial, relating to the business outcomes stated.

Effective investment appraisal and management requires full and accurate knowledge of the environment in which investments are being made and ventures are being considered. If the success of whatever is proposed depends on achieving a particular financial figure, then a full assessment of whether it is possible to achieve these figures must be undertaken at the outset; and this, in turn, must be undertaken in conjunction with an assessment of everything that could possibly or conceivably affect the ability to achieve these figures.

Returns on investment are normally expressed as a percentage of the total cost or value of the investment. As stated above, returns additionally need to be expressed in non-financial terms so that attention is drawn to the full context, and especially to the business purposes.

Cost–benefit analysis

Cost–benefit analysis is a concise ready-reckoner method of establishing the basis on which given initiatives and ventures might be feasible or profitable in both financial and non-financial terms. Cost–benefit analysis requires itemizing all of the costs and charges that could possibly be incurred in the venture and then setting them out against all the values and benefits that the completed initiative is expected to deliver.

Cost–benefit analysis is used widely in the consideration of public sector and commercial projects, and commercial ventures that bring wider social and economic benefits, as well as pure financial returns. Cost–benefit analysis is structured as follows:

- **action choices:** relating the purpose and outcomes of courses of action to each other;
- **time frames:** definitions of short, medium and long-term costs and the results to be accrued;
- **values:** both monetary values, and also in relation to wider economic and generation activities; and additionally, in terms of contribution to the public good;
- **priorities:** the priorities ascribed by all involved to the particular venture, and an assessment of some of the opportunities that might have to be forgone if circumstances change;
- **initiatives:** with especial reference to the effect that particular ventures and activities might have in terms of derived income and future prospects; and with reference also to less acceptable by-products such as effluent, waste and environmental damage;
- **risk and uncertainty:** consideration of the aspects of risk that must be built into the particular venture or initiative;
- **strategy:** aligning particular ventures and initiatives with organization strategy;
- **relativity:** the relative valuation and priority of different costs and benefits in terms of everything that is to be achieved;
- **income and expenditure:** relating what is being done to the cost and charges accrued, and to the immediate, apparent, potential and eventual returns made available (see Figure 14.2).

Action choice	Priority	Initiative
• Size • Capacity • Cost	• Policy driven • Vested interests • Motoring and transport lobbies • Green lobbies	• Integrated transport or isolated scheme • Job creation • Ending local and national benefits
Long term	**Strategic aspect**	**Risk**
• Facility usage • Upgrades • Short-term disruption and blight	• Transport improvement • Solve part of traffic problem • Part of national network	• Low as long as publicly financed • Materials availability • Expertise availability
Relative valuation	**Income–expenditure**	**Value**
• Government • Companies building it • Transport companies • Individual road users • Environmental lobbies	• Direct income only if tolls used • Derived income from greater usage and work generated • No direct returns otherwise	• To users • Negative value to environmental lobbies

Figure 14.2 *Cost–benefit analysis for a proposed motorway scheme*

Other numerical data

It is essential that managers are able to understand content, context and range of financial issues, how they interrelate with each other, and how they inform managerial thinking and judgement. It is also essential that managers know and understand how to look at other sources of data.

Primary and secondary data

Data can initially be categorized as primary or secondary:

- Primary data is obtained directly by organizations and individuals through observations, surveys, interviews and samples.
- Secondary data comes from other sources such as official statistics provided by government sources, and sectoral data gathered by employers' associations and marketing organizations.

It is essential to recognize that the use of secondary data always involves taking information that others have gathered, and interpreting it for purposes different from those that the original gatherers had intended.

This has to be balanced against the fact that gathering primary data is more time-consuming and expensive, though it is related directly to stated purposes.

It is therefore essential to be able to reconcile completeness and clarity of purpose with timescales and deadlines. The shorter the timescale or deadline, the greater the pressure to use existing data rather than primary sources.

The main sources of data available to management are:

- **Government statistics:** useful as general indicators of the state of national, business and economic confidence, direction and activity, and what is likely to happen in the foreseeable future.
- **Sectoral statistics:** produced by trade federations, employers' associations and professional bodies in the interests of their members.
- **Market research organizations:** which hold data on vast ranges of issues which they sell on a commercial basis to those requiring it; and which will produce data in response to organization requests.
- **Local government and other public bodies:** hold wide ranges of general data on the composition of society and people's standards of living and activities.
- **Public inquiries:** generate a great amount of information on particular initiatives (for example urban development and capital projects) that is often a useful point of reference for those planning other things in the area.

Whatever the basis, managers need to know and understand why specific information has been gathered and how it was originally to be used. It is therefore necessary to know and understand what methods were used to gather, store, analyse and evaluate particular information and any shortcomings that were either present at the time or have subsequently emerged. Managers need to know and understand the strength of the data and information from the point of view of:

- **Validity**: the extent to which the data and information prove, imply or indicate what was intended; if the data is invalid, this means it cannot be used to prove, indicate or imply the conclusions drawn.
- **Reliability**: the extent to which the data supports a single set of results only; or the extent to which the data can be relied on to support the fact or belief that the results would have been the same, wherever and whenever the information was gathered.
- **Currency**: the time lag between when the data was gathered and when it is being used; in general, the longer the time lag, the greater the scepticism with which it should be used.

Decision-making

The primary use of financial information and other data and statistics is as an aid to decision-making. All decision-making is a matter of judgement, and the greater the comprehensiveness and clarity of the data available, the greater the basis on which it can be used to inform and support particular decisions.

Many organizations now use business analytics and other data management activities to support and inform the critical areas of decision-making, risk analyses and market information evaluation. In particular, reliable and accurate financial data and other information are required to assist and support decision-making in the following areas:

- policy and strategy formulation, and the assessment of priorities;
- marketing activities and initiatives, measurable in increases or decreases in sales of products and services;
- output, productivity and delivery;
- identifying faults in particular aspects of products and services;
- successes and failures in staffing issues, employment relations, recruitment campaigns and staff retention rates;
- the effectiveness, or otherwise, of particular production, service and business process technologies;
- the effectiveness, or otherwise, of particular information technologies;
- the reliability and effectiveness of planning, forecasting and extrapolation processes.

It is additionally essential to have reliable and accurate data when considering specific problems and issues. For example, customer complaints, production, rejection rates, staff complaints and information database deficiencies all require accurate analysis and evaluation to consider:

- the nature and frequency of the occurrence of defects and complaints;

- the source of these defects and complaints;
- the time period over which the complaints and defects have arisen, and any trends within these time periods: for example whether the complaints have suddenly started to be made, whether they have risen or fallen on a regular basis, or whether the methods of logging them have changed.

The critical issue is the ability to use existing data to predict and inform decisions for the future, when there is clearly no data available from the future! All data management and data analyses have the flaw of using information from the past to assess the future; and so all forecasting and decision-making is subject to uncertainty. The expertise of managers and data analysts in relating what has happened to what has not yet happened is a critical factor in all forward planning, environmental assessment and strategic and operational decision-making.

Conclusions

The main conclusion to be drawn is in recognizing the difference between the work of professional accountants and statisticians in producing figures, and that of managers in using, interpreting, analysing and evaluating them. In many ways, the work of managers starts where that of the accountant and statistician finishes.

Managers need excellent and comprehensive sources of information that can effectively inform the whole of their range of activities (see also Chapter 2). Additionally, managers need to have proper knowledge and understanding of how figures are produced, what they mean, how they can be interpreted, and what they might state about the condition of the organization as a whole and its particular activities.

Effective financial management requires a high level of organizational and environmental knowledge and understanding. This is a key part of the capability to choose the right approach to finance in any particular set of circumstances, the right financial performance measures, and the right means for the assessment of the financial and quantitative aspects of management in particular situations.

In practice, the use of financial and other figures in management is often not helped by the resource allocation process that occurs within organizations. Data is used to emphasize partial points of view, or to emphasize the real, perceived and understood levels of performance in some areas relative to others.

There is also an enduring problem for those responsible for managing budgets. The point is made above that many budgets and financial resource allocations are set without any relationship to the levels of finance actually required or what they are to be spent on. This is certain to lead to many managers having to work within constraints that make it impossible to deliver the required levels of products, services and outputs.

Understanding the context, content, use and application of financial and other figures is therefore an essential part of managerial expertise, and one that it is essential to develop.

- It is essential to recognize the difference between accounts and financial management; accounts are drawn up by professionals for particular legal and regulatory purposes, while financial management is concerned with the whole range of organizational financial aspects.
- There are distinctive managerial approaches required in the assessment and evaluation of costs, charges, assets, liabilities and value. In particular, assets and liabilities from the managerial point of view can change from one to the other very quickly.
- Budgeting processes have to be seen as serving a clear and distinctive purpose – that of ensuring resources are necessary for departments and managers to carry out their activities effectively.
- All data and statistics have to be evaluated for validity, reliability and currency if they are to provide effective support for decision-making.
- Financial management, and the use of data and statistics, is an essential part of underpinning and supporting the manager's wider environmental and contextual knowledge.

Further reading

Arnold, G. (2010) *Corporate Financial Management.* Pearson.

Atrill, P. (2008) *Financial Management for Decision Makers.* Wiley.

Davenport, T. and Harris, J. (2007) *Competing on Analytics: The New Science of Winning.* Harvard Business School Press.

Knott, G. (2004) *Financial Management.* Palgrave Macmillan.

Marchand, D. and Davenport, H. (1999) *Mastering Information Management.* Macmillan.

Walsh, C. (2008) *Key Management Ratios.* Pearson (FT series).

Weetman, P. (2006) *Financial and Management Accounting: An Introduction.* McGraw Hill.

Organizational and managerial performance

15

'You can only measure anything for success or failure against what you set out to achieve.'

In this chapter

- identifying the need to measure all performance against objectives and intended outcomes
- the complexities of managerial and organizational performance
- using a range, diversity and complexity of measures to establish overall performance
- attending to different aspects of performance in order to build a complete picture

Introduction

Organizational and managerial performance is only measurable against what was intended or planned. It follows from this that organizational and managerial performance is a combination of priorities, aims and objectives, together with the capacity, capability and willingness on the part of everyone involved to do their best to achieve and to deliver what was intended. This has in turn to be seen in the context of whether performance is achievable in the present markets, locations and environment, with the present levels of staff and technology, and whether changes in all, or any, of these are required and desired; or conversely, whether changes in any, or all, of these would render it impossible to deliver what was intended.

In general terms, all organizations in every sphere of activity are concerned with the same thing.

- Maximizing customer, client and user satisfaction of their products and services over the long term.

- Maximizing the confidence of everyone involved or affected by the organization over the long term.
- Maximizing long-term owner/shareholder value and getting the best possible return on investment over the long term (and this applies to public services as well as commercial undertakings).
- Securing the long-term future and well-being of the organization.
- Working within the particular context and environment, with especial recognition of functions inside and outside the organization's control.

This all applies to private and commercial companies, public sector and service organizations, and the not-for-profit sector.

Prerequisites for successful and effective performance

Effective performance is only achievable if the following key elements are present.

- **Agreed aims and objectives, priorities, purposes and outcomes as above:** so that everybody knows and understands what is intended by the organization as a whole, and what the collective and individual contributions to this core purpose are to be.

point of view

Agreed aims, objectives and priorities

In practice, there is often an immediate problem with agreeing aims, objectives and priorities. For example:

- a hospital medical team has the treatment of patients as its priority;
- hospital managers have remaining within budget and delivering value for money as their priorities.

The first priority therefore is to reconcile the extent to which the differing aims and objectives of staff groups are capable of:

- full integration;
- partial integration;
- little or no integration.

Where full integration is possible or achievable, there is no problem at this stage. Problems do arise where little or no integration is possible. Organizations and their managers have to arrive at a view as to whether or not the differing aims, objectives and priorities should be reconciled.

In practice, this is very uncomfortable, and very often the decision is taken to 'muddle along' rather than clarifying particular positions. Failure to address this core issue normally leads to declining levels of performance and increased expense.

- **Clarity of purpose and direction:** knowing where you are going and how to get there; understanding the full implications and commitment necessary to achieve this.
- **Adequate levels of resources:** investment; information; technology; staff capability; expertise; willingness and commitment.
- **Knowledge and understanding:** of the markets in which activities and operations are to take place and what customers and clients want and expect from them; of what the organization's total capacity is; what it can and cannot achieve; and any operational implications arising; of the total environment in which activities are to take place.

This gives the broad context in which performance is measured. It cannot be measured effectively if this is not fully understood.

just a minute

It is essential always to look back at targets, aims, objectives and priorities to ensure that they deliver at least one of the above. Where this cannot be stated or clarified, you ought to be reviewing the targets, aims, objectives and priorities for viability, value and validity.

Components of successful performance

Organizational and managerial performance is measured in the following areas, again always against what was intended or what the organization set out to achieve.

- **Market standing:** overall organizational reputation; reputation of products and services; reputation of staff and expertise; size of market served; location of market served; specific needs, wants and demands.
- **Market position:** actual market position in relation to desired position; the costs and benefits of maintaining this; opportunity costs; returns on resources; returns on investment.
- **Innovation:** capacity for innovation; desired and actual levels of innovation; time taken for new products and ideas to reach the market; attitudes to innovation; percentages of new products and ideas that become commercial successes.
- **Creativity:** expertise of staff; versatility and ability to diversify; capability for turning ideas into commercial successes; new product/service strike rates; attitudes to creativity; other related qualities, above all flexibility and responsiveness.

- **Financial performance:** attention to levels of income over expenditure; the identification of specific cost and profit centres; attention to the nature and volume of returns on investment; identifying and managing fixed, variable and marginal cost bases; identifying the financial demands made by resources, processes, technology and staff.

- **Resource utilization:** efficiency and effectiveness; balance of resources used in primary and support functions; wastage rates; resource utilization and added value.

The chocolate factory

The chief executive of the Mars chocolate company was making a visit to one of the company's factories. There, he was horrified to find that some of the staff were working on a production line where the temperature was 55 degrees centigrade. He went round and asked the factory manager what was going on. Back came the explanation: 'The cooling system on the production plant is broken. I don't have the resources to repair or replace the equipment until the next financial year. The staff are therefore having to work in these conditions'.

The chief executive moved the factory manager's desk up into the production area stating that it would remain there, and the factory manager would work there, until the problem was fixed.

The problem was fixed the following day.

The lesson is that resource utilization should always be a matter of managerial judgement. Changes do have to be made from time to time. If essential work needs doing, resources always have to be found; and if necessary, taken away from areas and activities that have a lower priority.

- **Managerial performance:** total managerial performance; performance by function, department, division, group; performance at different levels of management – director, general manager, senior, middle, junior, supervisory, first line.

- **Management development:** areas of strength and weakness; progress and improvement; desired expertise and capability; actual expertise and capability; development of specific skills and knowledge; desired and actual attitudes and behaviour; priority of training and development.

- **Staff performance:** areas of strength and weakness; progress and improvement; attitudes and willingness to work; degrees of commitment; desired expertise and capability; actual expertise and capability; development of specific skills and knowledge; desired and actual attitudes and behaviour; attention to work patterns; commitment; extent and priority of training and development; targeting of training and development; attitudes to staff suggestions; specific positive and negative features.

- **Workforce structure:** core and peripheral; flexibility in attitudes and behaviour; multi-skilling; work patterns; general employability; continued future employability; relations between organization and workforce; relations between managers and staff; length and strength of hierarchies.
- **Wage and pay levels:** relationships between pay and output; relationships between pay, profits and performance; local factors and conditions; industrial factors and conditions; relationships between pay and expertise; pay as incentive; economic rent; known, believed and perceived areas of over and underpaying.
- **Organizational culture:** the extent to which this is positive/negative; identifying and removing negative factors; accentuating the positive; motivation and morale; staff policies; industrial relations; staff management; designed, emergent, strong, weak, suitable, unsuitable, acceptable, unacceptable aspects of organization culture.
- **Key relationships:** with backers; with staff; with suppliers; with distributors; with customers; with community.

point of view

Stakeholder interests and performance

Organizations inevitably have dominant stakeholders – those whose interests must be served above all else; or, more insidiously, those whose interests are served as a priority, whether or not this is the correct course of action for the particular organization.

The financial interest is invariably to be found as a dominant stakeholder; the best organizations also place their staff, suppliers and customers at this level. It is also true that any group that has cause to raise legitimate concerns about the organization and its activities should be treated as a dominant stakeholder until its problems have been resolved.

Serious problems can arise when the interests of the dominant stakeholders are served in spite of conflicting or divergent concerns from less influential sources.

The lesson is to know and understand which interest is being served. In particular, it is essential to know and understand whether specific interests are being served at the expense of others; or whether every interest is being served as far as possible. It is additionally essential to know and understand that, whichever line is taken, there are opportunities and consequences that are certain to affect both performance itself, and also the ways and means by which performance is achieved.

- **Public standing:** the respect and esteem in which the organization is held in its markets, in the community, among its staff, customers and suppliers; confidence and expectations; general public factor coverage.
- **Profitability:** levels of profits accrued; timescales; means of measuring and assessing products; scope for enhancement and improvement.

- **Ethical factors:** the absolute standards that the organization sets for itself; what it will and will not do; its attitudes to its staff, customers, clients, suppliers and communities; the nature of the markets served; standards and quality of the treatment of staff; management style; attitudes and approaches to customer complaints; attitudes and approaches to suppliers; quality of public relations; quality of community relations.
- **Other factors:** general efficiency and effectiveness; product and service quality and value; areas for improvement; areas where complaints come from; opportunities and threats; crises and emergencies.

Only three of the above areas identified are clearly and overtly financial. All the rest clearly contribute to the finances of the organization. However, drawing attention to this list of performance areas ought clearly to indicate the shortcomings of just concentrating on finances and figures without knowing and understanding – and addressing – the full context.

Additionally, many of the above areas overlap. In some cases, the same phrases are used under different headings. Without doubt, different words and phrases could be used to convey the same meanings. The mix and balance varies between organizations. However, every element is present in all situations to a greater or lesser extent. Initial lessons can therefore be drawn as follows.

There is no single effective measure of performance in any situation or organization. Even if a supervisor is working to a single daily production target, he/she must have the right staff, adequately trained and motivated; the right volume and quality of components; and somewhere to put the finished items. And given the normal nature of work – all work – all this has to be available on a steady and continuous basis.

A large proportion of the elements indicated are qualitative not quantitative. The main qualities necessary to evaluate such factors properly are therefore judgement and analysis. Success and failure are value judgements placed on events and activities based on high levels of knowledge and expertise. Seldom, if ever, is success or failure self-evident except in the immediate or very short term.

It follows in turn that the main attributes of those who measure business and managerial performance have knowledge, expertise and understanding: of results; of the environment; of people; of customers and the market; of the product/services offered; of the organization's general position. It is also the case that any situation can be turned to the organization's ultimate advantage if it and its managers choose to do so. Provided that the cause is not negligence or criminal activity, organizations can turn simple errors and omissions into profitable and effective ventures by ensuring that what has happened is fully analysed, and then used as a vehicle for learning and development.

Cock-ups can have a silver lining

Many organizations, and especially their top managers, find themselves unwilling to admit where, when or why mistakes are made. Invariably, they rather look for scapegoats, or else are inclined (if allowed to do so) to put failure down to 'factors outside their control' or 'volatile market conditions'.

Yet the theory of managerial cock-ups is the orphan of management studies. Innumerable books have been written on strategic triumphs and tragedies, but nearly all assume that the heroes or villains knew what they were doing. By contrast, the 'cock-up' theory holds that management moves, not from one considered coordinated ploy to the next, but by isolated lurches. These are governed, not by deep analysis and optimization of resources, but by impulse and unguarded optimism.

The 'cock-up' theory holds that problems always prove much greater than anyone expects. Financially, the potential killer is cost. If actual earnings fail to cover the true cost of capital and other resources used in particular ventures, the value of the company becomes eroded. Cock-ups might well be fewer therefore, if top managements were penalized when acquisitions, changes of direction, and other supposed brainwaves generated negative returns. Bonuses and long-term remuneration for directors and senior managers ought to be reduced in direct relationship to these negative returns. That is, after all, how many chief executives use remuneration systems to pressurize subordinates. What is sauce for the geese should surely apply to the ganders. But the 'cock-up' theory holds that this is where the whole bungling process begins – with the lack of checks and balances on over-mighty corporate rulers.

Cock-ups teach invaluable lessons. Management who have had their noses rubbed in the realities of the market and economic conditions tend to ensure that false assumptions are replaced by true facts. Necessary changes in people and policies are clearly indicated. Instead of indulging in corporate hand-wringing, there is a clear opportunity to assess why things went wrong, and from this, to take steps to ensure that specific, useful and practical measures of performance are instigated at the outset of any venture or initiative.

Source: Robert Heller (1998b).

The practice of performance measurement and assessment

Having identified the complexities of performance measurement and assessment, and the full range of areas in which attention is required, it is not surprising that things can, and do, go wrong from time to time.

From a human as well as a managerial point of view, the overwhelming pressure and perception is to simplify things as far as possible. Especially, by concentrating either on the finances or on production and output targets, something is available which is clearly recognizable and overtly measurable.

The simplified approach is then turned into other measurement activities such as performance appraisal, return on investment, hitting financial and output targets, and then handing a simplified and simplistic form of performance requirements on to staff.

The result is that very little attention is paid to the full complexity. The development of expertise in performance management in practice ought to be a major priority in management development activities. It ought also to be an area of prime concern for those in top, senior and key positions; all the while that the complexities are not addressed, performance (and what contributes to it) is not fully understood. Lack of attention and expertise in this part of management practice is likely also to lead to declining levels of organizational performance when measured in financial and production/output terms.

just a minute

Always remember that what gets measured gets done. If you concentrate on the full range of performance measures and indicators, life is more complicated but you provide the basis for developing sustainable and increasing levels of performance. If you concentrate on just one performance measure, everyone else will simply concentrate on this.

Information

Effective performance measurement and assessment is never possible without full, or at least adequate, information covering each of these areas and this must be constantly gathered and evaluated. Markets, technology and expertise are all constantly changing and organizations that do not respond have, at the very least, to recognize the effects that such a lack of response will, or may, have. Full information enables organizations and their managers to reduce uncertainty, analyse levels of risk, maximize chances of success, minimize chances of failure and assess the prospects and likely consequences and outcomes of following particular courses of activity. It enables projections to be made for the organization as a whole and for each of its activities. Summary positions are often established under the headings of **strengths, weaknesses, opportunities, threats**; and these are most effective when related to the organization as a whole, to its markets, to its backers and stakeholders, and to its competitors.

Effective planning is also based on full information. The value of planning is at its greatest when it allows organizations to:

- see the future as it unfolds, recognizing possible, likely and (more or less) certain developments;
- assess the continued performance of all activities and operations;
- assess the ways in which other people and organizations, especially competitors are operating.

Effective planning is a process, the purpose of which is to arrive at, and retain, continued clarity of direction. It involves the analysis of the information: thinking it through, testing ideas; examining what is possible and what is not. More specific schedules, practices, operations, activities, aims and objectives all then come from this body of knowledge and the understanding which arises from analysing it. Implementation and execution are then handed on to different people, functions, divisions and departments within the organization.

It should be apparent from this that there is a world of difference between planning and plans. Dwight D. Eisenhower, the United States general and president, once said: 'Planning is everything, the plan is nothing.' At their best, corporate and organizational plans are statements of what is now proposed as the result of information available; and subject to change, modification and, when necessary, abandonment as and when circumstances change.

At their worst, they are detailed statements covering the way that the world is certain to be extending into the far distant future. No such position is sustainable now – indeed, it probably never was in the past. This does not prevent large corporations, both public and private, and the policy units of public services drawing these up. At best, they are an irrelevance. More usually, they constitute a waste of organizational resources that would be better used elsewhere. At worst, they are indeed slavishly followed in the teeth of a changing world and competitive environment with immense adverse consequences for the organization.

Responsibilities

Organizational responsibilities

Specific organizational responsibilities exist in the following areas; and these areas provide the basis for where performance is to be evaluated and developed.

- Anticipating the future in terms of the changing environment; anticipating changes in customer demands and perceptions; recognizing changes in the nature of competition; recognizing changes in production and service technology; recognizing and anticipating changes in the nature of people attracted to work for the organization and the sector; recognizing and anticipating changes in the customer base.
- Investment as a continued commitment: in the areas of product development; quality improvement; management and staff training and development; production and service technology; the well-being of the customer.
- Organization development: in terms of its skills, knowledge, capabilities, attitudes and expertise; in terms of customer awareness and satisfaction; in terms of processes and procedures; in terms of supplier and distributor relations; in terms of its culture and structures.

- Training and development: of both management and staff in the skills, qualities, attributes and expertise necessary to secure the future; and in the key attitudes of flexibility, dynamism, responsiveness, willingness and commitment.
- Recognition of the fact that all organizations currently operate in a changing and turbulent environment; that historic and current success, efficiency, effectiveness and profitability is no guarantee that this will extend into the future. From this comes an obligation to ensure that all staff are capable of existing in this environment and that they are equipped with the resources and capability to do so.
- Openness: people respond to uncertainty and turbulence much better if they understand its extent and why they must constantly update and develop. Organizations therefore have a clear duty to inform, consult and provide detail on all aspects of performance in general; and in more detail, concerning things which directly affect specific members and groups of staff.
- Ethics: long-term existence, the ability to secure the employment of staff, and establishing a regular and profitable customer base are enhanced by taking, accepting, and understanding a view of the world as it really is. There is, therefore, a moral, as well as commercial, commitment.

Managerial responsibilities

Specific managerial responsibilities exist in the following areas.

- To develop (and be developed in) capabilities and expertise required by the organization; required by the nature of professional management as it develops; and which involvement in the particular business, industry or service requires.
- To take a personal commitment to organizational success as well as that of the department, division or function for which the individual is responsible. High levels of personal commitment are required of all professions and professionals, in all spheres of activity and expertise, and this is also true of management and managers.
- To develop the full range of managerial skills and qualities required by the profession of management. This currently means being able to solve problems; manage people; set standards of performance; understand where the manager's domain fits into the wider scheme of things and total organizational performance; use resources efficiently and effectively; set and assess budgets; recognize the constraints under which operations have to be carried out; and generate a positive, open and harmonious culture and attitudes.

At the heart of all organizational and managerial responsibility is the need to produce goods and services in the required volume and quality, at the right price, in the right place. This can only be achieved through having top quality, expert and highly motivated staff. This is the critical factor in which the long-term future of the organization is secured and all effective measures of organization and managerial performance have this at their core.

Expert and professional managers know and understand their key responsibility in the areas of performance assessment, evaluation, monitoring, review and development. A full understanding of all these factors is essential if performance improvements and enhancement are to be developed and sustained for the long term.

Priorities, aims and objectives

All performance has to be measured against what was intended, as above; and this is the reason for setting priorities, aims and objectives. Aims and objectives occur at different levels and, again, are set or inferred by each of the above groups to satisfy their particular points of view.

- **Corporate:** reflecting the overall scope of the organization; how it is to be run in structural and financial terms; how resources are to be allocated.
- **Competitive/business level:** how the organization is to compete in its different markets; which products and services should be developed and offered; the extent to which these meet customer needs; monitoring of product performance.
- **Operational:** how different functions of the organization contribute to total organizational purpose and activities.
- **Behavioural:** related to the human interactions between different parts of the organization; and between the organization, its customers and the wider community.
- **Confidence:** the generation of confidence and reputation among all those with whom it comes into contact.
- **Ethical:** meeting specific standards that may be enshrined in policy; the ability to work in certain activities, in certain locations; the attitude taken towards staff, customers and others with whom the organization comes into contact.

Aims and objectives should be a combination of the precise:

- **specific:** dealing with easily identifiable and quantifiable aspects of performance;
- **measurable:** devised in ways so that success and failure can be identified;
- **achievable:** striking a balance between maximizing/optimizing resources and output without setting standards so high that targets are unattainable and therefore unvalued;
- **recognizable:** understood by all concerned;
- **time constrained:** so that a continuous record of progress and achievement may be kept and problem areas identified;

and the imprecise, continuous and proactive:

- reconciling these differing and often conflicting pressures;
- attending to all aspects of organizational performance;

- providing distinctive measures of success and failure;
- enhancing the total performance of the organization;
- where necessary, reconciling the different and conflicting demands of particular stakeholders and interested parties;
- being prepared to adjust or alter direction and priority if the situation demands;
- establishing procedures for monitoring, review and evaluating all aspects of performance, and acting on the results.

Aims and objectives are required for the organization as a whole; and for each and every department, division, function, work group, location and individual. It is therefore impossible to set generic objectives. All aims and objectives must be drawn up against the organization's specific context and background if they are to have any meaning. Whatever they refer to, they must reflect the following questions.

- What contribution does this activity/set of activities make to total organizational performance; where does this fit into the broader objectives of the department, division or function concerned? Where does this fit into the wider purpose of the organization?
- What resources, equipment, information, technology and expertise are needed to carry it out successfully?
- What specific restraints are there – for example: can it be done straight away; are there other things that must first be done; how long does it/will it/must it take?

Aims and objectives therefore attend to both the broad and also the precise, including quantitative, qualitative and unquantifiable elements.

This is the broad context in which measuring all aspects of organizational and managerial performance takes place. It is not possible to do this effectively or successfully in isolation – and the fact that some organizations nevertheless attempt this, does not make it right. Without understanding this basis, both quantitative and qualitative performance measures have no meaning to those who are allocated more specific performance targets. Lack of any context is also one of the main reasons why staff, product and service performance appraisal and measurement schemes fall into disrepute. Whatever is done, must be understood, acceptable and valuable to those involved. Acceptability springs from understanding and this is based in turn on the effective communication of the right and required information to those involved.

The best managers do not set isolated performance targets. They know and understand the full context in which performance takes place in all situations; and they know and understand what happens to performance when elements of that context change.

Assessment and judgement

It is clear from the above that business and managerial performance measurement is largely qualitative. This is because organizations are created and staffed by people, and because their customers, clients and users are people also. Moreover, the most overtly mathematical and precise measures of performance have to be seen in the context in which they are established and then judged and evaluated by those responsible.

Performance measurement: Example

To illustrate the point, a 35% increase in sales is an overtly easy and straightforward measure of performance. There is a precise target to aim for, and whether or not it is achieved is easily quantifiable. However, the following elements have still to be addressed.

- The time period over which the increase is to take place.
- What constitutes bad, inadequate or unsatisfactory performance: whether this is 1%, 34%, 34.9% – or what.
- What the broader consequences of 'just failing' to meet the target are.
- What the consequences of achieving a 35% rise are (will this destabilize the rest of activities; is this a useful windfall; or what?).
- What the consequences of achieving a 100%/1,000%/10,000% increase are (again, is this a useful windfall, a serious destabilization of the rest of the organization's activities, or what?).
- Whether the 35% increase is required across the board, or whether an overall increase of 35% will do.
- Whether the 35% would be covered by a one-off purchase or windfall.
- Whether, if the 35% increase is fulfilled the following week, the target will be revised for the future.
- Whether this is a reflection of the capacity and capability of the rest of the organization.
- Whether this is within the workforce's capability, whether overtime will have to be worked, or whether new staff will have to be taken on.
- Any questions of location – are there any questions of specific market/localized constraints; the extent to which it is related to relative levels of prosperity in the market.
- The wider state of the market; the activities of competitors; whether the market is capable of sustaining this (or any other level of increase).
- Whether the 35% increase represents an increase in the total market, or whether it means taking market share from competitors.
- Finally, where does the figure of 35% come from; who decided it; and on what grounds?

So again, the full complexities and context have to be considered. Once this form of judgement and evaluation has been made, the behaviour of customers, consumers and clients has to be considered. For example, the buyer may come into the establishment, not receive instant service, and turn round or storm out. Or a salesperson may be so busy giving excellent satisfaction to one customer that the next customer is delayed, leading to dissatisfaction on their part. Or they may be dealt with by a good salesperson who has nothing to offer the customer; or by a bad salesperson, who nevertheless persuades the customer to buy, leading to an instant sale but subsequent dissatisfaction. The key lesson is therefore that the process cannot possibly be completely objective or rational; nor is it capable of being quantified in isolation from the need to apply judgement. Effective quali-fication and judgement of performance effectiveness and success therefore relies on each of the following, even if delivering a numerical target and outcome:

- recognizing the human signs of buyer behaviour and attitudes;
- recognizing the human signs of organizational behaviour and attitudes;
- recognizing the convergence and divergence of priorities and objectives;
- recognizing the importance and influence of stakeholders and participants.

The best approach is to identify the most likely outcome in the most sets of circum-stances; to concentrate primarily on this; and to deal with exceptions as and when they arise.

Priorities

Ideally, priorities are established to ensure concentration of organizational resources to best commercial or service advantage in the pursuit of long-term customer, client and user satisfaction. In practice, it is rarely possible to achieve everything desired or required.

Two basic approaches are possible (see Figure 15.1).

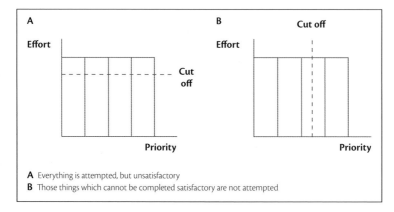

A Everything is attempted, but unsatisfactory
B Those things which cannot be completed satisfactory are not attempted

Figure 15.1 *Establishing priorities*

There is nothing intrinsically right or wrong with either approach indicated in Figure 15.1. The main issue at the outset is to know which approach is being taken and the opportunities and consequences of that choice.

Objectives

The objectives are:

- **organizational:** reflecting the overall purpose and direction;
- **departmental/divisional/functional:** reflecting the contribution that each is expected to make to the whole;
- **managerial:** reflecting the contribution that different managers are expected/ anticipated to make to the overall direction;
- **professional/occupational:** reflecting the need for professional and occupational satisfaction in different staff and work categories;
- **personal:** reflecting more general needs, especially those of job security, enhanced reward and prosperity, and advancement;
- **present priorities:** from whatever source they are driven;
- **future priorities:** those that begin to become apparent as the result of knowing and understanding the organization's preferred future direction.

Subjective and prejudicial convergence and divergence of objectives

It is essential to recognize the existence of these differing objectives. The best, most successful and effective organizations harmonize personal, professional and occupational objectives with those of the organization as a whole. Where this is not possible, a certain amount of dysfunction/malfunction occurs.

For example, a manager charged with responsibility for introducing a new education policy knows that this will take several years to evaluate for success. The manager's political masters want tangible results within three months. The next promotion in the manager's career is dependent upon the satisfaction of the political masters with their performance. The manager has therefore to reconcile the following:

- delivering the initiative professionally;
- advancing their own career;
- doing the work to the satisfaction of the political masters.

It is clear that doing the job properly requires persuading the political masters that a three-month measure is neither feasible nor legitimate in the circumstances. It is also clear that, on the face of it, there exists a real discrepancy between doing the job properly and receiving personal reward, recognition and advancement.

The greatest success is achieved where the potential problems have been recognized and steps have been taken to harmonize and integrate these different forms of objectives.

The lesson is that failure is likely where no or little recognition exists of the problem. Where it is not possible to integrate organizational and personal/professional objectives, recognition of the effects on performance (especially long-term performance) is essential. Problem areas for the future can then at least be more clearly identified.

Moreover, levels of motivation and morale are normally much higher where objectives in each category are harmonized. Where objectives do diverge and conflict, people always pursue their personal and professional objectives rather than those of the organization.

Conclusions

Each of the elements and factors indicated is an essential and legitimate area for managerial inquiry when assessing either total organization performance, or parts and features of it. Most of these elements and factors are interrelated. Several appear under different headings. Others are directly consequential – for example, it is impossible to have good and positive organizational attitudes without having clear standards established by top management. Taken altogether they reflect the fact that the performance of every organization, and every department, division and function within it, can always be improved.

This also underlines the complexity of measuring performance successfully. This is true even where supposedly simple or direct targets have been set – for example a simple increase in the outputs of a production line. Before such a decision can be taken, it has to be ensured that adequate volumes of components and supplies are available (or can be made available); that they can be stored; that any additional staff or overtime can be paid for; and that the increased output can be packaged, stored, distributed – and sold. It may be that such an increase adversely affects morale (for example, the need for additional production may be the latest in a long series of crises); or it may send morale sky-high, and this may subsequently lead to complacency if a positive, yet realistic, approach is not maintained.

So the role of the professional manager – whether chief executive officer, director, top, middle, junior or frontline and supervisory – is to understand this, and to continue to attend to each of the elements and factors indicated. This is equally important when things are going well, as the reasons why success is being achieved can be fully explained and understood. When things do go wrong, and problems begin to arise, they can be identified early and nipped in the bud. This in turn is best achieved if all managers understand the full range of inquiry that they need to make, and that nothing happens in isolation.

The measurement of organizational and managerial performance is complex and requires a high level of contextual knowledge and understanding, as well as the capability to choose the right qualitative and quantitative measures, and the required points of inquiry.

From this, managers are able to identify what contributes to successful, effective and profitable performance for their own organization, and that part of it for which they are responsible. They can also pinpoint:

- those activities that contribute to effective, successful and profitable organizational performance; the extent and nature of that contribution; and their effects upon each other;
- those activities that do not make any direct contribution to performance;
- those activities that detract from successful and effective performance; that destroy and damage it; that dilute its effectiveness;
- diversions from purpose; blockages and barriers to progress;
- the proportion and balance of steady-state activities with crisis handling.

It is necessary to recognize the range of parties, both internal and external, who have a legitimate interest in the organization, who measure it for success or failure, and the measures that they bring to bear from their own point of view. Long-term viability is much more likely where the concerns of each group can be addressed and reconciled successfully. One of the main tasks of top managers is to recognize the nature and legitimacy of the interests of the different stakeholder groups and interested parties, and to take steps to see that these are widely understood and satisfied as far as possible.

From this approach to performance, assessment and measurement comes a clear understanding of what the organization and its managers can control and influence, and what cannot be controlled or influenced. For example, it may not be possible to suppress a glut of bad or negative publicity and adverse media coverage. However, organizations can influence future coverage by responding as positively as possible in the circumstances, and by using this as a springboard to generate long-term positive interest.

Similarly, it is also not possible to control particular social, legal, economic and political constraints; but it is possible to recognize and understand the extent of their influence, and to work within them. It may also not be possible in the short to medium term at least, to influence the size or nature of markets served; and again, it is possible to recognize these specific constraints, and to provide products and services as successfully, effectively and profitably as possible within them.

in brief

- Performance assessment and measurement is complex. It can only be measured against what was intended, or what you set out to achieve in the first place.
- Performance assessment and measurement is a process, involving a range of complexities. If it is simplified, it is essential to remember that 'what gets measured gets done' and other things tend to be downgraded or ignored.
- Performance measurement and assessment ought to involve everyone, both as a continuous process and also in terms of formal reviews.
- It is always essential to prioritize activities; and from this, there is a clear choice whether to attempt everything or whether there are insufficient resources, and so some things have to be dropped.

- Performance assessment and measurement is a vehicle for organizational development, knowledge and understanding, and overall improvement in every aspect of managerial work.

Further reading

Armstrong, M. (2009) *Handbook of Performance Management: Making Performance Management Work*. Kogan Page.

Bourne, M. and Bourne, P. (2011) *Handbook of Corporate Performance Management*. Pearson.

Hutton, W. (2005) *The Productivity Report*. Vintage.

Kaplan, R. and Norton, D. (2002) *The Balanced Scorecard*. HBS.

Kent, B. (2006) *Performance Management*. Kogan Page.

Pettinger, R. (2005) *Measuring Business and Managerial Performance*. Pearson.

Enduring priorities in management

I f the drive for the future is towards the employment of fewer and much more expert managers, then it is essential that those aspiring to managerial positions know and understand where immediate and enduring priorities lie. Effective management in action requires all the knowledge, understanding and expertise indicated in Part One; the knowledge and understanding of collective and individual human behaviour addressed in Part Two; and the strategic capability and the marketing, financial, product and service knowledge and understanding covered in Part Three.

In order to be able to integrate all this knowledge and understanding into a basis for professional and expert performance, it is essential to be able to work within the constraints of the enduring priorities that have to be addressed on a continuous basis.

It has already been established that there are enduring organizational and managerial responsibilities. If organizations are to be able to sustain effective and profitable activities for the long term, then specific issues have to be addressed. These are:

- Risk, and how it is to be assessed: and from this assessment, expert judgement is required as to whether or not the risks can be accepted or mitigated, or whether they need to be avoided.
- The motivation of staff: if the position that much of management is concerned with is achieving things through and for people, then the nature of their commitment, and the factors that affect this (adversely, as well as positively) need to be known and understood.
- Reconciling the different pressures that are certain to arise on a regular basis; and ensuring that managerial capability and acumen are present in order to be able to deal with these pressures and issues when they do arise.

In addition, it is essential that those in managerial positions know and understand that, if they are to be recognized as professional and expert people, their knowledge, understanding and expertise need regular attention and development. It is essential that all those in managerial positions, or who aspire to management, take an active interest in and personal responsibility for the state of their own knowledge and expertise. As well as being involved in organizational management development activities, it is essential that all managers seek out opportunities for learning and development elsewhere, and ensure that they gain as much possible new knowledge from any situation in which they may find themselves. Furthermore, courses and conferences, and visits to other organizations and different parts of the world, all bring with them (or ought to bring with them) further knowledge and understanding on which to base expertise.

This in turn leads on to the question of managing in a global and international environment. Everyone in leadership and managerial positions has to know and understand the international as well as local environment. Many organizations now seek to expand overseas and into new and different markets; and so it is essential to know and understand the pitfalls and consequences, as well as the opportunities. As competition also expands, managers have to know where the next round of pressures are likely to come from, so that they can prepare their own responses for when the time comes.

Part Four deals with each of these issues in turn, and there is a chapter on each. As well as ensuring that everyone has a clear understanding of the enduring managerial priorities, and their influences on organizational and expert practice, these aspects integrate the foundations of management, and the knowledge of behaviour and strategy, into what ought to be a form of expert professional practice based on sound and ever-developing knowledge and understanding of what management is, what it ought to be, and how to go about continuously developing it for the future.

Risk 16

'Risk management ought to be a key discipline in all management practice.'

In this chapter

- knowing and understanding what risk is, and where risks exist and occur
- identifying the relationship between management and organizational behaviour and risk
- identifying and managing risks from the points of view of acceptance and avoidance
- developing collective risk awareness across the organization

Introduction

The purpose of this chapter is to introduce and illustrate that part of organizational, managerial and environmental knowledge and understanding that is concerned with those things that can, and do, go wrong from time to time.

The nature of risk is a reflection of the amount that is known and understood about a particular situation, as a precursor in deciding to do something. High levels of risk are incurred when little is known or understood; the more that is known and understood, the lower the level of risk; and this is because in the latter case, everybody knows and understands what they are letting themselves in for, and the opportunities and consequences that are likely to arise. Uncertainty exists where there is no knowledge of the particular situation. As a direct consequence, risk is insurable; uncertainty is not. The level of risk involved in something is therefore dependent upon the completeness of knowledge and understanding about it, its expectations; and this knowledge and understanding is then used to present the fullest range of outcomes possible in the given set of circumstances. In particular, a full evaluation is required of best and worst outcomes, so that those involved know and understand the opportunities and consequences of both success and also failure before anything is undertaken.

Uncertainty exists where there is no knowledge or understanding. One key part of managerial expertise is coping with uncertainty (see Chapter 1). The first step towards coping with uncertainty is to gather as much knowledge, information and understanding of what is not presently known or understood. This is to move the collective levels of expertise at least to relative familiarity; and from this, to begin to build a knowledge and understanding of the risks involved in whatever is contemplated, and to take active steps towards minimizing and, where possible, eliminating them.

The best managers get into the habit of analysing every situation in full for all of the risks involved, and everything that can possibly or conceivably go wrong. This is important in all situations; it is especially important where new ventures, new products and services, and new markets are being contemplated.

Risks and rewards

'The greater the risk, the greater the reward' is a cosy, easy and exciting mantra for organizations and managers to adopt. It is also dangerous nonsense. The best managers relate the assurance of rewards directly to the elimination of risks in so far as is possible in the circumstances.

Richard Branson and the Virgin organization

'We took incredible risks when we first went into the airline industry. We knew that we would be up against everything that the established airlines, the national flag-carriers, could throw at us. They tried to affect everything, from the availability of take-off and landing slots, to questioning our quality or commitment, or reliability – indeed, the very stability of the company as a whole.' (Richard Branson)

The picture that Branson paints is of a highly risky and very exciting venture. The perception, excitement and adventure surrounding the whole of the Virgin organization is enhanced by the very high profile adventures in which Branson himself has been involved in the past. For example, he has made three attempts to circumnavigate the world in a hot air balloon, as well as being shipwrecked in the Atlantic Ocean, before going on to claim the Blue Riband for the fastest Atlantic crossing by boat.

Lessons
Branson's statement should be rewritten to make clear that, because they knew there would be risks, the company would take (and did take) active steps to ensure that each of

these eventualities had been fully known and understood before the services were introduced. Consequently, the 'incredible risks' described by Branson were fully recognized, acknowledged and understood as a prelude to ensuring that they were minimized so that the Virgin organization would be able to operate within the given limits and constraints. It should also be noted that Branson took every step possible towards minimizing the risks involved in his ballooning and boating adventures so as to ensure that these too would have the greatest possible chance of success.

Source: Richard Branson (1998) 'The Money Programme Lecture', BBC.

The correlation between risks and rewards is therefore dependent upon seeing risks as obstacles to progress. These obstacles have either to be circumvented or removed. Their effects on what is intended require full acknowledgement and understanding as above; and if the obstacles cannot be removed, then there is a question of whether or not what is proposed should go ahead at all.

This reinforces the point that you need to know and understand everything that can possibly or conceivably go wrong. Especially where you do operate in a culture of 'the greater the risk, the greater the reward', you need to satisfy yourself that what is being done has a rationale and is not just a wild step into the unknown.

just a minute

Internal colloquy

It is essential to realize that even when something has been fully evaluated, and steps taken to minimize the risks involved or inherent, this is only the first step in the engagement of expertise in strategic and operational risk management. Before a detailed evaluation and implementation plan can be considered, the capability and willingness of staff and their expertise have to be assessed. Existing processes and systems have to be capable of delivering what the new proposal or venture requires; or else new systems and processes have to be designed and integrated with what exists already.

Collective and individual staff perceptions have to be managed. This is less of a problem where there is a collective, cohesive and positive culture. However, fundamental questions have to be addressed as to whether the new venture is known, believed and perceived to be glamorous and prestigious; whether it is a necessary evil (or a necessary good); and whether ultimately it represents a step on the road to progress. Fundamental issues of where the resources are coming from, and especially whether these are to be taken away from existing work, must be made clear; and if the staff do not understand or support this, then they may resist the idea itself.

It is essential that you see staff attitudes and receptiveness to ideas and proposals as a risk (or potential risk). Just because staff have been receptive to things in the past, does not necessarily mean that they will be as willing to progress in the future. Anything that is being proposed should therefore be accompanied by full staff communication and consultation.

External colloquy

A detailed understanding is required of what external stakeholders will make of what is proposed. Detailed knowledge and understanding is required of the likely and possible ranges of customer, client and end-user responses, not only for the new venture or proposal, but also in terms of the response to the existing range of products and services.

Shareholders have also to be satisfied that their returns will continue, ideally because of the new venture or proposal, and at least in spite of it. Shareholders need to know and understand the worst possible consequences; and shareholders normally need to be satisfied that they will at least get their money back over the long term. To that end they are entitled to see detailed forecasts and projections and are entitled to have questions answered, and any doubts and fears addressed. In particular, shareholders are entitled to be absolutely certain that their funds are not to be used in glamorous, exciting and untargeted ventures and adventures without additionally being satisfied that there are commercially viable prospects and returns available also. This is the full basis and context in which strategic and operational risk management is then learned in detail, and put into practice. It is increasingly usual to separate out the discipline of risk management into strategic and operational issues as follows.

- Strategic risk management is concerned with creating the conditions, attitudes and expertise for defining the organization's approach to risk; identifying those areas of risk with which the organization is, or may be, faced; and in ensuring that the desired approach is undertaken.
- Operational risk management is concerned with the detail of risk management in everyday activities; and this means addressing all of those things that can, and do, go wrong, and ensuring that steps are then taken to reduce, minimize and, where possible, eliminate risk from specific activities.

Strategic risk management

A strategic approach to risk management requires that the components of risk and uncertainty that can, and do (or may possibly), affect the organization and its environment must be studied so as to ensure that anyone in a top, senior or executive position understands the full range of issues that must be considered for any situation that could conceivably arise. In particular, a strategic approach to risk management requires the following.

- **Sectoral trends:** knowledge and understanding of whether the sector is growing or declining, either in size or prosperity; whether these trends are likely to continue; the nature of factors that are affecting particular trends at present; and the nature of factors that could conceivably affect these trends in the future.

- **Knowledge and understanding of substitutes and alternatives:** evaluating the possibilities of whether customers, consumers and clients could, or might, change their buying habits as an alternative to what the particular organization provides; and whether it is necessary both now, and also in the future, to have a range of responses available.

- **Knowing and understanding social, political and economic issues, drives and restraints:** in particular this means knowing and understanding the likely, possible and potential effects of changes in interest and exchange rates; credit squeezes; and overall purchasing power (for example, purchasing power is affected by such things as taxation increases, or increases in charges for transport, fuel, energy, gas and electricity).

- **The constitution of the organization:** the constitution of the organization is assessed and evaluated from the point of view of capability and willingness to undertake present ranges of activities in their present volumes; proposed ranges of activities in proposed volumes; and changes to internal structures and systems.

- **Evaluation of outcomes:** at a strategic level, this means that all initiatives, ventures and proposals require evaluation from the point of view of: identification of the best, medium and worst outcomes; analysis and evaluation of any critical obstacles or incidents; evaluating the capability to extricate oneself from the particular situation (or not) and the consequences of having to do this; assessment of the full range of costs and benefits to the organization and all its stakeholders.

- **Other behavioural and perceptual issues:** in particular the comfort and commitment which the staff are going to bring to present and envisaged ranges of activities, products and services; this is an especial problem where mergers and takeovers are proposed, or where there are radical shifts into new products and services.

- **Early warning systems:** early warning systems are based on the collective capability of the organization and its managers to have at their disposal the fullest possible data concerning the nature of organization activities, the quality and volume of products and services, and the present levels of activity within the markets and environments served. In particular, organizations ought to be able to know, understand and evaluate the likely, possible and potential effects on the overall ability to conduct business of: epidemics; strikes and disputes; wars and terrorist attacks; major incidents and disasters; and sudden unavailability of supplies, raw materials and information. Internally, there needs to be a strategic approach to organizational processes, databases and information systems.

At a strategic and operational level also, there are specific issues that have to be covered in terms of theft and fraud; dirty tricks; and human behaviour.

Theft and fraud

All organizations are susceptible to theft and fraud. This includes both petty pilfering by individuals, and also institutionalized larceny carried out by organized groups of staff.

An organizational view is required of what constitutes petty pilfering. This normally comes out in the extent to which the organization is prepared to tolerate the de facto theft of consumables such as pens and paper by staff; and also the extent to which the organization is prepared to tolerate the use of its telephones and computers for personal convenience. This sounds petty and trivial; however, it is essential to realize that small thefts can, and do, grow into grand larceny if not checked; and that the problems can, and do, grow as a consequence, and may become unmanageable if rules are not made clear and enforced.

Fraud on a grand scale may be carried out on an individual or institutional basis. In both cases, it is the institution and employees that suffer; and this invariably also leads to suffering on the part of staff, shareholders, backers, and suppliers. In many cases also, wider reputation is lost through adverse media coverage; and this can, and does, affect supplier confidence and the willingness of potential staff to come and work for the organization. This reinforces the need for clear and absolute sets of standards, behaviour and performance. Each of these has to be reinforced by the presence, implementation and enforcement of rules and procedures, reporting relations, and standards of conduct; and each of these in turn, has to be underpinned by sanctions when broken.

Dirty tricks

All organizations engage in competitive practices. Competitive practices exist in all areas of organizational and managerial activity, and are not simply confined to product and service delivery and performance. Organizations compete for assurances on the supply side; for technological advantages; for key staff and expertise; and for customer knowledge, understanding, acceptance and engagement. Companies and organizations engage in marketing and public relations; and some of this can be targeted at denigrating the competition and alternatives, as well as building up one's own position.

Problems arise when, again individually or institutionally, the line is crossed between legitimate competition (however aggressive) and criminal activity. Thus for example:

- it is legitimate to offer potential staff inducements to come and join a particular organization; it is *not* legitimate to induce them to breach their existing contractual duties and obligations;
- it is legitimate to market aggressively to potential customers and clients; it is *not* legitimate to tell lies about their present product and service providers;

- it is legitimate to transfer funds between budget headings within an organization; it is *not* legitimate to pay individuals bonuses out of these transfers at the expense of the future well-being of the organization and the rest of its staff;
- it is legitimate for top and senior managers to pay themselves (and be paid) bonuses in accordance with the constitution of the organization; it is *not* legitimate for those same managers to use the organization as a personal bank account, effectively to be looted for personal gain at the expense of the rest of the staff and stakeholders.

By the same token, it is additionally essential to guard against the risks inherent in talking up an organization's product, service, staff or share performance to the point at which it is neither sustainable nor true. This becomes a form of 'dirty tricks' when the organization, its managers and staff start to believe their own rhetoric, and to act as if their own rhetoric were actually the truth.

These forms of behaviour are often illegal; and they are always unethical. The risks involved are wide-ranging as follows.

- The trivial, normally consisting of passing media commentary on a blemish to the organization; and these are normally quickly forgotten if the matter is clearly a single aberration in an otherwise excellent organization.
- A series of events and issues become known and cause the media and other stakeholders to take an active interest in the organization's conduct and performance.
- Staff demotivation and demoralization caused by known, believed and perceived sharp practice within the organization; and this problem is compounded where these issues are known, believed or perceived to be allowed to exist and continue.
- Loss of customer, supplier and stakeholder confidence if the errors and crises persist; and again, the problem is compounded where it becomes known and understood that the organization is not tackling these issues.

The key lesson is to know and understand the full range of risks, outcomes and consequences which can, or might, occur as the result of choosing to go down such paths; or of doing nothing when it becomes clear that some organization functions are acting in these ways on their own initiatives. An organization-wide approach to theft, fraud and other malpractice is therefore clearly essential. This is to minimize the chances of things going wrong, as above, and additionally so as to be able to take remedial action quickly when they do occur.

Human behaviour

It is also essential that all organizations and their managers know and understand the key behavioural issues associated with risk management. These are:

- complacency, which occurs both as a corporate and collective as well as individual pattern of behaviour;

- vanity and arrogance, which leads to organizations having such utter faith in themselves that failings are neither recognized nor addressed;
- standard human failings of 'never quite getting around to things'; or not doing the jobs and work that they prefer not to do (or taking care to fill up their time with things that they do prefer to do, meaning that the rest get left anyway);
- laziness and indolence, in which people cannot be bothered either to do things, or do them properly;
- avoidance of difficult and unpleasant tasks and people, however essential it may be to do them or have dealings with them;
- unwillingness to go against collective or received wisdom: people have a great need to belong in all situations in which they find themselves, and so if they find themselves in the 'minority of one' position, there is great pressure to conform.

Additionally, some organizations have cultures that preclude people from raising concerns. This may happen on a departmental basis; and there may also be a wider culture of repression, in which any possible risk is known or believed to be 'off message'.

The consequence of all of the above is that problems do not (often cannot) get raised; and this is only ever sustainable so long as the company or organization somehow contrives to remain viable.

true story

Risk management and the UK banking crisis

The report into the causes of the UK banking crisis of 2007 onwards found that the root of the problem could be traced back to the way in which the Royal Bank of Scotland (RBS) and the Halifax Bank of Scotland (HBOS) were being run at the time. Both were led by chief executives who refused to look at the wider risks of what the companies were doing, especially in terms of their property acquisitions. These acquisitions were given value that could not be sustained; and this in turn led to the total assets and overall value of the banks and their resources being vastly overstated. Two key conclusions stand out in particular:

- that risk management was viewed as a constraint upon the business in both cases, rather than as being an integral part of a rigorous strategic approach;
- that effective risk management would have raised issues earlier; and would have, in turn, meant that there would have been no need for a taxpayer bailout in 2009 and 2010.

The whole crisis at both organizations arose because of the behavioural pressures, especially those imposed at the very top of the companies. Risk management policies and procedures were in place; staff were effectively ordered not to follow them.

Factors outside the control of the organization

Addressing factors outside the control of the organization is essential for effective strategic approaches to risk. Addressing factors outside the control of the organization means knowing and understanding the likely, possible and potential effects of events and actions, which include the following.

- Political instability, war and terrorist attacks: their effects on the ability of the organization to conduct business, and on the confidence of customers and consumers.
- Changes in the weather and consequent changes in customer and consumer behaviour: so that, for example, a very hot summer may cause a loss of trade to those depending on it as customers go overseas for their holiday; or the same thing may cause a glut of trade if customers choose to stay at home. It is not possible to predict absolutely which way events such as these will turn out; it is essential to take active steps to find out the likely outcome so as to be as well prepared as possible.
- Changes in currency values and exchange rates and their effects on consumer propensity to spend; and changes in interest rates and their effects on consumer confidence.

The result of a strategic approach to risk, and detailed consideration of the market and environment, criminal activities, and factors outside the organization's control, ought to be a detailed knowledge and understanding of the worst possible set of circumstances in which the organization might conceivably be required to operate. This reinforces the need for absolute standards, priority areas of attention, and the need to enforce conduct and behaviour with clear policies drawn up and implemented to meet the particular concerns of the organization. This fundamental approach is then translated into action through operational approaches to risk management.

Operational approaches to risk management

At an operational level, the priority is to know and understand which events are most likely to occur, where and why. It then becomes a priority for all managers, supervisors and section heads to take active steps to prevent these events occurring in so far as is reasonably practicable. The following areas for attention vary between, and within, organizations, departments, divisions and functions. The key areas for attention are:

- patterns of behaviour;
- accidents;
- single events and errors.

Patterns of behaviour

Risk management and patterns of behaviour mean that it is essential to be aware of the potential for, and effects of, bullying, victimization, harassment and discrimination. Each is damaging and ultimately destructive to motivation and morale if not stamped out immediately it becomes apparent. Each becomes more and more difficult to deal with the longer it is allowed to persist. The outcome internally is that resources and energy are consumed in dealing with these cases. Externally, customer and consumer confidence can be affected, especially when it becomes clear that such problems are endemic or institutional. People would rather not deal with organizations that conduct themselves in these ways.

Bullying, victimization, harassment and discrimination are extreme examples of collective and individual behaviour. As well as these extremes, operational risk assessments are required to ensure that overall standards of conduct and behaviour within departments, divisions and functions are assured and enforced. The need is to know and understand the effects on staff cohesion and working relations of allowing and, de facto, condoning different patterns of behaviour. It is essential to know and understand that there is a direct relationship between behaviour and performance; and to know and understand that failure to manage behaviour always affects performance adversely. It is therefore essential to be able to assess the likely and potential consequences of allowing particular patterns of behaviour to persist unchecked.

Accidents

Accidents occur everywhere. From an operational risk management point of view, the need is to ensure that accidents are kept to an absolute minimum. This part of risk management requires attention to the nature and quality of the working environment, patterns of work, specific health and safety aspects, and the use of technology. Health and safety management normally requires that all staff are trained and briefed in every aspect of the operational environment, especially in relation to technology usage and emergency procedures. It is impossible to eliminate the chance of accidents occurring; it is essential to take steps to ensure that accidents occur as infrequently as possible. An isolated accident is a cause for concern all round, but normally carries little subsequent long-term risk. Regular accidents are damaging to morale and performance, as above, and expensive in terms of resources and energy when they have to be dealt with, investigated and evaluated.

Single events and errors

Single events and errors are impossible to manage; they will always occur. The operational management priority is to ensure that the risk of single events and errors occurring is kept to a minimum. This is achieved through the creation of the right quality of working life and environment, patterns of activities and behaviour that ensure that overall risk is minimized. The whole is then enforced through inspection and supervision systems and procedures.

Single events and errors: Examples

- During routine maintenance, a paint scraper worth 30p was accidentally dropped into the torpedo chamber of the *USS Swordfish*, an American navy nuclear submarine. The paint scraper jammed the loading piston for the torpedoes. For a week, divers worked to try to free the piston while the submarine was waterborne but all attempts failed. The submarine had to be dry-docked. Subsequent repairs cost nearly £100,000.

- The *Mariner 1* space probe was launched from Cape Canaveral with the purpose of orbiting the planet Venus. All calculations were checked and double-checked; this was to ensure that the extremely complex and precise programme that had to be followed was fully accurate. The programme required that after 13 minutes of flight, a booster engine would give acceleration of up to 25,000 miles per hour to *Mariner 1*. After 44 minutes, 9,800 solar cells would unfold to provide further energy. After 80 days, the computer would calculate the final course corrections; and after 100 days, the space probe would circle Venus. Four minutes after take-off, *Mariner 1* plunged into the Atlantic Ocean. Inquiries later revealed that a minus sign had been omitted from the instructions fed into the computer.

- Pan Am, the American airline, undertook a security operation after it became worried that its staff were stealing miniature bottles of whiskey from the aircraft. The company wired up an alarm clock inside the drink's cabinet of one of the airliners. This was so arranged that it would stop whenever the door was opened. This, it was stated, would reveal the exact time of the thefts. However, the company management omitted to tell the cabin crew. As the result, on a flight between New York and Dubai, one of the stewardesses heard the ticking of the clock and assumed that it was a bomb. She alerted the pilot and the plane made a forced landing at Berlin. In the inquiry afterwards, it became clear that the thefts had amounted to no more than petty pilfering. The emergency landing cost the company £16,500.

The lesson is that each of these events, rationally considered, could have been prevented. Rationally, computer programmes for the space probe would have been checked again; additional decking would have been provided on the submarine; and the crew of the airliner would have been called to account, if necessary directly, rather than undertaking such a heavy handed approach. Each of the examples does however indicate the propensity for things to go wrong by chance. When chance occurrences such as these happen, it is essential that steps are taken to ensure that they do not happen again. However, as stated in the text above, it is impossible to eliminate every eventuality from working situations.

Analysing risk

Analysing risk requires the consideration of two key elements:

- What is the *risk* of particular events and circumstances occurring?
- What is the *probability* of the particular events and circumstances occurring?

It then becomes necessary to decide:

- whether to accept the risk;
- whether to avoid the risk altogether (and therefore do something else);
- whether to accept the risk and have responses in place for when things do go wrong.

The outcome of expert, comprehensive and effective risk analysis is the ability to take and implement informed decisions at all times. This is so that whether things succeed or fail, those involved will know and understand the reasons, and can use this knowledge and understanding to better inform future decisions, proposals and initiatives.

The techniques available for effective risk analysis are as follows:

- Specific factor analyses, in which a particular issue or factor is entered into a given scenario, proposal or set of circumstances, and its likely and possible outcomes and effects evaluated. Specific factors can be considered in either linear or complex terms; it is certain that anything that is finally implemented following specific factor risk analyses, will have to survive in a complex and changing set of circumstances.
- Random factor analyses, in which single or multiple issues and factors are entered by chance or at random into a given scenario, proposal or set of circumstances, and their possible and potential outcomes evaluated. Random factors can be introduced either by choice or by chance; or they may be drawn from a list using random number tables to select them.
- 'What if?' approaches; which are simpler to introduce because they can be started by a simple statement using any or all of the questions above. This approach is often limited, however, by personal, professional, collective or institutional lack of capability or willingness to consider the fullest possible range of issues and factors that could conceivably occur.

point of view

Rising fuel costs

In 2005, the price of all fossil fuels began to rise, and this has continued up till the present time. This was variously blamed on:

- the oil companies, who saw the global political instability as a way of driving up energy prices and therefore securing short and medium-term price and income advantages for themselves as a hedge against the day when prices would start to fall;

- oil market traders, who were using the media reportage of high prices together with the political uncertainty to drive prices higher;
- political initiatives undertaken by the USA and EU, which were deemed to drive prices up;
- the huge and increasing demand for fuel and energy in the emerging markets and economies of India and China;
- the use of fuel supplies by many of the main supplying countries (especially Russia and the Middle East states) as a bargaining chip to secure political advantages.

Each is worthy of analysis. However, from an organization management point of view, the main priority is the capability and willingness to be able to assess how high fuel prices might rise; how high they might conceivably rise; the point at which they will cause a crisis for the organization itself; and the point at which this one factor would drive the company or organization out of business. This then informs the risk assessment of entering into new ventures, investing in technology, or operating any plant or machinery. It will also help to inform transport costs and delivery charges; and may also give indications of possible upward changes in the costs incurred through heating and lighting for premises, and energy charges for activities.

Each approach is dependent for its effectiveness on the quality of the information available at the time of risk assessment; and this in turn is dependent on the overall understanding of the organizational and operating environment, and the circumstances that may cause this to change.

Each of these approaches can then be used to assess the probability of particular outcomes occurring. The establishment of probability or likelihood then needs further managerial evaluation and analysis to determine whether or not the outcome is mathematically certain or not. Where it is not (for example in the overwhelming majority of cases), managerial debate is then required. This then leads to an informed and expert judgement on which particular decisions can be taken; the risk of undertaking particular initiatives and proposals can be assessed; and organizations and their managers additionally develop a part of professional discipline that enhances their own detailed expertise and understanding in this critical area of activity.

Matalan

Amid difficult retail trading conditions, Matalan, the good value clothing and household goods chain, announced that it was having to make a special charge of £20 million to offset the shortcomings and underperformance of its computer-based operational and management information systems. This system had been installed on the advice of Kurt Salmon Associates, an information systems and management consultancy practice.

Matalan therefore considered suing Kurt Salmon in order to try and recoup some of the above losses.

The lesson is that any risk assessment and analysis carried out in advance of the installation ought to have considered:

- what could possibly go wrong with the installation and implementation;
- what costs and charges could possibly or conceivably occur as the result;
- the consequences of having to consider legal action against the consultancy;
- what it would then take to put matters right.

Such an approach would have helped to inform the choice of system made by the company, as well as providing a much clearer understanding of the basis on which the consultancy was being engaged, and the key results required. It is additionally the case that if organizations and managers comfort themselves with the thought that they can always prosecute if things do go wrong, they should be aware that litigation normally takes many years.

Applying risk management

Strategic and operational risk management is only effective if it is enforced. The Confederation of British Industry stated that over the period 1985–2005, the number of organizations with risk management policies had risen from 30% to 92% (CBI, 2005). However, this has occurred alongside a combination of organizational, institutional, strategic and operational errors which have nevertheless continued, and which the examples in this chapter illustrate.

The need therefore is to ensure that standards of conduct, behaviour and performance are related to the strategic and operational approaches to risk outlined above. Also as stated above, standards need to be enforced and this requires that sanctions are applied to those who breach them. This is only achievable if the organization's top and senior management know and understand that it is in their interests to do so. Top and senior management then need also to take the additional step of ensuring that risk management is an operational priority. Additionally, whoever is to be responsible for risk management within the organization requires genuine influence and authority, and the ability to impose sanctions for particular breaches of conduct, behaviour and performance. Such persons also require the ability to impose delays and investigations on operational proposals and initiatives when the matters of risk are concerned with the competitive environment, and new product and service development. There is an overall general need for all managers to know and understand that they operate within a risky environment, from the point of view of risk minimization as well as remedying adverse events and incidents.

Risk assessment

The outcome of applied risk management needs to be a clear understanding of everything that has to be considered and can possibly go wrong. Decisions are then required as follows:

- whether or not it is worth taking the risks identified;
- how the risks could possibly be avoided;
- what steps could be taken to mitigate the risks of events occurring;
- how to insure against specific risks (making sure that everything that has been identified is covered);
- whether everything that could truly happen has indeed been considered.

The wild and wacky

One of the major shortcomings of all organizational approaches to risk management is that they consider possible events and occurrences from a rational point of view only. It is necessary to consider also the absolute extremes of what could conceivably happen – the 'wild and wacky' – of which the following are examples:

- What if interest rates remain low, and then suddenly start to rise steeply?
- What if there is political instability in the European Union?
- What if there is a series of major natural disasters that affect the ability of companies, organizations, staff and individuals to move around easily?
- What if energy prices double? And then double again?
- What if computer technology, IT systems, and the ability to communicate are corrupted?
- What if customers suddenly stop buying Ford cars/McDonald's meals/Ryanair tickets?
- What if the demand for Ford Cars/McDonald's meals/Ryanair's tickets suddenly doubles?

This approach is designed to ensure that risk management is as broadly encompassing as possible. Not all of these events will come to pass (or come to pass immediately). On the other hand, some of them have already occurred, and have changed company and organizational practice, the behaviour of markets, and the demand for products and services.

Expert managers take the view that anything and everything can potentially go wrong, and therefore develop their risk management facility and capability accordingly. There is a clear body of knowledge and understanding in this, as above; it is also essential that risk management is developed as a managerial and corporate attitude.

Early warning systems

Managers at all organizational levels require early warning systems. Early warning systems are required in each of the areas of environmental assessment and organizational understanding as above. Early warning systems include:

- regular professional updates on the state of markets, the economy, product and service performance, the activities of competitors and alternatives, and technological advances and developments;
- regular scouring of the business, professional and news media so as to be aware of the events that they think are, or might be, important to the future. This is not to say that these events will be important in the future; expert managers will then be able to use this knowledge to help form their own judgement;
- early signs of dissatisfaction among staff about something; again this may, or may not, be important but knowing and understanding that there is a bit of trouble or grumbling is again useful information;
- early signs of increases in individual grievances and disputes, absenteeism and staff turnover;
- early indications of organizational costs beginning to rise in particular areas without apparent reason;
- declines in sales of products and services;
- increases in sales of products and services to competitors;
- early signs of rising levels of customer complaints;
- early signs of hold-ups and disputes on the supply side;
- early signs of malfunction with information and administration systems and processes.

The overall outcome is to ensure that managers know and understand every aspect of their domain; and in the context of risk management, they build their knowledge and understanding of where things can, and do, go wrong; and immediately, where things might be about to go wrong. Managers faced with these issues then construct a series of priorities designed to ensure that they are aware of the potential problems, and have a range of approaches that can be taken according to whether things do in fact occur; and how, when and where they do actually occur.

Early warnings systems at GEC

When he was the chief executive at GEC, Arnold Weinstock used to either meet with or telephone his top managers on a weekly basis. During these conversations, Mr Weinstock would question each manager closely about the performance of their divisions; and this would always include matters to do with costs, sales, staffing and supply-side issues. Failure to give precise assurances was always unacceptable; and this failure did, from time to time, result in some staff being 'transferred'.

The process had two clear outcomes. The first was that Mr Weinstock always new well in advance of where troubles might occur, he could then work through the matters with top managers and endorse their preferred lines of approach. The second outcome was that top managers new and understood that they were expected to do this and that failure to do so would always be a major omission, and could get them transferred elsewhere.

By the time of Mr Weinstock's departure from the company, he had generated a cash surplus of £2.5 billion, partially at least through ensuring that both he and his top managers paid constant attention to what could possibly go wrong and took early steps to remedy matters whenever they could.

Dealing with crises and emergencies

All organizations face crises and emergencies from time to time. Crises and emergencies are caused by:

- combinations of circumstances;
- series of accidents and chances;
- 'one of those things';
- as well as by ineptitude, incompetence, negligence, fraud and other criminal activity.

The managerial priority is to face the crisis or emergency; and a very fine balance has to be struck between providing a quick and effective response, and taking time to gather enough information to provide the actual response required.

Much of the work ought to have been done in advance through knowing and understanding the range of risks inherent in the particular situation; and having systems and procedures in place to respond as and when things do occur. The manager then deals thoroughly with whatever has occurred.

The organizational, managerial and human priority in all crises and emergencies is to ensure that whatever is done in response is clear, honest and effective as far as is possible. People expect to be treated honestly in response to their legitimate concerns. Failure to do so, and inability or unwillingness to do so, leads to an enhancement of organizational and institutional risk. This is because people do not, and will not, trust the managerial response to the crisis or emergency, and nor do they trust the managerial capability to resolve the matter.

Hurricane

In June 2005, the city of New Orleans, Louisiana, USA, was hit by a Category 5 hurricane. Overall, the city was used to dealing with violent storms. This one would have been little different except for the fact that the force of the storm breached one of the levees (protection banks) holding back the waters of the river. This breach caused the city to flood.

Instead of responding to the legitimate concerns of people who had lost everything, and especially addressing questions about the potential for pollution and disease, the US authorities concentrated on defending the strength of the levee and the fact that it should not have breached. Only following the resignation of top officials did it become clear that the levee was only constructed to withstand Category 3 storms, and that the city had in fact been at risk of flooding for many years.

In early 2006, the decision was taken to rebuild the levee to withstand a Category 4 hurricane. An absolute approach to risk management in order to minimize absolutely the risk of the crisis ever happening again would be to rebuild it to withstand a Category 8 storm, and then to see that it was fully maintained on a regular basis.

Other aspects of risk management

Clearly, things can, and do, go wrong in every aspect of organizational and managerial performance and activity. Of particular concern additionally to managers in all spheres and areas of activity ought to be the following.

- Technology performance, including the consequences of technology crashes and the loss of product and service delivery and information storage and retrieval. Alongside technological performance is the question of suitability and capability in terms of what the organization expects it to deliver.
- Managing over distances, referring to the risks inherent in devolving responsibility, authority and accountability to persons working in remote locations.
- Ensuring that drives for expansion into new products, services, ventures, markets and locations (including overseas markets and locations) are driven by organizational capability and willingness, and the prospects of profitable and effective activities; and above all, that these ventures are not driven solely by the excitement of the venture or the prestige of being international.
- Ensuring that the demands and obligations placed by everyone involved in outsourced business activities are clearly understood. It is essential that nobody's reputation or business performance is damaged as the result of the actions of other companies and organizations involved.
- Ensuring that a dominant position in a market or business relationship does not become a vehicle for sloppiness or laziness; even where it is possible to dominate a particular sector, the full rigour of resource management and attention to product and service quality and delivery are essential.
- Where a company or organization is in a dependent relationship, opportunities for other activities should always be considered. The fact that the dependent relationship may have existed securely for many years to the mutual benefit of all concerned does not alter the fact that this can change at any time.

- Ensuring a rigorous approach to new product and service development, again so that the drive is concentrated on commercial potential rather than pure creativity.

Risk management has to be seen as a key management discipline and critical foundation stone of managerial expertise. Risk management gives a critical perspective on everything that is being done.

Conclusions

It is clear from the above that the effective management of risk requires involvement in all aspects of organizational structure, activities, behaviour and performance. If anything goes wrong in any area, there is the potential for a knock-on effect that may ultimately affect every aspect of the organization. Serious problems can, and do, lead to loss of confidence in the organization and its products and services; and this in turn is certain to lead to downturns in performance, and can lead to bankruptcy.

It is true that a much greater attention than before is paid to risk management in all its forms. As above, 92% of organizations operating in the UK had risk management policies in place by 2005. This does not alter the fact that things can, and do, go wrong; risk and its management are therefore critical to future success and effectiveness.

It is essential in turn that everyone in the organization knows and understands the importance of constant attention to activities, behaviour and performance. This is a key part of the personal commitment and professional discipline required of managers in all organizations, in every aspect of business, industry and public services. This has to be tempered by knowing and understanding that it is impossible to plan for every eventuality; it is, however, necessary to learn from these eventualities when they do arise in order to ensure that the same thing never happens again, and so as to develop a broader understanding of the potential for problems in every area of activity.

'Opulence': The next glossy magazine

'Opulence' is the working title of a proposed new glossy magazine. The magazine is to be 160 pages long and presented in the same style, format and approximate size as *Vogue*, *Cosmopolitan* – and *FHM*.

The style therefore clearly draws from glossy magazines pitched presently at both men and women; and indeed, the magazine's proposed uniqueness and selling and branding point is to be the fact that it is to attract both male and female readers. The received wisdom is that this has never been tried before in the magazine trade, though it does work in other aspects of publishing. For example, Colin Forbes, the thriller writer, states that his readership is divided evenly between the sexes; and indeed, about half the people who buy *The Sun* newspaper are women.

'Opulence' is to be published monthly at £4.95. The proposed content of the magazine is as follows:

- editorial – 4 pages;
- celebrity interviews – 25 pages;
- book and music reviews – 10 pages;
- travel – 25 pages;
- finance – 6 pages;
- property – 6 pages;
- exclusive news scoops – 6 pages;
- advertising – 30 pages.

This leaves a certain amount of leeway for other features, editorial, advertorial and other matters that are certain to turn out to be of importance to the proposed readership.

'Opulence' is the brainchild of Graham Edwards. Graham has worked in the publishing industry for the past ten years on a series of glossy magazines in London and New York. His last post was as assistant managing editor of *Vanity Fair* in New York. Accordingly, he has experience of managing mass circulation, glossy and high value/high brand/high cost magazines for a wide variety of markets.

For several years, he has identified, as a gap in the market, the fact that there is no glossy magazine for men and women. In spite of the fact that, as stated above, the received wisdom of the industry is that it cannot be done, 'Opulence' is to fill the gap. Specifically, it is to be pitched at men and women of disposable income of £40,000 each/£60,000 per couple. These men and women are holding professional jobs in banking, retail, law, and management within these sectors; and also in engineering, travel, transport and public services.

The intended circulation is 120,000 per issue. At £4.95 per sale, the intended circulation brings in £594,000 per issue.

The minimum circulation is 60,000. At £4.95, the minimum circulation brings in £297,000. It is unviable to go below 60,000 because production costs rise as follows:

- 120,000 copies – 50p per copy;
- 60,000 copies – 80p per copy;
- 50,000 copies – £1.50 per copy;
- 20,000 copies – £2 per copy.

Additionally, the advertising revenues drop sharply if circulation falls below 60,000. At 60,000 plus, a single page advertisement can be charged at £8,000 per page; below 60,000, the charge drops to £3,000. Over several months, Graham met with six venture capitalists, all of whom turned him down for backing. Overall, there was a generally favourable response to the idea; but the crunch came on editorial and especially the market – on Graham's own admission, nobody had ever tried to produce this kind of magazine for a male/female split market.

The key lesson is that the risks have been known, understood and evaluated in full detail before the proposal or venture has gained life. Graham himself therefore, knows and understands where the risks lie; and he will be able to explain this if, and when, he ever gets backing for this particular product. In particular, both he and also anyone who can be persuaded to back the venture know and understand the barriers and obstacles to progress. Their first commitment is therefore to ensure that these barriers and obstacles can be overcome, otherwise there is no point in pursuing the venture at all. In particular, pitching the magazine at both male and female readers is in direct contrast to the past history of successful magazine launches. This means that there is additionally the question of where to locate the magazine on retailers' shelves, which tend to be divided on gender lines. This too is a critical question that has to be addressed.

- Risk management is a primary area of managerial expertise and ought therefore to be a key discipline in all management practice.
- There is a much greater awareness of the things that can, and do, go wrong, and of their effects on business practice and organizational performance.
- It is essential that all managers and organizations get into the habit of constantly asking: 'What can conceivably go wrong?' and 'What if?'
- Risk management and assessment is something that ought to pervade every aspect of organizational practice. Risk management ought to be used as a vehicle for staff and organization development, as well as an operational element.
- Expertise in risk management ought to be continuously developed so that collective and individual capability, knowledge, understanding and awareness are as high as possible at all times within all organizations.

Further reading

Blunden, T. and Thirlwall, J. (2010) *Mastering Operational Risk*. Pearson.
CBI (Confederation of British Industry) (2005) *Assessing and Managing Risk*. CBI Industrial Trends, July.
Crouhy, M. et al. (2006) *The Essentials of Risk Management*. Wiley.
Hopkin, P. (2010) *Fundamentals of Risk Management*. Pearson.
Hubbard, D. (2009) *The Failure of Risk Management*. McGraw Hill.
Marrison, C. (2002) *The Fundamentals of Risk Management*. Kogan Page.
Pettinger, R. (2000) *Investment Appraisal: A Managerial Approach*. Palgrave Macmillan.

Management and motivation

17

'People need continuing marks of success, as well as increases in rewards, in order to remain motivated.'

In this chapter

- understanding the nature of motivation and its applications in work and organization situations
- motivation as a 'joint venture' between organizations, managers and staff
- taking steps to motivate staff and keep them motivated
- developing motivation as a process to create a key condition for enduring levels of high and effective performance

Introduction

Motivation is a reflection of the reasons why people do things. All behaviour has a purpose (often several) and is therefore based on choice – people choose to do things that they do. Sometimes this choice is very restricted (for example sink or swim). Sometimes again, it is constrained by the law (for example stopping the car when the traffic lights are red). And again, it is constrained by the norms and processes of society – for example, people tend to wear smart clothes to a party where they know that everybody else will be doing so. In each case however, there is a choice, though the propensity, encouragement and direction to choose one course of action rather than the other in the examples given are strong, if not overwhelming. The nature of motivation and what people choose to do is constantly influenced by others; and it is also influenced by professional, social, economic and legal pressures.

Motivation may be seen as a combination of needs, wants, drives and incentives. Motivation can be defined as 'a process that starts with the physiological or psychological want, deficiency or need that activates behaviour or a drive that is aimed at a goal or incentive in the satisfaction of those deficiencies, wants and needs' (Luthans, 2002).

Some of these needs and wants are fundamental: the need to be warm, sheltered, fed and clothed. Some of these needs are social: the need to do things that are acceptable to those whose opinion is valued; the need to belong and be comfortable in group societies and locations; the need for self-respect and the respect of others.

In workplace terms, the need, want and drive is to earn an 'adequate' (whatever that may mean) wage or salary, and to receive recognition (at a human as well as occupational level) for work well done.

At the core of all this, there is a complexity of behavioural drives and incentives that cause people to commit themselves wholly or partly to their job, occupation and organization, and to the people with whom they work.

Source: F. Luthans (2002).

Workplace motivation

Workplace motivation is founded in a combination of:

- individual professions, occupations and expertise that need an outlet for development, success and achievement;
- the wage–work bargain, and the psychological contract between organization and staff;
- the nature of the working environment;
- the general feelings of well-being that the organization exudes as a whole;
- interpersonal, inter-group, interdepartmental and inter-occupational relations;
- relationships within the immediate department or location of work;
- the overall humanity of the organization and working situation, as well as its professionalism;
- the nature of the culture of the organization as a whole.

In this context, workplace, occupational and professional motivation is therefore a process. This process is based on a combination of internal drives from within the individual related to what the organization can provide to satisfy these internal drives; together with a commitment to the organization on the part of the individual in which the organization is entitled to expect that the individual will deliver their expertise in the ways required by the organization, and in the best interests of the organization, over an extended period of time.

Motivation is therefore a combination of mutuality of interest, capability and willingness. Motivation is one of the outcomes of the working relationship. If the employment conditions are right, known and understood, then organizations may expect high levels of commitment; if the working conditions are wrong, then motivation is certain to suffer. Similarly, if the individual has truly everything that they need or want in order to do their job properly, then the organization is entitled to expect these levels of commitment.

Many organizations directly address the reasons why motivation is low through a combination of ensuring that work practices are as open and positive as possible. Organizations support this as far as they can with full flexibility of working, and opportunities for advancement and achievement based on capability and willingness, and restricted only by the limitations of the organization and its activities.

Motivation and incentives

Many organizations mistake motivation for incentives. Organizations offer incentives, or directly targeted rewards, after which they then expect to receive an enduring commitment. Incentives provide specific rewards for short-term achievement only; and if the only step in the direction of motivation is the provision of incentives, then incentives have to be made available for every activity.

true story

Motivation and incentives in the central banking sector

The central banking sector is composed of the national banks of the countries of the world, together with overarching bodies, including the International Monetary Fund, European Central Bank, and World Bank.

Across the whole sector, there is a structural difficulty in attracting, recruiting and retaining people of expertise. Highly qualified staff come to work in the central banking sector; and then, attracted by the much higher salaries on offer, move to the commercial banking sector.

The sector as a whole concentrated on financial incentives, rather than on addressing the wider issue of capability and commitment. The incentives clearly fulfilled the ability to attract people into the sector; however, the problems of retention remained.

It required a fundamental shift of emphasis, concentrating on the positive benefits and attractions of working for these organizations. Rather than addressing purely the financial issue, some central banks started to present what was on offer in the sector in terms of:

- the ability to influence government and international economic policy;
- involvement in political processes;

- influence over how the retail, commercial and investment banking sectors themselves operated.

Of course, the salaries had to be right; and except in comparison to the commercial banking sector, pay and rewards were very good anyway. However, by concentrating on the job and work content, many institutions in the sector now started to attract – and crucially, retain – the staff that they needed to drive the sector forward into the future.

Motivation, goals and ambitions

Goals and ambitions must be present, realistic and achievable if satisfaction is eventually to occur. Problems arise when the goals set are too low (leading to feelings of frustration), or too high (leading to constant lack of achievement). They must also be acceptable to the individual concerned – in terms of self-image, self-worth, and self-value as well as work achievement – so they are likely to be positive and based on the drive for improved levels of comfort, capability and well-being. They must also be acceptable (or at least not unacceptable) to the society and environment in which the individual lives and works, and capable of being harmonized and integrated with them.

The need for recognition and achievement

A critical part of the motivation process lies in the nature and levels of recognition accorded to the achievement of particular goals. The need for recognition is therefore a drive. Individuals pursue goals that are of value to them; and it is essential therefore for organizations to match their objectives to that which is important to their staff, and to recognize their achievements.

point of view

Achievement

'Achievement' is largely subjective. Achievements fall into the following classifications:

- personal achievements, realized at different points in the life of an individual;
- professional achievements, usually based on job and occupational progression, and tangible deliverables;
- social achievements, in which personal and occupational fulfilment are recognized elsewhere;
- workplace achievements, in which as well as specific occupational deliverables, people are valued for their wider contribution to organizational well-being.

Whatever is 'achieved' is normally of value to the individual and the others with whom they interact (workplace and social). Indeed, some people do not value what they have succeeded at or done unless the recognition is forthcoming; for these people, the fact of success and achievement is not enough – they have to be recognized as well.

From the point of view of workplace motivation, it is essential to know and understand the staff sufficiently in order to relate what they are asked to do to their need for achievement. It is only possible to do this by asking them and then relating their hopes and aspirations to what is possible at the place of work.

The components of achievement are the anticipated and actual rewards that the fulfilment of a particular goal brings. High levels of achievement occur where these overlap completely. High levels also normally occur where real rewards exceed those that are anticipated. Low levels occur where the anticipated rewards are not forthcoming; this devalues the achievement. High or complete achievement is normally seen and perceived as successful. Low achievement or failure to achieve is seen and perceived as a failure.

Achievement motivation theory: D.C. McClelland

McClelland (1971) identified relationships between personal characteristics, social and general background, and work achievement.

Persons with high needs for achievement exhibited the following characteristics:

- task rather than relationship orientation;
- a preference for tasks over which they had sole or overriding control and responsibility;
- the need to identify closely, and be identified closely, with the successful outcomes of their action;
- task balance: on the one hand, this had to be difficult enough to be challenging and rewarding; to be capable of demonstrating expertise and good results, and gaining status and recognition from others. On the other hand, it needed to be moderate enough to be capable of successful achievement;
- risk balance: in which the individual seeks to avoid as far as possible the likelihood and consequences of failure;
- the need for feedback on the results achieved to reinforce the knowledge of success and to ensure that successes were validated and publicized;
- the need for progress, variety and opportunity.

Need for achievement is based on a combination of:

- intrinsic motivation – the drives from within the individual;
- extrinsic motivation – the drives, pressures and expectations exerted by the organization, peers and society.

It is also influenced by education, awareness, social and cultural background, and values. One potential problem was identified in relation to the appointment of high achievers to highly responsible managerial and supervisory positions. Because the higher achievement tended to be task rather than relationship driven, many did not possess (or regard as important) the human relations characteristics necessary to get things done through people, nor did they understand that they would need to develop these if they were to be successful in the future.

More generally, it needs to be recognized that the questions of:

- What is achievement?
- What is high achievement?

have to be addressed in individual cases and circumstances.

McClelland's findings above concentrate heavily on what individuals perceive as achievement; there is little in terms of what is understood and valued as achievement by workplaces, organizations or society. The overwhelming drive was the ability of the individual to present what they had done as 'achievement'.

Source: McClelland (1971).

The need for success and rewards

Additional issues now become apparent.

People need success. People therefore tend to aim their sights at what they know they can do, think they can do, or think that they may be able to do so that success is forthcoming. Genuine successes, victories and triumphs enhance feelings of self-esteem and self-value; failures diminish these.

People need rewards, both extrinsic (money, trappings and status) and also intrinsic (self-esteem and value). Rewards must be valued by both the individual receiving them, and also the wider society, organization, occupation and profession; and so to be fully effective, the rewards on offer must meet these needs as well as rewarding performance.

People need to be accepted, recognized and valued by others. The value (of self and others) arises as the result of a combination of pursuing things that the individual knows or perceives will be valued by those around them (as stated above) and also of seeking out those who will value the achievements for themselves. People need to develop and improve. If satisfaction is not forthcoming in one field, individuals are likely to lose interest and find something else to pursue. As well as matters of comfort and well-being, this also includes broadening and deepening experience and variety of life (including working life). It also includes developing new skills, capabilities and interests with the view to pursuing personal potential as far as possible.

Drives for success, achievement and recognition

As well as being workplace drives, these are wider social and behavioural needs, wants and desires. Each is influenced, developed and conditioned by societies and organizations, and groups within them. Each is based on more fundamental human needs as follows.

- **The need and instinct for society and belonging:** this is a reflection of the need for esteem, warmth and respect. More fundamentally, it is the need to belong, to interact and to have personal contact with those with whom the individual has identity, respect, liking and love. It also includes being drawn to those who have similar hopes, aspirations, interests and ambitions.
- **The need to be in control:** this is the ability to influence the actions and feelings of others; and the ability to influence the environment, to make it comfortable and productive in response to the particular needs, wants and drives. Control is a function of purpose – the organization and arrangement of particular resources (including other people) for given reasons.
- **The need to progress:** this is a reflection of the capacity to develop, to enhance knowledge, skills and capability. It includes:
  - economic drives for better standards of living, quality of life and enhanced capacity to make choices;
  - social drives to gain status, respect, influence and esteem as the result of enhanced capability and economic advantage;
  - personal drives reflecting ambition and the need to maximize/optimize the potential to achieve;
  - opportunistic drives – the identification and pursuit of opportunities that may become apparent and attractive to the individual;
  - invention and creativity – the ability to see things from various points of view and create the means by which quality of life can be enhanced.

Development, adaptation and creativity are also features of the needs for survival, society and control. They are a reflection of the extent to which the individual is able to influence their ability to survive, belong and control their environment.

Except at the point of life and death, when the instinct for survival is everything, these needs constitute parts of the wider process of adaptation and interaction. At given moments therefore, some needs will be stronger than others – there is no linear progression from one to the next.

Major theories of motivation

Human, workplace and occupational motivations have been extensively studied over the period since 1945. The overall purpose has been to identify what motivates and demotivates individuals and groups, and also to identify the conditions (social as well as occupational and organizational) that have to exist in order for people to feel motivated and committed to both life and work.

An illustration and evaluation of the major theories of motivation now follow. These theories are:

- Rensis Likert: System 4;
- Abraham Maslow's hierarchy of needs;
- two-factor theories;
- motivation and classification.

Rensis Likert: System 4

Likert's contribution to the theories of workplace motivation arose from his work with high performing managers: managers and supervisors who achieved high levels of productivity, low levels of cost and high levels of employee motivation, participation and involvement at their places of work. The work demonstrated a correlation between this success and the style and structure of the work groups that they created. The groups achieved not only high levels of economic output and therefore wage and salary targets, but were also heavily involved in both group maintenance activities and the design and definition of work patterns. This was underpinned by a supportive style of supervision and the generation of a sense of personal worth, importance and esteem in belonging to the group itself.

Likert identified four styles or systems of management, as follows:

- **System 1**: Exploitative Authoritative, where power and direction come from the top downwards and where there is no participation, consultation or involvement on the part of the workforce. Workforce compliance is thus based on fear. Unfavourable attitudes are generated, there is little confidence and trust, and low levels of motivation to cooperate or generate output above the absolute minimum.
- **System 2**: Benevolent Authoritative, which is similar to System 1 but which allows some upward opportunity for consultation and participation in some areas.

In both Systems 1 and 2, productivity may be high over the short term when targets can be achieved by a combination of coercion, and bonus and overtime payments. However, both productivity and earnings are demonstrably low over the long term; there is also manifestation of high absenteeism and labour turnover. In System 2, the basis of collective involvement can be developed through engaging a more consultative style.

- **System 3**: Consultative, where aims and objectives are set after discussion and consultation with subordinates; where communication is two-way and where teamwork is encouraged at least in some areas. Attitudes towards both superiors and the organization tend to be favourable especially when the organization is working steadily. Productivity tends to be higher, absenteeism and turnover lower. There are also demonstrable reductions in scrap, improvement in product quality, reduction in overall operational costs and higher levels of earning on the part of the workforce.

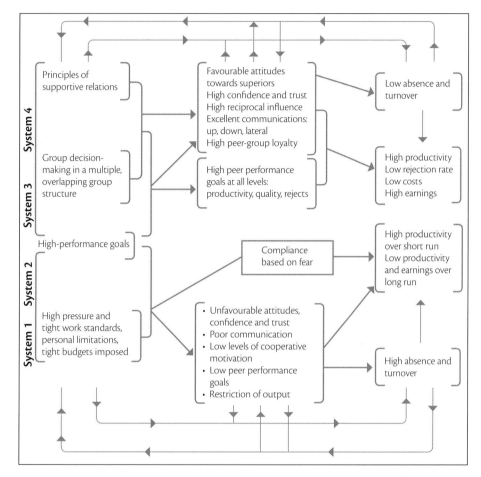

Figure 17.1 *System 4*
Source: Adapted from Likert (1967).

- **System 4:** Participative, where three basic concepts have a very important effect on performance. These are, the use by the manager of the principle of supportive relationships throughout the work group referred to above; the use of group decision-making and group methods of supervision; and the setting of high performance and very ambitious goals for the department and also for the organization overall.

Likert's two extremes – System 1 and System 4 – would appear to be major points of organizational and managerial inquiry and evaluation as the nature of work and workplaces changes. For those on flexible, non-standard and remote patterns and places of work, there would appear to be a critical need to ensure that, when necessary, short-term drives and demands can be made and met. The highly participative approach advocated by System 4 also requires attention through the creation and restructuring of managerial and supervisory approaches to ensure that the maximum possible engagement is achieved on the part of those who are not always present.

Likert's work centred heavily on creating the conditions in which high levels of motivation and achievement were possible; those responsible for designing and implementing flexible, non-standard and remote working patterns and relations need to be aware of these issues.

Abraham Maslow: A hierarchy of needs

Maslow (1960) presented a hierarchy of needs, which explained different types and levels of motivation that were important to people at different times. The hierarchy of needs works from the bottom of the pyramid upwards, showing the most basic needs and motivations at the lowest levels and those created by, or fostered by, civilization and society towards the top of it (see Figure 17.2). The needs are:

1 **Physiological** – the need for food, drink, air, warmth, sleep and shelter; basic survival needs related to the instinct for self-preservation.

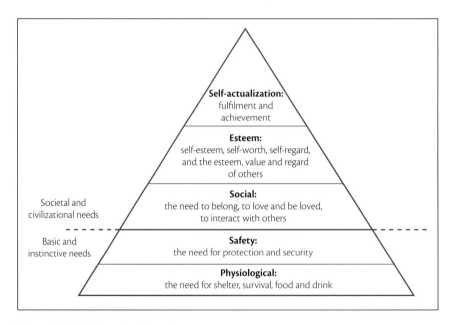

Figure 17.2 *A hierarchy of needs*
Source: **Adapted from Maslow (1960).**

2 **Safety and security** – that is, protection from danger, threats or deprivation and the need for stability (or relative stability) of environment.

3 **Social** – that is, a sense of belonging to a society and the groups within it, for example the family, the organization, the work group. Also included in this level are matters to do with the giving and receiving of friendship; basic status needs within these groups; and the need to participate in social activities.

4 **Esteem needs** – these are the needs for self-respect, self-esteem, appreciation, recognition and status, both on the part of the individual concerned and the society, circle or group in which they interrelate; part of the esteem need is therefore the drive to gain the respect, esteem and appreciation accorded by others.

5 **Self-actualization** – the need for self-fulfilment, self-realization, personal development, accomplishment, mental, material and social growth and the development and fulfilment of the creative faculties.

Self-actualization

Self-actualization refers to the ability and drive of individuals to realize their full potential, to progress as far as possible and to be fulfilled. This includes recognition and value by others. Self-actualization also addresses the need for challenge, responsibility and pride in work and achievement, as well as the technological or professional expertise.

Two views of self-actualization are taken. The first is that self-actualization is available only to the very few. It is limited by the inability to develop sufficient qualities and capabilities for this to take place. This is due to the limitations of the social background of many people and above all, of education, training and other means by which skills, knowledge and expertise are developed.

The second view is that self-actualization is achievable by almost everyone in their own particular circumstances. Whatever the limitations placed by society and education, individuals nevertheless exhibit a range of capabilities and qualities that have the potential of being harnessed and developed in the pursuit of highly rewarding lives in their own terms. Self-actualization is therefore an individual and not an absolute process.

The second view currently holds sway; and this is of particular value in understanding that everyone has needs for respect and esteem. Whatever the nature, level or content of work carried out, people will tend to seek variety and enhancement if this is at all possible. If it is not possible at the place of work, they will seek it elsewhere. This view tends to militate against traditional and classical organization features of task specialization and administrative hierarchies which expect individuals to restrict their capabilities, work as directed and operate machinery and systems, rather than develop and use their capabilities and talents to the full.

Two-factor theories

Herzberg (1967) identified two sets of factors affecting workplace motivation:

- those factors that led to extreme dissatisfaction with the job, the environment and the workplace; and

- those factors that led to extreme satisfaction with the job, the environment and the workplace.

The factors giving rise to satisfaction were called motivators. Those giving rise to dissatisfaction were called hygiene factors or dissatisfiers (see Figure 17.3).

The motivators that emerged were: achievement, recognition, the nature of the work itself, level of responsibility, advancement, and opportunities for personal growth and development. These factors are all related to the actual content of the work and job responsibilities.

The hygiene factors or dissatisfiers that Herzberg identified were as follows: company policy and administration; supervision and management style; levels of pay and salary; relationships with peers; relationships with subordinates; status; and security. These are factors that, where they are good or adequate, will not in themselves make people satisfied; by insuring that they are indeed adequate, dissatisfaction is removed but satisfaction is not in itself generated. On the other hand, where these aspects were bad, extreme dissatisfaction was experienced by all respondents.

Theory X and Y

McGregor (1970) developed the two-factor approach by identifying two distinctive sets of assumptions made by managers about their staff, as follows.

- **Theory X:** in which people dislike work and will avoid it if they can; they would rather be directed than accept responsibility; they must be forced or bribed to put out the right effort; they are motivated mainly by money, which remains the overriding reason why they go to work; their main anxiety concerns personal security, which is alleviated by earning money; people are inherently lazy and require high degrees of supervision, coercion and control in order to produce adequate output.
- **Theory Y:** in which people wish to be interested in work and, under the right conditions, will enjoy it; they gain intrinsic fulfilment from work; they are motivated by the desire to achieve and to realize potential, and to work to the best of their capabilities; they will accept the discipline of the organization and also impose self-discipline.

Effective work motivation was therefore a managerial responsibility. The core of this responsibility lay in understanding the collective attitudes of the organization and designing motivation and incentives around this. Organizations that adopted a largely Theory X approach could not expect long-term enduring high levels of production and output; organizations that adopted the Theory Y approach required much greater levels of investment in the behavioural, as well as operational, side of enterprises.

The work of Herzberg and McGregor has tended to encourage attention on such factors as:

- good and positive supervision which encourages and extends the workforce rather than restricts it;
- job satisfaction which can often be increased through work restructuring, job enrichment and job enlargement programmes;
- and the setting and achieving of targets and objectives based on a full understanding of what they are and why they have been set.

Some organizations have also concentrated on removing the dissatisfiers or hygiene factors to ensure that causes of intrinsic dissatisfaction with the workplace and its environment are minimized.

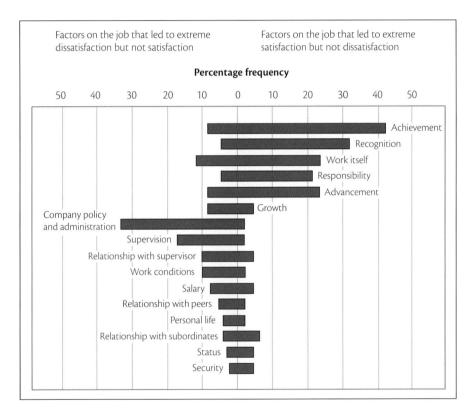

Figure 17.3 *Two-factor theory*
Source: Adapted from Herzberg (1967).

Absenteeism

Absenteeism is widely held to be a feature of the general level of satisfaction or otherwise at the place of work. The higher the level of absenteeism, the greater the level of dissatisfaction.

This translates as follows: for every hundred members of staff, every percentage point of absenteeism requires an additional person employed. Thus 5% absenteeism requires 105 members of staff to do the work of 100; or conversely it takes 105 days to do 100 days' work.

In order to manage the two-factor approach to motivation effectively, attention is essential in the following areas.

- Management style, attitude and approach to staff that is based on integrity, honesty and trust, whatever the nature, limitations or technology concerned in the work itself; and a suitable quality of working environment.
- The psychological contract and bond that exists between employer and employee (see Chapter 2), and which is a key factor in determining the nature, strength and integrity of all working relationships.
- General factors of status and importance that ensure that every member of staff is respected, believed in, treated equally and given opportunity for change, development and advancement within the organization.
- Effective and professional operational relationships between members of staff that in turn promote profitable and successful activities across the entire organization. This includes recognizing the existence of barriers and potential conflicts between departments, divisions and functions and taking steps to provide effective counters to these.

Pay and reward levels must meet expectations, as well as providing adequate levels of income so that individuals feel secure in both life and work. There are collective, cultural and social requirements to increase pay and reward levels; it is also becoming increasingly accepted that there is a moral responsibility placed on organizations to share the fruits of their success (for example through profit and performance-related pay). However, it is also necessary to recognize that high levels of pay do not make work more interesting or worthwhile – though they do certainly make it more bearable, especially in the short term.

Administrative support and control processes and mechanisms must be designed such that they make life easier for those working at the frontline, while at the same time providing the necessary management information. This particularly refers to the nature and effectiveness of the roles and functions of corporate headquarters and the relationships between these and the frontline operations indicated.

The work itself must be divided up fairly. There is particular reference here to those parts of the work that are looked upon with disfavour but which nevertheless must be carried out adequately and effectively.

People need to be confident in the security of their occupation. People need to be employed on a continuous basis as far as possible; and they need to have confidence in the stability and security of their occupation. Steps have to be taken to ensure that there is a steady and open flow of information so that when changes do become necessary, the staff concerned are both forewarned and positively responsive.

Honda UK

When the economic crisis struck the UK in 2008, Honda UK, like many other companies, found itself in crisis. Demand for the company's products fell by 60% over the first six months of 2009, and this resulted in a huge stockpile of unsold cars.

In response, the company consulted extensively with all parts of the workforce and staff. The extent of the crisis was made clear and the following series of actions were agreed.

- There would be a factory shutdown for three months. Over the period, all staff would continue to receive their full basic wage or salary.
- When production re-started, all staff would work an extra two hours a week in order to 'earn back' the salary that they had been paid 'up front'.
- Any member of staff who wanted to leave would do so on advantageous severance terms; however, there were to be no compulsory redundancies.
- The company would make it its business to inform all staff of any changes in circumstances. Especially, if the crisis was to continue (or even deepen), all staff would be summoned into work for a series of meetings and further consultations if these became necessary.

In late 2009, the crisis began to pass; and by the end of 2009, manufacturing was up to previous levels. The company achieved this without any formal dispute. No member of staff was materially disadvantaged.

Additionally, when work did pick up, the company had created the conditions in which it could legitimately call on the staff to re-engage very quickly.

Motivation and classification

Schein (1971) identified the relationship between motivation and commitment, and 'a classification of humankind', as follows.

- **Rational economic.** People are primarily motivated by economic needs. They pursue their own self-interest in the expectation of high economic returns. If they work in an organization, they need both motivation and control. As they intensify the pursuit of money, they become untrustworthy and calculating.

  However, there are those who are self-motivated and have a high degree of self-control. This is the group that must take responsibility for the management of others. They also set the moral and ethical standards required.

- **Social.** People are social and gregarious beings, gaining their basic sense of identity from relationships with others. People will seek social relationships at the place of work, and part of the function of the work group will be the fulfilment of this necessity. The role of management in this situation is therefore greatly concerned with mobilizing the social relationships in the pursuit of operational effectiveness and drawing a correlation between productivity and morale; and taking an active interest in the development of the work group.

- **Self-actualization.** People are primarily self-motivated. They seek challenge, responsibility and pride from their job and to maximize the opportunities that these bring. They are likely to be affected negatively by organizational and management style, external controls, scarcity of resources and other pressures. They will develop their own ways of working and objectives, and integrate these with those established by the organization. The inference is that this is strongest among professional, technical, skilled and managerial staff. However, all work groups have tended towards higher levels of motivation and morale when given a greater degree of autonomy at work.

- **Complexity.** People are complex and sophisticated. People have 'varieties' of emotions, needs, wants and drives driven by personal circumstances, interactions and adaptation. They have many differing, diverse and contradictory motives that vary according to the matter in hand and the different work and social groups in which they find themselves. They will not fulfil every need in any one situation, but rather require a variety of activities in order to do this. They respond to a variety of stimuli according to needs and wants at a given moment. Schein's view of 'complex man' in organizations is that of a psychological contract based on mutual expectations and commonality of aspirations (see Chapter 2). The nature of the working relationships is therefore that of a psychological as well as economic partnership.

The classification approach to motivation approaches the issue from the point of view of the people involved. This reinforces the need for all those in managerial positions to have the best possible knowledge and understanding of human, collective and organizational behaviour. The classification approach draws particular attention to the rational, economic and social needs that ought to be satisfied in all working situations. It also draws attention to the subjectivity of self-actualization and therefore the subjective need for achievement and recognition.

Additionally, managers need to understand the 'complexity' issue. Recognizing that people are indeed 'complex and sophisticated', it follows that they will have a variety of needs, wants, drives and concerns at any given time. When changes in behaviour are observed, managers ought to be able to at least initially relate this to the 'complexity' issue. For example, where a normally highly motivated member of staff is either distracted or else plainly not interested at a particular point in time, consideration needs to be given as to why this is so, rather than assuming that they have suddenly developed a bad attitude. There could be all sorts of reasons: personal problems; domestic issues; or even something as simple as a computer crash (leading to frustration).

The psychological partnership and contract

The psychological partnership and contract is based on the following.

- The motivation to seek out particular types of work, the determination to follow a particular career, to work in particular sectors, occupations, trades, professions and crafts.
- The motivation to apply for specific jobs, with specific employers, to complete the application process and to subject oneself to the recruitment and selection processes.
- The motivation to accept job offers, to accept the salary/occupation/prospects mixes of particular organizations.
- The motivation to turn up for work on the first day.
- The motivation to turn up for work on the second day and to continue turning up on a daily basis; and to start and continue to produce effective and successful work on behalf of the organization.
- The motivation to earn a living, and to both ensure and also increase the standard of living.
- The motivation to progress, develop and advance.
- The motivation for physical and occupational variety; and to apply skills and expertise in a range of situations, problems and issues.
- The motivation to work for the particular organization.
- The motivation to work with particular groups of colleagues.
- The motivation to give a measure of personal, as well occupational, commitment to the work in hand.
- The motivation that is generated by professional pride.
- The motivation that is delivered by a regular series of achievements.

The work itself has got to have known, understood and accepted value. Whatever the occupation, the contribution to the organization as a whole, and recognition for a job well done, must be universally applied.

It is also essential to ensure that the content of work and occupations can be developed as far as possible. Job and work development, enrichment, rotation, enlargement and empowerment ought to be known and understood, and employed wherever possible. If carried out successfully, motivation and commitment can be generated in any staff or occupational group, whatever the working situation and provided that the behavioural satisfaction aspect is also addressed.

Motivation, incentives and money

As stated above, a clear distinction needs to be made between motivation and incentives. Incentives are delivered in return for achieving specific targets; motivation is a broader process.

Nevertheless, monetary rewards and other material benefits are important in ensuring the levels of commitment required of the staff (see Figure 17.4). Wages and salaries are paid by organizations to individuals to reward them for bringing their expertise and efforts, and delivering these effectively. Financial rewards must therefore reflect the:

- specific levels of expertise brought by individuals, and the ways in which they are required to apply it;
- duration, quality and intensity of effort;
- effectiveness of individual performance; and the effectiveness of overall performance;
- locations where performance is required.

There is a strong perceptual relationship between pay and job importance and value. For example:

- a chief executive on an annual salary of £20,000 will be widely considered not to have a great deal of responsibility or authority;
- a marketing officer on £80,000 per year will be generally perceived to have a responsible and high powered job.

It is additionally the case that, in times of turbulence and uncertainty, the drive is for higher immediate rewards rather than the assurance of long-term stability of employment (which is certain to be less available during the periods of turbulence and uncertainty).

The effectiveness of pay and rewards management in terms of generating motivation and commitment is additionally limited or enhanced by:

- comparisons made with other sectors employing similar types or categories of staff;

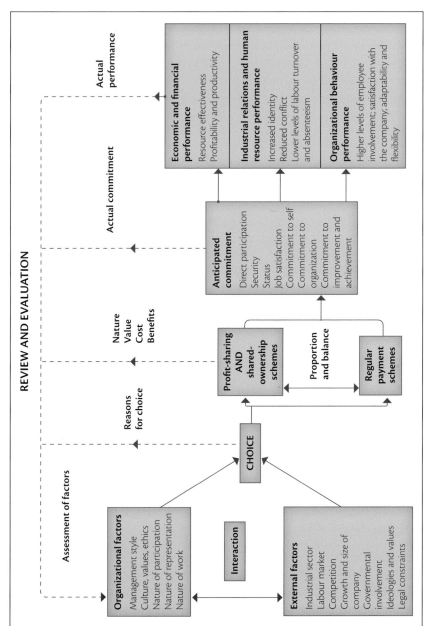

Figure 17.4 *The relationship between pay and performance*

- the going rate; and the going rate applies to both salaries and pay rises. In particular, if individuals receive a pay rise lower than 'the going rate', they tend to feel slighted; if they receive rises above the going rate, they will tend to feel that they have done rather well.

best practice

Effective pay and reward systems address motivation at the same time as targeting the performance required by the organization. Additionally, there is an increase in the number of organizations seeking to relate some part of pay and reward to organizational perform-ance. The purpose is to ensure that strategy, performance and motivation are aligned; and to ensure that staff are recognized and compensated for the efforts that they put in (see Figure 17.4).

Conclusions

Highly motivated and committed staff produce high quality work over long periods of time. The highest levels of motivation occur in organizations which:

- respect and value their staff as people; treat them equally; offer opportunities on an even and equal basis; concentrate on performance not personality; and pay and reward their people well;
- generate positive and harmonious culture; take early action to remove negative attitudes where they start to emerge; reward contributions to organizational performance;
- recognize that everyone has personal, professional and occupational drives, aims and objectives that require satisfaction; and taking steps to harmonize and integrate these with organizational purposes;
- balance the key behavioural features of expectation, effort and reward;
- recognize and rewarding achievement, development and progress;
- balance the attention given to the work in hand, the workings of work groups, and individual performance;
- recognize the prevalence and influence of those elements that, if right, tend to motivate; and those that, if wrong, tend to demotivate (see Table 17.1).

The fundamental concern is to have capable people on the staff who want to work. The best and most rewarding jobs in the world can be – and are – destroyed by negative styles and attitudes of management. The most overtly mundane jobs in the world can be – and are – transformed and made excellent by positive and supportive styles of management and by offering respect, value and recognition where it is possible.

High levels of motivation are indicated by the following:

- low levels of absenteeism;

- low levels of turnover;
- low levels of accidents, sickness and injury;
- few disputes, personality clashes, interdepartmental wrangles;
- open approach to problems; early recognition and attention to potential problems;
- active participation in consultation, organizational initiatives, suggestion schemes.

Table 17.1 *Managerial demotivators and motivators*

Demotivators	Motivators
• Management/supervisory style • Administrative overload • Length of chains of command • Attention to procedures rather than output • Bad communications • Lack of respect/value/esteem • Status/importance based on rank rather than achievement	• Value • Respect • Esteem • Responsibility • Progress • Achievement • Communications

In each case, these are reinforced by clear, open and participative styles of management; ready access to organizational, functional and personal information; and clear and simple systems and procedures.

Low levels of motivation are indicated by:

- high/increasing levels of disputes and grievances; high/increasing levels of disciplinary cases and the use of disciplinary procedures;
- high/increasing levels of accidents, sickness and injury;
- high/increasing levels of absenteeism and turnover;
- steady decline in quality and quantity of performance over the medium to long term. This is reinforced by the concentration of attention on procedures and systems rather than output; and by the proliferation of new systems, procedures, and monitoring and support functions.

These are the initial indicators of high and low levels of motivation. The key areas to address when assessing levels of staff motivation and morale are the:

- level and nature of identity that the staff have with the organization; and the extent to which status, esteem and rewards are issued for productive output as distinct from adherence to procedures;
- ability to offer fulfilment, recognition accomplishment to all levels and grades of staff.

Everyone has basic needs for a sense of belonging, self-respect and self-worth, the respect and value of others, and the need for growth, development and progress. Initial inquiries in this area are therefore to be made along these lines; and these are the key features to address where problems are found to exist.

- Motivation addresses why people do the things that they do, and the conditions necessary for them to be committed to particular organizations and courses of action.
- There is a difference between motivation and incentive: motivation is an enduring commitment; incentive is short term only.
- Motivation is fed by a combination of material and intrinsic rewards.
- The best organizations address particularly the reasons why people may become demotivated with a view to ensuring that demotivators are not present.
- Motivation is a process. People need continuing marks of success, as well as increases in rewards, in order to remain motivated.

Further reading

Herzberg, F. (1967) *Work and the Nature of Man.* Harvard.
Likert, R. (1967) *The Human Organization.* McGraw Hill.
Luthans, F. (2002) *Organizational Behaviour.* McGraw Hill.
Maslow, A. (1960) *Motivation and Personality.* Harper and Row.
McClelland, D. (1971) *Human Aspects of Management.* John Wiley.
Schein, E. (1971) *Organizational Psychology.* Prentice Hall.

18

Management on a daily basis

> 'A critical priority of all managerial practice is a continuous measure of performance against targets and objectives.'

In this chapter

- understanding the full complexities of the managerial role
- developing effective techniques of managing by walking about, remaining visible and accessible, and solving problems
- establishing the conditions under which things can be controlled as tightly as possible
- developing patterns of effective managerial and professional behaviour

Introduction

The purpose of this chapter is to bridge the gap between the acquisition of skills, knowledge, experience and expertise, and the complexities involved, in order to be able to combine them together to generate enduring effective and successful performance.

The managerial role

Managers are the figurehead, symbol, representation and point of identity and contact to everyone who works for them. Managers represent their departments at meetings; they carry the hopes and aspirations of the staff at all times in all dealings with the rest of the organization. It is the departmental manager's role and duty to fight the department's corner and to ensure that the interests of both department and staff are put forward and represented. In this function and according to the nature of the department in which they are working, it will additionally involve belonging to a wide range of professional associations, cluster groups and functional lobbies, and to be an effective operator in all of these.

Managers must have decision-making capabilities suitable to the purposes and functions specifically required. Decision-making is founded in expertise and experience; and this expertise and experience are then related to the particular matter in hand. An effective and expert decision-making process is required in particular for solving problems, whatever these may be. Whether it is consideration of a major departmental investment programme, or resolving an issue concerning a day off for a member of staff, the matter must be addressed effectively.

Effectiveness in any managerial position requires both understanding and capability in these areas. If these are present there are additional benefits in terms of the creation of identity and pride among departmental staff. All managerial actions constitute a critical part of creating the backcloth that is in all cases necessary to manage effectively in any work situation.

There are specific issues that have to be considered when seeking to manage effectively on a continuous basis. These are:

- attitudes and values;
- managing by walking about;
- wait a minute;
- control;
- time management;
- interpersonal skills;
- setting and maintaining standards;
- performance assessment;
- organizational survival.

Attitudes and values

To be truly effective, managers must foster an attitude of absolute equality, evenness and fairness of treatment and opportunity. Failure to do this means that staff are treated unequally and unfairly.

In this context, forming and nurturing the 'right' attitudes is an essential part of the managerial task, and any manager or supervisor must have a full grasp of this and be able to do it. If enthusiasm is infectious, so is negativity; it is only too easy to very quickly have a demoralized workforce if certain matters are not picked up. In both multinational and public and health services this is manifest in the 'canteen culture', and has been partly responsible for engendering and perpetuating negative and undesirable attitudes. The overall purpose must be that everyone is happy, harmonious and productive on the organization's terms and those of the manager and department in question. A clear and positive lead must therefore be given, and clear and positive attitudes engendered and formed.

Prevention of negative, unequal and unfair attitudes is achieved through managerial behaviour and example. It is reinforced through adequate and well-designed induction and orientation programmes so that every employee is given a positive set of both corporate and departmental values, a clear identity with the organization and its purposes and confidence in the rest of the staff. Ultimately, people wish to feel good about the organization and department for which they work.

The cure for bad attitudes is hard. In isolated or extreme cases, people who do not wish to work for the particular organization will be dismissed. In large or complex organizations they may be moved somewhere with the view of reforming their attitudes and getting a positive response from them. Marks of envy and jealousy must also be dealt with; for example, office executives who wish for the salespersons' cars should be informed that, without the efforts of the sales force, there would be no office job. Similarly, professional and technical experts may feel a much stronger loyalty and commitment to their expertise than to the organization that actually employs them to use it. In general, departmental managers will address such matters either at the point at which they first assume their post, or when new members of staff come into the department. They thus set standards of attitude and conformity to which all are to aspire in the pursuit of the goals of the department.

The hard line

The CEO of an organization can give clear guidelines to staff and stakeholders, as the following extract shows:

'I believe in as hard a line as possible being taken by the management on the staff, a harder line being taken by the owners on the management and the hardest line being taken by the owners on themselves. Creating this environment is very difficult and so a strong approach must be taken in every area. The working atmosphere must be tightly controlled and be all-pervasive or it will not work. This seems contradictory to the "soft" approach so often preached. I think it is necessary however, if their dreams of what people are capable of are to be achieved.

The vital ground rules must be ascertained (no more, no less) and then they must be stuck to absolutely rigidly. The Japanese conformity approach should be made to look weak when it comes to the ground rules. On the other hand, once these rules are adhered to, as much flexibility as possible should be allowed. In this way individuality is achieved through conformity. As long as the important things are taken care of, people can do what they want and express themselves freely through their jobs. I don't care how they do something as long as the end product is good. Mavericks who can work within the guidelines are welcome and a great source of creativity and inspiration.

It may be possible to summarise the ground rules into simply one thing. You must keep to your agreements. This encourages the development of the person's integrity, their ability to make choices and their sense of responsibility. It then gives us the opportunity to ask them to agree to what we really want, i.e., be at work at 8.00 a.m. If they agree to this, we will hold them to it precisely; 2 minutes past 8.00 is not 8.00, and providing we can maintain enough front (and maintain this level of integrity ourselves) then we will pull them up on it.

Reasons are not relevant (e.g. the bus was late). It then becomes a matter of "Personal Power" which we want to foster in the staff. It is possible to act as if you are responsible for everything that happens in your life whether it is true or not. Doing this eventually means it will end up as being true in your reality. It is possible to look ahead and manipulate the environment. If you expect traffic then you can leave earlier. If they were paid £100,000 just for turning up on time, they would be there. This principle can be applied to everything we want, and although it may seem strange, in the long-term it will benefit the individual as much as us.'

Source: Scott (1993).

Managing by walking about

Managing by walking about (MBWA) enhances visibility, and also creates opportunities for productive harmony, early problem and issue resolution, and improvements in communications.

In behavioural and perceptual terms, managers who are 'visible' are seen as approachable and acceptable. This will be reinforced by those who, while walking about, take active measures to approach the staff members, get to know them, understand their jobs, their problems and their concerns.

More specifically, MBWA underlines the essential qualities of trust, openness, honesty and integrity, as well as visibility. It fosters a communication forum and informal meeting point between manager and staff that demonstrates the manager's care and concern, and enables small issues to be brought up and dealt with on the spot before they become big issues.

MBWA is additionally an essential cog in the process of continually appraising the performance of staff. It enables any misunderstandings on the part of anyone concerned to be raised and rectified quickly.

just a minute

MBWA also fosters the quality of empathy in the manager or supervisor, and gives a full general knowledge and background to the hopes, fears and aspirations of those who work in the department. This is an essential prerequisite to the process of motivating the staff successfully.

MBWA reduces both the physical and behavioural barriers between the manager and staff. The closed door, large desk and executive trappings are not only physically imposing; they also present a perceptual barrier that the subordinate has first to overcome because they reinforce the differences in rank and status between the two: MBWA dilutes these.

Managing by walking about

Related to MBWA is the need to lead by example and set absolute standards. Good leaders and managers are always present, visible and accessible on a regular basis. Managers gain and improve respect among staff through their willingness to become fully involved as well as leading and directing. For example, Richard Branson of the Virgin Group regularly serves drinks and meals on his scheduled airline flights and train journeys. He also makes a point of regularly telephoning those staff whom he has not seen during the recent past. Additionally, he visits all of his different activities as often as he possibly can. Not only is he demonstrating his willingness, commitment and capacity, he is setting an example to, and for, the staff, as well as keeping an active eye on the daily operations of the Virgin organization. It is also excellent general PR and identity building among both staff and customers.

MBWA is an essential tool for managers, and one that must be in constant use. If it is not, the staff will develop their own patterns and ways of working, their own means of problem and issue resolution, and control will pass out of the hands and office of the manager.

In more sophisticated or complex organizations, and where there are flexible and non-standard patterns of work, managers need to reprioritize their schedule of activities in order to be able to maintain the visible face of the organization and its management. This is so that visibility and identity are built and developed whatever the working situation; and again, it helps to provide a full context for taking the day-to-day decisions and resolving minor and operational issues before they become major crises.

Wait a minute

All managers should have a mechanism in some shape or form that constitutes a 'wait a minute' facility. This will be present in the formulation of policy or direction; the taking of decisions; and in the implementation of strategy. At departmental and other junior levels the purpose is to ensure that no inconvenient operational precedent is being set by taking a particular line to resolve what may seem a simple and one-off problem. 'Wait a minute' is not an abdication of decision-making ability or of decision-making itself. It need not take a 'minute'. It is simply to ensure that what is to be done has been questioned from every conceivable angle. It is more generally part of the monitoring, review, early and late warning systems that should be integral to all aspects of the manager's task. The presence of a 'wait a minute' facility does not of itself ensure that the right decision is taken, but it does at least afford a moment's further consideration. If this is all that is necessary to confirm that what is being done is truly for the good of the organization and the fair and equitable treatment of the staff concerned, it is a moment well spent.

Wait a minute

- Nike, the sportswear corporation, tried to devise a global travel policy for its staff. In particular, the focus was on who should travel first class, business class or economy class on the world's airlines. Should this be based on – the distance travelled; the part of the world to which the executive was travelling; the length of the journey; or the volume or value of business to be conducted?

- John Stevens, an official at the London office of an international bank, asked to be able to take two years' annual leave back-to-back (a total of two months) to visit friends and relatives in Australia. His request was granted. Mary Phelps, an official in an equivalent position and with longer service at the same bank, put in the same request for the back-to-back leave to visit friends and relatives in Stornoway in the Western Isles off the coast of Scotland. She underlined the request by stating that it would take longer for her to get to her destination than for Stevens to get to his.

The 'wait a minute' facility would not necessarily address the issues raised in the Nike example, or change the decision about staff leave at the international bank. The 'wait a minute' facility would, however, ensure that the decisions had just been briefly reconsidered for integrity, fairness and transparency.

Control

All managers must have control mechanisms suitable to the department or unit concerned; and relating to the staff, resources and operations that are carried out within it. This must apply even where the work in hand is of a professional, administrative, technical or qualitative nature. The overall function of control involves setting desired standards and measuring actual performance against them: from this, analyses of differences between the two will be made and remedial action will be taken where necessary. It follows from this that objectives must be fully understood by all concerned so that involvement in the control of the work necessary and in any remedial action that becomes apparent is adopted and supported by everyone.

The methods and mechanisms to be used will therefore be department or task specific; and linked to, and in harmony with, the overall methods adopted by the organization. They must reconcile the need to produce clear results with the need to be flexible and objective in operation, and economical and simple. Presentation of control information in ways that everyone can understand and recognize is essential. It is necessary not only to indicate differences and deviations from required performance but also to provide the means of establishing the causes of these – where the failures are occurring, why this is so and what to do about them. Within this context, managers will draw up and use their own control methods. These will include:

- **Forecasts,** based on the resources – staff, financial and technological – available; and in relation to the outputs that the organization requires.
- **Risk assessment,** based on knowledge of the situation as it exists and with especial attention to what is not fully known about specific matters.
- **Resource allocation and usage,** based on what the department has, and can, get hold of; and based also on the resources that the department does not have and cannot get hold of.
- **Priorities,** and the basis of prioritization; in particular making clear to people what can, and cannot, be done.
- **Deadlines,** and the basis on which these have been arrived at.
- **Budgets,** for all the activities within the manager's sphere, covering such matters as staff, production, outputs, operational costs, administration, other overheads, cash and daily expenditure and possibly also an overall department reconciliation of these matters.
- **Management information systems,** including the gathering and promulgation of information within the department and the reconciliation of this with desired levels of performance; these also provide a vehicle for the manager's contribution to the information systems and requirements of the organization.
- **Reporting systems and relationships,** designed to highlight any deviations and problems immediately, and to identify means by which such situations may be remedied; in any case, they should be able to provide information that can be used on an organizational basis for future planning and direction setting.
- **Job and work design,** to ensure that work is allocated in order to ensure effective long-term organizational, departmental and individual performance; and that the bad or unattractive parts of the work are evenly shared out. This is likely to require attention to the ability of attracting and retaining staff; and to the design of effective (and often flexible) working patterns.
- **Performance appraisal, assessment and feedback:** part of the control process is the communication process that constitutes keeping the departments informed of its progress on a continuous basis. There is a control function inherent in the nature and content of feedback that is given in terms of recognizing any achievements and dealing with any shortfalls.
- **Conflict:** part of the purpose of having control methods and procedures in place must be to ensure that conflicts or disputes between members of staff are resolved as quickly and effectively as possible.

- **Control methods and means**: these should be integrated into the general review, monitoring and process assessment that should be in place in all departments. To be fully effective, they require full understanding on the part of all concerned – the manager, the staff and those other departments and units with whom they interact; they should also mirror the aims and objectives of the departments if they are to be fully effective.
- **Factors outside the manager's control**, which nevertheless have to be handled on a daily basis or as and when they arise. All managers need to do their best to in-build time so that they have a degree of flexibility and leeway in addressing matters when they do arise.

An airline manager working in the Middle East

This manager regularly fields questions from powerful and influential people in his region. Problems handled have included the following.

- Why the daughter of a diplomat had to wait 20 minutes for an orange juice on her flight back to London.
- Why packages and parcels carried by a worldwide courier organization had to go through security screening and not straight on to the aeroplane.
- Why it took two hours for a particular cargo to be cleared from the airport by customs.
- Why Europeans have to go through the full immigration procedure upon arrival in countries of the Middle East.

Each of these items is outside the manager's control. It is impossible to predict when these, and similar, issues will arise; they do, however, have to be dealt with on the spot. And if they appear (to outsiders) futile, trite and silly questions – nevertheless, managerial practice demands that they are dealt with. And everyone has similar things in their own situations that they do indeed have to deal with when they arise.

Time management

Time at the workplace may be divided into:

- productive time;
- non-productive stoppage or downtime;
- maintenance time;
- wasted time.

From this, priority, crisis, wastage, overload and underload can be identified; and a time–resource–energy dimension put on each. The purpose is to ensure that what happens in reality accords with what managers think happens. Other dimensions and variables will also be included. These include the complexity and difficulty of the task in hand, the importance of it, the urgency of it, and the frequency of it. The value of what is done, whether derived or implicit, will also have a time configuration to it. What is therefore required is an attitude of continued questioning of time usage based on the premise that anything and everything can always be improved and made more efficient and effective.

In order to maximize or optimize time usage, certain steps can be taken. The first is for the manager to be aware of the time issue. Part of the process that arises from this is:

- to set priorities for the department;
- to set a pattern of delegation of tasks and activities;
- to produce suitable and effective work schedules;
- to continuously assess the work in hand against time constraints, as well as against constraints placed by other resource implications.

Next the manager should identify those things that waste time. These may consist of:

- long, unnecessary or habitual meetings, or those which are procedural rather than executive in content;
- interruptions and the nature of these in his or her work;
- idle conversations; unnecessary bureaucracy, reporting systems and record keeping;
- the balance of travelling time against effective business conducted;
- task allocations – especially the allocation of the easy tasks which should be conducted on a basis that leaves those of high capacity and quality to carry out key, critical or other activities that match their capabilities, not filling up their work schedules with items that are well within them.

As stated above, managers need to be able to build in as much flexibility as is necessary in order to deal with interruptions and issues that have to be addressed immediately. Managers should also be aware of creative approaches to time management in terms of machine, equipment and plant usage; working patterns and shift arrangements; personal planning; the setting and maintenance of deadlines; and giving clarity of purpose to meetings. There are opportunity costs of time usage and especially time wastage that can never be made up. All managers and their departments should have a system of time measurement that is suitable to its purpose; and that encourages efficiency and effectiveness of performance in regard to this resource.

Interpersonal skills

Everyone has interpersonal skills. For managers, interpersonal skills additionally constitute a critical tool that is essential to them in the pursuit of their daily occupation. How interpersonal skills are used is instrumental in creating and reinforcing the management style adopted.

Interpersonal skills are used as part of the process of MBWA and the visibility that goes with this, reinforcing messages of honesty, openness and trust. Interpersonal skills have implications for general levels and states of communication within the department, and for conducting meetings and handling public presentations.

Crucially, managers need to be able to apply their interpersonal skills when dealing with performance or behaviour issues. They will never criticize members of staff either in public or on a personal basis when the problem is related to work. If there is a personal issue that requires managerial activity and concern, this will be conducted in private and remain a matter between the manager and the individual. If it is necessary to criticize somebody's work performance, then it must be done in a clear and straightforward way with the emphasis upon remedy rather than apportioning blame. Effective criticism is always constructive; the end result must be to reinforce the importance of the individual as a member of the department. If it is possible, such criticism should be reinforced by finding areas of work to be praised at the same time. In this way also, the work remains at the centre of the concern.

As well as dealing effectively with conduct and performance issues, the positive needs always to be emphasized. In particular, praise should be extended where it is due. It is a powerful form of recognition and a universal motivator. Every manager should avoid only dealing with staff when there are negative concerns. Praise makes the individual concerned feel identity, respected and important. It should be handed out whenever and wherever due, and it should be conducted in public.

Managers also use interpersonal skills to instil pride and enthusiasm for the job, the work and the department. The best managers inspire and generate pride and enthusiasm by the ways in which they behave in relation to the department's work and the people carrying it out. It is the manager's job to instil this feeling and to promote this attitude among the staff, and the interpersonal relationship with the staff is instrumental in this.

Always remember that all work should be a matter of enthusiasm, and a matter of enjoyment as well as fulfilment. Again, the interpersonal skills of the manager are instrumental in creating this background.

Other qualities of leadership that become apparent through the use of interpersonal skills are: the courage of the manager concerned; knowledge of the job; self-control and self-discipline; sense of fairness and equity; standards of personal conduct and behaviour that reflect the standards required in the department; and a sense of humour. It is also a reflection of the interpersonal qualities of the manager that ensures that the correct and appropriate standards of dress, language and manners are established. This is particularly important in departments and units where dealings with the public are an everyday feature, or where protective clothing must be worn.

Effective use and application of interpersonal skills is demonstrated when staff and manager each know where they stand in relation to each other. Effective and professional application of interpersonal skills provides the basis for effective work transactions, and organizational and departmental communications, ensuring that disputes and misunderstandings are kept to a minimum. Effective interpersonal skills, underpinned by integrity and transparency, also critically reinforce the manager's authority, confidence and trust.

Setting and maintaining standards

As stated above (Chapter 8), all organizations and managers have to be able to set and maintain standards of conduct, behaviour and performance. Much of this has to be done on a daily basis; as well as having procedures and policies that have to be followed, managers have to be able to visibly and effectively establish absolute benchmarks in the following areas.

- **Discipline**: establishing absolute standards of behaviour and performance based on both ordinary common decency and also absolute organizational demands; and ensuring that when disciplinary procedures are invoked, matters are dealt with quickly, fairly and effectively.
- **Dismissal**: ensuring that offences such as vandalism, violence, theft, fraud, bullying, victimization, discrimination and harassment are dealt with fairly and effectively; and that when these are proven, the perpetrators are dismissed.
- **Grievances**: handling and resolving issues rather than institutionalizing them; ensuring that the full facts of the case are covered; and ensuring that everyone understands what outcome has been reached and the reasons for this.
- **Health and safety**: creating and maintaining the conditions whereby a healthy and safe working environment exists; taking remedial action where unsafe practices and unhealthy aspects are found.
- **Occupational health**: above all paying attention to stress, repetitive strain injuries, and the causes of these; recognizing the potential for their existence; addressing and remedying working practices when these are found.
- **Risk management**: knowing and understanding where things can potentially go wrong, especially in terms of inter-occupational, inter-professional and interpersonal relationships; the integrity of computer and IT systems; production and service delivery issues where all of these are related to daily activities as well as organizational and institutional integrity.

In each of these cases, it is essential for managers to understand that there are procedures to be followed, and that failure to do so normally constitutes a breach of a employment law. Managers must therefore become fully knowledgeable in their content, and expert in their application.

Continuous performance assessment

Managers must be able to assess and evaluate levels and quality of performance in their departments, and to measure this against the required standards as follows.

- Where there are departmental problems, managers need to conduct full investigations to discover the reasons and to make judgements as the result. Investigations are likely to consist of:
  - a review of processes and procedures;
  - sampling of activities;
  - establishment of any shortfall in staff harmony and cooperation;
  - resource shortage;
  - identification of blockages;
  - identification of hold-ups in administration processes and procedures.

- At team level, it may be necessary to examine the extent to which there are problems of attitudes and behaviour. If serious conflicts have arisen, these must be addressed and remedied. If there are problems or blockages in communication, then there is the responsibility to ensure that team members are fully briefed.
- At an individual level, it is essential that managers attend to praise for good performance, and a quick and effective remedy for any shortfall.

All this should be underpinned by the approach taken to the general monitoring of the work of the department. As stated above, this is a crucial output of MBWA.

A critical priority of all managerial practice is a continuous measure of performance against targets and objectives, and the criteria against which the success or otherwise of departments and activities will be assessed. This reinforces the need for all managers to become actively and visibly involved in everything that concerns their department.

Survival and effectiveness

Managers have to create their own patterns of behaviour and networks of relationships in order to survive and be effective. It is impossible to apply any expertise in isolation from the particular situation.

Managers therefore need to become effective in operating within both the formal and the informal systems of networks and relationships that exist in every organization.

The formal networks tend to consist of regular meetings, and professional and occupational networks, all of which carry varying degrees of influence. Managers need to ensure that they become as effective as possible when working within the formal systems and networks so that they maintain, preserve and develop their own position and that of their departments, divisions and functions.

When working within the informal systems, managers need to find their own niches and from there, go on and develop networks and support as they require.

Managers need to develop a keen 'environmental' sense. This comprises:

- the ability to spot straws in the wind, indicating possible changes, developments, innovations or crises;
- the recognition of the departments and individuals where actual power and influence truly lie;
- sources of information within the complexities of the organization;
- 'managerial antennae' which are finely tuned to perceive any shifts in the other aspects or across the environment in general.

Managers will assess their own position in the pecking order, the competition for power and influence and the qualities that they bring to the organization's internal political situation. They will assess their own strengths and weaknesses in it, and the capabilities and capacities that are required in order to be effective and professional operators in the given situation.

They will identify where the inter-group frictions (and sometimes hostility) lie and assess the reasons for them. From this standpoint they will similarly assess the position of their department in the whole, and look to be able to lobby for support and influence where they are most likely to get it in the pursuit of these interests.

They must adapt their managerial style to the situation. For example, a highly open and task-oriented approach is not likely to work in a bureaucratic set-up. By adopting it anyway because of preference, the manager would simply throw away any advantages held and the political positioning necessary in order to operate in the environment. This would also impinge upon both the work and effectiveness of the department and its own regard in the organization.

Throughout the operational environment there will also be various agenda that are to be followed. Departments and their managers have secondary and hidden agenda, especially to do with the advancement of a particular course of action; but also, more generally, in the promotion of the department or its manager in the pecking order of the organization. Departments may engage in unhealthy, negative competition that has nothing to do with the pursuit of effective operations but rather, negatively encourages success at the expense of other departmental failures. It becomes a drive for power and influence in itself motivated by the need to gain the ear of the chief executive or in other spheres of influence.

The situation may be exacerbated by bad and inadequate communications and communication systems so that people find things out via the grapevine or other vested interests; in such situations especially, trade union officials prosper and flourish. There is a consequent increase in the numbers of disputes including those between departments; and an increase also in those disputes and grievances that are put on a formal basis and go either to arbitration or to the top of the organization for resolution. Rules and regulations in such situations become the end and not the means to an end. Where such situations are allowed to persist over long periods of time, bureaucratic superstructures are devised and additional staff and procedures taken on and adopted, and such interdepartmental and organizational wranglings become institutionalized and part of the ways of working.

Conclusions

The issues raised and discussed in this chapter are those common to all situations – projects, operations, and industrial, commercial and public services sectors. Whether or not written into organization strategy, policy and direction, each has to be addressed on a daily basis. It is essential therefore, that all managers ensure that they have their own ways of establishing specific standards in each of these areas, and uphold them.

The manager's performance in the eyes of their subordinates is underpinned by their determination to know and understand the field of operations in which they are working, even if they have no professional or occupational expertise in it. Preaching perfection, it is every manager's duty to ensure that they know as much as possible about the field of activities as a whole; the pressures and constraints on every activity for which they have direct responsibility; and of the professional and occupational boundaries for which they are ultimately responsible.

Cohesion of managerial activities with professional and occupational operations is essential if long-term effective organizational performance is to be sustained. This does not always happen – indeed, in some organizations, the overwhelming impression is that management and activities run parallel to each other with very little direct contact. The public services sector has an enduring reputation for this; indeed, many school head teachers and hospital ward managers can go for weeks without any direct contact from those to whom they are ultimately answerable.

Badrin Oil Ltd

Lack of managerial and professional contact is not unique to the public sector – many multinational and multi-site industrial and commercial organizations run in exactly the same way. For example, Badrin Oil Ltd, a large oil company, decided that it was going to undertake a programme of strategic change. Consultants were hired, and an outline strategy agreed. The consultants found that a key perception of those working as oil engineers in the field was that they did all the work, while head office spent all the profits. Accordingly, proposals were drawn up to make sure that nobody spent more than three years at head office without doing at least six months in the field somewhere in the world. The same year, the company reported a 0.5% decline in annual profits, even though turnover had risen by 7%. The company's top managers flew to a luxury hotel in South America to discuss the implications. The top managers decided that it was too much trouble to do anything about the oil engineers and their complaints. More critically, the company's managers dropped the proposal about doing six months in the field some-where in the world after three years at head office – contemplating this prospect was clearly highly uncomfortable. The consultants were paid off and everything went back to how it was before.

Finally, it is essential that all managers have a visibility and integrity of style and personality. This applies whether the manager is autocratic, democratic or participa-tive (there is no reason at all why autocrats should not also be honest and open). Participation and consultation should never be used as an excuse for sitting on the fence. Many managers use their overtly participative style as an excuse to avoid taking decisions or confronting awkward problems and individuals. Once the staff know, believe or perceive that a manager's style is solely concerned with the abdica-tion of responsibility – a 'hands-off' approach – the position becomes very difficult to retrieve.

In everything that managers do, the key qualities underlining all effective perform-ance are: enthusiasm; ambition; dynamism; flexibility; responsiveness; and the acceptance of responsibility and accountability. To these must be added: a willing-ness to be wrong and to admit mistakes; a willingness to put things right; and charac-teristics of integrity and truthfulness.

It is important to recognize that, however necessary it may be to behave according to the rules and norms of the organization, in the long term, integrity, professionalism and working relationships can be destroyed if absolute standards of continuous and daily managerial practice are not set and maintained.

in brief

- The position of visibility and identity in building effective managerial practice.
- The need for effective decision-making processes, both in terms of effectiveness, and in relation to what the context can support.
- The need to manage time effectively, and to be flexible in its usage.
- The need to be able to exert control over sets of activities, and the ability to identify and use effectively the means at the manager's disposal.
- The need to be able to recognize, understand and evaluate the organizational context in which activities take place; and the need to be able to develop expertise and presence so as to be able to survive and be influential in that context.

Further reading

Colley, J. et al. (2007) *Principles of General Management*. McGraw Hill.

Delves Broughton, P. (2007) *What They Teach You at Harvard Business School*. Penguin.

Drucker, P. (1986) *The Effective Executive*. HarperCollins.

Hayes, J. (2002) *Interpersonal Skills at Work*. Kogan Page.

Peters, T. and Austin, N. (1985) *A Passion for Excellence*. Harper and Row.

Semler, R. (2003) *The Seven Day Weekend*. Century.

Management development

> 'Management development is a partnership between the organization and the individuals ... the needs of both must be satisfied.'

In this chapter

- understanding the nature of management development, and its critical role in the professionalization of management
- developing all aspects of managerial expertise
- management development as a process; and as a personal as well as occupational drive
- understanding the value of different management development activities in the establishment and enhancement of professional practice and expertise

Introduction

If management is truly to become a profession, then managers and management have to be developed in line with gaining the body of knowledge, understanding and expertise required, and in order also to ensure known and understood levels of performance.

Like all expert practice, management development requires organizing along the following lines:

- **organizational**, reflecting the particular needs of the organization in which individuals find themselves;
- **occupational**, concerned with the needs of present and future positions within the particular organization;
- **professional**, concerned with organizational needs, and also with a wider view of what skills, knowledge, understanding and expertise ought to be developed;
- **personal**, concerned with organizational, occupational and professional development, and also attending to the preferred wider directions and interests of individuals.

Within this context, management development is concerned with the following activities:

- the development of managers and supervisors;
- the development of all staff through the activities of managers and supervisors;
- the development of overall organizational capability;
- identification of talent and potential;
- ensuring organizational succession and continuity;
- developing expertise in line with an individual's ambitions and aspirations.

The overall approach must therefore match organizational sustainability with developing the careers and expertise of the individuals involved.

Any discussion of management development has to start from the premise that the skills, qualities and expertise required of good and effective managers can be taught, learned and applied. The vast range of management courses, activities, expertise and qualifications would tend to support this view, at least to an extent.

For effective management development to take place, clearly the qualities have to be present in individuals as the basis for development. Plainly, some people are going to do better than others once the potential has been identified. However, this is just like all talented and expert people, while many have the expertise present within them, some turn out to be better footballers/actors/ plumbers/teachers/nurses than others.

The 'common sense' view of management

The alternative view offered to rigorous and professional management development is that management is 'common sense' and that therefore anyone can do it (see also Chapter 1).

The university of life

Those who take the view that management is 'common sense' and therefore anyone can do it point to the success of individuals such as Richard Branson. Clearly, Richard Branson has turned out to be an expert leader and very successful business person. However, Branson himself acknowledges his own shortcomings, going to a lot of trouble to surround himself with the highest quality available expertise in the fields in which the Virgin Group operates. Branson also acknowledges that had he gone to business school, he would have made far fewer mistakes in any case.

There are plenty of other examples – entrepreneurs who have succeeded in building vast organizations, and entrepreneurs who have succeeded in their own terms by building small organizations that can support their own lifestyle and ambitions.

Otherwise, the evidence is to the contrary.

Promotion paths

There has been a traditional approach in much of the Western world to promote the best professional or operative into the position of manager. Thus, for example, the best teacher became head teacher; and the best plumber, plumbing manager. What tended to happen was that the profession or occupation lost an expert practitioner; and the manager gained was of uncertain and untested knowledge and expertise – because they had no prior management training or development.

Other figureheads

Many other figureheads including Stelios Haji-Ioannou (who founded EasyJet), Michael O'Leary (who transformed Ryanair into the largest low-cost airline in the world) and Julian Richer (who founded the Richer Sounds chain of electrical stores) received business and management education. Most people who rise through the ranks to the top of their organizations have had some form of leadership or management training and development along the way. Those who reach the very top of their organizations normally at least undertake the executive development programme of the Institute of Directors; and many have either completed postgraduate business and management qualifications, or university-based executive programmes.

In practice, management development concentrates on:

- organization development and managing change;
- collective and individual development;
- the development of organizational understanding;
- the development of organizational, collective and individual behaviour;
- behaviour, attitudes, skills, knowledge, expertise and technological proficiency development;
- technical knowledge: finance, strategy, HR, marketing and ethics;
- knowing and understanding the environment;
- product, service and operational advancement and improvement.

In the first place, the knowledge, skills and expertise required of management and managers, as above, have to be developed and delivered in absolute terms. It then becomes necessary to ensure that this expertise can be delivered in the particular environment in which individuals are working. There are further demands that have to be met, ensuring that managerial expertise is integrated with organization, environmental and business pressures, opportunities and constraints. The development of organizational, collective and individual work ethics, including personal as well as professional commitment, has to be generated. Increasingly, managing across cultures and in transforming occupations, professions, industries and sectors is also a priority in all development activities.

Right or wrong?

A further problem becomes apparent when looked at from the point of view of change, environment and cultural pressures. For example, when an organization changes attitudes, priority or status (for example as the result of merger or takeover, privatization or techno-logical change) then it is *assumed* that present management expertise and qualities must be wrong. Those involved are therefore removed. Something has then to be put in its place. So long as this is different this is *assumed* to be right.

It is also the case that when there is a change of organization chairman, chief executive or other key figure, the new person coming in is *assumed* to be a right appointment. If this 'rightness' is to become effective, the new figure must have the skills, knowledge and expertise to become immersed very quickly and to begin to deliver results in very short time frames.

Finally, given that only 13% of mergers, takeovers, privatizations and technologically driven changes are wholly or mostly successful, there is an overwhelming need for attention in these areas and a managerial requirement to question these assumptions in the first place.

If nevertheless, this is to continue as organization practice, then it underlines the need for a distinctive body of professional knowledge and understanding so that managers can drop into a new job and become effective very quickly – a bit like a GP dropping into a new practice for the first time.

Sources: Industrial Society (1999); Institute of Management (1996).

The management development requirement is therefore twofold: to identify and develop a body of expertise; and to be able to apply it in whatever situation or environment required.

The professionalization of management

The best managers are committed and dedicated operators; highly trained and educated, with excellent analytical and critical faculties. Beyond this, there is a body of skills and aptitudes, knowledge, attitudes and behaviour that the effective manager must have and be able to draw upon.

Personal qualities are required of everyone who aspires to conduct their occupation to a 'professional' or expert level, and management is no different. For professional management practice, the personal qualities required include:

- ambition, energy, commitment, self-motivation;
- job, product and service knowledge;
- self-knowledge and self-respect;
- drive and enthusiasm;
- creativity and imagination;

- a thirst for knowledge;
- a commitment to improvement;
- a commitment to continuous development, both personal and professional;
- commitment to the interests of everyone involved;
- commitment to integrity and honesty;
- the ability to grow and broaden the outlook and vision of the organization concerned;
- a positive and dynamic attitude, self-discipline, empathy with the staff and everyone else concerned;
- a love of the organization and pride and enthusiasm in the job, its people, its products, its services, its customers and clients.

These personal qualities have to be present within the individual, and capable of being nurtured and developed, and they provide the springboard for the successful and professional operator.

Currently, much of the grounding for a professional approach is formalized and achieved through the study of business and management at school, college and university; and there are plenty of opportunities for everyone to develop this knowledge and understanding to professional levels. However, this is not yet a universal or formal requirement (see below).

Additionally, management is a global activity and lessons need to be learned from everywhere in the world. This includes Western Europe, North America, China, India, Japan, Korea, the Philippines, Malaysia, Indonesia, the Middle East, Australia, New Zealand and South Africa, where managerial practices are well documented.

It must be recognized finally, that management is currently being conducted in a changing and turbulent environment. This has itself changed over the period since 1945 and the reconstruction of the world damaged by the Second World War. Then, everything was arranged to try and bring order, stability and performance steadiness to business, service and the markets and spheres in which they operated. Today all that has gone and the processes of technological advance, management education, automation, technological and social change, and political development, together with the globalization of business and commerce, ensure that all concepts of management are in turn subject to continuous change and revision.

Truly expert and committed managers will therefore always ensure that they keep themselves up to date with everything that impinges on both their job and their chosen 'profession'. Many professional management bodies and institutions now insist that their members keep records of all continuous professional development activities that they undertake and, indeed, insist on this as a condition of continuing membership.

Professions

Having identified the range of knowledge, skills, expertise and qualities that expert managers need to have, it is then necessary to establish the extent to which 'management' can be truly professionalized. The 'classical' professions are always understood to be medicine, law, the priesthood and the military. The following elements were held to distinguish these occupations from the rest of society.

- **Distinctive expertise:** not available elsewhere in society or in its individual members.
- **Distinctive body of knowledge:** required by all those who aspire to practise in the profession.
- **Entry barriers:** in the form of examinations, time serving, learning from experts.
- **Formal qualifications:** given as the result of acquiring the body of knowledge and clearing the entry barriers.
- **High status:** professions are at the top of the occupational tree.
- **Distinctive morality:** for medicine, the commitment to keep people alive as long as possible; for law, a commitment to represent the client's best interests; for the church, a commitment to godliness and to serve the congregation's best interests; for the military, to fight within stated rules of war.
- **High value:** professions make a distinctive and positive contribution to both the organizations and individual members of the society.
- **Self-regulating:** professions set their own rules, codes of conduct, standards of performance and qualifications.
- **Self-disciplining:** professions establish their own bodies for dealing with problems, complaints, and allegations of malpractice.
- **Unlimited reward levels:** according to preferred levels of charges and the demands of society.
- **Life membership:** dismissal at the behest of the profession; ceasing to work for one employer does not constitute loss of profession.
- **Personal commitment:** to high standards of practice and morality; commitment to deliver the best possible in all circumstances.
- **Self-discipline:** commitment to personal standards of behaviour in the pursuit of professional excellence.
- **Continuous development:** of knowledge and skills; a commitment to keep abreast of all developments and initiatives in the field.
- **Governance:** by institutions established by the profession itself.

In absolute terms 'management' clearly falls short in most areas. Formal qualifications are not a prerequisite to its practice (though they are highly desirable and ever-more sought after). Discipline and regulation of managers is still overwhelmingly a matter for organizations and not management institutions. There is some influence over reward levels and training and development. Measures of status and value are uneven. Management institutions act as focal points for debate, and they also have a lobbying function; they do not act as regulators.

There is however a clear drive towards the 'professionalization' of management. This is based on attention to expertise, knowledge and qualifications, and the relationship between these and the value added to organizations by expert managers.

In 1993, Charles Handy proposed that all business school graduates should be required to take the equivalent of the medical Hippocratic Oath, thus committing themselves at all times to best practice and the highest standards and quality of performance. If management is viewed in this way, it is a highly professional activity and one that demands a set body of expertise and a large measure of commitment on the part of its practitioners. It requires active personal commitment; and it requires involvement in continuous professional development (CPD) so that individuals take a proactive interest in making sure that their capabilities remain fully up to date.

The body of expertise

Professions and professional occupations all have a body of knowledge, skills and expertise; and for managers and management this may be defined as follows.

- **Behaviour:** integrity, equity, respect and value; respecting and valuing the opinions and capabilities of others; openness, honesty; transparency; visibility.
- **Attitudes:** positive, enthusiastic, dynamic; concerned; flexible and responsive (as above).
- **Skills:** in developing the next generation of managers; in identifying and developing skills, qualities and aptitudes of all. Specific skills development is also required in the areas of: leadership, decision-making, delegation, performance measurement. In the specific case of employee and organization development, a part of management development must consist of identifying and engaging in organization, departmental, divisional, collective, group and individual development activities.
- **Knowledge:** keeping abreast of developments; reading; awareness; lessons from everywhere, in the key fields of strategy, marketing, ethics, technology, HRM, economics, market and consumer behaviour.
- **Expertise:** establishing targets and priorities; planning; organizing; motivating; measuring performance; communication; integration; accepting responsibility, authority and accountability; managing relationships.
- **Technological proficiency, knowledge and understanding:** understanding the capacity of technology; understanding its use, value and application; maximizing and optimizing output; scheduling maintenance; developing expertise in its usage; supporting those who use it.

Knowledge and understanding

A key feature of management knowledge is a full understanding of the environment in which managerial work takes place. For example:

- It is not necessary for managers to be able to type, file or make bookings if they have secretaries to do this. However, they must understand the pressures, constraints and volumes of work that secretaries have to undertake in these areas.

- It is not necessary for hospital managers to be expert doctors, surgeons or nurses. However, they must have a full understanding of the organizational and operational pressures and constraints of the professional staff under their direction (failure to ensure that senior and middle NHS managers do indeed have this full understanding of clinical and nursing practice is a major cause of NHS underperformance at the beginning of the 21st century).

There may also be cultural pressures and occupational expectations that have to be accommodated. For example, many sales executives need, behaviourally and culturally, to work for someone who already has a proven track record as a sales executive. The view is therefore taken that the best sales executives should be promoted into the managerial position. This must be accompanied by thorough and rigorous management training if the move is to be effective from everybody's point of view.

Induction is therefore critical. As well as bringing the managerial knowledge and expertise to bear on the particular situation, it is essential that mutual confidence exists between the new manager and the existing workforce as quickly as possible. Time therefore needs to be set aside so that each can get to know the other. Especially, time is needed for the new manager to understand the existing demands, pressures and priorities placed on the workforce.

It is important to understand that all these foundations and components of the body of expertise required can be developed – and this includes qualities of integrity, respect and value. (People can indeed learn to be honest!)

Very often, the approach taken is to parcel up the expertise and qualities into competency frameworks or clusters. The development effort is then concentrated on each of the areas defined in turn, so that the foundations of the expertise are laid and can then be built on. This approach is common in the structuring and organizing of professional management education programmes; and it is also used by organizations internally as the basis for development-led performance appraisal schemes.

Otherwise, the concern for all managers is to be able to take an enlightened and responsible view of each of these, and to identify their own strengths and weaknesses. Both require building on – strengths in order to become expert; weaknesses in order to become at least proficient.

In the wider context, organizations also need to take a strategic or collective view of their own pool of managerial expertise for the same reasons. Managerial audits (needs analyses and appraisals) identify areas of overall strength and weakness. A view can then be formed of what can or should be developed internally, and what needs to be brought in from outside.

Grow your own or buy in?

The question of whether to 'grow your own' or 'buy in' new talent from outside is another issue on which easy or universal answers are sought – and for which no rules exist. The principle is a balance of giving every possible opportunity to develop and enhance existing expertise with the need for fresh blood, ideas and talents coming in from outside to prevent introversion.

The keys as always are to examine each case on its merits and consider each managerial vacancy as they arise. Whether the decision is taken to promote from within, or bring in outsiders, the keys to acceptance are:

- the ability to explain, justify and support the particular case;
- the ability to get the individual working as productively as possible, as quickly as possible.

Whether organizations choose to 'grow their own' or to 'buy in' from outside, there are always potential problems. Too much emphasis on internal development leaves organizations vulnerable to the inability of accepting ideas from elsewhere. Known or perceived overemphasis on buying in from outside leads to feelings of frustration on the part of those who believe (rightly or wrongly) that they should be given their chance.

Buying in expertise is of greatest value when directors and senior managers come to a strategic and supportable view that the development of management now requires fresh talent and expertise; and that this will give those presently in the organization a positive and effective surge of energy. If this conclusion is genuinely arrived at, it must be publicly stated. The justification is then clear to all and the reasons understandable – even if there is some short-term disgruntlement and turnover.

Once you have reconciled the needs of the organization, you should aim at least to consider making appointments from within. Developing expertise in-house demonstrates commitment to existing staff and their capabilities, determination and motivation. This should never be ignored or forgotten, whatever the need for fresh talent and impetus. Once it is explained to them, most people understand this, provided that it is clear that their own value and worth are being recognized also.

Different approaches to management development

There are many different approaches to management development; and these are as follows:

- identifying potential and talent through internal processes including performance appraisal schemes;

- identifying clear paths into management from professional, technological and other occupations;
- identifying paths from one management job into another;
- using graduate employment and development schemes.

Whichever is used, there need to be clear aims and objectives, satisfying organizational, professional, occupational and career development demands.

Organizations need to define for themselves the body of skills, knowledge, understanding and expertise required whichever of the paths is used. Organizations can then structure particular development programmes, policies and activities so that they are clear about what they expect at the end of periods of development, and so that the individuals involved know and understand what they are going to be expected to do once they have completed the programmes and activities.

Specific organizational approaches: Examples

- All the UK major clearing banks require that staff on management development paths spend at least three months working at the frontline of operations. This includes planned periods of placements working on customer services desks and advising members of the public on particular financial products and services from an expert point of view.
- Those who wish to develop a management career at McDonald's must spend up to 18 months working in one of the managed branches (rather than franchise). They must also spend an extensive period of time at the frontline serving the public.
- Those who join any of the major UK supermarket or department store chains must spend periods of time working on the tills, in the stockroom and shelf-filling. This is so that they get to know and understand for themselves where the operational pressures lie.

In each of these cases, the companies involved have taken a clearly understood position for their management development schemes. Those who choose to go into these companies therefore know and understand what they are letting themselves in for and what they are going to have to do in order to succeed on these schemes.

Management qualifications

As yet, there exists no statutory or minimum management qualification. However, an ever-increasing number of organizations and individuals now undertake a wide variety of nationally recognized qualifications as follows.

- Higher National Diploma or Certificate and undergraduate business studies courses; and an increasing number of more traditional undergraduate courses with business or management elements (for example civil engineering with management; construction management; information management).

- Supervisory studies, Certificate in Management and other foundation courses in professional practice: similar in coverage to much that is taught in universities and colleges of higher and further education, though the approach is certain to differ. This is because such courses are normally pitched at those (with and without previously acquired academic or vocational qualifications) who already have several years' work experience. People take these courses as the result of their own drives and ambitions, those of the organization, or as one result of performance appraisal and needs analysis.

- Diploma courses in general management, and professional and occupational expertise: these courses are invariably pitched at either those who have done a foundation course as above; or those in professional occupations (for example marketing, technology, teaching, nursing) who now wish to enhance their professional employability or (with DMS – Diploma in Management Studies) look for opportunities to go into management.

- MBA (Master of Business Administration) and other Master's/postgraduate level qualifications: normally offered to those who already have substantial occupational experience, at least a diploma, and preferably undergraduate qualifications also. Best value is served by those wishing to acquire a substantial body of organizational, economic, behavioural, functional and environmental knowledge as a precursor to advancement into senior positions.

- Doctorate: attained by those with a combination of high quality managerial experience and substantial academic achievement as the result of extensive research and write-up of a major problem or issue.

- The vocational qualification route: those who prefer may undertake management development by attaining a set of work-based competencies and having these accredited through the production of a written portfolio of experience, evidence and workplace testing and observation.

The process of gaining formal qualifications and having expertise and achievement credited and recognized serves as:

- an accepted and understood level of achievement;
- a behavioural and perceptual benchmark of progress and opportunity;
- a springboard for the next step;
- a measure of value, respect and worth.

Many professional bodies (for example engineering, computer science, architecture, education) now have management elements that those following the courses have to take. This is because these bodies recognize that, as staff progress, they are going to have to deliver some element of managerial responsibility or activity in addition to enhancing their own professional practice.

Additionally, all management qualifications are now available on open, distance and flexible bases as well as traditional teaching, so that they are much more open to everyone than in the past. They can also be much more closely harmonized with organization and collective development, as well as individual enhancement. Many of these (especially certificate, diploma and Master's) bring project and secondment opportunities with them.

Organizational and environmental expertise

Managerial expertise, whether supported by qualifications or not, is required by all organizations whatever their size, location, sector or remit. A key management development problem remains ensuring that this expertise is used successfully and effectively in any given set of circumstances. Those who have managerial expertise therefore require environmental knowledge, understanding and capability as much as those who have worked in the particular situation for years and who nevertheless still need to develop managerial capability (see Figure 19.1).

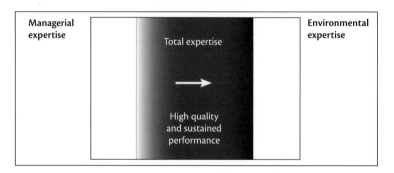

Figure 19.1 *The environmental–managerial expertise mix*

Fully effective performance is only possible in the shaded area. If there is a high level of both managerial and environmental expertise, there is a sound basis and high expectation of effective performance. If there is a low level of either, this means that:

- those with managerial expertise have no knowledge or understanding of how it should be applied in the particular organization, environment or situation;
- those with environmental expertise have no knowledge or understanding of what it takes to manage activities (though they will clearly understand the context in which activities have to be carried out, as well as the pressures and constraints that exist).

Whichever the gap, those involved are much more likely to be successful if they are prepared to learn and be receptive and bring a positive attitude. They are also more likely to be successful if they are fully supported by their organization, as well as committed to their own professional development. Additionally, anyone, on any development programme at all, ought to be open to suggestions and ideas from elsewhere as a part of their own commitment to enhancing their knowledge and understanding. Nobody should ever simply be prepared to stick to what they already know. As people are developed, they should always be prepared to modify their own preconceptions and, where necessary, change their own attitudes, behaviour and priorities.

Managerial openness

A survey conducted of managerial attitudes found that:

- 76% of managers surveyed believed themselves open, approachable and sympathetic to ideas and suggestions from elsewhere;
- 74% of the staff of managers surveyed stated that their managers were aloof, inaccessible and unreceptive to ideas and suggestions from elsewhere.

Clearly, there is some overlap! The core problem arises from ensuring that attention to managerial or environmental learning and development has a high priority both while it is being achieved, and also afterwards. Those in the situation require a mechanism that automatically asks the question *why* when rejection or a blinkered view is being offered. Another survey found that 90% of managers and supervisors who adopted an adversarial, aggressive, confrontational or absentee management style did so because it was how they had been treated themselves in junior positions, or because it was perceived or understood that this was the way to behave, or because they perceived or understood that this was the style to adopt if they wished to make further progress.

Source: Handy (1993).

Core managerial expertise can then be applied to the particular organization, situation and environment as follows.

- Developing this expertise in ways acceptable and applicable to those working in the environment and the pressures and constraints present.
- Developing behaviour, attitudes and values in ways that contribute to the positive development of the organizational and operating culture.
- Developing a state of visibility and access that promotes mutual confidence without being intrusive.
- Building on past positive experiences that professional, functional and operational staff have had with managers and supervisors.
- Rescuing past negative experiences that professional, functional and operational staff have had with managers.
- Maximizing the opportunities for staff, production and service development that arise as the result.

Rescuing the past

Part of the management development effort in these circumstances must be to understand why and how bad relations arose in the first place and to develop the environment, approach and standards of confidence necessary to rescue them and make them productive and effective for the future.

The keys to this are:

- regular visibility without intrusion;
- short, regular, formal meetings with collectively agreed agenda;
- asking staff for their priorities, issues and problems;
- delivering early, positive and recognizable results.

This is then reinforced by:

- levels of integrity, enthusiasm, ambition and drive exhibited by the manager on behalf of their staff;
- specific lobbying, cheerleading and advocacy when required;
- always supporting staff in public and resolving problems and issues privately and quickly.

This set of conditions and activities is a precursor to any attempt to rescue the past. It is a key feature of all management developments in large complex organizations, both public and private. Without it, little organizational, professional and occupational cultural or behavioural development is possible, and effectiveness of performance is always diluted.

Management development and product and service enhancement

The contribution of management development to product and service enhancement arises only as the result of understanding the nature of the working environment and the products and services delivered. The contribution then becomes:

- identifying, addressing and removing barriers to effective product and service performance;
- gaining staff commitment to new approaches through demonstrating the benefits and addressing any problems or issues inherent;
- consulting with a view to gaining active involvement and participation;
- addressing key staff priorities including pressures of work, periods of overload and underload;
- ensuring that the jobs that nobody wants to do are either subcontracted or else shared around equally;
- setting and reinforcing absolute standards of behaviour and performance that apply to everyone regardless of profession, status, occupation, length of service or hours of

work; and developing problem-solving capability and routes of access for staff so that when these issues occur, they are raised, dealt with and nipped in the bud.

'I must be seen to be impartial'

In the overwhelming majority of cases, managers that use this phrase when confronted with serious behavioural problems are understood to be avoiding the issue. Overtly, the word 'impartial' implies 'fair' or 'equitable'. The whole phrase implies: 'I would love to help but I cannot'. In practice therefore, this means that the issue will not be confronted.

If an employee makes an allegation about a colleague, the manager must develop a format that allows the employee to state their case and the alleged offender to respond on a basis of fairness and equality. This must be conducted face to face with each.

Once the two sides are heard, then the required action becomes apparent. Above all, if malicious and false allegations are being made, these are dealt with severely and may lead to disciplinary action or dismissal if proven.

Dealing with anything raised quickly in this way normally means that such incidents are kept to a minimum. Where it is known or believed that the manager 'must be seen to be impartial', there are widely held perceptions that nothing will be done.

This part of management development is therefore concerned with creating the conditions in which effective and sustainable high quality product and service delivery are possible. In directly operational and functional matters, effective development is concerned with knowing the jobs, tasks and outputs required, observing and analysing them, both to ensure that the present effective steady-state is maintained and to see where improvements can be made. These can then be discussed with the staff concerned and either implemented if truly practicable, or else killed off if those carrying out the activities come up with overwhelming operational reasons as to why they are bad ideas.

Management development must be concerned with understanding and improving customer, supplier and community relations. This involves creating the conditions in which all contacts with each of these groups are dealt with as a priority, and addressing specific issues, especially complaints, from the point of view of finding out what truly went wrong and why, and putting them right in ways that satisfy those who first raised them. If staffing or internal issues then become apparent they can be addressed separately.

Management development must be concerned with the operational details of the particular domain. This means knowing and understanding the following.

- **Tasks, occupations and work:** required and desired outputs, and the expertise and conditions necessary for these to be achieved; problem areas and blockages, and what causes these; deadlines and priorities.

- **Technology:** the influence of this on work patterns and behaviour (especially alienation); the consequences of breakdown or inability to recruit the required expertise.
- **Information:** availability and accessibility; quality, volume and value; contribution of information availability to effective, positive and productive decision-making and activities.
- **Organization:** formal structures and reporting relationships; cultural and behavioural issues that these may raise; the nature and expectations of those present.

Towards flexible and open organizations: MMRC

MMRC was a small but highly expert and profitable London advertising agency. It employed 50 staff on strictly traditional lines and reporting relationships. Everyone had clear job descriptions. From the most positive point of view, it was a role culture.

The company was taken over by a large firm, JWT. The new owners immediately destroyed the prevailing structure, culture and reporting relations. They brought in open-plan accommodation, flexible and open access to work stations (hot-desking), and fully portable technology. They also created a structure that meant there were two layers of supervision only.

Within six months all 50 MMRC staff had left. The senior partner at JWT commissioned a firm of consultants to contact the former staff and find out why. The key reasons given were as follows.

- The role culture had grown up over many years and was orderly and familiar. People had expectations and knew what could be achieved, and under what circumstances.
- The role culture was destroyed and the hot-desking introduced without consultation, and by people who were self-evidently working to a prescription rather than genuine understanding.
- Existing staff were given no idea of what was expected of them. It was clear to them that the new owners did not understand how the work was carried out, or the constraints and opportunities of the existing ways of working, technology or structure and culture.

There was a clear management development need at JWT. The new owners had simply not understood why MMRC had been so successful. JWT had assumed that with the expertise of MMRC, and the management presence of JWT, everything would go on successfully into the future.

This betrayed a clear lack of management knowledge and understanding. If the merged organization was to be successful for the future, there were management lessons to be learned.

- **Primary activities**: establishing aims, objectives and priorities; coordinating activities; integrating staff; communication and decision-making processes; planning for the present and future.
- **Key factors**: motivating staff; addressing individual and group needs, including development needs; knowing and understanding when and where to go for help when required; accepting and using power, influence, responsibility, authority and accountability; understanding the priorities, demands and constraints of the particular situation.

The use and value of management development activities

Specific activities need to be engaged in order to identify potential, and also in order to give those with career aspirations the opportunity to show their worth and value. The main activities are:

- *Mentoring*

Mentoring schemes exist in many organizations. In simple terms, junior members of staff with ambitions seek out more senior or experienced colleagues, and a relationship is generated enabling the mentor to pass on their experience, knowledge and understanding to the junior. The junior member of staff can access the mentor at any time for any reason; and so a relationship is built up. Part of the process of mentoring requires that a junior member of staff can ask for evaluation and feedback on particular tasks that have been carried out. The other part is to identify tasks and activities that ought to be carried out in the future; and the role of the mentor in this case is to help identify those tasks and to prepare the junior to carry them out, and then provide a sounding board for feedback and evaluation once they have been completed.

- *Project work*

Project work always ought to stretch the person or group carrying it out. The purpose of project work in the context of management development ought again be to identify potential, as well as giving the organization the opportunity to observe ambitious members of its staff in action. Project presentations, and review and evaluation, ought to be carried out during the project itself and also at the end. Evaluation of what has been learned should also always be carried out so that everyone involved knows what went well and why; and where mistakes were made and why. Project work should also always be seen as a process leading on to other opportunities.

- *Secondments*

Secondments are often built into management development structures (including graduate schemes). The purpose of a secondment is to give the individual the opportunity to broaden their experience and to give the department, division, function or location where the secondment is taking place the opportunity to benefit from fresh ideas, impetus and input. Secondment periods may last for a few weeks up to two years. Clearly once the individual has been through a secondment, especially one that lasts several months or years, it is unlikely that they will go back to their previous job with any degree of satisfaction. Secondment periods ought therefore to lead on to other things as long as the secondment is successful (and if the secondment is unsuccessful, this is likely to be apparent in a few weeks, which means that the matter ought to be remedied early).

Each of these activities ought to form the basis for developing managerial expertise, as well as identifying potential. Once individuals are on mentoring schemes, project work or secondments, there ought to be a fresh range of opportunities opening up for them and organizations ought to be supporting individuals in developing their potential along these lines rather than simply giving them mentors, projects and secondments to do – and then returning them to their old jobs. Nobody is going to benefit from this. Individuals become dissatisfied and frustrated; and the organization will therefore not benefit.

Continuous professional development

The increasing professionalization of management requires all those in these positions to take an active and personal commitment to their own development. The rewards for expert managers are now extremely high. In return for these, it is increasingly necessary to demonstrate and be able to engage genuine capability in the areas of: leadership; decision-making; strategic awareness and strategy design; market knowledge; organizational behaviour; and understanding people. The conflicting and divergent interests of organization stakeholders have to be balanced and accommodated. High and increasing value products and services must be delivered to ever-more demanding customer and client groups. Self-development therefore requires a commitment to:

- read widely about all organizations, industries and sectors to learn from their managerial practice and approaches;
- take professional qualifications and attend short courses by agreement with the organization as well as self-directed;
- meet with other managers at cluster groups and professional body gatherings;
- engage in continuous professional development and enhancement activities, whether at the behest of professional bodies, or self-directed;
- search constantly for areas where both individual management practice and also organization capability and output can be improved.

Of particular value are 'back to the floor' and 'action learning' approaches. More generally, managers must be prepared to go into other organizations at any time with a view to picking up ideas. They must be willing to try things out against their own self-generated and preset criteria. Some ideas and initiatives will succeed – others will fail or fall short of full success. As long as there was a genuine pre-evaluation of what was intended, failure and success can both be used as part of the learning process. This approach also tends towards instilling attitudes of self-development in the rest of the staff.

Succession and transformation

The role of management development in succession and transformation is to:

- ensure that there is a steady flow of ever-improving expertise and quality available to organizations to secure a future;
- identify potential capability and motivation in existing staff and to develop it for the present and future;
- recognize succession in its broadest terms.

This means addressing it from the point of view of:

- having a pool of staff to promote when required;
- having a fund of expertise and understanding as the organization goes through its own succession and transformation from one set of occupations, activities, markets, products and services to the next, including the ways in which these are delivered as well as what is delivered;
- taking a broader view of succession and transformation so that expertise and commitment are both available should they be required;
- looking for derived opportunities especially those that present themselves as the result of following one path of activities.

Traditionally, succession simply meant training the next generation of staff for supervisory, managerial and senior functional positions. Now it is essential that this includes attention to attitudes and behaviour so that qualities of positivity, flexibility and willingness are instilled and developed. Clear lines of progression through hier-archical organization structures are much less prevalent and subject to restructuring in any case. However, succession opportunities are, in practice, at least as widely available in terms of:

- rotation and progression through departments, divisions, functions, locations, projects and centres of activities;
- moving into a new job and being given the space, opportunity, resources and support to develop it in new ways;
- identifying potential in existing situations and ranges of activity.

Succession therefore, becomes broadened into progression and transformation. It is dependent on a positive view of the opportunities presently available, as well as those apparent for the future. Organizations that reflect and encourage this approach are certain to get much more out of their staff as long as they commit themselves to offering enhanced salaries and other rewards (which were always the key drives of those on structured promotion paths).

It is important to be able to offer genuine prospects of advancement and development. This approach, conducted properly, ensures that individual drives for progress are harmonized with organizational drives for greater effectiveness of resource utilization and maximization of staff capabilities.

Continuous professional development, and organization as well as individual commitment, ought to go hand in hand. In particular, a fully integrated and strategic approach to all forms of organizational, occupational and professional development ought to enhance product and service output, individual and collective levels of motivation, and enduring organizational viability and profitability.

Organizations and managers ought therefore to understand the mutual benefit that arises when professional commitment to continuous development is engaged. Continuous professional development is a partnership between organizations and individuals resulting in enduring mutual benefit.

Costs and benefits

As well as being able to make the case for management development in generally qualifiable and quantifiable terms, it ought to be possible to identify the costs and benefits more precisely. The costs and benefits of effective management development activities are as follows (see Table 19.1).

Table 19.1 *Costs and benefits*

Costs	Benefits
• Variable – in paying for courses and other support activities and periods of formalized training (on and off the job) • Fixed – in terms that management development requires a substantial amount of otherwise salaried and occupational time • Priorities – again a fixed cost – because managers must be able to block off periods of their time in order to *walk their job* and learn and understand their domain and environment	• High quality, enduring management–staff relations • Early identification of problems • Full organizational, environmental and operational understanding

best practice

Costs and benefits of engaging in organizational and management development depend on:

- the need for management development to be accepted by the organization as a whole;
- the costs and benefits being defined and evaluated;
- the strength of the joint approach between organization and individuals.

Conclusions

Effective management development depends on organizations recognizing the enhanced contribution and value that expert managerial staff deliver, as well as the derived benefits of generating motivation, commitment and capability in present occupations. It is fully dependent also on attending to the full range of behaviour, attitudes, skills, knowledge, expertise and technological proficiency; and respecting personal, professional and occupational, as well as organizational, drives.

Effective management development has a knock-on effect on attitudes to training across the rest of the organization. Professional, occupational, technological and 'unskilled' staff are much more likely to be given opportunities if these are available to those for whom they work. This enhances collective, group and organization development.

Highly developed and expert managers are also much more likely to understand and value the importance of induction, core programmes and initial job training. As stated above, these make major contributions to establishing the required levels of attitudes and behaviour, as well as performance, at the outset and in subsequently reinforcing these. Conducted effectively, management development is therefore all-pervasive, making a positive contribution to every aspect of performance.

in brief

- The need for continuous management development, including 'growing your own' from within and 'buying in' talent from outside must be known, recognized, understood and accepted.
- Management development is a partnership between the organization and its individual members; and the needs of both must be satisfied.
- Management development ought to be structured and based on a series of intended aims, objectives and outcomes, again satisfying the needs of both organization and individuals.
- Management development is a process that leads the organization forward. Especially when engaging in management development activities, there is a need for individuals to be moved forwards rather than returned to previous jobs.
- All management development activities, whether carried out in organizations or on the initiative of individuals, move 'management' towards a highly professionalized position.

Further reading

Gold, J. et al. (2010) *Leadership and Management Development*. Wiley.

Marchington, M. and Wilkinson, A. (2008) *Human Resource Management at Work: People Management and Development* (4th edn). CIPD.

Mayo, A. (2000) *The Human Value of the Enterprise*. Nicholas Brealey.

Owen, J. (2012) *Management Stripped Bare: What They Don't Teach You at Business School*. Kogan Page.

Pettinger, R. (2002) *Mastering Employee Development*. Palgrave.

Revans, R. (1967) *Action Learning*. Sage.

Senge, P. (1992) *The Fifth Discipline*. Century.

Managing in a global and international environment

20

'A key strategic need is the ability to manage diversity and manage across cultures.'

In this chapter

- understanding the nature of the global and international environment of business and management
- recognizing the opportunities and conditions demanded in order to be able to 'go global' and/or 'go international'
- developing an understanding of the cultures, habits and norms that exist elsewhere
- evaluating opportunities for expansion, and taking steps to ensure that these are exploited effectively

Introduction

Organizations that either seek a global or international presence, or else are maintaining and developing one, have to have the necessary command of the volume and quality of resources, expertise, capability and willingness in the first place.

This appears very trite. However, it is essential to consider the case from this perspective initially. This is because top managers of organizations with a strong domestic presence and peripheral activities in several other countries begin to describe themselves as global. It is a short step from this into getting sidetracked into exciting, glamorous, messy, dangerous – and costly – adventures in locations about which they know and understand very little, and often care even less, except from the point of view of easy financial returns.

So the need is to deal in some detail with what globalization is from a strategic management point of view, and then with the issues of resources, expertise, capability and willingness.

Always remember that globalization and internationalization are terms that are bandied about without a true perspective on what they actually are. Globalization is the process whereby organizations seek to establish a presence in the majority of countries, markets and communities of the world.

The foundations of globalization

Truly global organizations establish, maintain and develop their presence and influence in a variety of ways. Many of these are interrelated.

Global physical presence

Only three companies – ABB (the Swedish/Swiss engineering and power organization), Coca-Cola, and Microsoft – have carried out commercial activities in more than 200 countries of the world. Transport, travel and logistics firms have the capability of a truly global physical presence in terms of their ability to make deliveries and accept orders. Many banking and finance companies are able to access all parts of the world through partnership networks and relationships. Oil and energy companies also supply to all of the countries of the world, again through networks of local providers.

Global reputation

Global reputation comes in many forms, both positive and negative. On the positive side, Japanese manufacturing companies enjoy a high level of reputation for work practices and security of employment. Some banking and financial services companies have brought a lot of technological work and technology-driven expertise to parts of India, Eastern Europe and South Africa. On the other hand, there are persistent and enduring problems with employment practices in garment manufacture in the Asian, African and Central American factories used by the top brand clothing companies.

Global thinking

In management terms, genuine global thinking is very rare in the Western corporate world. Organizations with genuine global presence or influence clearly think globally and internationally to some extent. Others successfully achieve chains of global thinking that inform decision-making processes at head offices (see Figure 20.1).

Management thinking needs to be developed as new markets and locations are opened up. Management thinking needs to be informed by a full knowledge and understanding of the different demands of these locations, and demands placed on locations. It is also essential that global management thinking is informed by a full knowledge and understanding of local cultures, customs and habits.

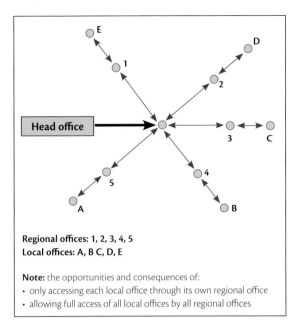

Regional offices: 1, 2, 3, 4, 5
Local offices: A, B C, D, E

Note: the opportunities and consequences of:
• only accessing each local office through its own regional office
• allowing full access of all local offices by all regional offices

Figure 20.1 *The chain approach to global and international management*

Global influence

Global influence arises from one or more of the following sources:

• technological standards;
• product and service standards;
• manufacturing and service delivery standards;
• the ability to command finance, information and other key resources in desired and/or major locations;
• command of rare or desirable raw materials (for example oil in Norway, Russia, Canada, the Middle East; diamonds in Southern Africa).

The global influence may also extend to the supply and manufacture of key components; and the supply, manufacture and delivery of the universally desired quality of products and services (for example Microsoft software; Coca-Cola soft drinks). Global influence may also be extended as the result of engaging in joint ventures, partnerships and outsourcing activities (see below).

Global standards

Global standards are established by a combination of best practice and the ability to dominate or influence the ways of working in particular markets, locations and sectors. For example, the global standards in financial services and banking are set in New York, London, Tokyo and Frankfurt; the global standards for air travel are set by companies such as British Airways, Cathay Pacific, American Airlines and Qantas. Companies such as Starbucks and McDonald's set distinctive standards in their own fields. Finally, fair trade has the purpose of establishing distinctive standards for companies from the developed world in their dealings with emerging markets.

Global access, reach and coverage

Global access, reach and coverage are claimed with full justification by companies such as the major airlines as above, and Federal Express, TNT and DHL in deliveries and logistics. It is claim also made by the major telecommunications, transport and delivery companies of the world, again through their networks of suppliers, local distributors and subcontractors.

The universality of internet coverage can lead companies, organizations and managers into thinking that they have global access and reach. It is true that you can log on to any company website, anywhere in the world. However, if this is to be translated into business activities, then the questions of product and service quality, access, location and convenience have to be considered from the point of view of standard business practices. A company in Paris is not going to do business with another in New Zealand just because they can log on to their website.

Global brand and/or identity

Global identity implies influence, standards and reputation. The 'golden arches' are the most recognized logo and symbol in the world. Coca-Cola is also universally recognized. Other examples include: IBM for perceived standards in the information technology, hardware and software sectors; Microsoft in the information software sector; Sony for quality standards and performance in the manufacture and provision of electrical goods; Unilever and Procter & Gamble for the production of detergents.

Other aspects of global influence

Other aspects that have to be considered are as follows.

- Global icon status: such as Walt Disney, setting standards for film production and delivery.
- Standards of consumer goods manufacturing, quality and durability have long since been set by Japanese companies.
- Global mobile telephone production is dominated by Nokia and Ericsson (Finland).
- Fashion design is dominated by exhibitions and trade fairs in London, Paris, Milan and New York.

- Hotel facility standards, which were originally set by Hilton and subsequently adopted by all those who sought a sustainable competitive position and commercial advantage in the sector.
- Individualized corporations where expansion and globalization are based on the individual and collective talents of those involved.

Any organization that sets or transforms any part of practice or activities has global influence. This may be extended to, for example:

- organizational and managerial principles and practice (for example Semco, Body Shop, Nissan);
- advertising (J. Walter Thompson);
- management consultancy (McKinsey);
- website development and commercialization (Amazon);
- search engines (Google);
- technology (Apple).

Global and international approaches to management must therefore be informed by as full an understanding as possible of the ways in which international and global presence are actually achieved and sustained; ensuring that a fully structured approach is taken for, during and after any processes of internationalization and the march to a fully global presence.

Fashion and fad in globalization

As well as expanding overseas for sound business reasons, it is also necessary to recognize that companies and organizations seek an international presence for any, or all, of the following reasons:

- it is exciting;
- it is prestigious;
- it gives managers the opportunity to travel to different parts of the world (ostensibly on company business).

Alongside this, in many industries there is a very great deal of peer pressure (and often shareholder pressure also). Companies and managers find themselves under pressure to have international locations just because everybody else is known, believed or perceived to have one also. Thus for example:

- pressure is exerted on clothing retailers to source their products from locations that are known, believed or perceived to be cheaper than local suppliers;
- financial services companies are pressurized into having technology management and call centres sourced overseas because these too are known, believed and perceived to be cheaper than local provisions.

Most insidiously of all, it is very often the case that cheaper provisions can be found in particular locations – but these are not always the locations of choice. For example, the overwhelming majority of UK call centre and technology management activities in financial services are in India. Equally expert and cost-effective provision is available in the countries of Central and Eastern Europe. However, India is perceived to be much more glamorous and exciting – and so companies and organizations tend to locate there anyway. And in the particular case of technology management and customer service in the financial sectors, costs in India have risen sharply (and continue to do so) simply because of the numbers of Western companies establishing activities there.

The axis of globalization

Whatever the desired or required global presence or influence, it is normal to establish and maintain a presence in the 'commercial axis' of the USA, EU and Japan; and from there, spread out into other localities around the world as follows (see Figure 20.2).

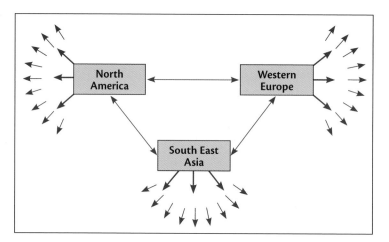

Figure 20.2 *The axis approach to globalization*

Organizations that establish a presence in each of the axis areas have to have the size, capability and reputation to establish price, quality, value and volume levels of capital and consumer goods and services, and standards of overall organizational performance. Large and dominant organizations in these areas establish levels of investment; staff rewards, terms and conditions of employment; quality of working life and labour relations; as well as strategic and operations management. Multinational and global organizations also have great influence on local, economic and political activities, the management of the environment, and the quality of social life in the locations in which they work.

A further and complicating issue is the emergence of what is called BRIC – Brazil, Russia, China and India – as locations of power, influence and economic and industrial size and scale. Many organizations presently find themselves needing a physical presence in each of these areas in order to maintain their own influence.

Specific issues with which organizations that establish themselves in the axis areas are concerned include the following:

- Supply side, in which supplies are sought from areas where they are most prolific and readily available; where the relationship can be dominated by the axis organization; or where there are commercial, economic and political advantages in dominating the supply side.
- Manufacturing, in which axis organizations locate or subcontract their manufacturing processes at places most suitable to serve their markets (for example Toyota and Sony in Poland); or where labour is cheap (for example branded garments and sportswear manufacture in South-East Asia and the West Indies; foodstuffs in South America).
- Distribution, in which axis companies place their distribution operations under flags of convenience allowing them to employ staff on expedient/favourable terms and conditions of employment and to operate to minimum standards of safety and security. This is standard practice in sea transport, and becoming more widespread in air and overland activities.
- Effluent disposal, in which organizations are able to pay developing nations' governments to relieve them of waste and effluent for a fraction of the cost of disposing of it effectively and in an environmentally friendly manner in the developed world, or of reprocessing it themselves.
- Switching costs, in which axis organizations are able, because of their command and their sheer size and volume of financial resources, to relocate to other areas in other short timescales simply because:
  - it is possible to undercut suppliers in the developing world due to the cheap price of labour and demand for economic activity and employment;
  - in order to be able to respond to political, social and economic problems and to be able to depart from areas in which there is suddenly war or strife without interrupting supply side, manufacturing, distribution or other economic activity.

Resources, expertise, capability and willingness

It is essential to ensure that sufficient volumes, qualities and flexibility of resources are available to gain the desired impact, presence and levels of activities across the world.

Financial size and technology availability are therefore essential. However, neither is an end in itself. These resources must be capable of energizing in the desired location and range of activities. Often insufficient attention is paid to the capability in particular locations to maximize and optimize resource potential and usage in the given context.

The result is therefore that operations and activities are energized at a loss rather than full efficiency and effectiveness. In the short to medium term, this may be an acceptable price for gaining a foothold in a desired location. If this is the case, then effectiveness and enduring operational capability are developed alongside the generation of the desired local reputation, scale of activities and productive capacity.

There is an enduring need to understand that few locations in the world are ever genuinely grateful that a large powerful international organization has come to work in the area. The need is to identify and build on a mutuality of interest; and this has to be based on:

- the provision of work and rewards for that work;
- the generation of mutual respect and value.

It is very easy to take a paternalistic and assumptive view of the working relationship, especially when the international organization is bringing much higher levels of economic activity and social provision to areas of relative deprivation. Enduring relationships are however only fully effective in the long term so long as there is a genuine respect for the prevailing local, social, environmental and cultural issues, customs and habits, as well as the generation of sustainable economic activity.

For this to be effective, local staff have to be trained and developed as well as rewarded. Part of the strategic outlay must involve contribution to the society at large in which activities are being carried out. Employment practices have to be designed and implemented so that employee protection, health and well-being are assured as well as enduringly high levels of production, capacity, output and quality.

Alongside this, however, is the constant stream of publicity generated as soon as it becomes known, believed or perceived that large organizations are responsible for unwholesome and unethical business practices in their subsidiaries or overseas operations. A response to this has to be managed, such that it avoids the negative aspects of:

- security measures so that investigative reporters, news teams and industry watchdogs cannot gain access;
- community domination in which the populations of the particular localities are bullied and frightened into not giving evidence or speaking against the Western company;
- political lobbying so as to ensure that whatever practices are being carried out are at least with the acquiescence of the particular local government and its officials;
- public relations, advertising and marketing initiatives to counteract the resultant bad publicity.

Many organizations and managers take a fully informed and enlightened view, and in turn take active steps to ensure that malpractice in any area is not tolerated. However, in many cases also, malpractice continues to persist and remains widespread.

Following the logo trail

Naomi Klein famously attacked corporate globalization culture in her book *No Logo*:

'As global brand-based connections gain popularity, the trail from the shops to the sweat-shop becomes better travelled. I certainly was not the first foreign journalist to pick through the laundry of the Cavite export processing zone in Indonesia. In the few months before I arrived there had been, among others, a German television crew and a couple of Italian documentary film makers who hoped to dig up some scandal on their home grown brand, Benetton. In Indonesia, so many journalists had wanted to visit Nike's infamous factories that by the time I arrived in Jakarta, the staff at the labour rights group Yakoma were starting to feel like professional tour guides. Every week another journalist would descend upon the area. The situation was the same at a factory I tried to visit outside Medan where child labourers were stitching clothes for Matel and Barbie. I met with local activists at the Indonesian Institute for Children's Advocacy and they pulled out a photo album filled with pictures of the NBC crew that had been there.

Elsewhere, family oriented brands like Disney and WalMart have been forced to confront the conditions under which real families produce their goods. Many more traditionally run companies are busy imitating Nike's model, not only copying the company's marketing approach, but also its 'on the cheap' outsourced production structure. Adidas followed a similar trajectory; the company shut down its own factories in Germany and moved to contracting out in Asia.

After four years of research, what I find most shocking is that so many supposed "dirty little secrets" are crammed into the global broom closet with such a casual attitude. In economic protection zones, employment violations are a dime a dozen – they come tumbling out as soon as you open the door even a crack.'

Source: Klein (2000).

Approaches to globalization

The main approaches for those seeking to expand and develop a global and international presence are as follows:

- corporate expansion;
- mergers, acquisitions and takeovers;
- local partnering;

- outsourcing;
- other collaborations;
- joint ventures.

It is essential to be clear which of these routes are being followed. Organizations and managers that go off into international ventures without due consideration of the basis and approach are certain to find themselves incurring heavy costs and charges (as well as potentially loss of reputation).

Corporate expansion

Corporate expansion is the process of establishing new offices, premises and centres of activity using only an organization's own resources, name, products, services and technology. This approach is found in retail and commercial banking, insurance and finance in the development of international branch networks and tailored financial products. Corporate expansion is also found in air and sea transport activities: large global airlines and shipping companies establish their own presence at the particular sea ports and airports of entry, and then normally develop this position through the opening of networks of agencies in the particular region served by the sea ports and airports.

Mergers, acquisitions and takeovers

When seeking a global presence, there are a number of legitimate reasons why mergers, acquisitions and takeovers are considered. For organizations that do have command of high levels of resources, in particular buying up other companies means that a presence can be established very quickly. Other reasons are as follows:

- to gain an interest in, or control of, a key source of, or outlet for, scarce raw materials, components, expertise or distribution;
- to gain control over supplies, components, distribution outlets and access;
- to gain entry into specific markets and locations;
- to gain market share and market dominance in specific markets and locations;
- to buy up customer, product, service and expertise bases in particular markets, sectors and locations;
- to speed up the process of market penetration in particular areas;
- to begin to develop a reputation, occupational base and expertise in a specific area.

As long as proposals can be legitimately considered from one or more of these points of view, then adopting the approach of merger, acquisition or takeover enables an advantage or potential advantage to be realized very quickly. Precise priorities, aims and objectives can then be directly related to whichever of these points the proposal is intended to address.

From a management point of view, problems with acquisitions, mergers and takeovers when seeking a global presence arise where one or more of the following are present.

- The proposal is acceptable to one dominant vested interest but not others. Invariably this is driven by stock market and short-term shareholder interests, industrial, commercial or sectoral pressures, or by the results of financial analysis. At the point of takeover the price of shares rises steeply, and, in many cases, this satisfies the immediate shareholder and financial interest. This process is fuelled by stockbrokers, shareholder representatives and financial analysts who gain commissions; and by rises in the share prices in the acquiring company because this is deemed or perceived to reflect the strategic acumen of its directors.
- The proposal is driven by certainties, hopes and expectations of assured market penetration, whether or not adequate market research has been carried out. Even where the proposal is driven by the ability to command key supplies of raw materials, components or information, these will hold full value only until alternative supplies become available from elsewhere.
- The financial advantage has been driven through with insufficient attention to the cultural and behavioural fit of the two organizations. Even where one organization is taking over a very much small operation, the ways of working, management style, logistics, operations and activities still have to be capable of harmonization and integration. Failure to do this means that the short-term financial advantage invariably evaporates. In more serious cases, there are interruptions on the supply, manufacturing and distribution aspects and these are nearly always caused by behavioural rather than financial problems.

Local partnering

Local partnering exists where the international organization agrees to go into business with an indigenous organization for a particular proposal or venture, or to develop the existing range of products and services from a particular local perspective, or to gain a foothold and presence, reputation and existence in a particular area with a view to developing further opportunities and giving substance to the general presence.

'Developing further opportunities'

Developing further opportunities need not be as general as it sounds. Provided that the statement is fully understood and supported at head office, there is no reason why this should not be effective. In particular, while 'further opportunities' are being identified, assessed and developed, those on the ground should be using the local partner to make contacts, establish a reputation and gain all-round general familiarity with the area and region.

In some industries, this process is essential to the future conduct of effective and profitable business and represents a critical element of the investment required. For example, in building, construction and civil engineering no overseas client, unless very hard pressed, is going to engage a foreign contractor without prior knowledge and understanding of their specific expertise, past history and track record.

This last point was mistaken by a large UK construction aggregates and civil engineering company when it went prospecting for work in Malaysia. The company's marketing director arranged a meeting with officials at the department of the Malay government responsible for allocating road, railway and major capital urban works projects. The government department was looking for further companies to participate in a centrally led programme of rapid expansion. The company was looking for overseas opportunities to help take up spare capacity.

Proudly, the marketing director announced who he was, his company and its record of public and commercial works in the UK. He then stated: 'We have built a cricket ground in Sri Lanka and an airport terminus in Canada. So we are truly a global company'.

The official from the Malay government replied: 'I have never heard of you. I doubt if you understand our needs, wants, demands or culture. But do take advantage of the rest of your stay to make yourself familiar with these things. Then come back and see us'.

The company won no work in Malaysia at the time, and nor has it ever worked there to date.

Outsourcing

Conducted effectively, outsourcing specific activities to different parts of the world enables organizations that wish to expand to gain a substantial foothold and clear understanding of the new location. A contractual arrangement is entered into, providing product and service levels and quality to be of mutual and lasting benefit to both organizations involved.

In practice, outsourcing takes place overwhelmingly because of a narrow drive to reduce the cost base. This leads in many cases to either malpractice (as above), or declines in service levels and quality.

Whenever outsourcing is being contemplated, it is therefore essential for managers to know and understand the full range of issues that have to be addressed so that the provision of products and services is enhanced, while at the same time the cost base is reduced and the integrity of the organization is preserved.

Other collaborations

Collaborating with specific organizations comes in a variety of different forms. These different forms include alliances, subcontracting, partnering and piggy-backing; and each is very effective in gaining a foothold, presence and experience in new markets provided that the following points are clearly understood:

- the needs of each party involved;
- the agenda of each party involved;
- the duration of the working relationship;
- the consequences of success and failure;
- sharing the rewards for success and the consequences of failure.

Sharing the rewards for success and the consequences of failure are particularly important. Where a venture succeeds in all aspects, the parties involved can then either agree to develop the relationship further or else go their separate ways. However, success may be the trigger for one party to wish to withdraw having achieved what it set out to do; while the other now wishes to carry on but needs the support and resources of the other to do so.

Failure needs to be paid for, both financially and also in terms of lost reputation and confidence. Again, how this is to happen needs to be made clear at the outset. While there is clearly no point in going into anything expecting to fail, the possibility and the resultant consequences should always be assessed and evaluated under the heading 'worst possible outcomes' before implementation.

Joint ventures

A joint venture is a contractual commitment by two or more parties for a particular venture, project, product range or range of services normally for a stated period of time. At the end of the period of time, the joint venture is then either wound up with the rewards of success or consequences of failure apportioned accordingly. The joint venture is a well-understood and familiar format in the defence, construction, civil engineering, aviation and electronics industries; and the format is driven by the needs for:

- scales of resources that many organizations simply do not have on their own;
- specific expertise that is required for the particular venture;
- the need to deliver particular projects, products and services by a given date or within a stated timescale; and this demand and drive leads to some organizations collaborating with each other, not because they do not have the full range of expertise themselves, but because they do not have this in sufficient volumes to enable the desired or required timescale to be met.

Clearly, many of the conditions and opportunities indicated above apply as much to any large or complex strategic management initiative, and are not confined to global drives. Where they are being used to pursue strategies of globalization however, specific attention is required to the following.

- **Cultural fit:** the ability of the two or more organizations and their staff to work together productively and effectively for the duration of the venture; and if required, in subsequent activities that have the purpose of building on progress made to date.

- **Financial stability:** the ability to sustain the venture for its duration and to accept the responsibilities inherent in supporting activities in remote and distant locations.
- **The standing of key staff:** especially the ability to manage any sudden arrivals or departures, changes in expertise, management and supervisory styles; and the ability also to accommodate any other shifts in strategic priorities.
- **Technological viability:** the ability to deliver, install, energize and maintain all equipment wherever it is being used; and the ability, whenever required, to integrate the technology and information systems of all those involved in the particular activities. Closely related to this is knowledge and expertise viability, the ability to deliver the specific expertise of particular groups and individuals in the locations, context, culture and environment required.

Dominance and dependence

All organizational, professional and business relations have elements of dominance and dependence; and for those concerned with global strategic management, this position has to be fully understood. The need is to balance the finance, resources, technology and brand strength that global and international companies have with the responsibilities that go with this. For example, the issues surrounding sweatshop labour in the clothing industry, and pollution and effluent caused by oil and chemical production are often the outcomes of the ability of the multinational corporations operating in these sectors to dominate their particular environment.

best practice

From a managerial point of view, dominating the business or operational relationship, or a particular locality, comes with a clear set of responsibilities and accountability. In particular, organizations that can and do dominate business relationships need to know and understand that while they can bribe or bully those in dependent positions for a short period of time, this is never the basis for enduring and viable activities.

From a management point of view, dominance and dependency need to be understood as follows.

- **Acquiescence:** where those involved have no particular respect or liking for the others, but are prepared to accommodate each other because it is in their present interests to do so, or because they have no apparent alternative. Acquiescent relationships do not produce enduring loyalty, though provided a fundamental mutuality of interest can be identified, effective work is normally possible.
- **Compliance:** a more positive approach than acquiescence but where the fundamental basis of the relationship remains the same. Compliance normally means a modicum of willingness to act in the interests of everyone involved, rather than the dominant organization alone.

- **Acceptance:** where each party involved is prepared to accept that there is a divergence of objectives and is prepared to accommodate these, at least as long as their own objectives are not compromised or damaged.
- **Formalization:** where contractual conditions are placed on the particular relationships or ranges of activity (for example, it is usual for joint ventures and subcontracted relationships to be formalized by contract).
- **Institutionalization:** where the prevailing norms, values and standards are capable of being adopted and translated into the particular situation and location in which work is to be carried out; and where these norms, values and standards are capable at least of acceptance by the particular locality.
- **Transcendence:** where the organization sets standards of attitudes, behaviour, performance and responsibility that transcend local difficulties; where customs, habits, norms and values of any locality can easily be accommodated.
- **Rejection:** where the organization finds itself unable to establish a foothold in a given location whatever its size and strength. This is normally because the particular location has its own distinctive set of social, economic and environmental habits, norms, customs and practices that either preclude it from interacting with the incomer or, because of recent histories with other organizations, cause it to reject the incomer.

Whichever approach is taken therefore, there are consequences. Coercive approaches remain effective only until alternatives for those being coerced are brought into being. This applies to monopoly supplies of water, gas, electricity, transport, foodstuffs and technology; and also to employment practices imposed by large or dominant employers.

Culture and behaviour

As stated above, organizations that seek a global or wide-ranging international position depend on a 'cultural fit' in order to be enduringly successful and effective. A key strategic need, therefore, is the ability to manage diversity or manage across cultures. To be effective, this requires acknowledging the differences in attitudes, values, behaviour and expectations of those who work in the various locations and activities; and harmonizing talents, qualities and expertise in accordance with overall policy, strategy and direction.

Clear standards of attitudes, behaviour and performance have therefore to be established at headquarters and enforced in different locations and circumstances at local and regional levels. Problems arise when there are known, believed or perceived variations and when organizations take advantage of lack of product, service, employment and environmental regulations to impose disadvantageous standards on those in particular locations. A key priority is harmonizing the strengths of the organization with the age, history, traditions and social customs of each locality and its patterns of work.

There are some key actions that can be taken:

- Developing and promoting local talent into managerial positions. This is likely to include culture and behaviour development as well as enhancing expertise because both commitment and capability are required. If this is to be effective, it is also essential that people from particular localities learn to understand, value – and influence – the activities of the parent company.
- Attracting and retaining local talent so that the bonds between the organization and its localities are reinforced and strengthened. Problems arise when axis management is imposed on localities. The purpose is to develop the whole global organization and not just local activities.

Specific attention is also required to:

- the attitudes to local partners, subcontractors and specialists and the basis on which these are engaged;
- the attitudes to local staff and organization development, and the extent of opportunities for promotion, development and full integration; and attention to specific local issues.

Many of the best managed international and global organizations finds themselves having to deal with specific local issues. In many cases, from a Western (and corporate) standpoint these issues are morally repugnant. However, in particular locations they are custom and practice. Organizations that are faced with these issues have therefore to be clear about how these are going to be tackled so that they begin to change prevailing customs, attitudes and values without compromising or destroying the social fabric of the areas in which they work. Of particular concern are:

- the use of child labour;
- the use of corporal punishment by local supervisors and managers;
- the length of working hours;
- the extent to which overtime is compulsory or not;
- the extent to which overtime is paid or not;
- the extent to which local activities can be developed to Western standards; and the extent to which Western standards can be translated into local activities;
- pay and reward levels, both in absolute terms, and also in terms of averages and values in particular markets;
- the frequency with which wages are paid;
- stoppages from wages and the reasons for these.

Effective culture and organization development requires attention to each of these aspects. This in turn means that corporate policies and standpoints are required. These must be based on a full understanding of all of the pressures inherent in each location and the ability to set standards ultimately that transcend them.

Responsibility and accountability

Specific global organization responsibilities extend to present and future generations of:

- backers, financiers and stockholders in terms of return on investments, return on capital employed, dividends and enhanced values;
- customers and clients as the ultimate beneficiaries of the products and services; and who in turn are to provide the financial returns required in order to ensure present and future stability and prosperity;
- staff, to provide all that is necessary for a long-term secure and productive relationship. Where this is not envisaged, staff always understand this. While it may be possible to gain the compliance of staff in specific situations, it will not secure their loyalty;
- suppliers and especially supply side management, the effectiveness of which has suffered in the past from (superficial) management wisdom as follows:
  - multiple sourcing is a 'good thing' because it keeps suppliers on their toes;
  - always buy from the cheapest source to keep costs down;
  - never pay on time;
  - it is possible to switch most suppliers at short notice if not instantly.

Global organizations can do any of these because of their sheer financial size. However, if these activities are unconsidered or unmanaged, future problems are stored up. Global organizations gain reputations for being bad for business on the supply, staffing, distribution and customer management side; and they gain a reputation for staying in particular localities only until the financial interest dictates or demands that they move on. This then quickly translates into a wider loss of reputation. Suppliers are unable to plan their own operations with any degree of certainty. They may become dependent for existence on the global organization and then have their own prices driven down. Customers and clients first become dissatisfied with loss of reliability of products and services and ultimately change their buying habits. This leads to pressures on staff. Ultimately, the financial interest also loses confidence in the situation because it can see that the envisaged returns (perhaps even returns hitherto generated) are no longer forthcoming.

Global management thinking

Global management thinking means the ability to interrelate the following elements.

- **Thinking globally**: adopting a perspective that envisages the organization's products and services on sale in the axis economies and also remote locations. A key perceptual test of truly global thinking is the present knowledge base that exists among top managers and strategic analysts. For example, can those responsible for strategy, policy and direction envisage working in: Anchorage, Alaska; Dundee, Scotland; Romney, England; Montevideo, Uruguay; or Antigua, Tahiti, Botswana or Sakhalin? However global the perceived approach may be, it has to be:

- on the one hand, capable of considering the whole world as having potential for activities and operations; and on the other hand, limited by where the priorities truly lie;
- fully appreciative of the true scale of effort, energy and resources necessary to generate a genuinely global presence.

- **Thinking locally**: requiring investment in cultural, social, behavioural and ethical understanding of the particular areas where business is envisaged. In particular, there may be strong religious customs or social norms, and patterns of work may be dictated by climatic extremes.

- **Thinking locality**: in terms of the nature of the business relationship that is to be developed and its basis in spending and consumption patterns; propensity to buy and consume local products and services; position and reputation of present providers; and forecast and projected investment levels and returns. This then needs developing into the basis of a mutually profitable relationship answering the key questions:
  - What do we gain from them?
  - What do they gain from us?

- **Thinking responsibly**: reflecting the need to manage the demands placed on particular localities by large and powerful companies; and reflecting the needs to generate a mutuality of interest, respect and value if long-term profitable activities are to be secured.

Global and international leadership

Leadership that is truly global transcends prejudices and preconceptions, acknowledges the subjective elements and matches and harmonizes these with the hard business drives and investment levels required.

The leadership of global organizations requires the following qualities:

- **Integrity** as the basis for all corporate and managerial activities and as the spine of organization culture and management style.
- **Humility**, recognizing that no corporation, however global, can possibly know and understand everything about all areas unless proper research and assessment are carried out; and recognizing that all organizations, managers and staff never stop learning and developing.
- **Enthusiasm**, the need for absolute commitment to all activities and locations; and where there are priorities, ensuring that everything is carried out with the

same degree of personal, professional and occupational enthusiasm, commitment and energy whatever the position in the priority order.

- **Respect**, recognizing that staff management in remote locations requires the same fundamental basis of value as those closer to head office. For example, the race and labour relations problems at Ford UK were compounded by the fact that for years nobody with real influence ever came from the company's head office in Detroit to see the situation for themselves. Respect must be earned. Those using powerful economic positions can gain entry more or less to the markets, sectors and locations of their choice. Maintaining and developing this presence means attending to the social and political elements, as well as market domination and exploitation. It is universally necessary to respect the fact that to those who live there, the Vietnamese/Thai/French 'way' is as important as the Swiss/American/ German 'way' is to those at headquarters.

A key feature of global strategic leadership is the need therefore to be prepared to travel, visit and understand the nature of activities, issues, problems and pressures in each location in which activities are carried out. In addition, those responsible for the guidance and direction of companies and organizations must be prepared to accept advice and guidance from those on the ground in particular locations.

Conclusions

A major issue is the level of commitment, knowledge and understanding required of organizations and their managers that seek international markets. Operating away from head office in a small country brings cultural, social and operational pressures. For example, east Londoners will state categorically that their culture is very different from that of north, south and west London; and so this must be true for all cities, towns and locations in the world. It is this kind of understanding and overall approach that is required if enduring, effective and profitable activities are to take place in unfamiliar territories.

It follows from this that senior, key and influential figures require levels of expertise and understanding that enable genuine cultural awareness and comfort to be achieved in short periods of time. This then forms the basis on which relations, knowledge, understanding and confidence can be further developed, as well as building a deeper cultural and locational appreciation and respect.

It is additionally worth pointing out that overseas markets and locations are likely to view any incursion from organizations operating within the axis locations of USA, EU and Japan with suspicion until their genuine commitment is proved and demonstrated. This is because many overseas markets and locations have had bad, exploitative or expedient relations with large Western and Japanese multinational organizations.

- Organizations that wish to expand into international and global markets and locations need to have the size and resources capable of doing so.
- There are some specific and well-understood paths – joint ventures, outsourcing, local partnerships – that enable organizations to expand carefully.
- Reasons for expansion must always be driven by business demands. Expansion should never be driven by excitement, vanity or prestige unless there are also substantial business reasons for doing so.
- Organizations and managers need to take a clear view of their attitudes and behaviour towards international and global markets and locations. If this attitude is purely dominant and exploitative, organizations and managers should at least be honest enough to say so clearly.
- Once an international presence is established, organizations should evaluate each location for potential business development exactly as in domestic markets.

Further reading

al-Suleimany, M. (2007) *The Psychology of Arab Management Thinking.* Trafford Publishers.

Bickerstaffe, G. (1998) *Mastering Global Business.* FT Pearson.

Deresky, H. (2007) *International Management: Managing Across Borders and Cultures.* Sage.

Haghirian, P. (2011) *Successful Cross Cultural Management: A Guidebook for International Managers.* Sage.

Lane, H. et al. (2009) *International Management Behaviour: Leading with a Global Mindset.* Routledge.

Luthans, F. (2011) *International Management: Culture, Behaviour and Strategy.* McGraw Hill.

Mead, R. and Andrews, T. (2008) *International Management: Culture and Beyond.* Pearson.

Managing
21 for the
present and
future

'The development of knowledge, understanding and expertise is ever-evolving, ever-increasing and lifelong.'

In this chapter

- understanding the need for constant and continuous development of management knowledge, skills and expertise
- recognizing the rapid pace of change in technology, markets, products and services
- understanding and being able to respond to pressures on resources and markets
- establishing 'managing for the present and the future' as a key professional drive for the whole of working life

Introduction

From every point of view, the drives in developing the future expertise and practice of management have at their core the need to gain ever greater results from finite, diminishing, scarce and expensive resources. For the foreseeable future, this means developing all the expertise required to ensure that there is:

- full knowledge and understanding of the environment, and that managers are comfortable and effective working within its constraints;
- full knowledge and understanding of individual, collective and organizational behaviour to ensure that the best and most enduringly productive ways of organizing and allocating work are achieved;
- full attention to the nature of rewards, and that people's aspirations are related as clearly as possible to organizational needs and wants;

- much greater knowledge and understanding of what organizational performance actually is and how this is to be achieved;
- an expert approach to balancing short-term demands for results with the need to ensure that organizations remain fully viable and effective for the long-term future.

All of this ought to ensure that both the demands placed on managers by organizations, and also the personal and professional commitment of managers themselves, lead to an ever-increasing awareness of the need for distinctive knowledge and expertise.

There is at present a very great range and volume of managerial literature, material, expertise and experience available to all. Expert and professional managers need to ensure that they take the fullest possible advantage of all this – learning, evaluating and using it (and sometimes discarding it of course) to their own best advantage in terms of developing their professional knowledge, understanding and practice.

There are specific areas in which all managers need to be knowledgeable and expert at present, as follows:

- the present and evolving nature of the environment;
- the use and value of technology;
- the use and value of the internet;
- creativity.

These areas represent a shift in the context of the knowledge, understanding and expertise required; how this knowledge and understanding is to be applied effectively; and how it forms one part of the basis for the evolution and development of professional practice.

The present and evolving nature of the environment

Those coming into leadership and management positions at present are doing so in difficult and turbulent times. Leadership and management in difficult and turbulent times require a detailed knowledge and understanding of the environment.

It is a key part of the professional duty and development of anyone in any field to keep up to date with everything that is going on in their area of expertise; and so it is with leadership and management.

It is essential to know and understand the effects on the organization, management and operating environment of:

- political and social upheaval in any part of the world;
- economic fluctuations that may cause either the collapse of markets at the one extreme, or the development of ever-increasing markets and demand at the other;

- the effects of natural disasters on markets and the environment, and on factors that affect the markets and environment (for example availability of resources, disruptions to supplies, fluctuations in stock markets and share prices, changes in currency values);
- the effects of weather extremes on the ability to conduct business effectively.

All these factors are wholly or mainly outside the control of leaders and managers; yet organizations have to be able to conduct their business as effectively as possible for as long as possible within these constraints. And it is not as though these factors are at all unknown; over the period since 2009, the following have all happened.

- Social and political uprisings in North Africa and the Middle East; enduring violence in India and Pakistan; terrorist attacks in Western Europe.
- Government and public support for the commercial banks and violently fluctuating asset valuations continue to reduce the amount of funds available to support capital ventures and corporate expansion (or to make these funds more expensive).
- The earthquakes in Pakistan (2009), Haiti (2010) and Japan (2011) all had effects on the availability of raw materials and transport.
- The cold weather in Western Europe in 2010 caused transport difficulties.
- The earthquake in Japan caused a run on stock markets and currency values, because there was uncertainty around how long it would take Japan to recover, and how much it would cost.
- The financial and trading uncertainty brought on by the Greek financial crisis of 2011 and the consequent destabilization of both the eurozone and other financial markets.
- The wider effects on world markets of declining and restricted economic and commercial activity have affected all economies and business activities, as well as affecting commodity prices and charges.

There is therefore a huge range of recent experience on which to build a professional and expert knowledge of what to do in the future when these things happen again. These factors affect everyone in all organizations regardless of size, location or activities. For example:

- a corner shop may lose the majority of its customer base if a business premises nearby closes down, and so people are no longer in the neighbourhood;
- declines in currency values often lead to interest rate rises, meaning that the cost of borrowing in the short and medium term and for mortgage funds rises (including for existing loans);
- declines in confidence always mean that the prices of loans and other sources of finance rise, and the conditions under which loans and finance are made available become more stringent;
- rises in oil, gas, electricity and water charges always make the cost of carrying out business more expensive.

The importance and value of expert environmental analysis, and the knowledge and understanding that arises from this, cannot therefore be overstated. No manager should ever be caught out by the fact of these events occurring in the future. Every manager should have a good understanding of the sorts of actions that are going to have to be taken when these events do arise.

The use and value of technology

The ability to lead and manage in technology-intensive and technology-driven organizations is certain to be a critical factor of expert and professional practice. Managers are going to need distinctive and detailed knowledge and understanding of whatever technology is used within organizations and within their own domain. This is so that they can assess every aspect of their ability to organize and deliver productive work. Knowledge and understanding are therefore required in terms of:

- what the technology does, and what it does not do;
- how much it costs to operate;
- how long it takes to work and produce what is required of it;
- how it processes data, raw materials and other inputs;
- how reliable its operations and activities are;
- how to manage problems, glitches and security implications;
- what to do about breakdowns, maintenance demands and schedules, upgrades and replacement.

Managers need to know and understand its actual and potential useful and cost-effective life, and the costs of the staff, expertise and energy needed to operate it. This is so that they can forecast accurately the quality, volume and cost of the products and services produced, and the operation of processes. It is also so that they can budget accurately for the total costs, fixed costs and variable costs of its usage. This means that, for example:

- Retail managers need to know and understand the security and integrity of till, stock management, sales and purchasing technology; and they need to be able to organize their operations in terms of the length of time that it takes to get stock into the shops. They need to know and understand the average length of time that it takes for products to be sold. They need facilities in-built, enabling the speeding up and delaying of supplies.
- Those who manage internet and intranet systems need to know and understand the present capacity, and the likely and potential capacity, demanded for the future. They need to know and understand the reasons for systems locking and breaking down. They need to know and understand the actual extent of stability and security, and where breaches could possibly occur. They need to know and understand the immediate and potential lasting effects on the business if the system crashes or is disabled for periods of time. And crucially, they need to know the costs of all of this.

- Hospital managers need to know and understand the costs and usage of all medical technology, and work out medical priorities on the basis that the technology is going to be used to maximum and optimum capability.

Hospital technology

There are major lessons in the development of professional managerial practice from the content and experience of those using medical technology. At present, 30% of NHS medical technology is underused and this is because of the staffing and expertise costs associated with using it to its full capacity. Much of the equipment, including scanners and microsurgery technology, continues to be underused or not used at all because the accounts and budgeting processes either fail to take into account the running and staffing costs, or because of the financial management conventions in the NHS that state that it is cheaper to have technology idle than being used. No organization can afford to have money tied up in capital goods that are then not fully utilized or exploited.

While this example is from the NHS, the lessons apply to all. This in turn therefore emphasizes the requirement for expert knowledge and understanding in terms of equipment purchase, usage and operating costs. Where managers do not have this expert knowledge and understanding, they need to go out and get it – or else change jobs.

The other critical factor in technology management is an appreciation of its useful life. This has to be seen in the context that:

- the capacity of microprocessors doubles on average every 18 months;
- technological developments may render obsolete existing technology (and its associated equipment) and so it has to be junked and replaced before the end of its anticipated useful life;
- new technology installations have to be compatible with what is already present;
- each time replacements and upgrades take place, the organization needs to expend time and resources to train and develop staff in day-to-day usage and managers in their general understanding of the new installation.

Managing in technology-driven organizations therefore requires a fresh, detailed and expert perspective on investment appraisal, costs and benefits, and operational and process effectiveness and efficiency.

The use and value of the internet

All organizations have websites; and all organizations use their websites at the very least for presentation purposes, giving information, providing points of contact, and as reinforcement of brand and identity.

Many organizations make much more use of their websites than this of course, using them for:

- recruitment and selection activities, including online application forms, tests and evaluations;
- sales of products and services, and after-sales activities;
- managing the supply side and ordering in products, services and information;
- information exchange through the use of forums, chatrooms, conferencing, e-mails and intranets;
- presentation of key results and achievements.

The concern for the immediate and enduring future is to assess and decide on how best to maximize and optimize the opportunities afforded by the internet presence without losing sight of the limitations that exist. Internet-based communications, HR activities and trading practices have to deliver the same value, confidence, assurance, integrity and quality of service that is expected when dealing face to face; and failure to do this means that the website is wasted.

Managers have therefore to know and understand what they need and want from websites in their own domains; and in turn to be able to work with technology and design experts to ensure that this is indeed maximized and optimized. Managers need to know and understand the costs and benefits, where problems are likely to occur, and the consequences of having to put things right. Managers need also to know and understand the possibilities and potential for the internet presence itself, and for the commercial and operational opportunities that could, or might, accrue.

Websites must be kept up to date both in terms of the content that is delivered and presented, and also in terms of operating capacity. And managers need to involve themselves in the wider aspects of technology and its management from the point of view of professional development and understanding so that when the time comes, they are able to make informed and effective decisions on future developments of the internet presence.

Whatever is done via the internet in terms of business practice and operations has to be enduringly viable. Using the internet for recruitment and selection, sales or managing the supply side requires the same attention to detail as face to face; and the outcomes need to be as assured as face to face.

Core business in the 21st century

Many organizations have found themselves diverted away from this by media, public relations and stakeholder pressures. They have consequently found themselves overcommitting to peripheral or unfashionable business in the pursuit of media coverage. Many organizations have created their own websites on the basis that they perceived they had to have one regardless of any contribution that it would make to long-term effectiveness, profitability and viability.

In an attempt to redress the balance, Porter (2000) wrote: 'At the end of the day there are no new business models or paradigms. There is no virtual industry. There are no easy rides, quick fixes or absolute certainties. Nothing can be fixed through public relations alone. There are no virtual markets. There is only competition – the pursuit of real customers for real businesses who are going to avail themselves of products and services at prices they are willing to pay.'

Source: Porter (2000).

Developing professional and expert practice

It is stated in Chapter 1 that the primary concern of management is to make best use of scarce resources in a changing and uncertain environment in order to cope with change and uncertainty. From that point of view, managing in the future is likely not to be all that different from managing at present and in the recent past.

It is certain, however, that a much greater understanding of what 'coping with change and uncertainty' actually means is required. Effective managers are going to be required to lead and direct change, to create structures and cultures that accommodate this, to do it profitably and effectively in the long term, and from the genuine point of view of the organization's enduring best interests, and those of all its stakeholders. This is certain to apply to all managers, whatever their level of responsibility, seniority or occupational position. Organizations can no longer afford the expense of large and sophisticated bureaucratic and administrative structures; and the consequence is that long-term effectiveness, profitability and viability are only possible if this approach is adopted universally.

Creativity

There is a view, wholly mistaken, that creativity in management is about dreaming things up and putting them into practice on a combination of whim, intuition and freedom of choice and expression.

Nothing could be further from the truth. Artists, musicians, writers, sculptors and designers all work very hard in professional and expert ways at their 'creativity'. Trying something out for the first time is never based purely on guesswork; there is always a strong element of knowledge and understanding that 'it ought to work', and this is based on prior knowledge and existing expertise.

All this ought to apply to creativity in leadership and management. 'Creative' decisions and approaches are based on existing knowledge, understanding and expertise in every other field. Expert leaders and managers therefore apply their creativity to develop their own ways of thinking, doing things, solving problems, and deciding on developments for existing ventures, products and services, and deciding on new developments. However, this has to be founded on strong existing expertise otherwise people are indeed simply guessing at what is required.

just a minute

'Genius and the creativity that goes with it is 1% inspiration, 99% perspiration.'
Thomas Edison

Having said this, it is essential that leaders and managers bring fresh approaches to bear on future problems and issues of:

- deciding which new products, services and ventures to become involved in;
- ensuring that ever-decreasing, and often evermore expensive, resources are ordered, used and consumed as efficiently and as effectively as possible;
- attracting and retaining the best staff and expertise;
- product and service design, delivery and execution;
- prioritizing organizational, departmental, divisional and functional activities, and developing ways of working ensuring that as far as possible and reasonably practicable everything is concentrated on operational priorities rather than processes.

The whole approach to professional creativity demands therefore a wide and ever-increasing expert knowledge and understanding. Expert managers ought actively to be considering possibilities, examining them, testing them – and then for the most part, discarding them! However, out of all this thinking, and the development of knowledge and understanding that goes with it, come the ideas that will work for the future, that can be tried, tested and implemented.

best practice

It follows from all this that truly professional leaders and managers need and must develop a rigorous, reflective and evaluative approach to their own practice. Reflective practice needs to be capable of evaluating:

- why things succeeded and went well;
- why things went wrong;
- what could, and should, have been done differently.

Clarity of purpose and direction

The aim of all organizations should be long-term effectiveness and profitable existence in a turbulent and competitive world. Lack of expertise in strategic management and organizational behaviour has meant that this has all too often become lost in the pursuit of short-term gain, or satisfaction of the financial interest alone.

Beyond this, full market, production, customer and client assessment is regularly not fully carried out. This in turn leads to:

- fashion-based drives: for example we must have a website, we must have every office/school/airliner equipped with computers and other portable technology as ends in themselves;
- hiring strategy consultants and accepting their findings unquestioningly and blindly;
- sending staff on unrelated professional, management, occupational and organizational development programmes without relating these to the needs of the organization or the individuals concerned;
- concentrating on peripheral rather than core issues.

Core and peripheral business activities

All organizations and their top managers must understand where the core activities lie. It is very tempting to draw attention, and therefore resources, away from these two fashionable alternatives, and to give the illusion of globalization. This varies between organizations. In some organizations the core business may not even be clear to top managers. Core business has to be assessed from the point of view of one of the following: what attracts, what sells, what makes money and why this mix should be so. Attention is needed in each of these areas, not just to the 'what makes money' narrow issue. From the point of view of attract/sell/make money, core business must also be seen in terms of enduring customer and client reputation, and brand loyalty and identity.

Dominant stakeholder drives

In industry and commerce, this refers to the desired priorities of shareholders' representatives, other financial interests, backers, and powerful and influential figures who drive their organizations into their own preferred core business. In public services, the dominant stakeholder is government, which sets performance priorities and targets according to political need. There is a divergence here from the majority stakeholder – the public – that wants high quality, enduring, good value public services. In the not-for-profit sector, many large charities now take the view that in order to provide the best possible service for their client groups, it is necessary to engage in fully commercialized fundraising activities; in these cases, the core business becomes the conducting of marketing campaigns.

It is essential to have a balance of primary and support functions with reference to resource consumption – what the organization values and rewards in terms of output and what it does not value; the effectiveness of administration and bureaucracy; and in many cases, the domination of administration and bureaucracy. In extreme cases, the 'core business' of organizations that are dominated by their support functions is effectively to provide career patterns for certain individuals within them.

Economic and social demands and pressures

Managing economic and social demands and pressures requires constant attention to the broader competitive environment. This is one reason why undertaking and using the Five Forces model (see Chapter 2) is so vital. This especially involves taking the broadest possible view of:

- Threats of entry: where new rivals or key players can conceivably emerge from, for example: 'If we can set up there, there will come a time when others can set up here.'
- Threat of substitution: where new inventions and ways of producing and delivering products render present business practices obsolete or at risk. For example, Amazon's online provision has radically affected the ways in which bookshops and music retail chains, especially, do business – bringing great pressures to bear.
- Threats of entry from players that used to conduct activities in an area or sector but have withdrawn for the time being. This especially applies to the re-entry of airlines into mothballed routes; re-entry of defence electronics companies into commercial and consumer products; re-entry of private hospitals into emergency and urgent surgery (this is going on at present by arrangement with the National Health Service in the UK, and may become a service that is purchased universally over the long term).
- Threats from suppliers become a problem when new players can command greater access to suppliers thanks to initial investment levels and willingness to pay. This may lead to supply auctions which some existing players may not be able to afford.
- Threats from customers and clients when product and service levels decline; where the existing is superseded by the same thing at better price, quality and value; where the existing is replaced by something altogether new.

Investment

The traditional – almost cultural – view of investment concerns the placing of finance and other resources into a situation or venture in the expectation of more or less certain and predictable returns. This is founded on the widely held behavioural aspect of placing money in individual deposit accounts, on which a rate of return is guaranteed or predicted. Even though this is less certain than in the past, and returns tend to be lower, the psychological drive to look at all investments from this point of view remains very strong, and this still applies to industry, commerce and public sector investments. For the future, however, a much more active managerial expertise and responsibility in this area is essential.

Investment in production, service and information technology must be undertaken on the basis that it may be necessary to discard it overnight in order to remain competitive and effective because new equipment is now available to competitors. Appraising potential investment in technology therefore requires that as full a projection as possible is available as to whether competitive activities around price, quality, output and retention of market share would be sustainable should alternative technology suddenly become available.

A key part of the management of investment in industrial, commercial and public service situations is therefore certain to require a continuous and active 'what if …?' approach – so that answers to questions such as:

'What if this technology becomes obsolete overnight?'
'What if we have to replace a particular system at short notice?'
'What if a competitor gains access to technology that can produce the particular product or service in a quarter of the time?'

are always kept at the forefront.

Greater expertise in forecasting a projection is required overall. This applies especially in those sectors that operate under mega-project conditions, where the true costs and returns on activities may not be realized for many years. Several current, and recent, high profile examples of this in the UK must cause a radical rethink of how projections and forecasts are carried out.

This also applies to investment in production, service and public sector technology by individual organizations and departments. This requires a much greater projected understanding of density and frequency of usage, speed and convenience of product and service, and quality enhancement and insurance as key elements of assessing returns on investment.

Investment in technology projects and expertise has therefore to be viewed as a sunk cost from a managerial point of view – one on which there may not be any direct or apparent returns. This flies in the face of the widespread current behavioural need to make simple and assured the calculation of return on investment: when investing in technology this is not possible. Moreover, the return on investment is in every case the subject of personal and professional evaluation as well as calculation, and these judgements may quite legitimately vary.

Investment in expertise is dependent at the outset on whether staff are valued as assets or liabilities, and the basis on which this is calculated. This also varies in each case; and is likely to vary within organizations according to:

- the nature of relative and absolute expertise of particular staff in different functions;

- the ease or otherwise with which individuals can be replaced or transformed through retraining and redeployment;
- specific industrial, commercial and public service advantages (and liabilities) that individuals bring. This is particularly true of highly capable and well-known key figures in industry and commerce (for example: Michael O'Leary at Ryanair; Alex Ferguson at Manchester United). It also applies to public services (for example: Magdi Yacoub and Robert Winston in health services; Peter Hall in town planning).

This is clearly a double-edged sword; individuals remain assets so long as they deliver their expertise in ways compatible with the priorities of their organization, and there may be a loss of confidence on the part of key backers and stock markets should such a figure suddenly move on. On the other hand, no organization should be dependent upon an individual, however great their expertise, for its future survival.

Investment in expertise is also required at the 'all staff' level. This consists of underwriting whatever steps are necessary to ensure that effective, productive and positive conditions are created, maintained, enhanced and improved so that high quality industrial, commercial or public service output may be maintained. It is also essential to ensure these conditions include the capability and willingness to transform when required.

Mergers and takeovers

All this is reinforced when considering the enduring managerial responsibilities to mergers and takeovers. Investment in mergers and takeovers requires managerial attention to the reasons behind the findings of two surveys carried out in 1996 and 1999 by the Institute of Management and the Industrial Society. These found that 87% of such ventures do not work at all or fully in the long term. The reasons for this were found to be exactly those considered elsewhere.

- Lack of attention to behavioural and cultural aspects.
- An assumption that these would simply fall into place once the financial deal was completed.
- Lack of attention to the long-term staff management, management style, human resource and industrial relations issues would have to be faced, coupled with the lack of requirement for, or understanding the necessity of, a long-term and sustainable staff management strategy as a precondition of the particular venture.
- Lack of precise definition of what synergies or economies of scale were projected or forecasted and the nature of investment necessary to achieve them. This especially referred to technological incompatibility; and again it was found that a lack of cultural fit and the necessity for culture transformation and change programmes were not sufficiently well thought out or costed.

- Design of the merger or venture to satisfy short-term financial demands, shareholder interest and the reactions of the media and stock markets, rather than long-term enduring customer satisfaction in terms of their relations with the new merged organization.

Those in senior positions with key responsibilities are therefore required to understand and acknowledge the full range of concerns when seeking opportunities and enhancements in this form of investment. It is also incumbent upon those in departmental, divisional and functional positions to understand the pressures that mergers and takeovers bring with them, especially if it is known, believed or perceived that overwhelming attention has been given to the narrow financial interest.

Structures and cultures

The demand here is that top managers take a continuous positive interest in the ways in which activities are carried out in order to ensure that the organization of staff continues to fit operational demands. Problems are caused when ranks and hierarchies work in favour of individuals and groups but cause blockages in operations and activities. It is therefore essential that questions of culture and structure change and development are addressed as part of any wider staff management strategy, and that these elements are related directly to organizational policy, priority, direction and performance.

A starting point for this is to look at structures and cultures from the point of view of the extent of fit. The initial inquiry is to establish whether structure, culture, strategy and staff management style:

- clearly fit and match;
- fit in some parts but not others;
- do not match and fit with strategy direction at all.

One clear indicator of this is to assess what is rewarded and punished, and what is not.

This inquiry causes attention to be drawn to the whole relationship between behaviour, operations, activities and direction. It is often not considered or not addressed fully because:

- its importance is not fully understood by directors and shareholders' representatives;
- there is a history of paying attention to 'the bottom line' rather than how the bottom line is achieved;
- it is not fully understood conceptually by top managers; or it is assumed that once direction is established, everything else will automatically fall into place;
- top managers take the easy way out, preferring to rely on a consultant's prescription, rather than tackling critical issues for themselves.

New fads

Structure, culture, strategy and staff management and integration often get handed on to consultants. This is all very well provided that a genuine brief is worked out with the consultants based upon full assessment of the situation. Many consultancy firms have taken advantage of this gap in organizational managerial expertise to sell off-the-shelf solutions such as:

- Business process reengineering, which is overwhelmingly taken to mean reductions in head count, de-layering, and increases in workload for the frontline.
- Downsizing, rightsizing, resizing, the outcome of which is normally a structured design suitable for the present rather than the future.
- Empowerment, normally resulting in pushing further responsibilities on to often overstretched frontline staff.
- Synergies and economies of scale – concentrating again on a narrow economic rather than broader context of behavioural aspects.
- Facilitation – guiding companies through extended programmes of change.

In many cases, this leads to a long-term relationship between consultants and client organizations. One way of looking at this is to consider 'the circular flow of consultancy'. This works as follows (see Figure 21.1):

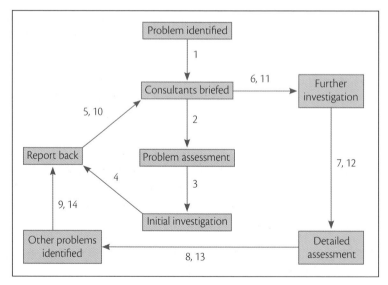

Figure 21.1 *The circular flow of consultancy*

Fee levels charged by top brand consultancies make it behaviourally very difficult to turn down their recommendations. There is also a collective perception that if fee levels are very high, then the consultants must necessarily know what is best for the organization. Many organizations and their top managers come, therefore, to depend on the consultants they have hired.

Effectively, consultants are asked to come in. They provide an initial organizational assessment leading to the conclusion that 'the organization needs some work doing'. Consultants then produce further investigations and a report to the effect that 'you need some more work doing'.

Management and organization development

The present view of management and organization development is that in order to professionalize and make expert the practice of management, and develop the expertise of individual managers, there is a body of skills, knowledge, attributes and qualities that must be learned and put into action.

These approaches are largely well understood and represent, almost by common consent, the known ways in which the required body of knowledge, skills and expertise is imparted.

To this must be added the following:

- Common standards of integrity in all dealings. This is an active collective responsibility as well as one placed on individual managers and supervisors. Moreover, while this may stand to reason in theory, in practice, many managers do not approach all their dealings from the point of view of this absolute standard. It needs to be clearly understood that customers, clients, suppliers and staff all come to know very quickly that the person or organization with whom they are dealing is trustworthy, and when this is not the case. When the person or organization is proved to be untrustworthy, given any choice in the matter, they will move elsewhere if they possibly can.
- The need to develop a distinctive, positive and collective management style. This reinforces culture, values, attitudes and behaviour, and is reinforced by the approaches and activities of individual managers. It matters much less that this is autocratic, participative or anything in between, than that it is common, open, honest and universally delivered.

The need is to develop the style, attitudes and behaviour of individual managers along the above lines. Key priorities therefore have to be:

- visibility;
- openness of communications;
- the building of the person, as well as the occupational and professional aspect of relationships;
- and the ability to develop suitable long-term work group cohesion, expertise and performance.

415

Additionally, there is a critical need for continuous professional development. Many professional and occupational bodies now demand this as a condition of continued membership. In any case, part of the professional and personal responsibility of all managers is to keep abreast of developments in the whole field, to learn lessons as they become available, and to study and evaluate practice in other organization sectors and locations. For example:

- One supermarket chain requires all its staff to go into competitors on a regular basis and to return with at least one example of what the competitor does better than them; to return and say 'there is nothing we can learn from them' is not acceptable.
- An internet-based travel agent, despairing at the lack of real customers, at last sent its staff into its high street competitors to study the real demand of customers; it consequently redesigned its approach and website to take account of these factors.
- A hospital reduced attacks on, and abuse of, its staff in its accident and emergency department by studying the management of long-stay customers and clients in airport lounges.
- A single location grocery store quadrupled its turnover in six months as the result of studying the range available at Tesco and Asda and increasing the perceived choice available to customers, as well as convenience.

All this is legitimate and effective as continuous professional development. It is as substantial as professional updates, technical studies, evaluation, and project work and secondment. Ideally, continuous professional development should be planned and reinforced with the opportunity to put it into practice. Ultimately this is a matter of personal responsibility, whether or not it is actively encouraged by particular organizations.

Conclusions

As stated above, the key drive must be towards managerial expertise in delivering performance and coping with change and uncertainty in whatever the context present. Organizations and their managers that blame environmental conditions for failings and shortcomings in their own expertise are therefore increasingly certain to get left behind by those that do not. All managers need to know and understand the effects of the following conditions, and be able to operate effectively when they change.

- Fluctuations in interest rates, inflation, retail prices indexes, currency values and other economic factors that 'simply could not be predicted or foreseen'.
- Currency collapses or surges making activities either too expensive to complete, or too expensive to contemplate.

- Turbulence in the global economy, especially competitive surges from different parts of the world.
- Changes in consumer demand and confidence caused by unfair trading practices on the part of manufacturers and service providers in areas of perceived cheap activities. It should always be remembered that the first countries to be accused of this were Japan on manufacturing; the Gulf States and Norway on oil production; and Switzerland on banking and finance industry practices.
- Resorting to public relations campaigns, rather than managerial inquiry, to counter the commentaries by media on organization and sectoral shortfalls.
- The practice of taking refuge in perceived sectoral league tables; this leads to the excuse that 'we are doing no worse than anyone else in our sector', or 'we are all beset by difficult trading conditions', as a substitute for active managerial responsibility.

There is likely to be a fundamental shift away from organizational, managerial and structural hierarchies with people rising through the ranks as they achieve the required standards of knowledge, understanding and expertise.

There will be hierarchies, but these will have fewer links and stages that previously existed. The driving force behind this is a combination of practice and expediency:

- practice, in that people at particular levels of the organization are going to be required to have a much greater knowledge, understanding and expertise at the level at which they find themselves, and to deliver critical performance rather than being constantly developed for the next job;
- expediency, from the point of view that organizations have all decided that middle managers are an expense that they can do without.

just a minute

Superficially attractive, the blanket removal of middle management grades and posts nevertheless removes also:

- career paths, meaning that it becomes less attractive for talented people to remain with, and commit to, the organization;
- knowledge and developing expertise, meaning that a void is likely to be left in some areas;
- a part of culture and organizational behaviour with which people are comfortable, and which the organization is used to.

In practice, there is enough management literature, training, development, understanding and awareness in all sectors, as well as overall, to ensure that each of these factors can be understood and accommodated. The most successful organizations in the long term are those that accept the constraints under which they have to operate, accept the potential for competitive and operational turbulence, and understand the factors outside their control within which they have to operate. In the future, the best managers are going to be those who take active responsibility for this, and continue to deliver high quality, high value, profitable and effective products and services, rather than those who take refuge in a ready-made list of excuses.

The most important lesson for all managers to accept is that coping with change and uncertainty, and achieving things through people, comes with a wide range of active responsibilities. Furthermore, the resources required for combining into productive, profitable and effective activities have to be gathered from a broader environment over which individual managers have very little control.

The purpose of this final chapter has been to illustrate the active steps that can be taken on a more or less universal basis in order to ensure the required capability and expertise in coping with change and uncertainty, organizing and directing people, and combining resources.

Above all, genuinely expert managers, those who accept and understand the constraints under which they have to work, and the expertise required as a result, are certain to become very much more highly prized in the future. As organizations come to query evermore precisely the actual added value of support functions and structures and hierarchies, the manager who can deliver enduring customer, client, supplier and end-user satisfaction is certain to become a most valuable commodity to organizations, and their expertise highly prized.

- It is essential that all those who aspire to be leaders and managers take a professional attitude to their own knowledge, skills and expertise.
- Management and leadership have increasingly clear bodies of knowledge, understanding and experience that all those who wish to practise need to acquire.
- The development of knowledge, understanding and expertise is ever-evolving, ever-increasing and lifelong.
- Management expertise is only delivered effectively if there is full knowledge and understanding of the operating environment; and the changes that take place in this.
- The effectiveness of managerial and leadership expertise has always to be seen in terms of how the organizations that they run perform, both for the present and also into the future.

Further reading

Ancona, D. (2003) *Managing for the Future: Organizational Behaviour and Processes.* Sage.
Drucker, P. (1999) *Management Challenges for the Twenty First Century.* HarperCollins.
DuPrey, R. (2010) *Work Place of the Future.* Jossey Bass.
Semler, R. (1993) *Maverick.* Century.
Tidd, J. and Beasant, J. (2009) *Managing Innovation.* Pearson.
Watson, T. (2006) *Organising and Managing Work.* FTPitman.

Summary
sheets

There is a summary (a crib sheet!) below for each chapter of the book. The purpose is to give you a short, quick and easy guide to looking things up; and also to remind you of the things that you will need to know and to be able to do, as you come to learn how to apply the principles and expertise of management. And it is also a very useful guide to exam revision.

Definitions

You need to have available a definition of all key terms that you are ever going to use. This is because:

- a great deal of management speak and jargon is devised so that people who use this kind of language do not have to make clear what they are talking about;
- terms such as strategy, culture, and employee relations have different perceptions and meanings attached to them; and so you have to be able to make clear the position from which you are addressing them;
- it is a question of professional discipline that you always need to be clear about what it is that you are addressing;
- it is a personal development issue that in order to know and understand things they have first to be clear in your own mind;
- it is a mark of professionalism that you do know these things and can define them, as a part of your commitment to your job, work and discipline.

Approach

While this section gives a summary for each of the chapters of the book, it is essential to know and understand that all aspects of management knowledge, understanding and expertise are interrelated – none of them stand in isolation from the others. So do approach any revision or knowledge development or professional enhancement from this point of view. You have to know and be able to apply the whole whether you work in a small company or a multinational; whether you work in HR or marketing or sales or web design; whether you work in commerce, public services or the not-for-profit sector.

Chapter 1 Introduction

The coverage of what management is and how it works: management is an increasingly professionalized discipline that consists of knowing everything about, and being able to apply:

- achieving things through and for people
- delivering performance
- coping with change and uncertainty

You should be able to debate the extent to which management is a profession – the need for expert knowledge and capability and the ability to apply this according to the situation and the organization and circumstances (with the need therefore for a 'professional' approach and commitment, including a personal commitment); and the extent to which it is not a profession – there are no entry barriers or pre-qualifications; there is no independent ability to regulate or to set reward levels.

Chapter 2 Organizations, managers and the environment

The main things to draw from this chapter are:

- knowing and understanding the environment and the constraints that are present and within which you have to work
- knowing and being able to do the analyses: SWOT, PESTLE, SPECTACLES, Five Forces

You have to be able to evaluate the results of the analyses also. You have to be able to form your own judgements and be able to support these judgements as to which are the overriding strengths and forces, which have to be accommodated and managed within, and which can be ignored (for the moment at least).

The other key lesson is that you need to be constantly scanning and evaluating everything around you. Things can and do change very quickly: someone comes up with new production technology; someone else comes up with a system that transforms industry standards; the bottom drops out of the market for a product or service line – you need to be able to anticipate these things happening, and you need to be able to have ideas about what to do if and when these things do happen. You also need to know (if you have invented or implemented a radical new technology or product or service line) how long you are likely to be able to sustain a competitive advantage before others catch up with you.

One word also about the legal issues: you always have the remedy of the law if someone offends; but you always need to remember how long it takes for things to come to court and finally be settled. On the day that this text was written, Microsoft announced the settlement of one of its numerous disputes with the EU; this particular issue had been going on since 1998, and so if you do think of legal remedies then be fully aware of how long the matter is going to take to resolve.

Chapter 3 Managing in a changing environment

As stated in Chapter 1, one of the key issues that managers have to face is the need and ability to cope with change and uncertainty. You need therefore to know:

- what is changing and what is likely to change
- the likely and possible effects of these changes

You need to be able to identify where the drives for change and barriers to change are going to come from; and you need to be able to assess and prioritize these and formulate propositions for building on and energizing the drives, as well as addressing the barriers and, where necessary, breaking them down.

You are going to need to know and understand how to go about changing people's resistances to change. This means that you need to know and understand why they are resisting, what they fear, and how to overcome these fears. You need then to be able to prioritize what to do and set out a clearly defined schedule and approach in order to tackle the things that you have identified.

During the course of your studies, you will see many case studies and examples relating to change and development. You need to get into the habit of evaluating these, seeing where success and progress were achieved, and what went wrong, and what could have been done differently and why.

You need also to recognize that there are no blueprints for successful change and development – there are principles that can and need to be followed; and you do need to have always in mind the mantra:

'Change, from what, to what, when, where, how and why'

Chapter 4 Ethics and corporate governance

You need to be clear about the standards that you set for yourself and why you have set these standards. You have to have a detailed and complex view of, on the one hand:

- the need to survive and be effective, and to be able to carry out your job and duties, how you will treat people – everyone: customers, staff, colleagues, peers, superiors, financiers, suppliers

and on the other hand, you have to relate this to your own view of:

- what is right and wrong, what you will and will not do and why, what your attitude is to dishonesty and duplicity.

You have also to know and understand how you are going to deal with the grey areas – things that are not quite true, not quite false, and not quite accurate (but not inaccurate). You must then be able to reconcile the different pressures and dilemmas that all this complexity brings, so that you can be comfortable as well as effective.

You have to recognize that everyone has their own set of ethics, moral compass and work ethic. You are entitled to have people do things your way – but only if you are not breaking legal, moral or social boundaries and pressures. You are entitled to have people work to the best of their abilities – you are not entitled to have them do wrong things, or break their own codes, just because you say so.

Chapter 5 The practice of management

The final part of any introduction and introductory part of any management text is to make clear that everything has to work in practice. There is therefore nothing esoteric or utopian about any of the material covered in Part One of this book – it has applications in every situation and set of circumstances.

However, there are pressures in terms of relating knowledge to practice; and so you have to be able to work within these pressures and constraints and be effective. These pressures come from:

- the company or organization and its resources and ways of working
- company and industry or sectoral matters
- staffing matters and issues, including people's hopes and fears
- the diversity of your people and staff
- the technology that you use and how this affects the patterns of work that you have

You have to be able also to work within specific constraints – the law, environmental pressures, getting to grips with sustainability, managing scarce, limited and finite resources, investing in and using technology to best advantage.

Everything has then to be related to the key managerial pressures of delivering performance, being effective, getting things done with and through and for people. You have to recognize where ideal solutions to problems will not be possible. You have to recognize that everything that you do or propose has to be capable of being sustained through the conduct of business.

You have to recognize that over time the practice of management and the practices used by managers have to change in order to meet new demands and opportunities – and new problems and issues. Especially as organizations grow and develop, you need to create the means for continued effective supervision and management – what might have been capable of being managed and organized and directed by one person may no longer be so, as either there are now too many staff functions to organize and direct, or the activities have now diversified to a point where the original management person or team is no longer knowledgeable enough to be able to do all this effectively.

Chapter 6 Culture

The key issues here are:

- recognizing the need for people to have a clear set of standards to follow and to work to
- recognizing that people have the need to identify with their place of work, and to feel that they belong to that place of work
- recognizing that if you do not set standards of conduct, behaviour and performance, then people will set their own
- recognizing that even if you do get a strong positive and inclusive culture, this comes with its own responsibilities – people will behave in the interests of the organization if this happens, and so those interests have got to be managed and discharged very effectively (remember that the Nazi SS had a very strong, positive and inclusive culture and so those who ran it were able to get the staff to carry out all of the repulsive crimes for which they were responsible)

Additionally, you should know the Handy and Harrison and Deal and Kennedy models of culture and you need to know the basis on which any organization culture is formed and developed.

Finally you need to recognize that culture change and development is a managerial responsibility. It is your role to set and develop the standards that you want – otherwise these standards will 'emerge' anyway, and be set by the staff.

Chapter 7 Communication

You need to know that this is one of the crucial management skills. You will probably never be recognized as a good communicator – you will always be recognized if you are a bad communicator! You need to recognize the strengths and shortcomings of each of the means and ways of communication shown in Figure 7.1; and recognize from this that there are very few fully effective ways of communicating – the key indeed is that the best way is for you to tell people things first hand, and then reinforce anything and everything with written documents if necessary.

You need to know that the non-verbal aspects are much more powerful than verbal – people will remember you rather than what you said; and people will remember pictures or being shown things, rather than words and being told things.

People recognize the messages that are really being given off, through a combination of language used, what is clearly stated and what is not, what is precise and what is not, the past history and track record of honest and dishonest communications, and what the agenda really is.

If you do not make clear what is going on and what is being communicated, then people will form their own judgements and make up their own minds. This reinforces the need for transparency and honesty – and if you cannot be fully honest, then never tell lies. You will be remembered for this forever!

Chapter 8 Management influence, power and conflict

The main things here to know and be able to work with are:

- how to establish and use your own influence, as the result of the position that you hold, and the respect with which you are regarded
- where the sources of power and influence that you have come from; and where the sources of influence that your people have come from
- why some people and groups are powerful and influential and others are not
- how to use and exercise power and influence responsibly

We have all come across bullies and tyrants; and we all hate them. In some cases people behave as bullies because they want to and because they can; in other cases they mistake this for being forward and forceful. The result is always damaging and destructive – and often very expensive in terms of loss of staff and production and output, and loss of staff morale, and damages to those who sue you!

It follows from this that it is necessary to recognize the potential for conflict in any organization. Conflict is a fact of human life; and so it exists in all organizations and groups of people. You have to be able to recognize the sources, causes and symptoms, and to be able to address the issues according to the situation and the personalities involved. You must be able to assess any conflict from the point of view of what you want the outcome to be, what the desired outcomes are on the part of everyone involved, and what the consequences of particular courses of action would be or might be.

Chapter 9 Human resource management

Human resource management (HRM) exists at strategic and operational levels in order to structure and integrate the staff effort with company or organization objectives, and to ensure that:

- people are properly selected and trained for work
- they are properly rewarded
- the collective and individual conduct behaviour and performance are kept up to standards
- the systems and procedures are structured and managed
- the place of work is healthy and safe

You need to know what the organizational perspectives are, and whether these are based fundamentally on consensus, cooperation, conformity or conflict. This assessment gives the full basis on which HRM is to be conducted. If it is based on consensus and participation, overtly so much the better, though this does bring with it a total responsibility for creating the conditions in which consensus and participation are possible and sought by the staff. If it is based on conflict, then you have to have effective and comprehensive systems and procedures in place to structure and manage the problems and issues and patterns of behaviour that are certain to arise.

The whole of HR is bounded by employment law and some very key principles. The areas of recruitment and selection, training and development, health and safety, pay and rewards, and employee relations are all bounded by both law and also principles that state the absolute standards to which you have to behave and perform, in terms of:

- equality and fairness of treatment
- diversity and recognizing and respecting people's differences
- fairness and reasonableness
- staff collective and individual representation
- natural justice
- transparency

There are minimum standards for wages, disciplinary and grievance procedures and health and safety practice. There are also sanctions for allowing, encouraging and participating in bullying, victimization, harassment discrimination, vandalism, violence and theft. Failure to follow and adhere to these minimum standards means that the company and its managers are normally found to be at fault, and there are statutory and discretionary remedies which are applied by courts and by employment tribunals.

Chapter 10 Leadership and management

The need here is to understand and be aware of what leadership is, how it impacts on managerial professional performance, and the part of management that is about 'leadership'. Leadership is additional to management and a part of professional managerial expertise in that:

- managers need to be accountable for their actions as well as responsible
- staff look to managers to give direction, confidence and assurance – 'leadership'
- the need for leadership is critical to the future effectiveness of organization practice and performance

It follows from this that leadership must be a combination of organizational situational and managerial knowledge; together with the ability to motivate and inspire, to address problems and crises and to take effective decisions at all levels and according to the needs of the situation or issue being faced.

There are leadership traits, styles, qualities and characteristics which have to be recognized and learned. Some of this comes more easily to some people than others; however, it is essential to understand that there is no such thing as a born leader – all of this can be (and must be) taught and learned.

Chapter 11 Strategy policy and direction

This part of the book is about what is done within organizations and by managers, and why. The main things to know and understand are:

- the need for clarity of purpose direction and priorities
- the ability to support and justify why the organization is pursuing its what and how

Beyond this, there is the need for a core foundation or generic position from which to compete. This is normally defined as

- cost leadership or cost advantage
- brand leadership or brand advantage
- focus or niche
- something else (for example convenience, reputation)

If this is clear then everything else flows from it – marketing, product and service, HR and technology strategies all have a clear basis for development. If the core position is not clear or precise, then everything else gets clouded also, and people (above all, customers and backers) become uncertain and so will gravitate towards those who do have a greater clarity.

The problems and issues with strategy are also identified: above all, the need for development and investment, and the incremental and radical approaches that some companies take; and the signs of failure (especially where costs are rising and income or sales are falling).

Chapter 12 Marketing

Marketing is the competitive process by which goods and services are offered for consumption at a profit. Marketing takes place at strategic and operational levels, and is concerned with developing a brand, image, presence and identity for the company and its products and services. It achieves this through:

- determining a position in relation to the core strategy as to whether the company will be first in the field or a follower
- using marketing mixes, which are:
  - the 4Ps – price, place, product, promotion
  - the 4Cs – customer, convenience, choice, cost

This position and mix are then further structured and developed through the use of marketing media – the internet, television and radio, packaging, design, colour, images, PR, posters, leaflets and sponsorship and endorsements.

Chapter 13 Managing operations and projects

All managers are involved to a greater or lesser extent with operations and projects, in terms of the demands of their own functional areas, and also in terms of the wider attention needed for business and organization development, and in maximizing and optimizing resource usage.

The need here is to be able to recognize where the priorities lie and how to address them. The main issues are attending to resources, defining the scales of production required and possible, and then ensuring that there is a good quality, healthy and safe working environment.

The scales of production are normally defined as:

- unit
- batch
- mass and flow

It used to be normal for a company to locate products that gained weight in the production process near to its markets, and those that lost weight during production near to the source of raw materials. With increasing globalization and internationalization, this is no longer a crucial demand.

It is essential to have a clear strategic approach to the supply side however. There are various approaches used, including just in time and the buying up of supply side companies; the critical factor is to ensure that you have as much command over the supply side as possible. Many companies and organizations go into extensive and complex contract arrangements with key and critical suppliers.

With all of this comes a distinctive expertise and set of responsibilities – the demands of each different place of work are different, and so a balance has to be struck between maintaining the highest possible standards of performance, with attending to the specific constraints of the particular situation and organization.

Chapter 14 Financial and quantitative aspects of management

You need to know how accounts are constructed and what they show you – and what they do not show you. You need especially to be aware of the fact that accounts are constructed for the purpose of meeting statutory requirements and demonstrating a summary of the company and organization financial performance – accounts are not a management information system, though you do need to read them in conjunction with other performance measures. You need to look at accounts also from the point of view of examining trends – for example:

- if costs are rising then the reasons for this need to be examined and agreed
- if profits are rising then you need to know what is driving this – is it all aspects of the organization's performance, or is it one or two activities only

And so on. Accounts are therefore a very useful and valuable starting point for addressing and assessing performance; you then need to relate what the accounts show to everything else that is going on.

You need statistical and mathematical knowledge in order to be able to make sense of all the data that comes your way, and again in order to be able to support and justify the decisions that you take and the assertions that you make about all aspects of business and management.

You need to be able to use data to support and justify and sometimes defend decisions and proposals that you make. You need to be able to use data and statistics to support project and operations management reports, sales efforts, production and productivity issues. Data is also needed for things like accidents, disputes and griev-ances and other HR matters.

You need to be able to have access to data that shows how long it takes for new products and services to get to market; the percentages of new products and services inventions and developments that do make it to market and profitability. You need data that shows where blockages and hold-ups occur, and the consequences of these in terms of lost production and output.

You need market knowledge and data that shows and supports your knowledge of customer behaviour and attitudes to your products and services, why they are loyal to you (or not), and what it is that makes them come to you (or not).

Chapter 15 Organizational and managerial performance

Organizational and managerial performance is a critical issue. You have to be able to assess and evaluate performance using multiple and often complex criteria. You have to be able to look at performance in terms of:

- overall aims and objectives
- specific and individual aims and objectives
- what you set out to achieve overall and whether or not this was feasible and reasonable in the circumstances
- what else was achieved and what happened as a by-product of your original aims and intentions
- what was not achieved

You have to be able to give reasons and a full justification for all of this. You have then to be able to relate it all to each aspect of the organization: finance; product and service performance; HR performance; marketing activities; and organization devel-opment and progress overall. You have to be able to relate all of these in turn to: timescales for evaluation; any milestones and critical positions along the way; and any problems and issues that arise along the way.

You have to have formal means and methods of performance management and appraisal (see also the HR chapter), so that people get clearly identifiable statements of performance, and clear and official statements of what is going well and why, and what is going badly and why. This is then reinforced through continuous discussions of performance, which need to take place as a part of daily organizational life.

You should finally note here that, because this is so complex and involved, there is a huge human pressure simply to look at the company or organization annual report and let the figures speak for themselves (it is less trouble than doing the job properly; and it is easier for everyone to understand – even if it is fundamentally wrong).

Chapter 16 Risk

Risk management is a major current issue and so you need to know:

- the nature of risk that is prevalent in all organizations

- the nature of risk that is prevalent in organizations that accounts for 'sectoral risk' or industrial risk
- the nature of human and behavioural risk
- the consequences of particular decisions and initiatives and actions

You need to be aware that the greatest risk to all organizations is that, collectively and individually, staff do not always get around to doing things; or that they concentrate on the tasks that they do like and avoid the ones that they do not like; or that they could not be bothered to do things; or that they could not see the value in doing things.

Each of these areas is a point of essential management intervention. The greatest contribution that anyone can make to effective risk management is to recognize where things are not getting done, and then to take steps to see that they are done.

Risk management requires expert environmental scanning to assess and evaluate the problems and issues from all sources; and then to take the earliest possible steps to address them. This additionally involves deciding whether you are going to:

- accept the risk because it is either very unlikely to happen, or because the consequences of it happening are very small
- accept the risk and take steps to mitigate it – which you will always do for things like health and safety issues and employee relations problems
- avoid the risk, which means that once the risk is recognized you decide that the consequences of the thing happening are too great and so you find alternative ways of achieving your objectives

Finally, you should note that the improved perfomance of companies in the past few years has come about at exactly the time that so many of them have introduced very comprehensive risk management policies. The problem with risk therefore lies not in recognizing it and having policies to deal with it, but in having the managerial will to address it and tackle it, and to implement the risk management policies that do already exist.

Chapter 17 Management and motivation

It is essential to know and understand motivation theories, especially those of Herzberg, Maslow and McClelland; and you need also to know the basis of expectancy theory – the relationships between expectation, effort and reward. You need to know the differences between motivation and incentives. You need to know the relationship between intrinsic and extrinsic motivation.

You then need to be able to relate all of this to overall assessments of what makes people happy and productive at work; and what does not make people happy and productive at work. You need especially to be able to assess different work groups and organizations and individual activities from the perspective of:

- why some people are very productive indeed in jobs that are neither well paid nor glamorous

- why some people who are very well paid and work in (perceived) glamorous industries and sectors are unproductive
- why some people are willing to work for an organization but others are not

You then need to be able to relate all of this to the overall management effort, and to the HR and people management effort in particular.

Chapter 18 Management on a daily basis

The purpose here is to show how much of what is learned of the principles and practice of management comes together. The key issues to recognize are:

- the unpredictability of much of the workload of managers
- the need to bring expertise to bear on a wide variety of different situations
- the ability just to take a moment to think things through before choosing a course of action
- that as so much of management is about achieving things through and for people, it is essential to have the interpersonal skills and understanding necessary to get things done with the minimum of fuss

The other factors covered in this chapter are all directly concerned with managing on a daily basis, and these are:

- the need to promote and develop the attitudes and values that you want to have in the place of work; and this is reinforced by the need for interpersonal skills, thoughtfulness, addressing a wide variety of different situations as above
- managing by walking about and being visible as often as possible; and this is because everything is addressed more fully and effectively face to face than through e-mail or other correspondence
- attending on a continuous basis to performance and its management; and again recognizing that visibility is likely to mean that performance issues are more likely to be picked up if management is visible and involved

Out of all this arise the questions of control and direction; and this is as much about how to control things as what to control. Certainly there is a balance to be struck between remaining actively involved, without getting in the way of progress.

Chapter 19 Management development

All managers have to learn their expertise; and all managers have to be developed: this is the basis of all management teaching and learning and education. This chapter and this part of management practice are about:

- continuous attention to expertise and knowledge development
- continuous attention to professional development
- relating what is known and understood to the demands of the business environment and company or organization performance

- relating knowledge and expertise to likely and possible future demands
- ensuring that there is a body of managerial (and leadership) expertise that is going to be of value to all companies and organizations for the future

The problems that arise often relate to the inability of organizations to release staff for development activities, and/or the inability of managers to take time out to make sure that they do remain fully up to date and continuously developed. It follows from this that there are needs to:

- integrate the development efforts with work on a daily basis
- structure development efforts so that there is a clearly identifiable and substantial approach to management development

The means and methods outlined – on the job training, off the job training, business school classes, project work, secondments – therefore need to be structured and organized so that everyone becomes as proficient as possible in their present job, and has the best possible basis for growing into future occupations as opportunities become available.

It is also essential to recognize that the need for fresh expertise can be addressed by bringing fresh talent and ideas in from outside as well as growing them from within; and the balance of this needs to be assessed and determined as a part of overall strategic management of the organization.

Chapter 20 Managing in a global and international environment

The purpose here is to ensure that you know and understand what globalization and internationalization are, and their effects on the principles and practice of management. The first thing to do therefore is to recognize just how far your company or the company that you are considering is truly global or international. You need to bear in mind that having a website does not make you a global business; and so you need some more tangible elements, as follows:

- global influence
- global physical presence
- command of resources
- global command of expertise
- global reach
- to set global standards

You then need to recognize the elements that have to be addressed if you are to be genuinely effective in a global or international environment:

- cultural recognition and the respect of people's differences
- language barriers
- time zones

- national borders and boundaries and the issues of managing according to the laws, customs and habits, and practices of others
- managing across distances

Finally, you have to recognize the extent and basis on which you are welcomed into the new and international arena overall, and the locations and countries that you go into in particular: if it is purely because you are big enough to do so, and to set your own rules and impose your own ways on different parts of the world, then recognize that you do have this presence and that you will not always be respected or welcomed. You need to be honest enough to state clearly the reasons for going into new markets; and if this is to exploit them and then depart, you need to be honest enough to say so.

Chapter 21 Managing for the present and future

The purpose here is to make informed, educated and (informed) speculative assertions and assumptions (and guesses) about how things are to develop over the immediate and longer-term future. In order to do this effectively, you need to know and understand the present and immediately unfolding state of the world because this is where you are starting from; and you need to know and understand what is to drive your future:

- the activities that you carry out and their present and enduring value to the customers that you serve
- the activities that you are intending to carry out in the future and their immediate and perceived enduring value
- the ability and willingness of management to look to the future and work within its opportunities and constraints
- specific resource pressures
- specific financial pressures
- problems in finding and retaining the expertise that you are going to need and want
- technology developments and their commercial prospects and potential
- technology and IT and their value for the future

You also need to be aware of any specific issues regarding the nature and location of your activities, and whether things are likely to change for the future.

You need all of the capabilities in strategy, marketing and finance; the ability to analyse and evaluate the environment, markets, customers and clients; the ability to organize and direct operations, products and services, in the context of things that are only partly known and assured. You have to have the capability and willingness to operate effectively as circumstances change and as existing activities and opportunities decline and increase, and as new opportunities come your way.

Above all, it is essential to have the attitudes that embrace the future, as well as the knowledge and expertise to deal with whatever comes up.

Bibliography and further reading

Adair, J. (1980) *Action Centred Leadership.* Sage.

Adair, J. (2000) *Great Leaders.* Arrow.

Adair, J. (2004) *Inspirational Leadership.* Arrow.

Adair, J. (2009) *Effective Communication: The Most Important Skill of All.* Arrow.

Adams, R., Hamil, S. and Carruthers, J. (2001) *Changing Corporate Values.* Kogan Page.

Adams, S. (2000) *The Joy of Work.* Boxtree.

Ahlstrand, B. (1990) *The Quest for Productivity.* Cambridge University Press.

al-Suleimany, M. (2007) *The Psychology of Arab Management Thinking.* Trafford Publishers.

al-Suleimany, M. (2011) *Cry for Help.* Trafford Publishers.

Ancona, D. (2003) *Managing for the Future: Organisational Behaviour and Processes.* Sage.

Anderson, M. (2010) *The Leadership Book: How to Deliver Outstanding Results.* FT Pearson.

Andrews, K. (1980) *The Concept of Corporate Strategy.* Irwin.

Armstrong, M. (1998) *Strategic Human Resource Management.* Kogan Page.

Armstrong, M. (2009*) Handbook of Performance Management: Making Performance Management Work.* Kogan Page.

Armstrong, M. and Baron, A. (1998) *Performance Management: The New Realities.* CIPD.

Arnold, G. (2010) *Corporate Financial Management.* Pearson.

Ash, M.K. (1985) *On People Management.* MacDonald.

Association for Project Management (2011) *Project Management: Body of Knowledge.* APM Publications.

Atrill, P. (2008) *Financial Management for Decision Makers* Wiley.

Bach, S. and Sisson, K. (2000) *Personnel Management: A Comprehensive Guide to Theory and Practice.* CIPD.

Baker, M. (1992) *Marketing.* Macmillan.

Baker, M. (2002) *The Marketing Book.* Wiley.

Barker, A. (2010) *Improve Your Communication (and create success).* Kogan Page.

Belbin, R. (1986) *Superteams.* PHI.

Bevan, J. (2007) *The Rise and Fall and Rise Again of Marks and Spencer.* HarperCollins.

Bickerstaffe, G. (1998) *Mastering Global Business.* FT Pitman.

Blake, R. and Mouton, J. (2004) *The New Managerial Grid.* Sage.

Blanchard, K. et al. (2010) *Leadership By The Book.* Sage.

Blunden, T. and Thirlwall, J. (2010) *Mastering Operational Risk.* Pearson.

Boddy, D. (2004) *Introduction to Management.* PHI.

de Bono, E. (1984) *Lateral Thinking for Managers.* Pelican.

Bourne, M. and Bourne, P. (2011) *Handbook of Performance Management.* Pearson.

Bower, T. (2003) *Broken Dreams.* Harper Business.

Bowman, C. and Asch, D. (1994) *Strategic Management.* Macmillan.

Boxall, P. and Purcell, J. (2003) *Strategy and Human Resource Management.* Palgrave Macmillan.

Boyatsis, R. (1982) *The Competent Manager.* Wiley.

Branson, R. (1998) *Losing My Virginity.* Virgin Books.

Brassington, F. and Pettit, S. (2006) *Essentials of Marketing.* Pearson.

Bratton, J. and Gold, J. (2007) *Human Resource Management.* Palgrave Macmillan.

Braun, E. (1999) *Technology's Empty Promise.* EarthScan.

Brech, E. (1984) *Organisations.* Longman.

Buell, V. (1990) *Marketing.* McGraw Hill.

Burnes, B. (2007) *Managing Change.* FTPitman.

Burns, T. and Stalker, G. (1968) *The Management of Innovation.* Tavistock.

Caplan, D. and Norton, A. (1996) *The Balance Scorecard.* Harvard.

Campbell, D., Edgar, D. and Stonehouse, G. (2011) *Business Strategy: An Introduction.* Palgrave Macmillan.

Carnegie, D. (1936) *How to Win Friends and Influence People.* Simon and Schuster.

Cartwright, D. (1958) 'Studies in Social Power'. Institute of Social Research.

Cartwright, R. (2000) *Mastering Customer Relations.* Palgrave – now Palgrave Macmillan.

Cartwright, R. (2001) *Mastering the Business Environment.* Palgrave – now Palgrave Macmillan.

Cartwright, R. (2002) *Global Organisations.* Wiley.

Cassidy, J. (2001) *dot.con.* Penguin.

CBI (Confederation of British Industry) (2005) *Assessing and Managing Risk.* CBI Industrial Trends, July.

Cellan Jones, R. (2001) *dot.bomb.* Aurum.

Chattell, A. (1995) *Managing for the Future.* Macmillan.

Cheatle, K. (2001) *Mastering Human Resource Management.* Palgrave – now Palgrave Macmillan.

Christensen, C. et al. (1987) *Business Policy.* Irwin.

CIPD (1999) *Managing Diversity.* Chartered Institute of Personnel and Development.

Clark, E. (1988) *The Want Makers.* Corgi.

Clark, P. (2011) *Beyond the Deal.* McGraw Hill.

Colley, J. et al. (2007) *Principles of General Management.* McGraw Hill.

Cooper, C. (1996) *Stress Management.* McGraw Hill.

Cornelissen, J. (2008) *Corporate Communication: A Guide to Theory and Practice.* Wiley.

Cornhauser, A. (1965) *Mental Health of the Industrial Worker.* Wiley.

Crane, A. and Matten, D. (2010) *Business Ethics: Managing Corporate Citizenship in the Age of Globalisation.* Oxford University Press.

Creaton, S. (2007) *The Ryanair Story.* HarperCollins.

Crouhy, M. et al. (2006) *The Essentials of Risk Management.* Wiley.

Cruver, B. (2003) *Enron: Anatomy of Greed.* HarperCollins.

Daft, R. (2005) *Management.* South Western.

Davies, H. (2002) *The Eddie Stobart Story.* HarperCollins.

Deal, T. and Kennedy, A. (2000) *Corporate Cultures.* Perseus.

Delves Broughton, P. (2007) *What They Teach You at Harvard Business School.* Penguin.

Deresky, H. (2007) *International Management: Managing Across Borders and Cultures.* Sage.

Donovan, T. (1968) *Report of the Royal Commission on Trade Unions and Employers Associations.* The Stationery Office.

Drennan, D. (1992) *Transforming Company Culture.* McGraw Hill.

Drucker, P. (1986) *The Effective Executive.* Warner.

Drucker, P. (1993) *The Ecological Vision.* Transaction.

Drucker, P. (1995) *Frontiers of Management.* Heinemann.

Drucker, P. (1996) *The Practice of Management.* Heinemann.

Drucker, P. (1999) *Management Challenges for the Twenty First Century.* HarperCollins.

DuPrey, R. (2010) *Workplace of the Future.* Jossey Bass.

Etzioni, A. (1964) *Power in Organisations.* Free Press.

Eyre, E. and Pettinger, R. (1998) *Mastering Basic Management.* Palgrave – now Palgrave Macmillan.

Farnham, D. (2000) *Employee Relations in Context.* CIPD.

Fayol, H. and Urwick, L. (1946) *The Principles of Administration.* Allen and Unwin.

Fiedler, F. (1967) *A Theory of Leadership Effectiveness.* McGraw Hill.

Fligstein, N. (2002) *The Architecture of Markets.* Princeton.

Fowler, A. (1999) *Induction.* CIPD.

Furnham, A. (1999) *The Psychology of Managerial Incompetence.* Whurr.

Gantt, H. (1919) *Organising for Work.* Harcourt Brace Jovanovich.

Gates, B. (1997) *Business @ the Speed of Thought.* Warner.

Ghoshal, S. and Bartlett, C. (1998) *The Individualised Corporation.* Heinemann.

Gilbreth, F. and Gilbreth, L. (1916) *Fatigue Study.* Harper and Row.

Goldsmith, W. and Clutterbuck, D. (1990) *The Winning Streak.* Penguin.

Gold, J. et al. (2010) *Leadership and Management Development.* Wiley.

Goldthorpe, J. et al. (1968) *The Affluent Worker: Industrial Attitudes and Behaviour.* Cambridge University Press.

Goleman, D. (2003) *The New Leaders.* Little, Brown.

Goleman, D. (2005) *Working with Emotional Intelligence.* Vintage.

Gratton, L. (2000) *Living Strategy.* FT Pitman.

Greenberg, D. and Baron, J. (2003) *Behaviour in Organisations.* Prentice Hall International.

Griseri, P. (1997) *Managing Values.* Macmillan.

Griseri, P. (2003) *Management Knowledge.* Palgrave Macmillan.

Griseri, P. and Seppala, N. (2010) *Business Ethics and Corporate Social Responsibility.* Cengage.

Gröschl, S. (2011) *Diversity in the Workplace.* Gower.

Groucutt, J. (2006) *Marketing Management.* Palgrave Macmillan.

Groucutt, J. and Griseri, P. (2004) *Mastering e-Business.* Palgrave Macmillan.

Guest, D. and Conway, N. (1998) *Fairness at Work and the Psychological Contract.* CIPD.

Guest, D. et al. (2002) *Effective People Management.* CIPD.

Haghirian, P. (2011) *Successful Cross Cultural Management: A Guidebook for International Managers.* Sage.

Hamel, G. (2005) *Leading the Revolution.* Harvard.

Hamel, G. and Prahalad, C.K. (1999) *Managing for the Future.* Harvard.

Hammer, M. and Champy, J. (1996) *Reengineering the Corporation.* Harvard.

Hancock, M. and Zahawi, N. (2011) *Masters of Nothing.* Biteback Publishers.

Handy, C. (1978) *The Gods of Management.* Arrow.

Handy, C. (1987) *The Future of Work.* Arrow.

Handy, C. (1994) *The Empty Raincoat.* Arrow.

Handy, C. (1993) *Understanding Organizations* (4th edn). Penguin.

Hannagan, T. (1998) *Mastering Statistics.* Macmillan – now Palgrave Macmillan.

Hargie, O. (2006) *The Handbook of Communication Skills.* McGraw Hill.

Harris, P. and Moran, R. (1991) *Managing Cultural Differences.* Gulf.

Harrison, R. (1995) *Collected Papers.* McGraw Hill.

Harrison, R. (2000) *Employee Development.* CIPD.

Harvard Business Review (2002) *HBR on Ethics.* Harvard.

Harvey, D. (2010) *A Companion to Marx's Capital.* Verso.

Harvey Jones, J. (1990) *Making it Happen.* Fontana.

Hayes, J. (2002) *Interpersonal Skills at Work.* Kogan Page.

Hays, C. (2004) *Pop: Truth and Power at Coca Cola.* Arrow.

Heller, R. (1998a) *In Search of European Excellence.* HarperCollins.

Heller, R. (1998b) *Management Today* (August).

Heller, R. (2000) *Management.* Dorling Kindersley.

Heller, R. (2002) *The New Naked Manager.* Coronet.

Hendry, C. (1994) *Human Resource Management.* Butterworth.

Henry, J. (1992) *Creative Management.* OUP.

Herz, N. (2001) *The Silent Takeover.* Arrow.

Herzberg, F. (1967) *Work and the Nature of Man.* Harvard.

Hilton, C. (1948) *Be My Guest.* HarperCollins.

Hoffman, D. (2002) *Managing Operational Risk.* McGraw Hill.

Hofstede, G. (1980, 2004) *Culture's Consequences.* Sage.

Hofstede, G. (2005) *Cultures and Organisations.* Sage.

Honey, P. and Mumford, A. (1986) *The Manual of Learning Styles.* Peter Honey Publishing.

Hopkin, P. (2010) *Fundamentals of Risk Management.* Pearson.

Huczynski, A. and Buchanan, D. (2003) *Organisational Behaviour.* Prentice Hall.

Hubbard, D. (2009) *The Failure of Risk Management.* McGraw Hill.

Hutton, W. (1995) *The State We're In.* Cape.

Hutton, W. (1997) *The State to Come.* Vintage.

Hutton, W. (2002) *The World We're In.* Little, Brown.

Hutton, W. (2005) *The Productivity Report.* Vintage.

Industrial Society (1999) *Managing Mergers and Takeovers.*

Institute of Management (1996) *The Long-Term Effect of Mergers and Takeovers.*

Jay, A. (1978) *Management and Machiavelli.* HarperCollins.

Jay, A. and Lynn, J. (1999) *The Complete 'Yes Minister'.* BBC.

Johnson, G., Scholes, K. and Whittington, R. (2009) *Exploring Corporate Strategy.* Prentice Hall.

Johnson, R. and Clark, G. (2009) *Service Operations Management: Improving Service Delivery.* Pearson.

Kanter, R. (1985) *When Giants Learn to Dance.* Free Press.

Kanter, R. (1990) *The Change Masters.* Free Press.

Kaplan, R. and Norton, D. (2002) *The Balanced Scorecard.* HBS.

Katz, D. and Kahn, R. (1978) *The Social Psychology of Organisations.* Wiley.

Kennedy, C. (2000) *The Merchant Princes.* Sage.

Kent, B. (2006) *Performance Management.* Kogan Page.

Klein, N. (2000) *No Logo.* Picador.

Knott, G. (2004) *Financial Management* (4th edn). Palgrave Macmillan.

Kotler, P. (2009) *Marketing Management.* PHI.

Kotter, J. (1996) *Leading Change.* Harvard.

Kotter, J. (2009) *What Leaders Really Do.* Harvard.

Lane, H. et al. (2009) *International Management Behaviour: Leading with a Global Mindset.* Routledge.

Lawler, E. (1990) *Strategic Pay.* Jossey Bass.

Legge, K. (1995) *Human Resource Management: Rhetorics and Realities.* Macmillan.

Lessem, R. (1987) *Intrapreneurship.* Wildwood.

Lessem, R. (1989) *The Global Business.* Prentice Hall.

Lewin, K. (1951) *Field Theory in Social Science.* Harper and Row.

Likert, R. (1967) *The Human Organisation.* McGraw Hill.

Lockyer, K. (1992) *Quantitative Production Management.* Pitman.

Lockyer, K. (1996) *Project Management.* Penguin.

Lupton, D. (1999) *Risk.* Routledge.

Lupton, T. (1984) *Management and the Social Sciences.* Penguin.

Luthans, F. (2002) *Organizational Behaviour.* McGraw Hill.

Luthans, F. (2011) *International Management: Culture, Behaviour and Strategy.* McGraw Hill.

Mabey, C., Salaman, G. and Storey, J. (1998) *Human Resource Management.* Blackwell.

Machiavelli, N. (1986) *The Prince.* Penguin Classics.

Major, J. (1998) *John Major: The Autobiography.* HarperCollins.

March, J.G. and Simon, H. (1958) *Organizations.* John Wiley.

Marchand, D. and Davenport, H. (1999) *Mastering Information Management.* Macmillan.

Marchington, M. and Wilkinson, A. (2008) *Human Resource Management at Work: People Management and Development.* CIPD.

Marchington, M. and Wilkinson, A. (2009) *People Management.* CIPD.

Marrison, C. (2002) *The Fundamentals of Risk Management.* Kogan Page.

Maslow, A. (1960) *Motivation and Personality.* Harper and Row.

Mayo, A. (2000) *The Human Value of the Enterprise.* Nicholas Brealey.

McAlpine, A. (2000) *The New Machiavelli.* Wiley.

McCormack, M. (1983) *What They Don't Teach You At Harvard Business School.* Fontana.

McGregor, D. (1970) *The Human Side of Enterprise.* Harper and Row.

McClelland, D. (1971) *Human Aspects of Management.* John Wiley.

Mead, R. and Andrews, T. (2008) *International Management: Culture and Beyond.* Pearson.

Mendzela, J. (2003) *Managing Change in the Central Banking Sector.* Central Banking Publications.

Merrick, N. (2001) *People Management.* CIPD.

Mintzberg, H. (1979) *The Structure of Organisations.* Prentice Hall.

Mintzberg, H. and Quinn, D. (2000) *Strategy.* Prentice Hall.

Mintzberg, H. et al. (2003) *Strategy Safari.* Prentice Hall.

Monbiot, G. (2001) *The Captive State.* Penguin.

Morita, A. (1987) *Made in Japan: The Sony Story.* Fontana.

Morton, C. (1994) *Becoming World Class.* Macmillan.

Moss Kanter, R. (1992) *The Change Masters.* Free Press.

Mullins, L. (2005) *Management and Organisational Behaviour.* FTPitman.

Noon, M. and Blyton, P. (2002) *The Realities of Work.* Macmillan.

Ohmae, K. (1986) *The Mind of the Strategist.* Penguin.

Ouchi, W. (1981) *Theory Z.* Addison Wesley.

Owen, H. (1990) *Myth Transformation and Change.* Routledge.

Owen, J. (2003) *Hard Edged Management.* Kogan Page.

Owen, J. (2012) *Management Stripped Bare: What They Don't Teach You at Business School.* Kogan Page.

Packard, V. (1957) *The Hidden Persuaders.* Penguin.

Packard, V. (1960) *The Waste Makers.* Penguin.

Pascale, R. (1989) *Managing on the Edge.* Simon and Schuster.

Pascale, R. and Athos, A. (1983) *The Art of Japanese Management.* Fontana.

Payne, D. and Pugh, D. (2001) *Managing in a Corporate Environment.* Penguin.

Peters, T. (1986) *The World Turned Upside Down.* Channel Four.

Peters, T. (1989) *Thriving on Chaos.* Pan.

Peters, T. (1992) *Liberation Management.* Pan.

Peters, T. and Austin, N. (1985) *A Passion for Excellence.* Harper and Row.

Peters, T. and Waterman, R. (1982) *In Search of Excellence.* Harper and Row.

Pettinger, R. (1999) *Organisational and Managerial Performance.* FTPitman.

Pettinger, R. (2000) *Investment Appraisal: a Managerial Approach.* Macmillan – now Palgrave Macmillan.

Pettinger, R. (2002a) *Mastering Employee Development.* Palgrave – now Palgrave Macmillan.

Pettinger, R. (2002b) *Managing the Flexible Workforce.* Cassell.

Pettinger, R. (2002c) *The Future of Industrial Relations.* Cassell.

Pettinger, R. (2004) *Contemporary Strategic Management.* Palgrave Macmillan.

Pettinger, R. (2005) *Measuring Business and Managerial Performance*. Pearson.

Pettinger, R. (2007) *Introduction to Management* (4th edn). Palgrave Macmillan.

Pettinger, R. (2010) *Organisational Behaviour*. Routledge.

Pinchot, G. (1984) *Intrapreneuring*. Sage.

Porter, L. and Lawlor, E. (2000) *Management and Motivation*. Harper and Row.

Porter, M. (1980) *Competitive Strategy*. Free Press.

Porter, M. (1986) *Competitive Advantage*. Free Press.

Porter, M. (1999) *Competitive Strategy and the Internet*. Harvard.

Porter, M. (2000) 'Competition in the 21st Century'. *Harvard Business Review*, Jan–Feb.

Pringipas, C. (2001) 'Individual Customisation of Mass Offering Products' (Graduate thesis). UCL.

Pugh, D. and Hickson, D. (1996) *Writers on Organisations* (5th edn). Penguin.

Quirke, W. (2008) *Making the Connections*. Kogan Page.

Randall, G. (1992) *Marketing*. Routledge.

Ratcliffe, S. (2009) *Leadership Plain and Simple*. FTPitman.

Reddin, W. (1970) *Leadership and Management Behaviour*. McGraw Hill.

Revans, R. (1967) *Action Learning*. Sage.

Rice, J. (2000) *Doing Business in Japan*. Penguin.

Ries, A. and Trout, J. (1997) *Marketing Warfare*. Wiley.

Roddick, A. (1992) *Body and Soul*. Ebury.

Ross Sorkin, A. (2009) *Too Big to Fail*. Penguin.

Sheen, B. (1988) *The Herald of Free Enterprise*. HMSO.

Schein, E. (1971) *Organizational Psychology*. Prentice Hall.

Schein, E. (2010) *Organisational Culture and Leadership*. Jossey Bass.Schiller, R. (2003) *The New Financial Order: Risk in the 21st Century*. Princeton.

Schlosser, E. (2002) *Fast Food Corporation*. Harper.

Scott, D. (1993) Artisan Group Ltd Business Plan.

Semler, R. (1993) *Maverick*. Century.

Semler, R. (2003) *The Seven Day Weekend*. Century.

Senge, P. (1992) *The Fifth Discipline*. Century.

Shapiro, D. (2004) *Conflict and Communication*. Kogan Page.

Silbiger, S. (1996) *The Seven Day MBA*. Piatkus.

Simon, H. (1967) *Organizations*. Harper and Row.

Slack, N. et al. (2009) *Operations and Process Management*. Pearson.

Stanley, A. (2009) *Leadership and Conflict Management Styles*. Sage.

Stanton, N. (2009) *Mastering Communication*. Palgrave Macmillan.

Sternberg, E. (1995) *Just Business*. Warner.

Storey, J. (2001) *Human Resource Management: A Critical Text*. Routledge.

Sun Tzu (2000) *The Art of War*. Free Press.

Sutton, C. (1999) *Strategic Concepts*. Macmillan.

Taylor, F. (1947) *Scientific Management*. Harper and Row.

Thompson, J. (2002) *Strategic Management*. Thomson.

Thomsett, M. (2009) *The Little Black Book of Project Management*. Jossey Bass.

Thurley, K. and Wood, S. (1983) *Industrial Relations and Management Strategy*. Cambridge University Press.

Tidd, J. and Besant, J. (2009) *Managing Innovation*. Pearson.

Torrington, D. and Hall, L. (2002) *Personnel Management*. Prentice Hall.

Trevor, M. (1992) *Toshiba's New British Company*. Centre for Policy Studies.

Trott, P. (2007) *Innovation Management and New Product Development*. FT Pitman.

Tyson, S. and York, A. (2000) *Essentials of HRM*. Heinemann.

Vroom, V. and Deci, E. (1990) *Management and Motivation*. Wiley.

Walker, J. (1992) *Human Resource Strategy*. McGraw Hill.

Walsh, C. (2008) *Key Management Ratios*. Pearson.

Warr, P. (1987) *Psychology at Work*. Penguin.

Watson, T. (2006) *Organising and Managing Work*. FT Pitman.

Weetman, P. (2006) *Financial and Management Accounting: An Introduction*. McGraw Hill.

Weightman, J. (2002) *Managing People*. CIPD.

Wheeler, D. and Sillanpaa, M. (2000) *The Stakeholder Corporation*. FT Pitman.

Wickens, P. (1990) *The Road to Nissan*. Macmillan.

Wickens, P. (1998) *The Ascendant Organisation*. Macmillan.

Wilkinson, R. (1996) *Unhealthy Societies*. Routledge.

Whittington, R. (2009) *What is Strategy, and Does It Matter?* Thomson.

Williams, A., Dobson, P. and Walters, M. (1990) *Changing Culture*. CIPD.

Williams, A., Dobson, P. and Walters, M. (2000) *Managing Change Successfully*. Thomson.

Woodward, J. (1961) *Industrial Organisation: Behaviour and Control*. OUP.

Wright, M. (1990) *Financial Management*. McGraw Hill.

Index